MW01026182

ICAN SOUTH SERIES
R. *Varon and Orville Vernon Burton, Editors*

FACING FREEDOM

FACING FREEDOM

An African American Community in Virginia from Reconstruction to Jim Crow

Daniel B. Thorp

University of Virginia Press   *Charlottesville and London*

University of Virginia Press
© 2017 by the Rector and Visitors of the University of Virginia
All rights reserved
Printed in the United States of America on acid-free paper

First published 2017

9 8 7 6 5 4 3 2 1

Library of Congress Cataloging-in-Publication Data

Names: Thorp, Daniel B., author.
Title: Facing freedom : an African American community in Virginia from
    Reconstruction to Jim Crow / Daniel B. Thorp.
Description: Charlottesville : University of Virginia Press, 2017. | Series: The
    American South series | Includes bibliographical references and index.
Identifiers: LCCN 2017025186 | ISBN 9780813940731 (cloth : alk. paper) |
    ISBN 9780813940748 (ebook)
Subjects: LCSH: African Americans—Virginia—Montgomery County—History. |
    African Americans—Virginia—Montgomery County—Biography. | Montgomery
    County (Va.)—Biography.
Classification: LCC F232.M7 T47 2017 | DDC 305.896/0730755785—dc23
LC record available at https://lccn.loc.gov/2017025186

Cover photo: James and Harriett Carr late in the nineteenth century. (Used with the permission of Lois C. Teele)

For JACK GREENE, who showed me how to be a serious historian,

and

HAROLD LIVESAY, who taught me not to be too serious

CONTENTS

ILLUSTRATIONS

ACKNOWLEDGMENTS

I WOULD LIKE TO EXPRESS my deep appreciation for the support I have received over the years from so many members of Montgomery County's African American community. I especially want to thank Lois Carter Teel, Gladys Sokolow, James Dow, Charles "Sonny" Johnson, Nan and John Hairston, Aubrey and Mary Mills, Jessie Eaves, Sarah Carter, Raymond Bishop, N. L. Bishop, Richard Wade, and Cora Pack for the information they shared with me and for the help and encouragement they provided. I also owe a debt to the Rev. Jimmie Price, a dogged researcher into the history of northwestern Montgomery County with whom I often crossed paths at the courthouse and who shared willingly his deep knowledge of local history and his profound respect for the contributions that African Americans have made to it. I would also like to thank Erica Williams, Montgomery County's Clerk of the Circuit Court, and salute several current or former members of her staff. For almost five years, I spent every Friday in the clerk's office, where Laura Wren, Bridget Adams, and Allen Worrell provided both moral support and practical assistance. At Virginia Tech, I want to thank Peter Wallenstein for his help and support over the years and my department, the College of Liberal Arts and Human Sciences, and the Office of the Provost for financial support toward the publication of this work. Finally, I wish to thank my wife, Elizabeth, for letting me spend so much time in an alternate world that often seemed to exist only in the mass of papers scattered around our basement.

FACING FREEDOM

INTRODUCTION

THE SEED FOR THIS BOOK was planted in 1981, though I did not realize it at the time. I was a graduate student then, still finishing my dissertation, and thinking only of Moravians in Colonial North Carolina. I had recently been hired to fill a one-year position at Virginia Tech as a visiting instructor of history, and my wife and I had moved to Blacksburg from the Maryland suburbs of Washington, D.C. While I had been working on my dissertation, my wife had been supporting us as an elementary school teacher in Prince George's County, and soon after we moved a former colleague of hers came with her children to spend the weekend in Blacksburg. Sometime during their visit we all went to McDonald's for lunch. Looking around the restaurant, our friend's ten-year-old daughter asked a question that may have occurred to all of us but that only a child was brave enough to ask: "Why do they call it Blacksburg? Everyone here is white."

Blacksburg was certainly white, but that was hardly unusual in Montgomery County in 1981. Only about 4 percent of the county's population was African American at the time, and few members of that small community lived in Blacksburg. Moreover, the local narrative suggested that Montgomery County had always been that way, that the region had been settled by sturdy, yeoman farmers—Germans, English, and Ulster Scots—who had worked the land themselves and rarely held slaves. This narrative had never included many African Americans. Few historians had ever paid much attention to the county's African American community, and histories of the county and of the region continued to emphasize its "frontier" roots and "mountain" culture.[1]

Over the next decade, however, I gradually came to see that this local narrative contained significant elements of myth and that a key element of Montgomery County's early history had been nearly forgotten by those writing its history. My term as a visiting instructor ended in 1983, and I left Blacksburg for several years but returned in 1986 as a member of the regular faculty in Virginia Tech's history department. In that capacity I often taught an undergraduate course in research methods and began to incorporate local history and local sources into the class. In doing so, I first learned that Montgomery County had a significant African American population during the nineteenth century. I was surprised to find that in 1860 nearly a quarter of the county's residents had been black and that more than a fifth had been slaves. Moreover, a number of those African Americans had remained in the county for years after the Civil War. While many of their descendants did move north in the late nineteenth and early twentieth centuries, others remained and formed the core of a small but proud black community that could trace its roots in the county back more than two centuries. This realization, however, is not what led me to write this book. That took Nikki Giovanni.

By 2008, Nikki was an Alumni Distinguished Professor at Virginia Tech. She was also a force to be reckoned with. When she publicly challenged the university to deepen its connection to the local African American community, the administration took notice. One early sign of this was an effort by university officials to work with alumni of the Christiansburg Institute, a black school that had operated in the county until 1966, to preserve the history of that institution and to make its story more widely known. I was then the chair of Virginia Tech's history department, so I was a logical candidate to serve on a university working group that also included members of the Christiansburg Institute Alumni Association and representatives of several local governments. Together, we started looking for ways to meet Nikki's challenge. As a historian, I became increasingly interested in the story of the African American community that had supported the Christiansburg Institute and, as a teacher, I started thinking maybe I could find enough information about that community to offer a public lecture as part of an ongoing local history series. Once I began looking, though, I quickly realized that there was more than enough material for a lecture. I began thinking about an article, and before long I knew there was a book in it.

And I knew exactly what sort of book I wanted to write. I had originally trained as an American colonial historian and did so in the wake of John Demos, Kenneth Lockridge, James Lemon, and Darrett and Anita Rutman. I cut my historical teeth on their groundbreaking community studies, and it quickly became clear to me that the history of Montgomery County's African American community offered a wonderful opportunity for just such a study. The county has existed as a corporate entity since 1776 and has generated an impressive body of records. More importantly, it has never suffered a major loss of those records. No flood, no fire, no invading army has ever destroyed the courthouse, and while some records have gone missing over the years, most have survived. Deeds, wills, county court minutes, criminal and civil court records, indentures, election records, censuses, and the records of births, deaths, and marriages all remain intact and available in the office of the court clerk. Complementing the county's rich public record is a range of other sources. Private correspondence, business records, the records of fraternal organizations and churches, school records, newspapers, military and pension records, records of the Freedmen's Bureau and those of various philanthropic agencies during and after Reconstruction, and oral histories have also survived to help tell the story of African Americans in Montgomery County. From these scattered pieces it is possible to construct a remarkably complete picture of African American life in Montgomery County.

It was not just *possible*, however, to produce a community study of Montgomery County's African American community; it was also important to do so. Scholars of African American history have long recognized that as slavery emerged and expanded in the American South, environmental factors led different subregions to focus on different crops. This, in turn, led to the emergence of several "Souths" and to significant variations among them. These variations extended to, among other things, patterns of labor, demographics, family structure, religion, and material culture among the regions' enslaved workers, and to differences in the relationship between those workers and those holding them in bondage. Such variations did not vanish when slavery did. Regional variations persisted for years and meant that the postemancipation experiences of African Americans in the cotton South were often quite different from those in the tobacco South, mixed farming regions of the mountain South, or the urban South of Richmond or New Orleans. Fully understanding these differences requires an intimate understanding of each community, which is difficult to accomplish in regional or national studies.

Community studies can help provide that intimate understanding. Among the sources Herbert Gutman used in *The Black Family in Slavery and Freedom, 1750–1925*, for example, were censuses and marriage registers compiled by local agents of the Freedmen's Bureau in seven Virginia counties — including Montgomery. Gutman used them to describe some characteristics of black families in these counties before and after the Civil War but noted that "deficient enumeration procedures prevent us from knowing the exact interior composition of these households, and nothing can be learned about kin connections between immediate households."[2] This is certainly true when the documents are considered in isolation, which was all Gutman could do given the broad scope of his research. A community study, however, allows one to combine these documents with other sources to make them far more illuminating and provide answers to some of the questions that Gutman raised but could not address. This is the great value of community studies. Focusing on a particular community makes it possible to gain an intimate familiarity with the multitude of fragments that have survived from that community, to recognize how those fragments fit together, and to provide a level of analysis that is simply not practical when working with larger populations.

No community study, however, should ever exist in isolation because no community does. They are all parts of larger worlds and must be seen in the context of those worlds. Most importantly, members of Montgomery County's African American community were African Americans, and this book is about *them*. Over the past half century scholars have produced an abundance of valuable works that focus on the social, cultural, political, economic, and demographic experiences of African Americans between the Civil War and the Great Migration. Leon Litwack and Edward Ayers, for example, have produced sweeping studies of black southerners' experiences during the eras of Reconstruction, the New South, and Jim Crow,[3] while scholars such as Herbert Gutman, Jacqueline Jones, William Cohen, and Steven Hahn have also explored broad regions and eras but have concentrated on particular aspects such as family, labor relations, or politics.[4] These are all important works, and they provide essential elements in our understanding of the African American experience after the abolition of slavery, but their broad geographic focus sometimes makes it difficult for them to capture local variations within the big picture.

Meanwhile, other scholars have written about particular African American communities after the Civil War and have emphasized both the differences and the similarities that existed among them. As valuable as these studies have been, though, they have often been rather narrowly focused. Some scholars have restricted their chronological scope. Roberta Sue Alexander, Lynda Morgan, Dylan Penningroth, and Susan O'Donovan, for example, have each explored the experiences of freedpeople from multiple perspectives—legal, social, political, economic, and demographic—but each of these authors has closed her or his study with the restoration of conservative control during the 1870s.[5] Thus they have missed the continuing efforts of black southerners to adjust to their new world after 1876. Others studies are broader chronologically but more narrowly focused topically. Jeffrey Kerr-Ritchie, Sharon Holt, Jane Dailey, and Hilary Green, for example, have all looked past 1876, but each has done so for a single aspect of the African American experience: economics, landholding, politics, or education, for example.[6] These works, too, make valuable contributions to our understanding of the transition from slavery to freedom, but by focusing on a single facet of that transition they do not capture as effectively as they could the connections among different elements of African American life in the postwar South.

Facing Freedom seeks to combine the approaches found in a number of the works cited above in order to explore more fully the transformation of Montgomery County's African American community across time and from multiple perspectives. It starts with the fundamental understanding that Reconstruction in Virginia did not end in the 1870s. Like Stephen Hahn, William Cohen, Hilary Green, and others, I want to make clear that the process of remaking southern society continued through the 1880s and 1890s and into the twentieth century. Military Reconstruction in Virginia ended in 1870, and the restoration of white, conservative control over the state's politics certainly altered the pace and direction of change in the political lives of black Virginians, but political change did not stop in 1870, and the conservatives' return did not mark the end of African American involvement in Virginia politics. Nor did the end of Reconstruction stop the economic transformation of Virginia or that of the position African Americans occupied in that economy; indeed, extensive economic changes were just beginning when Reconstruction ended in the commonwealth, and they continued in the decades that followed. Similarly, by 1870 black churches and schools were just beginning to emerge in Virginia, and they continued to grow and develop in important ways over the next thirty years.

Equally fundamental is a recognition that this Long Reconstruction of the South took place on multiple fronts simultaneously. Remaking the South to include several million African Americans who were no longer enslaved was not a single process. It was multiple, interrelated processes — demographic, economic, social, legal, educational, religious — moving at different speeds and even in different directions at particular moments in time. *Facing Freedom* is predicated on this view and organized to highlight these different processes and their differential rates of change. Chapter 1 offers a brief overview of developments in the county between 1865 and 1902 and establishes the broad demographic, economic, and political contours of the African American experience there. After that, separate chapters focus on specific elements of that experience: families, economic activity, the development of black schools within a white-controlled public school system, the emergence of distinct and separate black churches, and the continued — if reduced — roles of African Americans as citizens in Montgomery County and as members of the body politic. In this way it seeks to capture the full complexity of the African American experience in Montgomery County.

Of course the story of Montgomery County's African American community is not just a part of African American history; it is also part of the history of southern Appalachia. Montgomery County is part of Appalachia, and *Facing Freedom* also seeks to broaden our understanding of postemancipation African American history in that distinctive region. Appalachian history has now moved far beyond the stories of rugged pioneers that dominated it for so many years. John Inscoe, Kenneth Noe, Charles Dew, Wilma Dunaway, Martin Crawford, and Steven Nash have broadened and deepened our understanding of the mountain South by including African Americans among its inhabitants. Their works have certainly illuminated important elements in the history of race and slavery in southern Appalachia before, during, and immediately after the Civil War, but they have said much less about the experiences of African Americans in the region after the 1870s. There have been exceptions, of course. Gordon McKinney included African Americans among his Southern Mountain Republicans and explored their role in the region's politics through the end of the nineteenth century. Similarly, Ronald Lewis and Joe Trotter have written extensively about black coal miners in Alabama and West Virginia during the late nineteenth and early twentieth centuries. Such studies, however, have been relatively rare, and much of the story of blacks in the mountain South remains untold. More often, historians of southern Appalachia have presented the region's history during the final quarter of the nineteenth century largely as the processes of whites settling grievances among themselves that arose from wartime divisions between Unionists and pro-Confederates and of local whites reacting to the growth of national political power and the expansion of industrial capitalism in a region that had little prior experience with either. African Americans do appear in these histories, but they often do so as an undifferentiated mass of black voters or black workers and as the victims of white violence or the object of white fears rather than as individual actors in their own right. Moreover, these works generally say little about the black *community* and its distinctive institutions. In many studies of post–Civil War Appalachia, African Americans seem to be an abstract category rather than actual residents of the region.[7]

But African Americans were actual residents of the region. They constituted a significant presence in southern Appalachia during the decades after the Civil War, and their story needs to be told more fully. *Facing Freedom* strives to incorporate African Americans into the broader history of Appalachia between the Civil War and the early twentieth century and situate their history into that of the region. It does so, however, from *their* perspective and emphasizes *their* particular experiences. *Facing Freedom* highlights the stories of men and women like James and Harriett Carr. Born to slavery in the 1840s, James Carr and Harriett Souder both came of age in Montgomery County as the Civil War was breaking out. They married during that war and soon afterwards celebrated "a new birth of freedom" when the Confederacy fell and slavery ended in Southwest Virginia. In the decades that followed, they and their children established themselves economically, participated as citizens in the county, and served as members and leaders in newly established black schools and churches. By the time James and Harriet died, early in the twentieth century, they and their family were still far from equal, but they were free and prosperous members of an established African American community. Moreover, that community had developed by then a range of resources and institutions that helped its members survive in a world that grew increasingly hostile toward them over the next fifty years. Men and women like James and Harriet Carr laid the foundations of a new African American community in Montgomery County that survived the horrors and humiliation of Jim Crow, and their descendants have remained in the county to this day. *Facing Freedom* is their story.

PROLOGUE

FOR MARY BROWN, slavery ended with a whimper. In April of 1865, Brown was an enslaved cook, living with and working for Floyd and Catherine Smith on their farm in the Childress Store neighborhood of Montgomery County. A native of the county, Brown was forty-six that spring and the mother of six children. At least three of her four daughters—Celia, Ellen, and Eunice—lived with her on the Smiths' farm, though her husband, Tom, was a slave elsewhere in the county, and her sons had been sold following the death of an earlier owner. Her great-granddaughter later recalled: "They sold the boys to what's called nigger traders and they took em off down south and they never seen em anymore."[1] Montgomery County was far from the front lines, but the Civil War had been raging for four years, and slaves in the county knew what the fighting was about and how it was progressing. Charles Hunter, who was also enslaved in the county during the war, declared that slaves there "[often] talked about the prospect of getting free by the war" and that he "gloried in the hope of the yankees gaining the day." Earlier that month Union cavalry had spent several days in the county tearing up rail lines and destroying bridges, and shortly after they left, word reached Christiansburg, the county seat, that General Lee had surrendered. William Moon, a free black living in the county, was happy to hear the news: "I was glad at the surrender and glad the colored people got their freedom." Stephen Ash and Wilma Dunaway have both suggested that slave owners in Virginia sometimes tried to keep their slaves from learning of the surrender and of their emancipation, but

Floyd Smith made no such effort. Soon after Lee surrendered, he simply told the hands: "Well you all's set free today." [2]

Montgomery County lies in the mountainous southwestern region of Virginia and because of its location had never been one of the state's major slave-holding counties. The land and climate of the county were certainly well suited to a range of agricultural pursuits for which enslaved workers might have been put to use. Both the eastern and western edges of the county include extensive bottomland along the North and South Forks of the Roanoke River in the east or the Little and New Rivers in the west, and several of the creeks feeding these rivers flow through broad valleys that are level enough to plow and plant a variety of field crops—including tobacco. Even land that was too rocky or steep to crop was often quite productive; the mixed forest offered timber, and all but the roughest mountain terrain lent itself to raising cattle, sheep, or pigs. As the seller of one tract in the county put it, land there was "somewhat broken, but . . . well adapted to the growth of Corn, Wheat, Oats, and Tobacco, and cannot be surpassed for a grazing farm." [3] *Producing* marketable goods, then, had never been a problem in Montgomery County; getting those goods to market, however, had remained a challenge into the 1850s.

This is not to say that farmers in Montgomery County did not partici-pate in national or international markets before the 1850s. They certainly did, but they did so at a lower level than many other Virginians because of the difficulty they faced getting their products to market. This far up-stream, the Roanoke River was too shallow for commercial traffic, and the New River, while useful for intraregional trade, was interrupted by rapids and falls farther downstream that limited access from Southwest Virginia to the rest of the Ohio/Mississippi river system. Thus, for many years the best option for moving goods from Montgomery County was overland some ninety miles to Lynchburg and then onward via the James River or, after 1840, the James River and Kanawha Canal. This raised the price of goods from Montgomery County and made them less competitive in eastern markets, which discouraged residents from investing in more slaves and expanding production. That changed, however, when the rail-road arrived. [4]

Advocates of internal improvement had tried for years to establish a railroad through Southwest Virginia. Their hopes were finally realized in 1849, when the General Assembly granted a charter to the Virginia and Tennessee Railroad. Ground was broken at Lynchburg in 1850, and over the next six years crews worked from east and west to construct a two-hundred-mile-long link between Lynchburg and Bristol. Montgomery County residents did not have to wait for the line's completion, for it reached the county seat, Christiansburg, in April 1854, and that was enough to link the county to the world. The Virginia and Tennessee Railroad connected Christiansburg directly to Lynchburg, and from there other railroads and the James River and Kanawha Canal led onward to Richmond, Baltimore, and beyond. Completion of the rail link provided large new markets for crops and products from Montgomery County by reducing significantly the cost of getting the county's products to those markets. As a result, agricultural production in the county soared. Between 1850 and 1860 wheat production tripled and that of tobacco rose fifteenfold (1,582 percent). New markets also appeared for millstones, coal, and wood, which the railroad itself needed for ties and to fuel its locomotives. [5]

None of these activities required slave labor, but they often created opportunities that benefited from slavery. For those who could afford them, owning slaves reduced even more the cost of producing a variety of goods that thanks to the railroad could now be moved profitably to eastern markets. And slaves were certainly available. Many planters in Tidewater and Piedmont Virginia had more workers than they needed. For years they had been selling slaves to planters in the expanding cotton belt or had moved there themselves. Now they did so in Southwest Virginia, expanding their operations by sending sons and slaves to Southwest Virginia or selling slaves to farmers already living there. As a result, the number of slaves in Montgomery County rose dramatically between 1850 and 1860. The 1850 census found 1,471 slaves in the county, while a decade later there were 2,219—an increase of 51 percent—and they made up 21 percent of the county's total population. [6] This figure is still well below the 30 percent that slaves represented in Virginia's total population, but if one considers, instead, the percentages found in each of Virginia's 148 counties in the 1860 census, Montgomery ranks seventy-seventh—slightly below the median, which was 24.2 percent. [7]

Most of the county's slaves lived in a wide band running from northeast to southwest through the county's center, between the parallel chains of mountains that mark the county's northern and southern boundaries. Within this zone, Christiansburg, the county seat and its largest town, had the greatest concentration of slaves; nearly one in three residents there was in bondage. Christiansburg also had the highest level of slave ownership in the county; countywide 18.5 percent of white households owned or rented at least one slave in 1860, but in Christiansburg 41 percent did. The vast majority of slaves in the county, however, did not live in towns such as Christiansburg. As was common throughout Virginia, towns in Montgomery County had a higher *percentage* of slaves in their populations, but the *numbers* involved were often relatively low because the towns were so small. Christiansburg, for example, had just 704 residents in 1860; slaves there made up 31 percent of the population, but they numbered only 220. Despite the greater concentration of slaves in the county's towns, well over three-quarters of the slaves in Montgomery County lived in the countryside beyond those towns.[8]

The distribution of slave holdings by size was similarly skewed, and this has often led to a significant misunderstanding of slavery in Montgomery County. In 1860, the median slave-holding in the county was five, and almost 20 percent of slaveholders owned or rented a single slave. The fact that so many masters had just one slave has often led local historians to conclude, erroneously, that slaves in Montgomery County were mainly domestic servants. Focusing on their owners, however, obscures the experiences of the slaves themselves. Most owners may have had just a few slaves, but most slaves lived in fairly large groups. Only one county resident, James R. Kent, had more than one hundred slaves in 1860, but twenty-three individuals in Montgomery County owned twenty slaves or more that year and thus qualified as "planters." They alone held more than a third of the county's slaves, and two-thirds of all the slaves held in Montgomery County in 1860 lived on holdings of ten slaves or more. Thus, the "average" slave in the county lived in a unit that was twice the median size. By the last decade of the antebellum era, Montgomery County was not a society of yeoman farmers with a handful of slaves; it was a fully articulated slave society and one in which slavery was expanding rapidly.[9]

This is the world that came to an end in April 1865. The announcement that they were free signaled the start of entirely new lives for Mary and Tom Brown, for their daughters, and for the hundreds of other African Americans—both slave and free—living in Montgomery County at the close of the Civil War. This is certainly not to say that attitudes toward African Americans or the condition of their lives immediately changed for the better with the fall of the Confederacy. Indeed, the Confederate defeat led briefly to heightened concerns among the county's white residents and increased efforts to ensure that former slaves did not threaten public safety. Elizabeth Payne, whose family lived near Shawsville, recalled that "the County was in the greatest state of Anxiety and unrest" as word spread of Lee's surrender. Payne herself claimed not to believe that former slaves were a major concern; "The negroes, of course were freed," she later wrote, "but we did not seem at the time to regard that." Others did regard it, though. When the county court met for the first time after Lee's surrender, on May 1, it ordered justices in each of the county's four districts to establish patrols "for suppressing riots and preventing lawless depredations" and directed them "[to] take into their possession all the arms found in the hands of children and servants." It seems unlikely that members of the court were particularly concerned about armed gangs of children roaming the county. "Servants," however, were another matter, and while justices used the word "servants" in that case, in others they left no doubt what they meant. That same session of the court also handled the cases of "'John,' a slave the property of William Pearl and 'Major,' a slave the property of William Byers." Such attitudes should hardly be surprising. All the members of the county court, as well as other public officials who had governed Montgomery County under Confederate authority, had remained in office after the Confederacy fell, and all the laws of antebellum and Confederate Virginia restricting the lives of nonwhites remained in force. As the court was ending its May term, though, the wheels of change were gradually beginning to move.[10]

Virginia already had a state government waiting to fill the void left by the collapse of Confederate authority. "The Restored Government of Virginia" had been established in Virginia's northwestern counties in June 1861 in opposition to the secessionist government in Richmond. It had remained in Wheeling until 1863, when West Virginia entered the Union as a separate state, and then moved to Alexandria. There it continued to function for the next two years, holding elections, convening a "state" legislature, and drafting a new, more democratic, constitution that abolished slavery throughout the state. Few people either in Virginia or in Congress had taken it seriously, though, and its reputation and authority had slowly waned. Just as the war was ending, however, President Lincoln indicated that he regarded the restored government as the legal government of Virginia, and this was later confirmed by President Andrew Johnson's executive order of May 9, 1865. Armed with this new authority, the state's "restored" governor, Francis H. Pierpont, called for elections in July to select new local officials and to begin preparations for statewide elections in the fall. None of Virginia's African American residents voted in the July election—Virginia law still restricted the franchise to white men—and many incumbents were simply reelected. Before resuming office, though, each was required to take new oaths to uphold both the US Constitution and "the government of Virginia as restored by the convention which assembled at Wheeling on the 11th day of June 1861."[11]

Voters in Montgomery County also cast ballots in July and elected a mix of new and returning county officials, but by the time those officials assumed their duties the balance of power in the county was changing dramatically. Even as the restored state government was taking steps to establish a functioning political structure in Virginia, military and federal officials were fanning out across the state and coming to play an increasingly important role in reshaping its social, political, and economic landscape. Reconstruction was under way, and in Montgomery County its face was initially that of J. Irvin Gregg, a captain in the Union army and assistant provost marshal in Lynchburg. Gregg traveled to Christiansburg early in July and spent several days administering oaths of allegiance to prominent residents of the county seeking presidential pardons for their participation in the failed rebellion, oaths that required them to support the Constitution of the United States and "all laws and proclamations which have been made during the existing rebellion with reference to the emancipation of the slaves." An even more significant development came at the end of the month, when the new Bureau of Refugees, Freedmen, and Abandoned Lands—better known as the Freedmen's Bureau—opened an office in Christiansburg.[12]

The Freedmen's Bureau had been established by Congress in March 1865 and was originally charged with "control of all subjects relating to refugees and freedmen from rebel states" for the duration of the war and for one year after hostilities ended. It was reauthorized by Congress twice in the next five years and officially functioned until the summer of 1872, though by 1870 its operations were confined to settling claims in its Washington headquarters. During the spring and summer of 1865, assistant commissioners were appointed for each state, and local agents, most of them Union military officers, opened offices throughout the South. Initially, these agents concentrated on providing medical care and emergency supplies of food and clothing to freedpeople, helping to reunite families separated by slavery or war, and overseeing contracts and labor relations between former slaves and their former owners. A year after the war ended, in 1866, the bureau was also authorized to supervise and encourage the establishment of schools for freedpeople, and in response to the passage of Black Codes in many southern states, agents of the bureau assumed a much wider role supervising a range of legal, economic, and political activities in an effort to prevent the abuse of freedpeople's rights. The bureau was also authorized to employ its own courts or military courts if necessary to carry out its mandate. Such powers were short lived, though, and the bureau's operations were sharply curtailed after 1868. Beginning January 1, 1869, its local offices closed throughout the South, and each state's assistant commissioner was restricted to overseeing education and the settlement of claims by black veterans.[13]

In Virginia, the Freedmen's Bureau began operating in June 1865 under the direction of Assistant Commissioner Orlando Brown, a physician and recently colonel in command of the Twenty-Fourth US Colored Infantry. The state was soon divided into ten districts and each of these into a number of subdistricts with bureau agents appointed to each. Montgomery County was part of the state's Eighth District, which initially had its headquarters in Christiansburg, and late in July, Captain Buel C. Carter, a New Hampshire native and a Yale graduate, arrived there with some two dozen soldiers to reestablish federal control in the seven counties for which he was responsible. The district's headquarters moved to Wytheville in September, though, and for the next six months the bureau's presence in Montgomery County was sharply reduced. The following spring, however, the Christiansburg office resumed operations, and Captain Charles S. Schaeffer arrived in May 1866 to assume command of a division occupying Montgomery, Giles, and Pulaski Counties. Schaeffer, a native of Germantown, Pennsylvania, and a veteran of the First Delaware Infantry, was also a devout and active Baptist (figure 1). For a decade before the Civil War, he had been a member of Philadelphia's Tenth Baptist Church, and his work with the church and with the Philadelphia Tract Society had brought him into frequent contact with the city's large black community. He was deeply and personally committed to the welfare of African Americans, and he directed the Freedmen's Bureau in Montgomery County from May 1866 until it ceased operations at the end of 1868.[14]

To many of Montgomery County's white residents, the arrival of Captains Gregg and Carter and the opening of an office of the Freedmen's Bureau in Christiansburg marked the beginning of what one resident called the "humiliation incident to Yankee subjugation." To freedpeople such as

E. P. HIPPLE,   820 Arch Street, Phila.

FIGURE 1. Charles S. Schaeffer, ca. 1863. (Courtesy of the Photographic
History Collection, Division of Culture and the Arts, National
Museum of American History, Smithsonian Institution)

Mary Brown, on the other hand, federal officials offered hope that emancipation would lead to real change in their lives. No one represented Montgomery County at the Colored State Convention that met in Alexandria in
August 1865, but freedpeople in the county probably shared the delegates'
concern about the return to power of Virginia's antebellum white elite. In
an address to the loyal citizens and Congress of the United States, convention delegates explained: "We *know* these men—know them *well*—and we
assure you that, with the majority of them, loyalty is only 'lip deep,' and
that their professions of loyalty are used as a cover to the cherished design
of getting restored to their former relations with the Federal Government,
and then by all sorts of 'unfriendly legislation,' to render the freedom you
have given us more intolerable than the slavery they intended for us." Con-

vention delegates believed that only a government of the "military persua-sion" could ensure the security of freedpeople until the federal and state constitutions could be amended so that black Virginians were guaranteed the vote and could protect themselves through the ballot box.[15]

In the case of Montgomery County, neither assessment proved entirely accurate. "Yankee subjugation" there was mild and brief. The county's antebellum leaders were not swept aside by the Civil War; they retained much of their status and eventually regained most of their power. As for the Freedmen's Bureau, its agents certainly wanted freedpeople to enjoy the benefits of democracy and capitalism, but they had in mind particu-lar forms of both. Schaeffer, for example, clearly shared the patronizing and paternalistic attitudes toward African Americans that were common among white Americans of his day. He believed that freedpeople needed protection from their own moral and human shortcomings as much as they did from the evil designs of their former owners and other white southerners. Moreover, the Freedmen's Bureau did not remain in the county for long. It certainly played an important role in Montgomery County immediately after the Civil War, but its office there closed at the end of 1868. And while Schaeffer remained in Christiansburg and worked with and for the county's black community until his death, in 1899, he had little authority or power beyond moral suasion.

As it did throughout the postbellum South, change came slowly for African Americans living in Montgomery County. Formal Reconstruction ended in 1870, with Virginia's readmission to the Union, but the process of reshaping African American life in the state—the Long Reconstruction—stretched through the turn of the century. And progress was neither rapid nor constant. While blacks in Montgomery County gained their legal free-dom almost immediately, it took them years to acquire the political, social, and economic wherewithal to begin making that freedom real, and even when they did make gains, these often proved temporary and were some-times reversed. And while the Freedmen's Bureau and other government agencies helped to effect some of the changes that took place immediately after emancipation, much of what happened in the decades that followed was the result of long, hard work by the county's black residents them-selves. Emancipation was a start, but it was only a start.

1 PEOPLE AND COMMUNITIES

JAMES DOW MOVED TO Montgomery County sometime between 1870 and 1876. Born a slave in Roanoke County in 1850, he left no account explaining why he decided to move, but it may have been for a woman. Three years after his emancipation, in April 1868, Dow began working as a laborer for the Virginia and Tennessee Railroad. He was living near Salem at the time, on the western edge of Roanoke County, but from there the section crew to which he belonged moved east and west along the rail line performing regular maintenance on the track and roadbed. This brought him into eastern Montgomery County, and there he met Frances Taylor. Frances, who went by Fanny, was the daughter of John Taylor, a farm laborer living near Big Spring, and his wife Charlotte, and like James Dow, she had been born a slave. When and how James and Fanny met remains a mystery, but they married in 1876, when he was twenty-six and she was seventeen, and spent the next half century building a life together in Montgomery County.[1]

James and Fanny Dow initially lived with Fanny's parents but eventually moved into their own home in the Brake Branch neighborhood, just outside of Big Spring, or Elliston, as it was renamed in 1890. James continued to work for the successors of the Virginia and Tennessee Railroad, retiring from the Norfolk and Western in 1918 after fifty years as a section laborer (figure 2). He and Fanny also farmed the small tract of land on which they lived and raised twelve children born between 1877 and 1904. As their children came of age, though, the younger Dows found themselves living in a county and a state that offered African Americans

FIGURE 2. James Dow (*front row, center*) in 1930. The photograph was
taken at the time of his inclusion in the Colored Division of the Veterans
Association of the Norfolk and Western Railroad in recognition of his fifty years
of service to the company. (Courtesy of the Norfolk Southern Corporation)

fewer economic and political opportunities than it had in their parents'
day and in which racial attitudes were hardening and growing more bitter.
Some of the Dows' children remained in Montgomery County, and some
of their grandchildren and great-grandchildren remain there still. Others,
however, elected to leave in search of better opportunities in West Virginia,
Ohio, and Pennsylvania.[2]

The story of the Dow family encapsulates the broad demographic
history of Montgomery County's black population in the half century following the Civil War, and this chapter provides a broad overview of how
and why that history unfolded as it did. For some two decades after the
Civil War, the county's African American population grew as individuals
and families moved into the county and with those living there already
established and maintained African American schools, churches, social
organizations, and neighborhoods throughout the county. These institutions and communities were always distinct and often separate from their
white counterparts, but they were never isolated from the larger society of

which they were a part. By 1890, though, black migration into the county had slowed while that out of the county had begun to accelerate. By the dawn of the twentieth century, Montgomery County's black population had started to decline and would continue declining until the 1960s. Like the children of James and Fanny Dow, members of Montgomery County's black community often moved out in search of better opportunities, but like the Dows, the county's black community never disappeared. Today, more descendants of James and Fanny Dow live in other counties and other states than in Montgomery County, but the family remains part of the county's African American community, and that community remains an essential part of the county and its history.

During the course of the Civil War the black population of Montgomery County had declined significantly. John Inscoe and Gordon McKinney have found that slave populations in western North Carolina often rose during the war as residents of the region bought slaves from panicked owners farther east or as easterners fled west with their slaves, and Jaime Martinez has noted that wartime demand for salt brought more slaves to labor in the salt works of Southwest Virginia. In Montgomery County, however, there was little evidence of such inflows. There were white refugees who may have brought slaves into the county. Isaac White Sr., for example, moved from Upshur County, in what became West Virginia, to Montgomery County during the war and may have brought some of his slaves with him when he relocated. And after the war the Freedmen's Bureau did provide transportation from Christiansburg to Atlanta for two girls "who refuged here with a Mrs. Sullivan during the war."[3] Overall, though, the war led to a decline in the number of slaves and free people of color in Montgomery County. More than one hundred of the county's slaves or free men of color were impressed or hired to work for the Confederate government or military during the war, and hundreds of enslaved men, women, and children fled the county when Union troops passed through in 1864 and 1865.[4] Evidence of both the absolute decline in population that occurred during the war and the broad nature of that decline appears in a census of Montgomery County's "colored population" conducted by the Freedmen's Bureau in August 1865, just a month after opening its Christiansburg office. The bureau found a total black population of just 1,573 — down a third from the 2,366 reported on the federal census in 1860. It also found that the age and gender distribution within that population was still quite close to what it had been in 1860. Males age fifteen years and older, for example, still made up 26.1 percent of the county's black population in 1865; this was down from the 27.4 percent reported in 1860, but not dramatically.[5]

The 1865 enumeration certainly overstated the decline, though, as it missed a number of freedpeople known from other sources to have been in the county that summer.[6] Moreover, whatever the exact level of the decline, it was quite short lived; another census, taken in 1867, showed that the county's African American population had already begun growing again. By 1867 it had regained its prewar size, and it continued to grow steadily for at least another fifteen years. By 1870 it had grown to 2,882 — up more than 80 percent from its wartime nadir and almost 22 percent above its 1860 level. It grew by another 47 percent between 1870 and 1880, to 4,227, and probably grew for several more years after that before starting to decline. The best estimate of the county's population between decennial censuses comes from the annual reports of public school enrollments, and by that measure Montgomery County's African American population probably peaked during the 1882–83 school year at an estimated 4,400.[7]

Such growth in absolute numbers is not surprising. Gordon McKinney found that throughout the mountain South, the number of African Americans rose between 1870 and 1900. What is unusual, however, is that in Montgomery County African Americans also increased as a percentage of the total population. They made up 23 percent of the county population in 1870 and 25 percent in 1880, compared to 22.4 percent in 1860. After peaking in the 1880s, however, both the number of black residents and their share of the total population percentage began to decline, falling to 3,515 (19.8 percent) in 1890 and 3,381 (17.1 percent) in 1900. It is difficult to express properly the rate of decline in the county's black population at the turn of century because Radford, which had about five hundred African American residents at the time, became an independent city in 1892. Whenever one makes that adjustment to the county's population, the black population shows a precipitous and misleading drop. Adjusting for that one-time drop, however, does not change the overall story; the final years of the nineteenth century saw what Jeffrey Kerr-Ritchie called "the roots of the later Great Migration." Montgomery County's black population began to decline by about 1885 and continued to decline steadily until the 1960s.[8]

Both the growth and the decline in Montgomery County's black population after the Civil War were due, in part, to natural demographic factors — births and deaths — but the main factor driving it was migration. In the decades after the Civil War, hundreds of black men, women, and children moved into or out of the county, and sometimes did both. Obviously, the volume and direction of migration changed over the years, but so did the factors driving it. Three factors seem to have been most evident during the decades following emancipation, though their relative importance shifted over time. Family provided a very strong motive to move, at first, but then declined and soon became a factor reducing the likelihood that an individual would migrate. Economics was the most consistent factor. African Americans were always looking for better access to land and better job opportunities, but whether that served to attract them into the county or pushed them to leave changed over time. It seems to have drawn them into the county for the first twenty years after the Civil War but by the mid-1880s seems to have become an important factor leading to out-migration. The third factor—racism, race relations, and the status of African Americans in the county—also seems to have fluctuated as a factor influencing migration out of Montgomery County. As Steven Hahn found elsewhere in the South, racism often triggered black emigration in the late 1860s and again at the turn of the century but was a less important factor for much of the 1870s and 1880s.[9]

In the years immediately after emancipation, the most powerful factor behind black migration into and out of Montgomery County seems to have been the desire to reunite families broken by slavery.[10] Slave families in antebellum Virginia had often been separated by sale or by forced migration with their owners, and the expansion of slavery in Montgomery County during the 1850s had brought hundreds of new slaves to the county, many of them from Virginia's Southside region. The county's cohabitation register, compiled in 1866 to legalize slave marriages and families, indicates that just 47 percent of the adults who had been enslaved in Montgomery County had been born there. This figure rises to 60 percent if one also includes the counties immediately adjacent to Montgomery—a sort of "Greater Montgomery County"—which might be more appropriate in light of the fact that several large landowners on the eastern and western edges of the county also owned land in Roanoke or Pulaski County.[11] Still, the cohabitation register suggests that at least 40 percent of the adult slaves living in Montgomery County in 1860 had been brought or sent there. Some of these traveled alone and left all of their relations behind, but even those who made the journey in family units left more distant kin near their former homes, and those who did not arrive in complete families often left parents, spouses, and children as well. Meanwhile, slave families that were already established in the county were sometimes broken as members were sold or manumitted or escaped. Susan Lester, for example, was manumitted by Mary Wade in 1860 along with her two younger sons. Wade retained Lester's older sons, however, and they remained in Virginia when their mother and brothers moved to Ohio later that year.[12]

Numerous studies have shown that restoring family ties was a critical priority among freedpeople following their emancipation. Throughout the antebellum South, slaves had run away to rejoin family, and as soon as the Union army began to occupy parts of the Confederacy, slaves escaped to Union lines and began searching for family. As early as 1862, the *Christian Recorder*, a newspaper published by the African Methodist Episcopal Church, began carrying announcements from former slaves asking for information about family members sold away. It continued to do so well into the 1870s, as did a number of other papers. Only one resident of Montgomery County is known to have used the *Christian Recorder* or similar outlets to look for family, but others also showed their determination to reunite families broken in slavery. Susan Lester, for example, explained her decision to return to Christiansburg by telling her banker in Ohio: "In slave time I left Va. and going back now I have two sons there and other relations and I would like to have my home there."[13]

Agents of the Freedmen's Bureau were often interested in family reunification as well, and among the first records generated by the bureau's office in Christiansburg was an accounting of money provided by Captain Buel Carter during the summer of 1865 to cover the costs of railroad travel for reuniting several families in Southwest Virginia. When Charles Schaeffer took over as the agent responsible for Montgomery County in May 1866, he also demonstrated a desire to help reunite the families of freedpeople. As Heather Williams has recently pointed out, though, even bureau agents who wanted to help reunite black families had very limited resources with which to do so. Bureau policy was to provide financial support only for those who were truly destitute and, even then, only if the failure to do so would force the government to support them. Those who could work would have to pay their own way. Schaeffer, therefore, was able to cover the cost of bringing Sarah Winfrey, "an aged colored woman," from Bristol, where she was "without home or friends," to join her daughter and son-in-law near Blacksburg in late 1866. But when Henry Poor, a freedmen living in Lynchburg, asked Schaeffer for help bringing his ten-year-old son, Lewis, home from Montgomery County, it was a different story. Schaeffer helped arrange the boy's passage to Lynchburg, but his father had to cover the cost himself. Bureau policy was not to provide financial assistance except in "extream cases," and Lewis Poor did not qualify.[14]

The extent to which family reunification brought freedpeople into Montgomery County is most evident, perhaps, in the county's cohabitation register. The register indicates that approximately a quarter of married black adults in the county in 1866 had moved there since gaining their freedom. Some of these moved to rejoin a spouse or children. Thomas Baker, for example, apparently moved to Montgomery County from Spotsylvania County to join his wife, Martha, and three of the couple's children. In other cases, freedpeople who had been born in Montgomery County and had been taken or sent elsewhere moved back to rejoin their extended families. Frank McNorton, Frank Moon, and Ellen Fraction Raglin, for example, had all been born in Montgomery County but seem to have been among the slaves that Catharine Jane Preston took with her to Pittsylvania County when she married George H. Gilmer in 1845. They remained in Pittsylvania after Catharine Preston Gilmer died, but following their emancipation they returned to Montgomery County and brought with them spouses and children born elsewhere.[15]

Immediately after emancipation, then, family reunification was a major factor motivating freedpeople to move to Montgomery County, but by the early 1870s it was probably a less significant factor than economics was. Growth of the county's black population was greater during the 1870s than during any decade in the county's history except the 1850s, when slavery had expanded so dramatically following completion of the Virginia and Tennessee Railroad, and the early 1880s marked the high point for African Americans as a percentage of the county's total population, at 25.3 percent. Much of this growth seems to have been a result of young adults moving to the county in search of better economic opportunities.

Most of these opportunities were in agriculture. In many parts of Tidewater and Piedmont Virginia, the tobacco-based economy had faced severe challenges long before the Civil War. Wartime destruction, weather, and white opposition to free black labor added to those challenges, and parts of eastern and central Virginia often saw large numbers of unemployed freedmen immediately after emancipation.[16] In Montgomery County, on the other hand, commercial agriculture had really begun to expand only when the railroad arrived, in the mid-1850s, and still had room to expand when the war ended. Moreover, while some of the region's infrastructure had been damaged or destroyed during the war, destruction there was modest compared to that seen elsewhere. As result, agriculture in Montgomery County escaped the postwar decline seen in many parts of Virginia. Statewide, improved acreage in Virginia fell by a quarter between 1860 and 1870 and then rose by just 4 percent in the following decade. In Montgomery County, though, improved acreage rose by 9 percent between 1860 and 1870 and by 24 percent between 1870 and 1880. And though whites in Montgomery County sometimes complained about free black labor and occasionally threatened to replace black workers with white immigrants, most quickly realized that if they wanted to make their land profitable they would have to employ freedmen. Moreover, unlike white landowners in some parts of the postwar South, those in Montgomery County were also willing to sell land to freedpeople.[17]

Rising demand for labor in other sectors of the economy also meant that black families in Montgomery County could complement farming with other employment, as the family of James Dow did. The Virginia and Tennessee Railroad, which became part of the Atlantic, Mississippi, and Ohio in 1870 and the Norfolk and Western in 1881, used black labor extensively on its section gangs—men who maintained the track and roadbed—and also as brakemen and as laborers around its depots. Increased construction throughout the county also meant more jobs for black men during the 1870s. Both Christiansburg and Blacksburg expanded significantly during the decade, which meant new buildings, and the establishment of the Virginia Agricultural and Mechanical College in 1872 meant additional construction on its Blacksburg campus.[18]

Many of the African Americans who migrated to Montgomery County during the 1870s were young men moving in from other counties in central and western Virginia. This is most evident from the information included on applications submitted for marriage licenses in the county. During the decade 1870–79, 357 black men living in Montgomery County applied for marriage licenses there. Of that number, 57 percent (205) had been born beyond "Greater Montgomery County"—Montgomery and the five counties immediately adjacent to it. This compares to a level of 49 percent among married men on the cohabitation register, and suggests that migration had increased since the antebellum era. It also suggests that young black men were more likely to migrate than young black women were, as the percentage of brides born outside Greater Montgomery County, 37 percent, was well below that of grooms. Young couples also moved to

Montgomery County during the 1870s; Pink and Emma Henderson, for example, did so shortly after they were married in Caswell County, North Carolina. They seem to have been outnumbered, though, by unmarried adults.[19]

Just as economics seems to have encouraged migration into Montgomery County and helped to increase the county's black population during the 1870s, it seems to have been a major factor in the decline of that population that began during the 1880s and accelerated during the 1890s. One factor in this decline was the apparent reduction in economic opportunities for black men in Montgomery County during the final decades of the nineteenth century. Many parts of southern Appalachia saw during these years what Ronald Lewis called "the penetration of industrial capitalism," and in some this led to greater opportunities for black workers.[20] This was not the case in Montgomery County. The Norfolk and Western did continue to employ black workers there, but beyond that neither industry nor mining in the county grew significantly, and neither employed more than a handful of black workers. Meanwhile, opportunities for black farm workers seem to have stagnated or even declined. Improved acreage continued to rise but at a slower rate than it had before 1880, and the production of sheep in Montgomery County began to increase during the 1880s and 1890s, which may have reduced the demand for farm labor. As a result, migration into Montgomery County slowed during the 1880s. During that decade, the percentage of grooms marrying in Montgomery County who had been born outside Greater Montgomery County declined to 44 percent from the 57 percent seen during the 1870s, while the figure for brides declined to 29 percent from the 37 percent seen during the preceding decade. And this trend accelerated during the 1890s.[21]

At the same time, greater economic opportunities elsewhere led to increased migration out of Montgomery County during the 1880s and 1890s. As early as 1880, the *Christiansburg Messenger* reported "a large number of able bodied colored men left this week for West Virginia, to work on the railroad and in the mines." Well into the twentieth century men from Montgomery County moved to West Virginia because coal mines there were much larger and much more willing to hire black workers. Nor was West Virginia their only destination; mining companies in Ohio and Iowa also attracted men from Montgomery County. Consolidation Coal Company, for example, recruited heavily in Virginia during the 1890s and brought black workers from the state to its mines in Muchakinock and

Buxton, Iowa. Years later, Frank Bannister explained why many of his kin had left Montgomery County and gone to Buxton: "See there's transportation paid your way. Jobs opened up, a whole lot of folks left." Even more attractive to black workers may have been the new cities of Roanoke and Radford. Roanoke, which was chartered in 1884, grew explosively over the next twenty years as the Norfolk and Western Railroad established facilities there and expanded its operations. During the 1880s and 1890s, Roanoke was the fastest growing city in Virginia, and thousands of African Americans migrated there, including many from Montgomery County. Radford had actually been part of Montgomery County until 1892, when it was chartered as an independent city. Here too, railroad expansion during the 1880s—in this case a branch line to coal fields in the New River valley—led to rapid economic expansion that attracted significant numbers of black workers by the last decade of the nineteenth century.[22]

Still others headed to eastern and midwestern cities that offered wider opportunities for relatively unskilled black labor. According to surveys conducted in Philadelphia and New York early in the twentieth century, almost half of the southern blacks who had migrated to those cities had done so for economic reasons. The links between Montgomery County and eastern cities extended back to the antebellum era. Baltimore, for example, had been a major source of manufactured and imported goods at least since the opening of rail links to the county, and the only free black storekeeper known to have operated in antebellum Montgomery County, William Campbell, had traded with merchants based there. Other eastern cities, such as New York, Philadelphia, and Washington, D.C., also attracted a steady stream of migrants from Montgomery County during the final decades of the nineteenth century. Meanwhile, the postwar growth of rail connections also led black men and women from Montgomery County to midwestern cities such as Chicago and Columbus, Ohio, in part because they hoped to find work there.[23]

The decline in Montgomery County's African American population that began during the 1880s was not just a result of declining economic opportunity, though. It was also influenced by growing frustration in the black community with the status of African Americans in the county. To be sure, racism and discrimination had been common in Montgomery County throughout the postwar years, but the pattern of racial discrimination there seems to have followed one similar to that identified by scholars such as C. Vann Woodward, Gordon McKinney, Jane Dailey, and Steven

Hahn. As discussed more fully in later chapters, racial discrimination was particularly intense during the five years immediately after the Civil War, then seems to have declined somewhat during the 1870s and early 1880s, and grown ever more virulent during the last fifteen years of the century.[24]

Racial tensions in the South rose immediately after the Civil War as black and white southerners, their new state governments, and the government of the United States all wrestled with the postemancipation world and their respective places in it. In this pattern of escalating racial tension after the Civil War, Montgomery County was no exception. As described more fully in chapter 6, Freedmen's Bureau officials in the county reported white hostility toward freedpeople and occasional episodes of violence during the early years of Reconstruction. In 1866–67, for example, Robert T. Preston waged a prolonged vendetta against Thomas and Othello Fraction, former slaves of his who had escaped, served in the Union army, and then returned to live in the vicinity of Preston's farm outside Blacksburg. As Othello Fraction later recalled, "Our master said if any of his 'niggirs' went to the army & came back he would kill them and he tried hard to kill [my] brother." More broadly, the election of delegates to the state constitutional convention in October 1867 led to rising tension, and the spring of 1868 saw a brief outbreak of Ku Klux Klan activity that was probably sparked by the appearance of at least one Union League chapter in the county and a desire among conservative whites to intimidate black voters before the constitutional referendum.[25]

This tension and violence may have been a factor in the interest shown by several black families in emigrating from Montgomery County to Liberia in 1867. After sharply reducing its activity during the war, the American Colonization Society (ACS) had resumed its work in 1865 and was aggressively recruiting former slaves to settle in Liberia, which it described as a natural home for African Americans and as a last, best alternative to continued racism and discrimination in the United States. Most of those it sent after the war came from states south of Virginia, though one party of 172 freedpeople from the Lynchburg area did sail for Liberia in November 1865. The leader of that party, according to the ACS, "could do as well in the United States as any of his race" but wanted "a country and nationality of his own people." The same, perhaps, could be said of some of those from Montgomery County who, in the summer of 1867, inquired about the possibility of their emigrating to Liberia. Almost half the group were members of Ellen Campbell's family, one of the largest and longest-settled black families in the county. They had been living there as free people of color since the end of the eighteenth century and in 1867 were among the wealthiest African American families in the county. They had no obvious financial or family incentive to move to Liberia but may have shared the view of the ACS that life in Liberia promised them liberty and dignity they would never have in Virginia. Ultimately, just one member of the group, Thomas Campbell, left for Liberia, and it is unclear when he did so.[26]

Race relations in the county then seem to have improved during the 1870s, not because blacks were more respected or much closer to being treated as equals, but because the initial disputes over their legal and social status had been resolved, and whites in the county felt secure enough to relax a bit. As Gordon McKinney wrote of African Americans in the mountain South at this time, "Their small numbers apparently freed the mountain whites of the fear of 'Negro Domination.'" Public schools had opened to blacks, but they were segregated, and spending per black pupil was well below that spent on whites. Blacks had gained the right to vote, but they were still only a quarter of the county's population, and it was unlikely that any black man would hold public office there. African Americans had also gained the right to testify against whites in court, but they were still kept off the bench and out of the jury box. Thus, while full-blown segregation did not yet exist and the races mixed on a daily basis in a variety of ways, it was clear in Montgomery County that whites were firmly in control.[27]

As described in more detail in chapter 6, however, a biracial political coalition of black Republicans and white Readjusters briefly challenged the racial status quo in the early 1880s. This led to modest changes in the political and legal position of African Americans in Montgomery County but was then followed by a renewed assault that was especially evident in increased restrictions on black voting. The Walton Act, passed in 1894, mandated a complicated voting process, barred the use of party symbols on ballots, and disenfranchised large numbers of black voters. Then, in 1902, conservatives finished the work of disenfranchising Afro-Virginians by drafting and adopting a new state constitution that included a combination of tax and literacy requirements guaranteed to keep nearly all blacks from voting. This was also the era in which racial segregation became more established in Virginia. Between 1900 and 1912 the General Assembly passed legislation authorizing or requiring the segregation of steamboats, streetcars, and railroads and permitting cities to enforce residential segregation.

Without black newspapers or politicians, it is difficult to capture the response of blacks in Montgomery County to the increasingly evident racism of the late nineteenth and early twentieth centuries. The limited evidence that is available, however, suggests that persistent or increasing racism was a factor in the decision by a growing number of the county's black residents to emigrate. First, where they chose to go speaks clearly of a desire to escape the grip of Jim Crow; large numbers went in every direction except south. A few left Montgomery County for cities in Virginia such as Roanoke or Norfolk, but most of those who can be traced went to Maryland, Washington, D.C., New Jersey, Pennsylvania, West Virginia, Ohio, Illinois, Iowa, Montana, and California. The North and the Midwest were hardly paradise for African Americans in 1900, but they were certainly an improvement over Virginia. Ronald L. Lewis has written that in the coalfields of West Virginia "blacks came closer to finding economic equality than in any other coalfield, and perhaps anywhere else in America," and black miners in Iowa, note modern scholars, "faced no barriers in renting or building homes, in finding employment, or in patronizing public institutions and private businesses."[28]

Even more eloquent are accounts that have survived from the emigrants themselves. These capture vividly the mix of racial and economic incentives that led so many men and women of color to leave Montgomery County. In 1892, for example, George W. Hopkins wrote to his wife from Chicago excitedly describing what he had found there and urging her to join him: "Everybody is white here. I am just as white as any body." Seven years later, in 1899, George Washington sent a much angrier letter from his new home in Chicago to his wife and her "white friends" back in Christiansburg explaining why he left: "The old white people there sold me out making out that they wanted to pay my debts and they are liars, they just did it to get money for their own pockets." Similarly, people who knew William McNorton reported that he left Montgomery County in the late 1880s and took up land in western Montana to escape the "prejudice against Negroes" that marked his birthplace. In July 1938, shortly before McNorton's death, a local Montana newspaper reported, "He recounted to his friends that he had left Virginia and sought his fortune in the west so that he would not be restricted from opportunity by racial prejudices as he would be in the south." Race relations in Chicago or Montana were certainly not perfect in the 1890s, but cities and regions in the North and West did offer greater economic and personal opportunities than many African Americans saw at the time in Montgomery County and in other southern communities. Moreover, by the 1890s the extreme poverty that had hindered their emigration immediately after emancipation had improved somewhat, and the movement north that would surge in the early twentieth century had clearly begun.[29]

The decades following the Civil War also witnessed significant changes in the geography of black life *inside* Montgomery County. Not only did African Americans move into and out of the county during these years, they also moved within the county. Immediately after their emancipation, the great majority of freedpeople continued to live where they had been enslaved. An 1865 census of freedpeople in the county indicates that almost 90 percent were still living with their former owners, and two years later 18 percent still were. Stephen Ash, Susan O'Donovan, and Wilma Dunaway have suggested that such persistence was often because owners in regions more distant from the armies, such as southern Appalachia, deliberately withheld from slaves news of the war's end and of their emancipation and held them in quasi slavery for months after they were supposed to be free. Dunaway, for example, claimed that "many mountain slaves were not liberated until eighteen months or longer after the war ended." There is little evidence of this, however, in Montgomery County. No descendants of slaves in the county reported their families being held after April 1865, and the register of complaints maintained by the local office of the Freedmen's Bureau, beginning in August 1865, includes just one complaint that a former owner "refuses to recognize the freedom of the negroes."[30]

But moving off of the farms and plantations on which they had been enslaved required economic resources that most former slaves simply did not have.[31] Freedpeople needed houses in which to live and the means to support themselves, and immediately after emancipation few former slaves had independent access to either. Janie Milton, for example, recalled that her great-grandparents, Mary and Tom Brown, chose to stay on the farm on which Mary and her daughters had been slaves because they had housing there. Only after Tom Brown could find another house for the family did they move.[32] Similarly, the great majority of freedpeople in Montgomery County continued to live with their former owners for months, if not years, following their emancipation. By the late 1860s, though, the racial geography of the county had begun to change. Like African Americans throughout the South, many in Montgomery County moved from farm to town in the decades following their emancipation.[33] Between 1870 and 1900, the county's black population became increasingly concentrated in or adjacent to the towns of Christiansburg, Blacksburg, and Radford (known until 1887 as Lovely Mount or Central Depot) and increasingly segregated in distinct black neighborhoods in both urban and rural sections of the county.

Slaves and free people of color had never been distributed evenly across Montgomery County. Before the Civil War, both groups had been over-represented in the county's "urban" sector, especially in Christiansburg. In 1860, the county seat had been home to 6.6 percent of the county's total population but to 9.3 percent of its slave population and 27.2 percent of the free people of color. In all, 10.4 percent of Montgomery County's African American population had lived in Christiansburg in 1860. That and the smaller community in Blacksburg combined to bring the total "urban" share of the county's African American population to 12.7 percent in 1860. This had changed little by 1870 and even by 1880 had risen only slightly, to 13.3 percent. Census data show, however, that over the next twenty years, as the county's economy shifted away from agriculture and as the county's African American population began to decline, those who remained were much more likely to live in town. By 1900 26.4 percent of the county's black residents were living in one of its towns.[34] The urbanization that took place after 1880 was not, however, just a continuation of the pattern seen before then. By 1900, the county's urban hierarchy had changed entirely and with it the geographic pattern of black town life in Montgomery County.

Christiansburg had long been the county's largest and most important community, but it declined in both regards during the last quarter of the nineteenth century. Much of this decline was a result of town leaders' earlier decision not to allow the Virginia and Tennessee Railroad to pass directly through town. Instead, they convinced the line to lay its track and build its depot a mile from downtown Christiansburg in what was then farmland. A decade later the neighborhood around the depot gained its own post office and a separate identity as Bangs—later changed to Ronald and finally to Cambria—and in the final decades of the century it grew steadily as the railroad gained significance to the local economy. Christiansburg, in the meantime, saw its role as a central place decline after the Civil War. It remained the seat of government for Montgomery County and still boasted a number of its leading merchants, but its importance to the local economy declined substantially with the growth of Cambria, and by the end of the century both Christiansburg and Cambria were being overshadowed by the rapid growth of Roanoke, to the east, and Radford, to the west. Not surprisingly, the population of Christiansburg declined along with the town's significance. It fell by almost a quarter between 1870 and 1900.[35]

Christiansburg also got whiter during those years. In 1860, the town had been nearly 35 percent black and was still a third black in 1880, but by 1900 African Americans made up just 17.6 percent of the town's population. There was no policy mandating racial segregation in Christiansburg at this time, and African Americans who could afford to could live anywhere in town they wished. In 1869, for example, Charlotte Calloway bought a lot two blocks south of the town square and built a house for herself in what a real estate handbill of the day called a "desireable" neighborhood. Her neighbors there included William C. Hagan, first superintendent of schools in the county, and Charles A. Miller, minister at the town's Presbyterian Church. Certain parts of town, however, were clearly blacker than others in the decade or so following the Civil War. The northern end of Franklin and Center Streets was the heart of what was then called Campbell Town—the largest black neighborhood in Christiansburg—though its residents were not all black. Free people of color, many of them members of the Campbell family, had begun buying land and building houses there during the 1850s, and in the years immediately after the Civil War it remained the largest black neighborhood in Christiansburg. There were also a number of African Americans living at the western ends of Center Street and Railroad Street, though neither of these areas was exclusively black either.[36]

During the final two decades of the nineteenth century these original black neighborhoods in Christiansburg shrank and new ones emerged just outside of town on both its eastern and western edges. The latter of these, along the Mud Pike, was the smaller and less distinct of the two. East of Christiansburg, on the other hand, the area known as Zion Hill was by 1900 the largest and best-known African American neighborhood in the Christiansburg area. At the end of the Civil War, this had been a largely undeveloped area between Christiansburg and the railroad depot, but in 1867 Charles Schaeffer acquired land on Zion Hill on which to erect the first structure in the county built to be a school and church for freedpeople. Over the next thirty years, Zion Hill became a part of the expanding Bangs/Ronald/Cambria community. It also attracted more black residents and became the center of black life in Montgomery County. Zion Hill was home to the county's largest and best black school, the Christiansburg Institute, until the school moved a mile north in search of more land on which to expand its industrial department. It was also home to the county's largest black church and to a growing number of middle-class black families. It was never an exclusively black neighborhood, though, nor were its black residents all middle class. Census schedules from 1880 and 1900 show that the Zion Hill neighborhood was about half black and quite mixed in terms of race and class. Small clusters of black families alternated with small clusters of white families, and some black residents were homeowners while others were servants living in white households.

The situation in Blacksburg after the Civil War was both different from and similar to that found in Christiansburg. In contrast to Christiansburg, Blacksburg grew both larger and blacker between 1870 and 1900. Antebellum Blacksburg had been considerably smaller than Christiansburg and had a much smaller African American population. Slaves made up just over 11 percent of Blacksburg's population on the 1860 census, and the three free people of color in town brought its total African American population to just under 12 percent. Not surprisingly then, Blacksburg had little in the way of an African American community before the Civil War and no African American neighborhoods. Slaves and free people of color certainly associated with one another at church or on the streets of town, but both populations tended to live in fairly small groups, often in white households, and were scattered widely through town. And with just three free people of color in 1860, all of whom lived in white households, antebellum Blacksburg had nothing like the Campbell Town neighborhood that was emerging in Christiansburg. Few freedpeople moved into Blacksburg immediately after emancipation; it was still a small village with relatively few job opportunities for black workers. That changed, however, with the establishment of the Virginia Agricultural and Mechanical College in 1872. The town's population and economy both began to expand, and they attracted a growing number of African Americans to the town. By 1880, Blacksburg's population was a quarter black, and it remained so through the end of the nineteenth century.[37]

As the number of black residents in Blacksburg increased, three separate black neighborhoods appeared, though, as in Christiansburg, the largest and best known of these actually developed just outside the town's legal limits. The first black neighborhoods to emerge in Blacksburg were on the east side of the town's original core. The African Methodist Episcopal (AME) Church organized a congregation in town shortly after the Civil War, a black Baptist congregation was established there early in the 1870s, and several different black schools operated during the 1860s and 1870s. All of these institutions were on the eastern side of town, and they became the anchors for two small black communities that had emerged by the early 1880s: one around the AME Church, in Blacksburg's northeast corner, and the other near the Baptist Church and a black primary school, on the southeastern edge of town. Each was fairly small and fairly compact, but each remained a distinct neighborhood into the twentieth century.[38]

Blacksburg's largest black neighborhood, however, did not develop around either of the town's black churches or its black school. Instead, it grew up near the Virginia Agricultural and Mechanical College, just northwest of town, where both jobs and land became available during the 1870s. Though small when it opened, the college experienced a growth spurt during the 1870s and needed both laborers and servants, which attracted black workers. At the same time, developers began dividing up farmland adjacent to the town and college and selling it in small lots. Among those who bought lots in what was originally called Clapboard Town were a number of black men who may have come to work at the college or for those who were building it. About half of these were former slaves from the region around Blacksburg, but at least half were men who cannot be found in Montgomery County before the mid-1870s and seem to have moved into the county after emancipation. The name Clapboard Town, or New Town as it was soon known, may have originally referred to the entire development of new lots and homes northwest of Blacksburg's original core. At some point, though, it came to mean just that section including Gilbert Street and an adjoining alley in which the overwhelming majority of the residents were black. This New Town—home to black laborers, servants, and craftsmen—remained an almost exclusively African American community into the mid-twentieth century.[39]

The increased concentration of Montgomery County's black population in the county's towns was certainly pronounced during the decades following the Civil War, but it still involved less than a third of that population.

A majority of the county's African American residents remained in the county's rural districts well into the twentieth century. That does not mean, however, that the human geography of those rural districts remained as it had been before the Civil War. In antebellum Montgomery County, slaves and free people of color had been widely distributed through all of the county's farming districts except in the more mountainous northern third of the county, where neither slaves nor free people of color were very numerous. This pattern changed after emancipation, though.

After the Civil War, black laborers continued to work some of the county's the best land, along the valley bottoms, but they did so mainly for its white owners. They rarely farmed such land for themselves, and they rarely lived on it. Instead, black families lived farther up the hillsides or in the narrow valleys known as hollows. This seems to have been a result of white landowners' disinclination to sell their better land to black farmers; so as more black families sought to buy land, they could often only get it farther up the hillsides or up hollows that had little of the best cropland. When Jerry Watson and Violet James bought twenty-five acres on Pilot Mountain, for example, the deed indicated that their land ran along a hollow "to near the top of said mountain." Similarly, the surveyor who laid out Gordon Mills's land on the slopes outside of Blacksburg described it as "very rocky steep land." This pattern tended to concentrate the county's rural black population more than it had been before the Civil War. While the population of slaves had been distributed widely through the county's rural districts, in the postbellum era black residents were more often clustered in distinct black neighborhoods that emerged between 1865 and 1890.[40]

The best known of these black, rural neighborhoods in Montgomery County is Wake Forest, which remains a distinct and recognized community (if no longer an exclusively African American one) almost 150 years after its creation. James R. Kent, the owner of Kentland plantation and the largest slaveholder in the county in 1860, had quarters for some of his slaves on or near the land on which Wake Forest was built. This land was arable but hiller and rockier than bottom land nearer the New River, and tradition among the community's residents is that Kent permitted freedpeople to settle the area after the Civil War and hired them to work at Kentland. Thus, the Kents retained the plantation's best land for their own benefit and a labor force to work it, while the freedpeople found steady work and home sites on which they could also farm a bit for themselves. According to this tradition, after Kent told his slaves they were free, "they went onto the wooded area, you know, seemingly all wood, which was a forest. And overnight, they built a community out of the forest and logs and what have you. And that's how the Wake part of it come, like, like, you, you [sic] go overnight, you wake up the next morning and the community is there." Even if it did not it arise in a single night, Wake Forest was clearly a well-established and recognized African American community by early 1869 because in May of that year the Virginia Conference of the AME Church appointed a minister to the congregation there and later that year a school opened there.[41]

Wake Forest may be the best known of these historically black rural communities that emerged in Montgomery County after the Civil War, but it was not the only one. As figure 3 shows, about a dozen such communities appeared during the last decades of the nineteenth century. They were located throughout the regions of the county in which slaves had been concentrated before 1865. In many cases, in fact, former slaves from several farms or plantations in a particular region of the county settled together in a new community near the farms or plantations on which they had been enslaved. Former slaves from Kentland, as described above, often settled in Wake Forest. Similarly, some of the former slaves from the Hoge plantations, in Ellett Valley, lived in Nellies Cave, on the mountain above their former homes, and a number from the Payton and Edmondson plantations, between Shawsville and Big Spring, lived in Dark Hollow and Brake Branch. None of these communities was a town, or even a village, and none merited a post office. Officially, they were just rural neighborhoods in which a dozen or two dozen black families lived near one another without formal incorporation or legal boundaries. They often had their own black schools, churches, cemeteries, and other institutions, though, and were widely recognized by both black and white residents of the county as distinct communities. Like Wake Forest, they had names and recognized (if rather general) physical boundaries that often survived over several decades and in a few cases have survived more than a century.

Montgomery County's African American community was more than places, though. It also included distinctly African American institutions, practices, and leaders described more fully in later chapters. Churches and schools were the most common black institutions in postwar Montgomery County, and almost every black neighborhood, urban or rural, had one or both soon after its founding. As discussed in chapter 4, the Freedmen's Bureau and northern aid societies established a handful of schools for

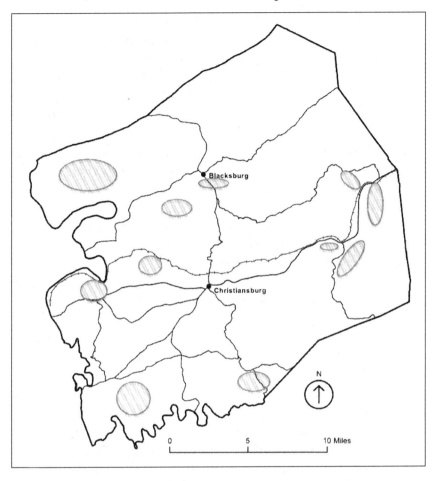

FIGURE 3. Rural African American communities in Montgomery
County, ca. 1890. (Base map by Matthew Layman)

freedpeople in Montgomery County between 1867 and 1870, and most of
these became public schools after 1870. The number of schools then rose
and fell as the county's black population did and as the state's economy
did, but for most of the period 1871–1902 there were sixteen to eighteen
black schools in the county in any given year. Black churches were at least
as common as black schools during these years. As described more fully
in chapter 5, freedpeople in the county largely withdrew from its white-
controlled churches almost immediately after emancipation and quickly
began to establish their own predominantly or entirely black churches.
Not all of these survived, but between 1865 and 1900 at least twenty-

two black churches opened in the county. In later years, as the county's black residents began to establish themselves economically, a number of black social and mutual aid organizations also appeared. Some of these were closely linked to particular churches. The Good Samaritan Society in Blacksburg, for example, was affiliated with the AME congregation in town. Others, however, were local chapters of national, nondenominational organizations. The Prince Hall Free and Accepted Masons, a black order of Freemasons that had begun in Massachusetts during the American Revolution, opened St. John's Lodge No. 35 in Christiansburg in 1877; the Grand United Order of Galilean Fishermen, which began in Baltimore in 1856 as a benevolent society and then came to focus on business and economic development, established Zion Sons & Daughters Tabernacle No. 89 in Christiansburg in 1891; and the three lodges of the Grand United Order of the Odd Fellows, a mutual aid society established by free blacks during the 1840s, opened in the early twentieth century: in Blacksburg (1905), in Christiansburg (by 1907), and in the Brake Branch community adjacent to Big Spring (date unknown).

The leaders of these institutions—ministers, teachers, and lodge officers—seem to have been the most visible leaders of the communities in which they lived and of Montgomery County's black community. There were a few entrepreneurs among the county's early black leaders. Minnis Headen, who was the first black man in the county to stand for elected office, earned his living as a blacksmith and held two patents for improved treadle hammers, while Joshua Webster was a successful house builder. Both men, however, were also church trustees before they became successful in business. Similarly, Alexander Hopkins was the only other black man in the county known to have stood for public office before the twentieth century, but before that he taught school, attended seminary, and was licensed by the Baptist Church. In Montgomery County, education and religion seem to have been just as important as wealth or property as criteria for leadership among the county's African American residents in the decades following the Civil War.[42]

A few of these postwar black leaders, both former slaves and free persons of color, had been prominent during the antebellum era. Richard Taylor, for example, had been a well-known slave preacher in the county. He had served as a Methodist lay preacher and had performed marriage ceremonies among slaves in a rural district southeast of Blacksburg. After emancipation, he became an ordained Baptist minister and led the congregation in Christiansburg for a decade before his death in 1879. John Campbell may also have been a leader among the county's antebellum free people of color. A carpenter living in Big Spring, he was a landowner by 1853 and the county's wealthiest free person of color in 1860. After the war he remained a successful carpenter, but he was also ordained a Baptist minister and played a leading role in the Big Spring church. Both Taylor and Campbell, as well as Minnis Headen, another former slave, were among the men identified in 1867 by Charles Schaeffer as "the most intelligent of the Freedmen belonging to Montgomery County Va. in whom both races have confidence." Other black leaders of the 1870s and 1880s were younger men who only emerged as leaders after the Civil War. Alexander Hopkins, for example, was just twenty-three when the Civil War ended, and Joshua Webster was not only young when the war ended, twenty-five years old, but seems to have migrated into the county between 1865 and 1870.[43]

Missing from the ranks of postemancipation black leaders in Montgomery County were Union veterans. More than a dozen men from the county had escaped slavery, joined the Union army, and survived the Civil War. Ira Berlin and others have noted that the experience of wearing their country's uniform, carrying a rifle, and sometimes serving as noncommissioned officers often had a transformative effect on black men. Many came home with a different sense of themselves and of their place in southern society. Returning veterans brought experience and confidence to their communities and often emerged as leaders in those communities during the postwar years. Men from Montgomery County known to have served in the US Colored Troops generally mustered out in March or April of 1866, and those who returned to the county did so later that year. Most went on to lives of modest success. None, however, emerged as leaders in the black community, perhaps because those most likely to do so left the county after repeated confrontations with the prominent and powerful Preston family. Thomas and Othello Fraction came home in 1866 and immediately demonstrated the sort of transformation described by Berlin. As described more fully in subsequent chapters, however, this brought them into conflict with Robert Preston, the owner of a large plantation near Blacksburg on which the Fractions had previously been enslaved. They successfully stood up to Preston several times in 1866 and 1867, but by 1870 they had left the county and never returned.[44]

Finally, members of Montgomery County's African American community also celebrated events with a special significance to their community or in ways that were distinctive to it. January 1, 1863, the date on which the Emancipation Proclamation took full effect, was marked by annual celebrations among Christiansburg's black residents for at least twenty-five years after the Civil War. Independence Day, July 4, was also sometimes marked in black communities with particular enthusiasm. In 1874, for example, the *Messenger* reported a large "Negro celebration" near Vickers, west of Christiansburg, at which an American flag and a portrait of George Washington were prominently displayed. The most distinctive temporal marker of the county's black community, though, seems to have been the continuing pattern of celebrating marriages during the Christmas holiday. This had been common among slaves throughout the antebellum South, including Montgomery County. Among the marriages recorded on the county's cohabitation register, 15.5 percent had taken place during the last ten days of December. In Montgomery County, at least, this pattern was explicitly identified with African Americans and continued long after slavery ended. In January 1869, the *Christiansburg Southwest* commented on the number of marriages that had taken place in the county during December and declared, "Cupid must be using grape shot on the Hams in our midst." And the pattern continued long after slavery ended; 15 percent of black couples who married in the county between 1870 and 1899 married during the ten days around Christmas.[45]

Montgomery County's postwar African American community was never as large or as complex as those found in some of Virginia's other counties, and it had already begun to decline in size by the end of the nineteenth century. The population would continue to decline until the second half of the twentieth century, while the community faced mounting pressure from the passage of Jim Crow legislation and a rising tide of overt racism. Through declining numbers and rising white antipathy, though, the community survived. That survival was largely a result of institutions maintained or established by the county's black residents between 1865 and 1902—institutions that helped to unite them in the face of continuing social, political, and economic challenges. The oldest and most significant of these institutions was the family.

2 FAMILIES IN FREEDOM

THADEUS MORGAN AND AMANDA PRICE married on Christmas Day 1865. Morgan, who was twenty-three at the time, had been a slave of Henry Fowlkes until the end of the Civil War, eight months earlier. This was, apparently, his first marriage. His bride, also twenty-three, had been a slave of Waller Staples, a lawyer, politician, and planter who owned land about three miles from that of Henry Fowlkes. Her background is less clear. Her marriage license says Amanda Price was a widow, and a census taken during the summer of 1865 shows that at the time she married Morgan she had two children with two different surnames: seven-year-old Ann Eliza Mott and two-year-old Abraham Black. She might have been widowed twice, might have borne her daughter before marrying the first time, or might have described herself as a widow to help the children avoid the stigma of illegitimacy. And there is no way of knowing whether her prior marriage (or marriages) had been arranged by her owner or was a union of the couple's own making. With Thadeus Morgan, though, Amanda had the chance to marry a man of her own choosing.[1]

Unfortunately, their marriage did not last long; Amanda died in childbirth in 1873, leaving Thadeus with a newborn, named Amanda after her mother, and six other children or stepchildren to care for. His mother-in-law, Parthenia Price, moved in to help with the children and the housekeeping, but six years later, in April 1879, Morgan remarried. His second wife, Sallie Cox, was single and fifteen years his junior when they wed, and their union proved neither long nor happy. Soon after they married, according to Thadeus, Sallie Morgan began to engage in "lewd and adulterous conduct with various persons in the neighborhood." By October 1882 Sallie had left Thadeus, and the couple divorced early the next year. Ever the optimist—and with six children to care for—Thadeus Morgan married again just ten months after his divorce from Sallie. At age forty-two, he wed Julia Ann Forrow, who was twenty-six and single. This union proved his most successful. Thadeus and Julia Morgan had at least seven children together over the next twenty years and were still married when Thadeus died, in the fall of 1904.[2]

Thadeus Morgan was one of many African Americans in Montgomery County making the transition from slavery to freedom after 1865, and the story of his effort to build and maintain his family demonstrates a number of features that were common among those who made this transition: a strong desire to establish and maintain traditional, patriarchal families; the challenge of constructing such families from the parts of preexisting families that emerged from slavery; the influence of racism on family formation; and the variety of strategies by which Afro-Virginians established, reestablished, and maintained families in the face of it. Above all, Thadeus Morgan's story shows that, in spite of the challenges facing them in postwar Montgomery County, African Americans could and often did succeed in establishing successful, autonomous families.

Families, of course, had also been an essential element of black life in Montgomery County before the Civil War. Scholars have long understood that most American slaves lived in families, though these were not always the male-headed nuclear units that white observers associated with "families." Slavery and the property rights of slave owners meant that slave families were subject to their owners' control. Owners determined if slaves would marry, who they would marry, and whether or not the resulting families would remain intact. In abroad marriages—unions in which the partners lived in two different locations—they also controlled to some extent how often and for how long the partners could see one another and how often the nonresident parent (usually the father) could see the couple's children. As a result, slave families were often headed by women whose partners visited their wives and children when they could, and in the absence of blood or marital kin, slave families often relied more on fictive kin than white families did. Such strategies did not, however, reduce the importance of families in the slave community. Nor did slavery reduce the desire for families among the enslaved. Slaves saw families as valuable sources of emotional and physical support—an important weapon in their battle against the potentially dehumanizing effects of chattel slavery. Masters too, precisely because slavery did turn humans into property, were often willing to encourage family formation among their bondsmen and women. Families created emotional ties that helped to keep slaves from escaping, and the children born to slave women represented future workers or sources of capital.[3]

In antebellum Montgomery County, at least, free black families had also been subject to a significant measure of white control. In part, this was because free blacks in the county often married slaves, but even if two free people of color married, their union enjoyed only partial recognition. Antebellum law in Virginia was entirely silent on the issue of marriage by free people of color except to declare void "all marriages between a white person and a negro," and no marriage between free blacks or mulattos was ever recorded officially in Montgomery County.[4] Such unions did occur, however, and seem to have been recognized by white neighbors. Unfortunately, no evidence has survived from the county to show whether or not the widows, widowers, or children of free people of color were considered legal heirs or could inherit their property, though the absence of legal disputes over such matters suggests that they did. More telling, however, is the county court's apparent recognition of free people of color's parental rights in the cases of their children's indentures. Hercules Marrs, for example, successfully approached the court in 1854 with a request "to bind his son Andrew . . . to Elizabeth Taber & Whitley J. Taber according to law." Six years later, county officials also recorded an agreement by which Marrs bound his son Chapman to serve Edwin Linkous in exchange for "suitable clothing & medical care" for the boy plus $25 paid to Chapman and $160 paid to his father. Such actions suggest that the county's white community may have accorded the marriages and families of free people of color a sort of de facto common law status.[5]

This all changed following emancipation. Freedpeople could suddenly establish families without white permission and with much less interference from whites, and in this new environment, marriage and family took on a political significance they may not have before. Marriage and family for African Americans now became legal matters, and freed*men*, in particular, considered their new rights as husbands and fathers to be important elements in the freedom they expected to emerge from the abolition of slavery and the reconstruction of southern society. The assertion of these rights and their recognition by whites often became a marker of freedmen's status as citizens and as men.[6] Dylan Penningroth has shown that freedpeople sometimes employed extralegal mechanisms to resolve questions of family or property rights, and there is some evidence that they did so in Montgomery County. Far more often, however, freedpeople there sought *legal* remedies to such questions and did so in the face of significant economic, social, and legal challenges.

The most fundamental challenge was the complete absence of any legal framework in Virginia by which to establish or reestablish African American families immediately after emancipation. Herbert Gutman observed in *The Black Family in Slavery and Freedom* that how freedpeople learned about the laws governing marriage in the chaos surrounding the collapse of slavery and the Confederacy "remains one of the many hidden 'stories' about ex-slaves." What also remains hidden is just how government officials handled the issue. Virginia law at the time required that any couple seeking to marry first secure a license from the clerk of the court, and it required the clerk to record all marriages after receiving notice from the person officiating that the marriage had been performed. The law said nothing about the race of the parties entering into the marriage, though. Its authors had simply assumed when they drafted the law that it would only apply to whites, but the world had changed in 1865. In the immediate aftermath of general emancipation, it seems that no one in Montgomery County knew if freedpeople were bound by the same requirements as whites. At least five black couples in the county began living together as husband and wife between April 14 and August 31, 1865, but none of these couples secured a license, and none of their marriages were registered by the clerk of the court. It is impossible to say, however, whether or not these couples simply took up together, as slaves often had, or tried to get licenses and whether or not the clerk refused to grant them licenses or to register their marriages.[7]

By September the situation had finally begun to change, perhaps because by then the Freedmen's Bureau had opened an office in the county. On September 1, Oscar Johnson and Nancy Duke became the first African Americans known to have obtained a marriage license in Montgomery County. This did not, however, make things much clearer. After obtaining their license, Johnson and Duke married in Blacksburg, on September 9, and their marriage was entered in the records of the Methodist Church there. The minister also submitted his return to the clerk of the court, but the clerk never entered the marriage in to the county's official register. Such irregularities were common for the rest of the year. During the last four months of 1865, at least ten black couples married in Montgomery County. Six of the ten obtained marriage licenses, and five of the ten marriages were entered in the county register, but only three couples among the ten met both of these requirements, and two met neither. It seems that no one really knew what was required and that individual couples or the clerk of the court simply did as they wished on a case-by-case basis. In February 1866, the state finally acted to require that black couples follow the same procedure white couples did; it then became normal in Virginia for black couples to obtain licenses, though as discussed further in chapter 6, the county clerk was still sometimes slow to register their marriages. This new regimen was clearly still a work in progress. In Montgomery County, at least, the clerk continued to use forms that dated to 1861 and, thus, had no place to enter the couple's race; so he entered the information in a variety of places on the license, or not at all. Moreover, he still had not settled on a term for the county's nonwhite citizens; thus "Freedman," "Colored," and "African" were all employed on marriage licenses in the county during 1865 and 1866.[8]

Even without a proper legal framework, African American residents of Montgomery County immediately set about the task of safeguarding their families. Sometimes this was a relatively straightforward process. In the spring of 1865, for example, Steward Collins left the farm of Pitt Woodroof, where he had been a slave, and traveled to Danville to bring his wife and three children back to live with him in Montgomery County. At the same time, Gilbert Vaughn, formerly a slave of Mary Wade, moved his wife, Charlotte, and their four children from Robert Miller's farm, where Charlotte and the children had been slaves, to live with him on land he was sharecropping for Hamilton D. Wade, the nephew and heir of his former owner.[9] At other times, however, freedpeople in the county faced a range of obstacles in their effort to establish successful, autonomous families.

These obstacles sometimes included their ostensible allies in the Freedmen's Bureau. The establishment of stable black families was certainly an important goal of the Freedmen's Bureau in the years after emancipation, and it often worked with freedpeople to reunite their families by helping to locate members and by paying the costs of transportation necessary to effect reunions. The first agent to arrive in Christiansburg, for example, almost immediately began asking for funds to pay the travel costs of freedpeople searching for their spouses or children. The bureau's priorities, however, were not always the same as those of the freedpeople it sought to help. The latter wanted to establish stable relationships with partners to whom they had an emotional attachment. The Freedmen's Bureau, on the other hand, was sometimes more concerned with what it considered to be the morality and legality of a marriage and was disturbed by the willingness of freedpeople to dissolve what the bureau regarded as "a sacred obligation." Charles Schaeffer, the agent in Christiansburg, wrote, for example, "The cases which give me the greatest anxiety and trouble are those growing out of the marriage relation; as it is a difficult matter to get the colored people to fully understand the binding obligation of their pledges to each other."[10]

In fact, freedpeople understood exactly what they were doing, and their actions were often taken in order to promote the very pledges about which Schaeffer seemed so concerned. Dick Johnson, for example, had apparently been separated from his first wife and their children by sale or migration while they had all been slaves. He had then remarried, either as a slave or soon after slavery ended, and by 1868 was living near Christiansburg with his second wife. To Schaeffer, this second wife was Johnson's legal wife. Thus, when Johnson left her to rejoin his first wife, in Spotsylvania County, Schaeffer's initial response was that Johnson had "deserted his lawful wife . . . and is supposed to have married another woman contrary to law" and that he should be prosecuted for his actions. Only after learning the details of Johnson's situation from the agent in Spotsylvania does Schaeffer appear to have accepted the situation.[11]

Many of the bureau's agents were also concerned by the impact that family unification might have on the local supplies of labor. Freedmen leaving to search for spouses, freedwomen refusing to work in the fields as they had under slavery, and couples demanding control over the lives and labor of their children all threatened to reduce the hands available to work for white landowners and employers. Scholars such as Mary Mitchell and Mary Farmer-Kaiser have noted that if these landowners and employers complained, agents of the Freedmen's Bureau sometimes sided with them at the expense of black families' autonomy or parental rights. This does not seem to have been common in Montgomery County, though. Schaeffer did try unsuccessfully to indenture a twelve-year-old boy without the consent of his mother because, he claimed, the boy wanted it, but this was an exception. Records of the Freedmen's Bureau in Christiansburg indicate that, generally, Schaeffer was much more likely to support the rights of black parents than he was to side with white employers anxious to secure workers. For example, he actively sought to return Isaac Cox, a young orphan held by a white man near Bristol, to his "proper guardians"—the black couple "who have raised the child as their own son"—and in other instances he worked to reunite black children with their parents or assured freedpeople that their parental rights would be protected.[12]

Legal and institutional challenges certainly complicated the efforts of freedpeople in Montgomery County to establish autonomous families after their emancipation, but for many the greatest challenges were economic. Even those freedpeople whose families had remained intact under slavery faced enormous economic challenges. Establishing truly autonomous families required resources that few former slaves enjoyed immediately after emancipation; they needed jobs and housing. As shown in the preceding chapter, this meant that the great majority of freedpeople in Montgomery County continued to live with their former owners for months if not years following their emancipation. This meant that their families often remained divided, too. This is clear from a census conducted by the Freedmen's Bureau in August 1865. The census suggests not only that four months after their emancipation most of the freedpeople in Montgomery County were still living on the same farms and plantations on which they had been slaves but that few were living in family units. In all, 280 of the 1,573 individuals named on the 1865 census can be identified as members of 78 different families, and most of these families were still living apart. Allen and Nancy Wright, for example, had been married since 1857 and had at least three children in 1865. As slaves, Allen and Nancy had belonged to Nathaniel Harvey and Thomas Childress, respectively, and the census shows that in August 1865 both were still living with their former owners and that the children were living with their mother on Childress's farm. Of the seventy-eight families that can be identified on the 1865 census, fifty-four (69 percent) seem to have been living apart that summer, and among the minority that were living together, most had probably been together before they were emancipated. The twenty-four couples found together on the 1865 census include twelve in which, as slaves, the husband and wife had belonged to the same owner and five in which one partner had been a free person of color. These seventeen couples had probably been living together before 1865. Thus, only seven of the seventy-eight families that can be identified on the 1865 census seem to have lived apart as slaves and to have united their families by August 1865.[13]

The 1865 census captures Montgomery County's African American community very early in the process of asserting its identity and establishing its families. In the two years that followed, the process of family formation continued rapidly, and freedpeople in the county demonstrated widespread and strong commitment to traditional patriarchal families. As described above, in February 1866 the General Assembly amended the statute regulating marriage in order to include those of freedpeople. More importantly, the same law that required black couples to obtain marriage licenses also sought to clarify the legal status of existing families formed under slavery. The statute declared that any African American couple that had previously agreed "to occupy the relation to each other of husband and wife" and was still "cohabiting together" when the law was passed "shall be deemed husband and wife." It also made the children of such couples legitimate "whether born before or after the passage of this act" if their parents registered their marriage. The law left a number of issues unresolved, though. It legitimized, for example, the children of couples that had ceased to cohabit by 1866 if the father acknowledged them but said nothing about children whose fathers had died, had been sold to distant states, or who simply chose not to acknowledge their former families. Nor did it make clear whether or not "children" included stepchildren, a large category in slave families due to the frequency of remarriages following deaths or sales. More fundamentally, it included no provision for identifying cohabiting couples or recording their unions. That void was filled only when Colonel Orlando Brown, assistant commissioner of the Freedmen's Bureau responsible for Virginia, directed bureau officials throughout the state to inform the freedpeople in their districts of the law's passage and to call on them to appear before their local agents to include their marriages in county cohabitation registers.[14]

Not all of the couples living in Montgomery County registered. Some may not even have known of the opportunity to do so. It was still difficult to disseminate information among freedpeople in the county in 1866; most of them lived in rural parts of the county, and at that time there were no schools and few churches or other institutions through which to reach them. Others may have found it too difficult to reach the recording officer, either because they were working or because of the distance they had to travel. Still others may not have wanted to register. Couples who had been joined only at the insistence of their former owners, couples in which one partner preferred to reunite with a prior spouse from whom he or she had been separated, and couples who had simply grown weary of one another could cease to cohabit, decline to register at the appointed time, and secure de facto divorces. Still, 324 couples with a total of 872 children did record their marriages and families that summer. It is impossible to say precisely what percentage of the county's adult freedpeople that represented, but it was certainly more than half. The 1865 census had identified 826 African Americans fifteen years or older in the county, of whom an estimated 670 were eighteen or older, while an 1867 census found 1,206 freedpeople aged eighteen or older. Assuming the adult population in 1866 fell somewhere between the two—a thousand for example—then approximately two-thirds of adult freedpeople in the county were married, and even using the 1867 population, more than half were.[15]

In the years immediately following emancipation, marriage and family were not just common among the freedpeople of Montgomery County; they were also important, as the case of Alexander Saunders demonstrates. In the summer of 1867, Saunders was a fifty-five-year-old farm worker living outside Christiansburg with his wife, Sarah. According to Charles Schaeffer, local agent of the Freedmen's Bureau, Sarah Saunders was "seduced" that summer by Whitford (or Whitfield) Goff, a black farm worker, thirty-five years old and, reportedly, a man "of bad reputation." Goff then attempted to clear the way for further "licentiousness" with Sarah by having her husband arrested. The details of Goff's behavior may already have been known, but they certainly came out when a county magistrate heard his complaint against Alexander Saunders. The magistrate, therefore, described Saunders as the injured party and threw Goff's complaint out. Saunders, however, demanded more.[16]

Like many other freedmen, Alexander Saunders was willing to employ both legal and extralegal remedies to right a wrong. After "having the peace of his family destroyed" by Whitford Goff, Saunders was not satisfied with the court's decision, and when the hearing ended he asked the magistrate for permission "that he might take with him a party of the boys, to punish Goff, with a good switching." The magistrate refused, explaining that such an approach was against the law. Saunders, however, declared "that he must have some redress, that he could not live under the burden that oppressed him; and that he would go to the boys, and see

what could be done." In response, the magistrate warned Saunders that if
he and his friends took action against Goff, "they had better be very careful
not to injure him" and reiterated that "the law would hold them responsible." Saunders took this as license to act and told "the boys" they had
permission "to give Goff a good switching, but not to injure him." A group
of freedmen, therefore, decided to punish Goff "for destroying the peace of
the old man's family, and the dishonoring of his wife."[17]

The next night, August 15, Saunders and a number of other men—most
in their twenties or thirties and several married—went in search of Whitford Goff. They eventually found him hiding at the home of his employer,
a white house builder named Chapman Johnson, who made no effort to
stop them. Johnson later told Schaeffer that he had already helped Goff
out of "a number of scrapes" and that after the last he had told him that if
he continued to act "badly," he would have to face the consequences. Goff's
captors then took him to Saunders's house, where "they tried his case in
the presence of the woman." After finding him guilty, the men stripped
Goff and began whipping him with "a small switch . . . cut from the limb of
a dog wood tree." This was presumably so as "not to injure him," and after
delivering fifty to seventy-five stripes the men released Goff with orders to
leave the county within twenty-four hours—which he did.[18]

Three weeks later, Saunders and five of his accomplices were indicted
by the grand jury for their assault on Whitford Goff. When the accused
appeared in court, early in November, they were ordered to post bond,
and the neighbors who stepped forward to provide security for the men
demonstrate the breadth of support that they and their action enjoyed
in the county's African American community. At least eight freedmen,
including several of the most prominent men in the community, and one
freedwoman came forward to guarantee the bonds. Clearly, many in the
local community believed that Saunders had a moral right to defend his
manhood and the honor of his marriage and family, even if he had no legal
right to do so. Ultimately, an all-white jury convicted some of the men
who had actually whipped Goff but acquitted Alexander Saunders, and
Schaeffer wrote that if the accused had been white, they would all have
been found not guilty.[19]

While the Saunders case was unfolding, freedpeople in Montgomery County were also demonstrating the strength of black families in a
more peaceful way. During the summer of 1867, the Freedmen's Bureau
conducted a second census of the county's African American population.

Individuals on the 1865 census had been organized by the employers for whom they worked and with whom they lived, and the enumerator had largely ignored family units. In 1867, on the other hand, the document was organized alphabetically, and it highlights families. At the most basic level, the 1867 census captures the effort of freedpeople in Montgomery County to establish their family identities more clearly through the use of family names. As Leon Litwack has noted, this was not just a practical matter that made it easier for freedpeople to deal with government officials; it was also a matter of pride. Family names, Litwack wrote, "[were] an essential step toward achieving the self-respect, the personal dignity, and the independence which slavery had compromised."[20] This was not a matter of choosing a name, though. It is clear from a variety of antebellum sources that most slaves had surnames, even if their owners rarely knew or used them.[21] And in marked contrast to widespread popular belief, few slaves in Montgomery County shared names with their former owners. Many Americans, both black and white, continue to believe that former slaves commonly took the names of their former masters.[22] In fact, very few did in Montgomery County. On the 1865 census it is possible to identify 555 African Americans with surnames, and only 14 of these (2.5 percent) bore the same name as their former owner. The cohabitation register tells a similar story. Time has rendered some of the entries illegible, but the register includes 613 individual adults with legible surnames. Just twenty of these (3.3 percent) bore the name of their last owner. Moreover, names on the 1867 census make it abundantly clear that the families to which they belonged were distinctly patrinominal. When the county cohabitation register was compiled in 1866, it included a column for "Name of Wife." Of the 312 women on the register, 311 provided both a first name and a surname, and the surnames they provided were not those of their husbands. Instead, they gave their birth names. In 1867, however, every married couple had a single surname, and it was invariably that of the husband.

Unfortunately, the census taker did not assign numbers to either families or households, which makes it difficult to distinguish solitaires from unrelated individuals living together and to identify orphans and evaluate their experiences. Still, the 1867 census offers the first comprehensive portrait of black families in Montgomery County after the Civil War and shows clearly both the determination of freedpeople in the county to establish or reestablish their families and the extent to which the legacy of slavery shaped their ability to do so. The desire to form families is evident from the fact that the 1867 census found 370 married black couples in the county, a number representing 61 percent of the county's adult black population.[23] As described more fully below, this figure is quite similar to that seen in the county's African American community over the next thirty years, which means that within two years of general emancipation freedpeople in the county were establishing families at a rate that would be normal for the rest of the nineteenth century. Unfortunately, it is impossible to compare the postemancipation marriage rate to that seen in the county under slavery. It is tempting to believe that one could estimate the marriage rate for slaves from the cohabitation register, but it is simply not possible to do so with any degree of accuracy. Freedpeople had been moving into and out of the county for more than a year by the time the register was compiled; so it is difficult to say how many of the couples identified on Montgomery County's register had actually been enslaved in the county. Moreover, an unknown number of slave marriages had been broken by sale before 1865, while others broke up after emancipation and never appeared on the cohabitation register.[24]

While it remains impossible to identify precisely the men and women whose unions had been broken by sale while they were enslaved or by de facto divorces afterward, clear evidence of their presence emerges from the 1867 census. At least 449 adults on the census appear to have been unmarried, though only about half of these were explicitly identified as "single." In 215 cases, just over 17 percent of all adults named on the census, the enumerator did not identify the individuals as either "married" or "single," the only two categories employed on the schedule. He did not overlook these people, however. In each of these cases, the enumerator placed a dot in the "married" column, and while no man or woman identified as "single" on the census had children, almost two-thirds (138) of these "dotted" individuals did. The dot, it seems, indicated that an individual had been involved in some kind of relationship prior to 1867 but was no longer.[25] Some of these were widows or widowers; thirteen subsequently identified themselves as such when they remarried. Nineteen, however, identified themselves as single when they remarried, and most of these already had children in 1867. Unfortunately, it is impossible to determine the status of most of these "dotted" men and women. Some of the women had probably been raped; some had probably entered consensual, short-term relationships; some of them, however, were men or women whose spouses had been sold while they had been enslaved or who found themselves in unions they did not wish to continue when slavery ended.[26]

The marital status of African American adults, of course, also influenced the environments in which their children were raised. The 1867 census found a total of 1,249 African Americans under the age of eighteen in Montgomery County. Sixty percent of these children lived in two-parent black households. Many of these were traditional nuclear families. Peter and Millie Morgan, for example, had married in 1840 and in 1867 were living with six of their children on land they were sharecropping. Others were blended families in which some of the children lived with a stepparent. Peter and Millie's son, Thadeus, for example, lived in just such a family with his wife, Amanda. It included a son born since Thadeus and Amanda's marriage as well as two children born to Amanda before she married Thadeus. In still other cases, it seems, black couples were also raising the children of relatives or friends. Gordon and Ellen Mills, for example, appear on the census with their children James, Walter, and Gordon Jr., all of whom had been identified as children of the couple on the cohabitation register the year before. Living with them in 1867 were two other children, Hamilton and Russell Mills, who do not appear on the cohabitation register as children of Gordon and Ellen. Moreover, when Russell applied for a marriage license in 1876, he identified his parents as Sampson and Betsy Mills. No record of Sampson or Betsy Mills has yet come to light, but Sampson may have been Gordon's brother. If that were the case and if both Sampson and Betsy had died or been sold away before 1865, it would make sense that Gordon and Ellen took in their nephews, Hamilton and Russell.[27]

Another 21 percent of the black children living in Montgomery County in 1867 were living with unmarried African American adults. A small number of these single-parent households were headed by men, but the great majority (97 of 114) were headed by women. These included widows as well as women who had been separated from their partners during their years as slaves, had separated or been abandoned after their emancipation, or had never had a long-term partner. By whatever path they reached this status, in 1867 they found themselves solely responsible for the care of their children, which may have meant greater economic hardship for the children in these families. In this regard, however, the number of single-parent households may be somewhat misleading, because some of these mother-child units seem to have been parts of multigenerational house-holds. Frances Day, for example, was twenty-two years old, the mother of a two-year-old son, John, and employed as a servant of Henry Ribble. According to the census, Albert and Martha Day and their sons Hugh and Joseph also worked for Dr. Ribble, and it seems likely that Frances was ei-ther their daughter or widowed daughter-in-law. Though a single mother, Frances was probably in a position to call on family for help raising her son. Cases such as the Days' were a minority, though; most of the single parents living in the county in 1867 seem to have been on their own.[28]

The remaining 19 percent of the black children living in Montgomery County in 1867 lived in a variety of circumstances. Some, such as Thomas Jones and Eliza Hoge, seem to have been living with older siblings. Oth-ers, such as Washington Jenkins and William Crockett, lived with black adults to whom they were not obviously related, though some of these may actually have been children who went by the names of their deceased or departed fathers while living with their mothers. More than half of these children, however, (just over 10 percent of all black children in the county that year) apparently lived on their own in white households. Studies of Reconstruction elsewhere have shown that white southerners often regarded all black or mulatto children as a source of cheap labor to be exploited as fully as possible and that agents of the Freedmen's Bureau sometimes encouraged such behavior through their determination to keep as many freedpeople as possible off public support. Children who had been separated from their families by sale or whose parents had died were es-pecially vulnerable, but even children whose parents were still alive and present in the community were sometimes declared orphans by unscru-pulous local officials and bound to white "guardians" for whom they were expected to provide years of service.[29] The presence of so many nonwhite children in white households on Montgomery County's 1867 census could suggest that white residents of Montgomery County and officials of the Freedmen's Bureau adopted similar attitudes and employed mechanisms by which white families in the county assumed the responsibility of car-ing for black and mulatto children in return for the fruits of their labor. A more thorough examination of the records, however, suggests that the situation was more complicated.

Records from the Freedmen's Bureau and from the county court identify very few black or mulatto children who were bound out legally to whites in Montgomery County during Reconstruction. One "Record of Indentures" has survived from Virginia's Eighth District, which included Montgomery County, though it only covers the period between December 1865 and January 1867. It documents 166 contracts approved by bureau officials, and just 5 of these appear to have involved children from Montgomery County. It is, of course, possible that whites held children without the benefit of legal indentures, but neither county court records nor those of the Freedmen's Bureau include many complaints of children in the county being held illegally or under questionable circumstances. One boy whose parents had died was reportedly taken in 1865 by a contractor working for the Virginia and Tennessee Railroad and held near Bristol for more than a year without the consent of the boy or his "proper guardians"—a black couple who had raised the child after his parents' death. In three other cases, questions arose concerning the circumstances under which an African American apprentice was bound to a white master. In one case, the mother of a young boy was dead and it was unclear if a man claiming to be his father really was; in the second, a girl's father sought to free her from an indenture negotiated by the girl's mother; and in the third, a mother objected to her twelve-year-old son's agreeing to enter an apprenticeship without her approval. In two of the three, bureau officials canceled the indentures, and in the third case the outcome remains unknown.[30]

Further clouding the picture is the fact that a significant number of the black and mulatto children living with white families in 1867 seem to have been too young to provide any real economic benefit to the families with whom they lived. Of the 131 children who seem to have been living as "orphans" in white households, just 35 were described on the census as workers of any kind (mostly servants). Moreover, sixty-three of them were ten years old or younger, and children that young were *very* rarely employed for wages at that time in Montgomery County: only six children that age on the entire 1867 census were employed. Thomas Montague, for example, was a white farmer living near Christiansburg who did employ six African Americans during the summer of 1867. George, Wyatt, and Richmond Brown were all between the ages of sixteen and twenty-one, were all described as "farmers" receiving wages or shares, and may have been siblings living on land belonging to Montague. James Mason, age twelve, was identified as a "servant" receiving wages and probably lived with Montague. The census also indicates that Charlotte and Millie Jones lived with Montague. The Jones girls were black, ages eight and four, and the census shows neither an occupation nor any form of compensation for them. When Millie Jones married, in 1879, she identified Montgomery County as her place of birth and her parents as Gabriel and Jane Jones, neither of whom appears in any other county record. There is no obvious reason for Millie and Charlotte Jones to have been living with Thomas Montague in 1867, but Montague's father, Rice, had owned twenty-eight slaves in 1860, and the girls—as well, perhaps, as James Mason—may have been the children of former slaves who had died or been sold out of the region.[31]

In the years that followed, some of the nonwhite children found with white families in 1867 remained with white families, some went to live with African American families, and at least one went back and forth. Henry Morrison, who was seven in 1867, was apparently living just outside Christiansburg with Emaline Craig, a white widow. Three years later, in 1870, he appeared on the federal census in the household of Joseph Jones, a black farm worker who lived in the same general neighborhood, but in 1880 he was back with the widow Craig. Records, however, are simply too incomplete to show what happened to most of these individuals as they grew up. Some may have changed their names, some no doubt died, and some probably left the county. Few appear on subsequent censuses, though, and fewer than a third seem to have married in Montgomery County. As result, it is simply not possible to say with any certainty who they were or why they were living where they were in 1867.[32]

Whether living with their families or not, more than a quarter of the African American children living in Montgomery County in 1867 were, apparently, considered "illegitimate" by the Freedmen's Bureau. The 1866 statute legalizing the relationships and children of nonwhite couples in Virginia living together at the time of the law's passage also legalized children whose parents had ceased to live together before 1866 "in consequence of the death of the woman, or from any other cause" but only if the children "[were] recognized by the man to be his." This meant that if a man refused to admit paternity or was absent for any reason, and thus unable to admit paternity, his children became illegitimate in the eyes of the law. Charles Schaeffer, who represented the Freedmen's Bureau in Montgomery County, had reported the presence of 121 "illegitimate offspring" in the summer of 1866, probably on the basis of information gathered while compiling the county's cohabitation register. The following year, in taking the census of freedpeople, he seems to have employed a pattern of dots to identify 356 children whose fathers could not or would not admit their paternity. These included children with no parents in the county—whether as a result of death, slave sales, or the chaos of war and emancipation—but also included the stepchildren in newly formed families if their biological fathers were dead or absent. The census showed Thadeus and Amanda Morgan, for example, had two illegitimate children in 1867 although the couple had legally married in December 1865. These were, apparently, Amanda's children by previous relationships, but because their father (or fathers) was unable or unwilling to acknowledge them, Schaeffer considered them illegitimate.[33]

This view of legitimacy could have led to serious problems in later years, when parents died and children sought to inherit their estates. It did not, however, because the community and the courts took a less rigid stand than the law seemed to require. They apparently accepted these children as legitimate, even if their fathers had never officially acknowledged paternity. Sallie Patterson Leftwich, for example, was the daughter of William Patterson and Chaney Birchfield. Her parents had married as slaves but then separated during the 1850s, when William "took up with another woman." After emancipation, William Patterson registered his marriage to that other woman—Clara Owens—but seems never to have legally acknowledged either of the two daughters surviving from his relationship with Chaney Birchfield. By the statute of 1866, then, Sallie Patterson was illegitimate. William Patterson did, however, acknowledge to others in the community, both black and white, that he was Sallie's father. By the time William Patterson died, in 1895, Sallie was already dead, but she had married William R. Leftwich in 1876 and had eight children with him before her death. Thus, when William Patterson died without leaving a will, Leftwich sued Patterson's estate on behalf of the children born to him and Sallie. They were the children of William Patterson's daughter, Leftwich claimed, and thus entitled to shares in the estate. After taking depositions from both black and white witnesses who had known the parties to the case and who reported that William Patterson had often said that Sallie Leftwich was his daughter, a commissioner of chancery determined that Sallie Patterson Leftwich had been one of her father's "heirs at law," and the court ordered that her widower and children receive a share of Patterson's estate equal to those of the two children William Patterson had by a later wife. Whatever the law or the Freedmen's Bureau said, in the wake of emancipation, people in Montgomery County seem to have recognized the marriages of slaves and free people of color as binding unions as long as the individuals themselves did.[34]

These and other court proceedings clearly indicate that in the decades following emancipation, citizens of Montgomery County and county officials accepted slave marriages as binding, even if they had not been entered on the cohabitation register, and that they recognized the legal rights and obligations of the parties involved in these marriages and those of their children. Samuel Pincus found a similar attitude at the state level, noting the Virginia Supreme Court's "willingness, even eagerness to extend the constitutional and statutory mandate of legitimacy to as many black families as possible." This could, of course, serve as a means to control what whites considered "immoral" behavior among their black neighbors. One sees this, for example, in criminal proceedings against Lewis Brown. Brown and Millie Howard, both enslaved at the time, had married in 1861 and registered their union in 1866. As a result, Lewis was charged with bigamy in 1871 when he tried to marry Emaline Gray while "his lawful wife [was] then living." More often, though, it worked to the advantage of African Americans in the county, as the case of Sallie Leftwich demonstrates.[35]

Many of the marital and family patterns evident on the 1867 census of freedpeople in Montgomery County continued over the three decades that followed. Historians, sociologists, and others have long debated the extent to which slavery did or did not influence African American attitudes toward marriage and family.[36] Did the fact that slave families were often broken by owners and by the operation of the slave system motivate freedmen and their descendants to establish and protect the families that slavery denied them? Did slavery make broken families so common in the black community that the pattern seemed normal and continued even after slavery ended? Evidence from Montgomery County seems to suggest that both attitudes existed simultaneously. In the decades following Reconstruction, patriarchal nuclear families did remain the norm among African Americans in Montgomery County. Freed from a system in which the needs of black families had come second to those of their white owners, many black residents of Montgomery County wanted, expected, and rewarded stable, nuclear families in their community. Moreover, these black families shared many of the same middle-class attitudes toward the family and about gender roles within it that white Americans did. Not all of the county's African American residents, however, shared this desire for traditional nuclear families. A significant number chose not to marry. Nor were those who did marry always able to realize their ideal; the nature of the work they did often made it difficult for the county's black residents to maintain stable nuclear families. As a result, they also adopted variations from that ideal when doing so helped to provide an appropriate environment in which to raise children or helped to ensure the physical well-being of individual men, women, and children.

Marriage and the establishment of patriarchal nuclear families remained the norm among African Americans in Montgomery County between 1870 and 1900, though it was far from universal. Throughout this period, the percentage of blacks and mulattos in the county age eighteen and older who were married at the time of a particular census remained between 59 and 64 percent, while another 5–10 percent (widows, widowers, and divorcees) had been married previously but were not at that time. As noted above, a number of slave couples may have dissolved their unions immediately after emancipation, but this was followed by a significant increase in marriages during the 1870s as young people wed for the first time while older people remarried. During the first half of the 1870s nonwhite marriages made up about a third of all marriages recorded in Montgomery County, although African Americans made up only about a quarter of the county's population. This overrepresentation may have been partly a result of a reduced number of marriages in the white population due to the number of men killed during the Civil War, but there was also a clear and substantial increase in the number of black marriages in the 1870s. By a wide margin, more African Americans married in Montgomery County between 1870 and 1879 than during any other decade in the county's history; the 386 marriages recorded during those ten years exceed by almost a quarter the number recorded between 1880 and 1889, in spite of the fact that the county's black population was greater during the 1880s than it had been during the 1870s. After this flurry of weddings, the rate of marriage among the county's black residents slowed, and the number marrying each year settled to a level close to their share of the county's total population.[37]

In fact, after rising during the 1870s, the percentage of black adults in Montgomery County who were married at a particular time declined slightly during the final decades of the nineteenth century; census returns from 1880 and 1900 show that among those eighteen years and older, the percentage of blacks in the county who were married at the time of the census fell from 63.9 percent in 1880 to 60.2 percent in 1900. The age at which Montgomery County's African American residents first married did not rise significantly during this period, though. For men, it fell from a mean of 25.4 years among those who married during the 1870s to a mean of 24.6 years among those who married during the 1880s and then rose again to 25.3 during the 1890s. Among women, the mean age at first marriage remained virtually unchanged; it was 21.4 years during the 1870s and 21.5 years during the 1880s and 1890s. Nor did the percentage of black adults identified as single on the federal census rise during this period; in fact, it declined slightly from 30.3 percent in 1880 to 28.6 percent in 1900. What did rise were the numbers of widows and widowers in the county's black population and the percentage of black marriages that were not first marriages. The 1880 census found that 5.9 percent of African Americans in the county aged eighteen years and older were widows or widowers, while by 1900 the figure had risen to 10.3 percent. Consistent with this is the fact that the percentage of marriages in which at least one party was widowed or divorced rose from 16.2 percent during the 1870s to 19.4 percent in the 1880s and 21.3 percent in the 1890s. Both of these trends are consistent with a population that was getting older. Between 1867 and 1900 the percentage of Montgomery County's African American population aged twenty-one years or older rose from 37.6 percent in 1867 to 40.3 percent in 1880 and 46.3 percent in 1900. African Americans in Montgomery County continued to marry in the decades following the Civil War, but more and more young adults seem to have left the county after they did so.

With some modest fluctuations, then, the frequency of marriage among adults in Montgomery County's African American community may have remained broadly the same after emancipation as it had been before. The age at which women in that community married, however, changed quickly and dramatically, and the change seems to demonstrate clearly the greater agency African Americans enjoyed after 1865. It is not possible to establish an average age at first marriage for slaves in Montgomery County because the cohabitation register does not distinguish between first marriages and remarriages. It is still clear, however, that enslaved women married at a younger age than free women did. Among the 254 women on the cohabitation register for whom the "Date Cohabitation Began" is legible, 54 (21.3 percent) were sixteen years old or younger when they married, and 36 (14.2 percent) were fifteen or younger. After emancipation, brides that young quickly became much less common, and their number continued to decline through the end of the century. In the decade 1870–79, only 4.1 percent of black or mulatto women who married in the county were sixteen or younger and just 1.5 percent were fifteen or younger, and by the decade 1890–99 these rates had fallen to 3.9 percent and 0.9 percent, respectively. This pattern is also evident in the most common age reported among non-white women marrying in the county. On the cohabitation register it was seventeen; by the 1870s it had risen to eighteen, and in the 1880s and 1890s it was twenty-one. The ages at which men married showed much less change. On the cohabitation register, the most common age for men entering relationships was twenty. During the final three decades of the century, the most common age for men at their first marriage rose from twenty-one during the 1870s and 1880s to twenty-two in the 1890s, while the average age at first marriage moved from 25.4 during the 1870s to 24.6 during the 1880s and 25.3 during the 1890s.[38]

In the decades after the Civil War, then, marriage remained both desirable and common among African Americans in Montgomery County, and their expectations concerning those marriages seem to have been quite clear and quite traditional. Like other Americans of the time, African Americans in Montgomery County generally expected husbands and wives to remain faithful to one another, expected husbands to provide financial and material support for their families, and expected wives to care for the home. Obviously, there were cases in which one or both parties failed to meet this middle-class standard. Husbands sometimes abused their wives, both husbands and wives sometimes committed adultery or abandoned their spouse entirely, and some couples needed both partners' earnings to survive, but the ideal seems to have been traditional, monogamous, patriarchal families. Such expectations had appeared almost immediately after emancipation, as the case of Alexander and Sarah Saunders showed in 1867, and they remained common through the end of the century.

Ironically, the best source of information about what African Americans in Montgomery County sought and expected in their marriages comes from those who failed to find it: couples who went through divorce proceedings. Between 1870 and 1900, at least forty-five nonwhite couples entered divorce proceedings in Montgomery County.[39] In a majority of these cases, twenty-six of the forty-five, the husband was the plaintiff. Enough wives petitioned for divorces, however, to provide a fairly balanced view of marital expectations. Obviously, those seeking a divorce had a vested interest in making their spouse look bad. Moreover, divorce complaints are somewhat formulaic, and these particular complaints were written by white lawyers in an effort to convince white judges. The depositions from black witnesses in these cases, however, and the limited evidence that has survived from other sources do provide a window into the ideals of black couples in the county at the time.

The most basic assumption among both men and women of color in Montgomery County was that couples would remain faithful to one another. Whether husband or wife, most of the plaintiffs seeking a divorce complained that their spouse had abandoned them or had committed adultery. John Beverly, for example, filed for divorce in 1882 after his wife, Caroline, left him and began leading "a life of shame" in Roanoke County with a man named Samuel Taylor. Similarly, Lucinda Cephas filed for divorce in 1885 because her husband, Andrew, "was too intimate with Sallie Shelton," a woman described by one witness as "a strumpet . . . [who] lies with the lowest order of colored people." In the case of wives, at least, this expectation of moral integrity could also include their behavior before the wedding. When, for example, William Leftwich married Gracy Watson, in January 1872, the groom believed his bride "to be a chaste & virtuous woman." Within a few days of marrying her, however, he discovered that she was actually several months pregnant by another man and had "carefully concealed her condition from him . . . for the purpose of inducing him into a matrimonial alliance." On learning of his wife's deception and her prior immoral behavior, Leftwich moved out. He filed for divorce soon after the child was born, and it was granted in the 1873.[40]

African Americans in Montgomery County also expected married couples to follow the gender norms of Victorian America. Under slavery, even married women had invariably worked outside the home, either in the fields or in someone else's home. Such labor was considered unbecoming of a proper woman in nineteenth century America, which is precisely why it was often expected from women of color. After gaining their freedom, therefore, freedpeople throughout the South moved quickly to establish families that reflected their new status by keeping married freedwomen in their own homes. For freedwomen this was a mark of their status as proper women, while for their husbands it was a sign of their masculinity to exercise control over the females of their household.[41] As a result, just two years after the war ended the Freedmen's Bureau found that only half of the married black women in Montgomery County were working outside their homes, and by 1870 the figure had dropped to 6.7 percent. It remained less than 8 percent through the end of the century. Certainly, as described more fully in chapter 3, unmarried, black women in post–Civil War Montgomery County continued to work outside the home. A wife's place, however, even if she was black, was in the home, and her role there was to ensure her husband's domestic comfort. Thus, when Robert and Mary Scott divorced, in 1888, Howard Sherman, who had lived with the couple, testified as to "what kind of a wife" Mary had been. "She treated her husband as kind and lovingly as anybody I knew of," Sherman told the court. "Had his meals prepared regularly. Obeyed him & never went anywhere without his permission & fixed up his clothes for him."[42]

Husbands, for their part, were expected to provide for their families. When, for example, Taylor Walker sought a divorce from his wife, Lucy, he assured the court that he had always "provided well to her." Even when Taylor was taken ill while visiting relatives in Henry County, "he left ample provisions & arranged with Mr. J. K. Montague with whom he lived to furnish her what she needed during his absence." Even poverty did not excuse an African American husband from fulfilling his duty. James Briggs identified himself as a servant when he married Alice Oglesby in 1882, and when he petitioned for a divorce fifteen years later, he claimed that he had always supported her "as best he could for one in his station of life." Such expectations were especially clear in the cases of men who failed to meet them. Julius Twine, for example, married Georgiana Jefferson in 1879, and over the next fifteen years the couple had at least five children together. By the early 1890s, though, it was evident that Julius drank to excess and had given up any effort to provide for his family; so Georgiana took a job cooking to support the family. Julius Twine also physically abused both his wife and his children. His daughters, Esther and Maggie, described their father beating Georgiana and the children, threatening to kill them, denying them food or firewood when he had both, and driving the children out of the house on several occasions. Neighbors who saw this and the doctor who treated Esther after her father struck her with a smoothing iron confirmed the girls' testimony and declared that Julius was "mighty rough to his wife & children." One neighbor noted: "I have a dog that is better treated than his children by him." Neighbors did intervene when Twine ran his children out one night. John Lewis and his wife took the children back and told Julius "this would not do," but only when more of the neighbors showed up did Twine relent and let the children stay. Finally, in 1894, Georgiana Twine secured a divorce and, apparently, left the county with her children.[43]

Even men who tried to provide for their families sometimes found that the nature of the work they did undermined the stability of the very families they were trying to support. New River boatmen and railroad workers were often gone for long periods of time, which sometimes made it difficult for these men to maintain their family relationships. Edward Armstrong, for example, was a boatman on the New and Kanawha Rivers in the decade following the Civil War. In that work he "[went] from place to place . . . only returning home once or twice a year." Railroad workers also spent long periods of time away from home. Some, such as Thomas Fuqua, who was a fireman on the Atlantic, Mississippi, and Ohio Railroad, seem to have been home fairly often between runs. Others, however, were gone for months at a time. Asa Radford left his wife and daughter in the county and went to work as a laborer on the Chesapeake and Ohio Railroad for five months during the summer and fall of 1872, and Daniel Mitchell worked for twenty months as the cook on a material train in the early 1870s while his wife Maria and their children remained in Central Depot. It was not just transportation workers who left home to earn a living, though. Lowry Jones went to Alabama and worked for eighteen months in 1873–74 before returning to Montgomery County. He did so "with the consent of his wife . . . it being supposed by himself & wife that he could obtain better wages for his labor in that state." Even men who owned their own land sometimes left their families and traveled beyond the county to earn additional income. Charles Clark and Thadeus Morgan were both farmers on their own land, but both also worked away from home for periods of time during the 1880s. Clark worked on the railroad for several years while also helping to farm his family's thirty-one acres in the Vickers community whenever he could get home. Thadeus Morgan also owned his own farm. Morgan bought sixty-two acres outside of Christiansburg in 1875 and had a mortgage to pay, so in the early 1880s he "left his wife and some of his children in possession of the land, and with his team went to the lead mines to earn money to aid in the payment of his debt."[44]

Some of these relationships endured despite the couple's separation. Daniel Mitchell's marriage seems to have survived his stint on the material train, and Charles and Julia Clark remained together in spite of the fact that Charles was often away from home, working on the railroad.

"Whenever I did not come home after payday," he recalled, "I sent the money to her." No doubt, many other couples experienced such separations and remained together, but because so much of the surviving evidence comes from divorce cases, most of the known cases ended badly. Lowry Jones, for example, returned from Alabama to discover that his wife "had heard & believed [him] . . . dead" and had taken up with another man, and Thadeus Morgan found on his return from the lead mines that his wife had "engaged in lewd and adulterous conduct with various persons in the neighborhood and about Christiansburg." Both men, therefore, sought and obtained divorces. It was not just wives who behaved badly, though. Edward Armstrong, the boatman, wrote a friend asking him to sell a horse that Armstrong had left in his care, to use part of the proceeds to settle a debt, and then to turn the remaining cash over to another friend "for the benefit of my children." In another letter, he asked friends to convey "my love to all my children." He made no mention in either letter, however, of his wife, which no doubt contributed to her suspicion that Edward had married another woman (which his friends denied) and to her seeking a divorce. In the case of James Mason, there seems to have been no question that the husband strayed. Mason was a schoolteacher and Baptist preacher in Blacksburg who went to preach in Frankfort, Kentucky, early in the 1880s. While he was there, he fell in love with another woman, eloped with her to Birmingham, Alabama, and abandoned his wife, who also sought a divorce.[45]

Cases such as these were one factor contributing to the large number of female-headed households in Montgomery County's postemancipation African American community. Divorce, however, was not the chief factor driving the phenomenon; widows outnumbered divorcees in the county by a considerable margin. Railroad work was open and attractive to black men, but some of it was also extremely dangerous. So too was mining, which a number of black men from Montgomery County went to West Virginia to pursue. Fatalities among railroad workers and miners no doubt contributed to the rising number of African American widows in the county; the 1880 census found 77 (7 percent of the adult women of color in the county that year), and by 1900 the number had risen to 122 (13 percent). Even if their husbands did not die, black and mulatto women were often left alone to care for their families for extended periods of time while their husbands worked elsewhere. The census found thirty-six married women in the county with no husband present in 1880 and forty-nine in 1900. Still other women, it seems, simply chose to live on their own. Charlotte Calloway, for example, seems never to have married. She lived in Christiansburg from 1867, if not before, until her death, in 1893, and had no children of her own, though she raised her niece, Olivia Smith, as her "adopted daughter."[46]

Women like these consistently accounted for a significant share of non-white heads of household in Montgomery County during the nineteenth century. As slaves, of course, many black families had been separated. The county's cohabitation register suggests that well over half of married female slaves had lived apart from their husbands, and at least 70 percent of these women had children. The number of female-headed households in the county did drop markedly after emancipation, but they remained a significant minority through the end of the century. The 1867 census of freedpeople did not specifically identify households. However, on the basis of surnames, employers, and the order in which names were recorded, it seems to include approximately 585 African American households. Of that number, 178 (30 percent) seem to have been headed by women, and more than half of these included minor children. Countywide, the number of African American households headed by women remained fairly constant on censuses over the next thirty years—31 percent in 1870, 25 percent in 1880, and 29 percent in 1900. Their distribution through the county, however, did not remain constant. Female-headed households became much more common in towns. In 1870, just 21 percent of nonwhite households in Christiansburg were female headed; by 1880 that figure had risen to almost 30 percent, and it reached more than 40 percent in 1900. This is hardly surprising. The vast majority of working women of color in Montgomery County worked as cooks, washerwomen, housekeepers, and servants, and jobs such as these were much easier to find in towns than in rural districts of the county. As Georgiana Twine discovered when she set out "to earn a living for herself and children" in 1894, she could only find work in Christiansburg.[47]

African American families in Montgomery County could certainly be larger and more complex than simple nuclear or female-headed units. Blended, combined, and multigenerational families appear on every census. Indeed, a single family might pass through multiple forms over the years. As described at the start of this chapter, Thadeus and Amanda Morgan had formed a blended family when they married in 1865, as Amanda already had two children when she married Thadeus. In the decades that followed, Thadeus Morgan's family became increasingly complex. It became multigenerational sometime after 1870 with the arrival of Amanda's mother, Parthenia Price, and even more complex as Morgan married Sallie Cox (in 1879), divorced her (in 1883), married Julia Farrow (in 1884), and began fathering children by her. But at most times and for most members of Montgomery County's African American community after the Civil War, family meant nuclear, patriarchal, two-parent families. This was both the ideal and the reality for the great majority of the black men, women, and children living there in the decades immediately after emancipation.

In spite of rising racial discrimination, continuing economic challenges, and increased out-migration, African Americans living in Montgomery County continued to believe that marriage and family were the proper state in which to live. As a result, they continued to marry in large numbers and attempted to establish and maintain families that reflected and promoted the gender and social norms of Victorian America. While far from universal and far from flawless, these families proved a key element in the formation and survival of a viable African American community in the county.

3 LABOR, LAND, AND MAKING A LIVING

By THE TIME GORDON MILLS DIED in 1891, he and his wife, Ellen, or Nellie, had managed to establish themselves and their children on thirty acres of land just outside of Blacksburg. It had not been easy, though, and their status as landholders was still tenuous. Gordon and Nellie Mills had been in their early thirties when slavery ended. They had been married since 1856 and in 1865 had two children to support and a third on the way. They had no education beyond the practical skills they had acquired as slaves on the farm of Daniel Hoge, and they owned nothing beyond their clothing and a few personal effects. Like the vast majority of freedpeople, the Millses began their new lives with little in the way of human or economic resources. It would be a long, hard struggle for the Millses to grasp even the lowest rung of the ladder to success, but they had family in the county, a network of friends among the Hoges' former slaves, and the trust of several white families in the neighborhood where they lived. Using these resources, and their own hard work, they set out to claw their way up that ladder.[1]

Like many freedpeople, they began by working for the family that had held them as slaves. In partnership with Dennis Hopkins, another of the Hoges' former bondsmen, Gordon sharecropped land belonging to his former master along the North Fork of the Roanoke River. Nellie earned additional income for the family by washing laundry for the Hoge family. Over the next twenty years, the Millses moved slowly and haltingly toward establishing themselves as an independent farm family. They apparently

FIGURE 4. Ellen Mills in front of the house that she
and Gordon built. (Author's collection)

lost the first tract of land they acquired in 1875, probably to satisfy an unpaid debt. In 1878 they tried again. Gordon arranged to buy thirty acres
from Hamilton D. Wade, a prominent farmer and businessman in the
county, for $600 to be paid over the next six years. The land was uphill
from the Hoge farm, on the slope of the mountain leading toward Blacksburg, and was not particularly good farmland. Mills, therefore, continued
to rent land from the Hoge family on which he raised corn, wheat, and hay.
His hope was to earn enough farming the Hoge land to pay for the Wade
land, on which the family settled and built a house (figure 4). A decade
later, however, the Millses' homestead was still not paid for.

Mills and Wade then renegotiated their deal in 1888, and Wade agreed
to take just $400 for the thirty acres and the bonds that Gordon Mills had
signed ten years earlier. Even these better terms presented a challenge,
and the Millses paid just forty dollars toward the purchase before Gordon died in 1891. Nellie and her sons, however, continued the struggle.
Hamilton Wade agreed to restructure the sale yet again, reducing both the

acreage and the price, and in the years that followed, the Millses finally paid off the land on which they had been living since the 1870s. By 1910 they owned sixteen acres free and clear. Since then, many of Gordon and Nellie Mills's grandchildren and great-grandchildren have left Montgomery County and settled in West Virginia, Ohio, and New York, but more than a century later their great-great-grandson still lives on part of the land that Gordon and Nellie Mills worked so hard to acquire, and the neighborhood in which he lives is known today as Nellies Cave.[2]

The story of Gordon and Nellie Mills is not unique. In the decades following the Civil War, dozens of African American families in Montgomery County made the same transition: from slaves to free laborers and from abject poverty to modest material success. A few did even better, reaching genuine middle-class status. In making this transition they faced a variety of challenges, some because of their race and others because so many of them were farmers in a time and place that made farming difficult. And they made the transition in a variety of ways. Some did it as farmers, others did so by giving up farming altogether, and many combined farming with other activities. Whatever the labor at which they toiled, their stories resembled that of Gordon and Nellie Mills in a number of important ways. African Americans living in Montgomery County during the decades after the Civil War often faced resentful white neighbors and always operated in an environment of severe legal, social, and economic challenges. Nevertheless, many improved the economic and material condition of their lives through hard work, through cooperation with family and friends in the black community, and through extensive interaction with the white community around them. Moreover, while some of those interactions with their white neighbors were exploitative, many were mutually beneficial.

Initially, antebellum patterns of labor and economic relations in Montgomery County changed very little. In the months immediately after the fall of the Confederacy, most of the freedpeople in Montgomery County continued to work for their former owners. As noted earlier, there is little evidence that any of the county's slave owners attempted to suppress the news of Lee's surrender and continue holding African Americans as slaves. Instead, most of the county's white residents acknowledged the end of slavery and invited their former bondsmen to continue working for them. Thus, soon after arriving in Christiansburg, Captain Carter reported "a disposition on the part of the citizens to accept the new order of things with a good grace and to be willing to assist in regulating the labourers and their families." Some, however, did so with more good grace than others. Janie Milton recalled that her grandmother, Ellen Brown, told her that her master, Floyd Smith, had told his former slaves, "Now just keep on a doin' what you doin'. But when you feel like you want to venture out I'll do all I can to help you." Others were less graceful. Pitt Woodroof, who with his wife had owned nineteen slaves in 1860, wrote the Freedmen's Bureau in 1866, "At the time of the surrender I gave them all their choice either to leave or have a certain portion of the crop."[3]

Whatever the tenor of their offer, most white landowners were undoubtedly thinking first of their own economic interest when they offered to employ former slaves as free laborers. Like white landowners throughout the South, many in Montgomery County owned more land than they and their families could cultivate alone. Without someone to work that land, it would earn them nothing.[4] At least some whites also saw the employment of freedpeople as a matter of public safety because it soon became clear that African Americans in the county were not going away. While some freedpeople left in search of family or better opportunities, most stayed and seemed likely to remain. Moreover, others migrated in. In the months after emancipation, rumors sometimes circulated that freedpeople might emigrate to Liberia or take advantage of the Homestead Act to take up land farther south. Indeed, Charles Schaeffer reported in 1866 that "a very large number" of white residents *hoped* the county's freedmen would leave. Few did, though, and if freedpeople were going to stay in the county, they would need to find work. As John Etzler concluded early in 1867, "We must give them a chance to make living, or they will beg or steal."[5]

Staying put also made sense from the perspective of the freedpeople themselves, at least in the short term. Immediately after the war, most had few attractive alternatives to remaining with their former owners. Though they had gained their freedom, most freedpeople in the county found themselves with no land, tools, livestock, or housing of their own. Fewer than half of the county's free adults of color had owned any taxable property in 1863, and only nine had owned any land.[6] Slaves had owned even less; the homes in which they lived, the tools with which they worked, and the land on which they might raise food for themselves all belonged to their former owners. Thus, most freedpeople lacked the resources necessary to use the skills they possessed to establish themselves as independent farmers or craftsmen in postwar Montgomery County. They also lacked the resources to move in search of better opportunities. They clearly lacked the material resources. Even a year later freedpeople from Montgomery County declined the offer to take up homesteads in Florida, Mississippi, or Louisiana because they would be unable to feed their families before making their first harvest and the government was unwilling to provide assistance.[7] In addition to material resources, however, most freedpeople also lacked the human capital to move—the connections or reputation that would help them find work beyond the community in which they had been enslaved. The antebellum experiences of free people of color had repeatedly shown that although white Virginians were suspicious of "free blacks" as a category, they often treated individual men or women they knew with a modicum of respect. Leaving a neighborhood in which they were familiar rendered African Americans "strangers" who could not be trusted and were less likely to be employed.[8]

For some of Montgomery County's freedmen, railroad work offered an immediate, though short-lived, alternative to remaining with their former owners. Soon after the fighting ended, the Virginia and Tennessee Railroad hired workers to rebuild the track and bridges destroyed by Union cavalry during the final weeks of the war. For freedmen in Montgomery County, this did not require a long move; in fact some of the work was done right in the county. Nor did it require the resources that homesteading would; railroad workers used company tools and lived in camps where the company provided food and housing. The real draw, however, seems to have been the wages. The railroad itself claimed to be paying fifteen dollars a month, though Frank Dean earned just ten dollars and his board when he signed on at the end of April. Even ten dollars, however, was near the top end of the range that farm workers received at the time. A few men in the county earned fifteen dollars a month that summer for agricultural labor, but most received between five and ten. Most farm workers, however, got no wages at all in 1865. The vast majority received their upkeep or shares in the crop, and as John Langhorne discovered, freedmen often preferred wages to board or shares. Langhorne farmed seven hundred acres outside Shawsville, and when the war ended, he offered his former slaves "a part of the crops if they would work for him." According to his daughter, the freedmen wanted "steady money" and went to work for the Virginia and Tennessee. Most of these jobs, however, ended by late July, when the rail line was rebuilt to Lynchburg, and many of the men employed by the Virginia and Tennessee, including John Langhorne's former slaves, came back to Montgomery County in search of work.[9]

Thus, immediately after their emancipation most of Montgomery County's freedpeople continued working for their former owners. In August 1865, when the Freedmen's Bureau arrived in the county, Captain Carter reported that "the freedmen in this district as a rule are willing to work for their former masters," and a census completed that month confirms it. The census found 1,462 freedpeople employed in the county, and of that number 1,419 (97 percent) were described as "employed by former owner." According to the census, only thirty-nine freedpeople in Montgomery County worked for someone other than their former owner and another four were self-employed. The census, however, exaggerates somewhat the extent to which freedpeople in the county continued to work for their former masters. It includes, for example, children as young as two years old among those "employed." Moreover, it seems from information collected on the cohabitation register that some of those described as working for their former owners in 1865 may actually have been working for their spouses' former owners or for employers with whom they had no prior connection. Even with these adjustments, though, it seems that Captain Carter was right. During that first summer of freedom, at least 85 percent of adult freedpeople working in Montgomery County continued to work for the men and women who had held them as slaves.[10]

It also seems clear that the vast majority of freedpeople in the county that summer were still being compensated like slaves; in return for their labor, they received their upkeep and that of their families rather than wages or even shares of the crops they raised. In all but a few cases, the 1865 census reported the form of compensation provided to each freedperson, even children too young to work on their own, and almost 90 percent were compensated with "board & clothes." Even among freedpeople aged fifteen years or older, almost 84 percent of those working in Montgomery County during the summer of 1865 received their food, housing, and clothing in exchange for their labor. Given the shortage of cash in the local economy that summer and the attitudes of white landowners toward freedmen, this pattern is hardly surprising, but such echoes of slavery help to explain why John Langhorne's former bondsmen preferred "steady money." After years of enslavement, they were anxious to enjoy their status as *free* men, and that was much harder in a system in which a man and his family received their housing, clothing, and rations directly from a white employer, just as they had from white masters under slavery.[11]

The most common alternative to "board & clothes" was "shares of the crop." According to the census, fifty-four freedpeople aged fifteen years or older (6.5 percent) received shares in return for their labor during the summer and fall of 1865. In later years, as African Americans acquired animals and tools of their own, sharecropping could provide them somewhat greater autonomy than working for wages. Sharecroppers might still be obliged to raise crops selected by the landowner, but they might have more control over when to plant them or how to tend them and could determine their own daily schedule and hours. They could also decide for themselves whether or not to call on family at times such as harvest when the demand for labor was greatest. In 1865, however, this was probably not the case. None of the actual agreements for shares that summer have survived, but given the economic and political conditions prevailing at the time, it seems likely that working for shares was simply a form of in-kind wages. Workers probably still lived in quarters provided by their employers, used their employers' tools and animals to raise the crop, worked when and how their employers directed, and received a share of the harvest as wages in kind. Another thirty-seven freedpeople (4.5 percent) clearly earned wages in kind (a set quantity of corn, for example) or a mix of wages and board, and twenty-seven (3.3 percent) worked for cash. Even to men working for wages, however, their situation may have seemed very much like slavery. Agreements often involved entire families, and many employers still exercised direct control over the well-being of their workers' families. In January 1866, for example, Andrew Hicks agreed to a contract with William and David Edmundson by which Hicks, his wife, and three of their daughters were to work for the coming year. In return, the Edmundsons agreed "to give the said Andrew Hicks one hundred dollars and find his wife & three daughters with the customary clothing & food."[12]

Even when the Freedmen's Bureau did arrive in Montgomery County, its oversight of labor relations was initially quite loose. The bureau did not set "prescribed" wages for any district. Rather it left to agents in the field the responsibility to determine what was "fair" in individual cases, though it did suggest that each agent should have in mind "minimum rates for his own guidance." Written agreements between freedpeople and their employers were "desired" but were not required, and in Montgomery County, at least, they were quite rare. They were also quite vague or quite one-sided. Wyatt and Rose Price, for example, agreed to work for Edmond Christian from April 1865 until Christmas. In return, Christian promised to pay "what ever was just and right, and in proportion to the wages paid to other colored people at that time." Joseph Nelson and David, Alfred, and Andrew Moore negotiated a more precise written agreement with William and David Edmundson, but it was hardly balanced. The freedmen agreed "to perform [hon]est & constant labor, holding themselves at [all] times in readiness promptly to obey the orders [of] the said Wm. R. & D. Edmundson" from mid-August 1865 until January 1, 1866. In return, each man was to receive twenty dollars, ten bushels of corn, and "the customary winter clothing." After that the terms of the agreement became even more one-sided. For "dereliction of any of the duties herein specified" the men would lose "such deduction from their wages . . . as shall be deemed just by their said employers"; the Edmundsons could dismiss any or all of the men at any time for "any neg[ligence], willful waste or disobedience" on their part; and in such cases, the man or men dismissed would also be banished from the Edmundson plantation—on which they were presumably living—and "forfeit all or so much of his or their [compensation] as to the said Wm. R. & D. Edmundson shall [seem] proper."[13]

It is, of course, hardly surprising that the county's postwar labor system retained elements reminiscent of slavery. It took shape at a time when neither Union troops nor agents of the Freedmen's Bureau were present in the county. Until midsummer, local control remained entirely in the hands of a government established under Confederate authority that in the name of "suppressing riots and preventing lawless depredations" quickly took action to maintain white control.[14] The system was not, however, simply a postwar effort to control free black workers; it was part of an economic system that had long operated alongside slavery in the mountain South. Throughout the antebellum era, large planters in the region had engaged white workers under very similar terms. In 1844, for example, William and David Edmundson's father, Henry, had promised to pay Andrew Howard, a white man, $106.50 "to labour faithfully and diligently" for the year on Edmundson's farm. The contract also stipulated that Edmundson would "furnish the said Andrew with provisions for the use of himself and his family," that should Edmundson find Howard's labor necessary on the turnpike that crossed his farm "the said Howard is bound to execute any direction to such an effect, promptly & faithfully," and that "the said Howard is not to absent himself from the business of the said Edmundson, especially in planting, sewing, and *more* especially in harvesting the crops unless it be on necessary business, and on proper occasions."[15]

Officials of the Freedmen's Bureau certainly recognized that landowners

and freedmen were not negotiating as equals and conceded the possibility
that freedmen would be exploited. They took comfort, however, in point-
ing out that the situation could be worse. "Suffering may result to some
extent," concluded a July 12 circular from Washington, D.C., "but suffering
is preferred to slavery." On the ground in Montgomery County, Captain
Carter and his successors demonstrated a similar attitude and took comfort in the fact that things could be worse. "Fair wages as a general thing
are voluntarily [furnished] by employers," Carter wrote in August, and in
another letter that month he concluded, "generally the negroes are well
off [in this district], much better than in the eastern portion of the State."
However, the Register of Complaints maintained for Carter's district between August 1865 and January 1866 does include a number of references
to freedpeople in the county "in a suffering condition for want of subsis-
tence." It also describes a number of cases in which freedmen were deprived of their due, including ten cases of freedmen who were dismissed by
their employers, ordered off the premises, and not paid for the work they
had done. There were "many fair exceptions," Carter noted at the end of
August, but even he conceded "the general effect of the conduct of employers & former masters is to *create distrust* rather than inspire confidence."[16]

Labor relations in Montgomery County became somewhat more struc-
tured during the course of 1866, as the Freedmen's Bureau grew more
organized in the region and as Charles Schaeffer assumed command of its
office in Christiansburg. The system remained far from perfect, though.
Steward Rollins, a former slave of Pitt Woodroof, was still working for
Woodroof in 1866 and was frustrated by his continued dependence on
his ex-master. According to Woodroof, "[Rollins] cursed me & the Freedmans Bureau & said why don't they free me good." At least some in the
Freedmen's Bureau, however, were almost as frustrated by the system
as Rollins was. When Charles Schaeffer took over the bureau's office in
Christiansburg, he did acknowledge that "the larger portion of them [the
freedpeople] are fully supplied with the necessaries of life" and did note
that the minority of freedmen in the county who had sharecropping arrangements were doing particularly well. "Some have done exceedingly
well and have sufficient to support themselves and their families for the
next twelve months," he wrote near the end of November. But he was still
quite concerned about the vulnerability of most freedmen to the whims of
their white employers. In July, two months after his arrival, Schaeffer complained to his superiors in Richmond that few employers in his subdistrict

followed bureau procedures or Virginia's new contract law in the employment of freedpeople and that he still had no authority to require "proper
written contracts." "Almost invariably the contracts are simply writings
drawn up by the employers," wrote Schaeffer, "without complying to the
form of law, and in almost every instance, there has been no witness to the
agreement. If the Freedmen make objection to this mode of procedure,
they are immediately refused employment and state that they are obliged
to accept the terms of those employing them, or go without work. Others
are working under verbal contract, and state they are unable to obtain employment in any other way." He also noted that because written contracts
were not required, he was only aware of problems when freedmen brought
them to his attention. As a result, he concluded, "Under the present state
of affairs it is quite certain that many of the freedmen will be defrauded
out of their honest compensation for labor—and unless it is made obliga-
tory upon the Employer to come forward and make Lawful Contracts, the
Freedmen will lose the greater part of their honest wages—and perhaps
[be] turned off in the midst of winter, without food or quarters."[17]

The full extent of that danger finally became clear in the spring of 1867,
when Schaeffer conducted a second census of freedpeople in Montgomery
County. This census provides the first comprehensive survey of African
Americans' employment in the county after the abolition of slavery and
reveals both the extent to which labor relations and the experience of black
workers in the county had changed since 1865 and the extent to which they
had remained the same. The census form includes a column headed "How
Employed" that provides occupational information for every adult and for
a number of older children in the population of freedpeople. For most of
those employed in the county, it also details the nature of the relationship
with a landowner or employer—lease, shares, or wages—and identifies the
owner of the "plantation" on which he or she worked, and probably lived.

According to the census, the great majority of freedmen in the county
still worked as farmers in 1867. Among the 595 men aged eighteen years
or older on the census that year, almost 78 percent (463) were identified as
"farmers," a description that included a variety of different categories. Most
were hired hands, though as detailed below, nearly a third were sharecroppers or farming independently on leased land. Another 13 percent of
freedmen were servants (forty-two) or laborers (thirty-eight). Thus, more
than 90 percent of adult male workers were farmers, servants, or laborers.
Just 43 men (8 percent of the total) reported other occupations in 1867:

15 blacksmiths, 9 carpenters, 5 shoemakers, 3 wagoners, 3 boatmen, 2 millers, 2 barbers, and 1 each a tanner, a tobacco roller, a cabinetmaker, and a bricklayer. Among freedwomen, the distribution was similarly lopsided, but in their case it was away from agriculture; Amanda Lee was the only freedwoman in the county described as a "farmer" in 1867. The census also shows very small numbers of midwives, cooks, and spinsters, one weaver, and one teacher, but the vast majority of employed freedwomen in the county, 440 out of 450, worked as servants, seamstresses, or washwomen. Scholars such as Mary Farmer Kaiser have noted the decline of women as farm workers after their emancipation, and the 1867 census may demonstrate just how rapid and how complete that transition was in Montgomery County. The term "servant," however, is broad enough to cover a range of activities, including farm work, and unlike the census bureau, the Freedmen's Bureau issued no instructions explaining how to categorize an individual's labor. It *seems* that by 1867 freedwomen in Montgomery County had generally "retired from the fields," but it is impossible to say for sure.[18]

It is possible to say with certainty, however, that many fewer freedwomen in the county worked outside their homes by 1867 than had been the case for enslaved women. As described in chapter 2, freedpeople often marked the end of slavery by establishing family patterns in which wives worked only in the family home. This effort did not keep all married freedwomen in Montgomery County out of the workforce in 1867. It did, however, reduce their numbers significantly. Among the 370 married freedwomen identified on the 1867 census, just 181 (49 percent) appear with an occupation. Among unmarried women, in contrast, the rate was almost 90 percent. In all, almost two thirds of black or mulatto females in the county aged eighteen years or older were "employed" in 1867, though fewer than half of married freedwomen were.[19]

The role of children in the workforce is less clear. Like their elders, most of the African American children named on the 1865 census had been shown receiving their "board & clothes," and like their elders, most of these children had been described as "Employed by former owner." Children younger than three years old had generally not been identified as workers, though some two-year-olds had been; anyone three years or older, however, had been marked as a worker. It is, of course, highly unlikely that such young children could actually perform any useful labor, but calling them workers was a means by which whites could continue asserting a claim to control them. By 1867, this illusion of or claim to children's labor had faded. A few children younger than sixteen years old, some as young as ten, did appear among those employed for wages in 1867; they were shown with specific occupations, generally that of "servant," and probably did work outside their family home. Most children younger than sixteen, however, appeared on the census with neither an occupation nor any form of compensation. They might, and probably did, continue to work for their own families, but it seems that part of the process by which freedpeople asserted their identity as families and their roles as parents was to withdraw their children from the workforce whenever possible.[20]

Whatever their occupation, gender, or age most of the freedpeople in Montgomery County who did work outside the home in 1867 still worked for white employers, either for wages or through lease or sharecropping agreements. Of the 1,092 freedpeople shown with occupations on the 1867 census, 1,063 (97.3 percent) had white employers. A few worked for corporations controlled by white managers and shareholders, such as the Virginia and Tennessee Railroad (nine) or for one of the mineral springs in the county (three), but most worked for individual white employers. In a change since 1865, however, it seems that by 1867 most of the freedmen in the county had left their former owners' employ. Married men appearing on the cohabitation register all identified their last owners before emancipation, and comparing where and for whom these men worked in 1867 to the names of their last owners shows that among the 226 men for whom it is possible to make this comparison, 171 (76 percent) had left their former owners' employ by 1867. In addition, at least fourteen freedpeople—ten craftsmen and four farmers—were apparently self-employed in 1867. Most of these were men, though the group also included four unmarried women working on their own as seamstresses. Another fifteen freedpeople, including three women (one of whom was married), worked for other freedpeople. Their employers were generally self-employed freedpeople, such as Norbourn Banks. Banks was a fifty-year-old former slave working as a self-employed carpenter in 1867 and employing five other freedmen as farmers as well as two freedwomen, a weaver and a midwife. The women, Crecie Ann Phillips and Nancy Lewis, were the wife or mother of men working for Banks as farmers and may actually have worked on their own and simply lived with Banks. At least one of the freedmen working for another freedman, however, worked for a sharecropper. John Edmundson, who was black and worked on shares for a white landowner, hired another freedmen, George Deskins, to work for wages. Such variations were exceptions, however, and the overwhelming majority of Montgomery County's freedpeople still worked for white employers in 1867.[21]

How freedpeople were compensated for their labor also changed between 1865 and 1867, and here too some reminders of slavery faded quickly while others lingered. The most dramatic change, perhaps, came in the practice of employers compensating freedpeople entirely through their upkeep. Almost 90 percent of freedpeople on the 1865 census had been working for "board & clothes" only, and even among adults the rate was almost 84 percent. In 1867, however, not a single freedperson in Montgomery County was described on the census as working simply for his or her maintenance. This may not be entirely accurate, as Schaeffer did report in February that women sometimes received just food and clothing for their labor. Still, according to the census, more than 80 percent of African American workers in the county worked for wages in 1867, though the census does not say whether they were paid in cash or in kind. Nor does it report the level of any wages, though Schaeffer reported in June that freedmen in his subdistrict generally earned eight to fifteen dollars per month and women five to eight dollars. The shift to wages, however, did not mean that employers no longer directly controlled their workers' access to housing or food. Many contracts, Schaeffer noted, still provided "suitable food and quarters," and this meant that losing one's job could still mean losing one's home as well. Anderson Carter, for example, was forced to move during the winter of 1866–67 when the white landowner for whom he had worked in 1866 hired another worker in his place. Fortunately, Carter was able to find work and housing on a neighbor's farm, but he remained vulnerable because his new employer also provided housing as part of his compensation.[22]

Not all freedpeople worked for wages, though; 7 percent of those identified as workers on the 1867 census worked for shares. This does represent an increase from the 4.5 percent receiving shares in 1865, but it remains well below the level found in Virginia's tobacco counties. More noteworthy, though, is the fact that by 1867 the nature of this relationship had changed. Immediately after emancipation, "working for shares" often seems to have meant receiving one's wages in kind. This may or may not have been in exchange for farm work (the 1865 census did not specify what work an individual did), and many of those working for shares that summer were women (19 percent) or children (13 percent). By 1867, in contrast, working for shares in Montgomery County was almost exclusively the more familiar form in which a laborer used land and perhaps tools belonging to a landowner in return for a set percentage of the crop raised on that land. Moreover, in Montgomery County at least, by 1867 sharecropping was limited to men. Among the seventy-nine freedpeople in the county shown as working for shares on the 1867 census, all were men and almost all were farmers; Frank Sanders, a miller, was the only nonfarmer working for shares. By 1867, then, working for shares in Montgomery County had generally come to mean *farming* for shares, farming had come to be almost exclusively *men*'s work, and sharecroppers represented 15.8 percent of African American men farming in the county.[23]

Unfortunately, it is not clear who or what the driving forces were in the change to farming for shares. Such arrangements had existed for years in southern Appalachia and were certainly familiar to large landowners in Montgomery County. Financial records left by the Edmundson family, for example, suggest that they employed sharecropping agreements on land in eastern Montgomery County both before and after the Civil War. It was, to them, simply one of several means by which they engaged labor to make their land profitable.[24] As for the choice by freedmen to work for shares rather than wages, scholars elsewhere have suggested that freedmen often preferred sharecropping to working for wages because it gave them greater control over their schedule and working conditions, and nothing suggests that freedmen in Montgomery County dissented from that view. Both white landowners and black workers, then, had cause to enter sharecropping agreements after slavery ended in Montgomery County. Writing in late 1866, Charles Schaeffer reported that freedmen and their employers "find it to their mutual interest to adapt the share system, by which more work is performed, larger crops obtained, and both parties greatly benefitted."[25]

Only scattered evidence has survived concerning the details of early sharecropping arrangements in Montgomery County. The most common form was an annual agreement, though some were longer, and freedmen generally received one-third to one-half of the harvest plus the use of a house and a garden plot. There is no evidence in these agreements of what Lynda Morgan called "shared management," by which, for example, sharecroppers helped to determine what to plant.[26] The most complete early sharecropping agreement that has come to light from Montgomery County is one drawn up in 1868 between William and David Edmundson and a white sharecropper named James Taylor. This made no reference to Taylor working *for* the Edmundsons, and he seems to have planted, tended, and harvested his crops according to his own schedule. The contract did, however, stipulate that Taylor would plant "about eight acres in tobacco and about thirty five acres in corn."[27] If a white sharecropper had such restricted control over his farming activities, it seems unlikely that freedmen were any less restricted. At best, it seems, during the first several years after emancipation, black or mulatto sharecroppers might have been able to establish their own work routines but did not make larger management decisions concerning the mix or marketing of the crops they raised.

Another 7.9 percent of the freedpeople working in Montgomery County in 1867 did so under lease agreements by which they seem to have rented land or shops and retained their earnings for themselves. Most of those with leases were farmers. Of the eighty-three freedpeople shown with leases on the 1867 census, seventy-eight were farmers. Indeed, almost 16 percent of all farmers on the census that year had leases. Most of these ran for a single year, though some were longer, and rent was paid in a variety of ways. Some men, such as Isaac Banks, paid their rent in cash, while others, such as Jones Brandon, paid a share of the harvest. Still others paid their rent through labor. John Lawson, for example, entered a three-year lease agreement with John Gibson in June 1867 under which Lawson was to receive all of the crops he harvested off land he cleared for Gibson. The agreement was to run "until he [Lawson] receives three crops from off all the land he cleared," after which Gibson would regain control of the land that Lawson had improved. Farmers were not the only ones with leases, though. Two carpenters and two blacksmiths on the census also had leases, perhaps to their shop facilities, and one washwoman, Parthena Price, had a lease, perhaps to a shop or to the house in which she worked and lived.[28]

The 1867 census of freedpeople shows that some things in Montgomery County had changed since emancipation, but it also showed Captain Schaeffer and the Freedmen's Bureau that black and mulatto workers in the county remained vulnerable to abuse by their white employers. Previously, Schaeffer had expressed concern that the absence of written contracts could leave freedpeople vulnerable to exploitation by their employers. The census revealed just how widespread that risk actually was. Writing in May to federal officials in Richmond, Schaeffer reported: "I had found on taking the census of Montgomery County, that only one tenth of all the colored people, who had contracted for twelve months or more service, had been furnished with written articles of agreement." In fact, written agreements were even less common than Schaeffer reported; according to the census, just sixty-one workers out of nearly eleven hundred in the county (less than 6 percent) had such agreements. Moreover, Schaeffer observed, many of these written agreements "were illegal, unjust and unequally binding upon the parties." As a result of information gathered on the census, Schaeffer ordered a tightening of supervision by the local office of the Freedmen's Bureau of the labor arrangements between freedpeople and their white employers. He issued a circular from his Christiansburg office requiring all persons who hired a freedperson for more than two months to have a written agreement—"properly made out in accordance with the existing laws"—and to provide a copy to the freedperson. Schaeffer then checked these new contracts to ensure they conformed to "law and justice." Surviving records do not suggest that the rate of compliance was particularly high, but there were fewer complaints from freedpeople in 1867 than there had been in 1866.[29]

Of course, the greatest protection freedpeople could have from abuse by white employers was to own their own land, but in 1867 this was practically unheard of. Fewer than a dozen freedpeople in the county are known to have owned any real estate in 1867, and many of those who did had been free people of color who purchased it before the war.[30] Immediately after emancipation it was nearly impossible for freedmen in Montgomery County to acquire land. In part, this may have been a result of the fact that little land was available for purchase. In August 1865, soon after his arrival in Christiansburg, Captain Carter reported "there are no lands in the market in this vicinity." Carter did not explain why no land was available. It may have been an unwillingness among white landowners to sell to freedmen, as was sometimes the case in the postwar South, or it may have been a wider unwillingness to sell at all until the economic situation was more clear. Carter's 1865 letter, however, remains the only such comment known to have come from Montgomery County. When Charles Schaeffer arrived in 1866, he wrote nothing about whites refusing to sell land to freedmen and by 1868 was able to report that "one gentleman in this county is selling out all his property (a small farm) at a fair price to the colored people, feeling it his duty to assist them all in his power." Even if land was available, though, most freedmen lacked the means to purchase it immediately after their emancipation. Just 34 of the 292 African Americans on the county tax roll in 1867 reported owning any taxable property at all, and the median amount they reported was valued at less than thirty dollars. Thus, even if Schaeffer's unnamed "gentleman" wanted to sell land to freedmen at "a fair price," few could afford it.[31]

Just twelve freedpeople in Montgomery County are known to have purchased land between the end of the Civil War and Virginia's readmission to the Union, in January 1870. This number is not entirely accurate, however, as at least two of the twelve were apparently obtaining deeds to land they had owned since the 1850s.[32] On the other hand, it is also seems that additional freedpeople purchased land for which no record has yet been found. The Freedmen's Bureau, for example, reported payments of rent to Minnis Headen, a freedman, for an office in Christiansburg, but there is no record of Headen's owning any real estate at the time.[33] Among the sales involving freedpeople that are known, one is known only from an unrecorded deed and one from a chancery case brought fifteen years after the sale. It is quite possible, then, that other sales may have escaped discovery, but it still seems clear that the number of freedpeople in Montgomery County who purchased land before 1870 was extremely small.[34]

Even this small number, however, includes a range of individuals and experiences. One of the twelve, Ellen Campbell, had been a former free woman of color; the other eleven had all been held as slaves until April 1865. Most had been slaves in Montgomery County when the war ended, but at least one, Harrison Jones, had moved to the county following his emancipation. These first postwar landowners were also divided almost evenly between men and women; among the twelve freedpeople who bought land in the county before 1870 were seven men and five women. All of the men except Robert Beverley and Norvell Curtis were married when they bought land, and they ranged in age from twenty-nine to sixty-six in 1867, with half between thirty-four and forty-eight years old. The women were slightly older—between thirty and seventy-two in 1867, with most over the age of fifty. All of the women seem to have been unmarried at the time they purchased land, though three of the five seem to have been widows. Several of the men were skilled craftsmen, who might be expected to have had an easier time earning a living after gaining their freedom. Alfred Walker and William Poindexter were both blacksmiths, Robert Beverly was a shoemaker, and Spencer Haden was a barber. Monroe Bailey, however, was a farmer and Harrison Jones a laborer. Among the women, no occupational information is available for Anne Taylor or Ellen Campbell, but the others were all servants or laundresses. And while most of these early purchases were for small lots in or adjacent to Christiansburg, Robert Beverly bought five acres on the North Fork of the Roanoke River, east of Christiansburg, and Harrison Jones bought twenty-five acres on Crab Creek, west of Christiansburg.[35]

These early purchases also capture parts of the extensive web of economic and personal relationships existing between whites and freedpeople during the years of Reconstruction. At least four of these early sales depended on credit extended to freedpeople by whites who knew them and in some cases employed them. Catherine and Norvell Curtis, for example, paid for their house and lot in the town of Christiansburg with four bonds guaranteed by their employers—Waller R. Staples and D. David Wade, a prominent lawyer and doctor, respectively, in town. Indeed, Staples later recalled, "my impression is that I superintended the whole matter for them," which was perhaps true, as neither of the Curtises could read or write at the time. Two other sales may actually have been gifts to freedmen in the form of sales. Allen Phizor, for example, sold Robert Beverly five acres "in consideration of the sum 1 dollar"; there is no evidence that either Phizor or his family had ever owned slaves, but the price he charged for five acres suggests that he may have had some sort of prior relationship with Robert Beverly that led him to sell the land for such a modest price. It was not just freedpeople, however, who benefited from interracial relationships. Charlotte Calloway, a freedwoman, not only paid $250 in full and in cash when she bought a Christiansburg lot from her employer, William C. Hagan, but did so at a time when Hagan desperately needed money "for the maintenance of Mrs. Margaret J. Hagan [his wife] & her children."[36]

In addition to these early land purchases by freedpeople in Montgomery County, at least one African American family in the county received land as a gift from a former owner. Stories of such gifts have long featured in southerners' memories of Reconstruction, and in the case of Montgomery County it is certainly true that a small number of white residents did provide land to some of their former slaves, but most who did so waited decades before acting. Clear evidence has survived of just one such gift in Montgomery County before 1870. In April of 1867, Margaret Taylor gave Allen and Charlotte Lewis two hundred acres near Vickers, a small community on the rail line west of Christiansburg. The Taylor family had lived in Montgomery and Pulaski counties for decades before the Civil War and owned land and slaves in both counties. Margaret, who never married, had inherited both land and slaves from her father in 1856, and in 1860 she owned hundreds of acres of land in Montgomery County and sixteen slaves, including Charlotte Lewis and seven of her children. Allen Lewis had been the slave of Hiram Hornberger, who owned land adjacent to Taylor's Montgomery County holdings, and the couple had been married since 1840. When Taylor transferred some of her land to the Lewises, she did so through "a deed of gift" and, she wrote, "in consideration of faithful service and in the further consideration of a desire to aid the said Allen & Charlotte Lewis."[37]

Other whites in the county *may* have given land to their former slaves or sold it at nominal prices, but conclusive evidence that they did so has not survived. As noted above, elements of the sale to Robert Beverly suggest that sale may have been more than a simple economic exchange. Moreover, oral histories from the Wake Forest community recall that it began soon after the Civil War ended when James R. Kent told his former slaves "to go into that wooded area and to plot a piece of land, claim it their own, and he would give um deed to it." Freedpeople certainly had access to land in the Wake Forest area almost immediately after their emancipation; a school and church for freedmen were both operating there by 1869. Kent, however, died in May 1867, and his estate remained tangled in lawsuits for almost twenty years. As a result, no deeds transferring land from the Kent family to any of their "old and faithful family servants" are known to have been executed before 1889. Similarly, descendants of Gordon Mills believe that he received land from his former owners, the Hoge family, after he and Nellie were emancipated. No evidence of such a transfer has yet come to light, but in 1874 Mills did secure two loans with a deed of trust on property that included four acres of land adjacent to that of Daniel Hoge, deceased. Because land sometimes changed hands in Montgomery County even if deeds did not, it is entirely possible that Gordon Mills did receive land from the Hoge family but lost it when he was sued for debt in 1875.[38]

Overall, the era of Military Reconstruction brought only modest change to the economic lives of African Americans in Montgomery County. By 1870, very few families had acquired land of their own and only a minority had gained even partial economic autonomy as leaseholders or sharecroppers. While married women were much less likely to work outside their homes than had been the case in 1865, unmarried women still worked, overwhelmingly as domestics in white households, and the great majority of black men still worked as farmhands for white landowners. Both men and women, however, generally received payment of some kind for their labor and did have the option to change employers if they chose. Most of the county's African American residents still lived in quarters that either resembled those they had known as slaves or were, in fact, former slave housing, and they remained among the poorest members of the local community. They were, however, slowly gaining modest holdings of livestock, household furnishings, and other personal property. Like Gordon and Nellie Mills, freedpeople in Montgomery County had begun moving slowly and haltingly toward greater economic independence.

That process accelerated over the next thirty years. Between 1870 and 1900, African Americans in the county continued to make modest economic gains. Landownership increased, nonagricultural employment became more common, and a small number of black families attained middle-class status in terms of income, housing, and material possessions. The most noteworthy of these changes was the increase in land ownership. Owning their own land—the fabled forty acres and a mule—was the great ambition of many former slaves. Owning land, they hoped, would bring them economic and political independence and the respect that went with such independence.[39] Many freedpeople believed that only landownership would bring them genuine freedom; thus, throughout the postwar South, African Americans toiled and sacrificed to join the ranks of freeholders. As shown above, the effort began in Montgomery County almost immediately after the abolition of slavery but made relatively little progress during the first few years. After 1870, however, the pace of black land acquisition in the county increased significantly. Years later, Susan Lester recalled the change. Lester and two of her sons had been manumitted in 1860 and had immediately moved to Ohio. She returned to Christiansburg in 1871, however, and found when she arrived that "there was colored people at that time purchasing homes."[40] Indeed, the year Lester returned, 1871, saw twice as many African Americans buy land in Montgomery County as had in any previous year in the county's history. And the process was just beginning. Between 1870 and 1900 black ownership of land in Montgomery County increased more than twentyfold. At the end of 1870, only 18 African Americans in the county are known to have owned any real estate, but the 1900 census reported that 374 black heads of household owned the property on which they lived. This is not as great as the increase Loren Schweninger found for the state as a whole, but the growth in the number of black landowners in the county was still impressive.[41]

As they had during Reconstruction, freedpeople in Montgomery

County continued after 1870 to acquire land in a variety of ways. A very few received land from their former owners, often long after their emancipation. Margaret Taylor gave land to two more former slaves, Jackson and Lucy Ford, in 1876; the Kent family, in 1889, was finally able to honor the wish of Elizabeth Kent to provide land to her "old & faithful servants" and gave sixteen acres near Wake Forest to Amos and Granville Sherman; and in 1895, Ferdinand Roer sold Samuel Brown one hundred acres near Snowville for one dollar "and the further consideration that Saml. Brown was once my slave and rendered me valuable service as such." At least one other county resident, Waller R. Staples, sold land at reduced prices to some of his former slaves. Staples's executor, Archer A. Phlegar, reported that Staples "either gave, or sold at low prices, to his former slaves adjoining parcels of land" south of Christiansburg, and at least two deeds bear this out. In 1890, Staples sold seven acres to Robert Carter for forty dollars, well below the price per acre generally seen in the county at that time, and three years later he sold three acres to Anderson Carter for twelve dollars.[42]

Most former owners, however, offered no such help to their former slaves, and others set limits on their gratitude. Harvey Black, a prominent physician in Blacksburg, had served in the Confederate army for several years, and for part of that time an enslaved man named Abraham Vaughn had cooked for him. In 1873, Black bought nine acres of land outside of Blacksburg in order to resell it to Vaughn and two other freedmen, George Washington Russell and Robert Saunders. The three agreed to pay for the land over several years and provided bonds to that effect. Six years later, in 1879, the men still had not finished paying for the land, so Black brought suit. Black claimed in a letter to his son that he did this to bring about a court-ordered sale of the property in the hope it would sell at "a very reduced price" and permit him to buy it cheaply for Vaughn. "If I can finally secure it to Abe I will do so," wrote Black. Unfortunately, the land sold for $300, which the commissioner overseeing the sale described as "high," and Abraham Vaughn never got it back. Instead, Harvey Black bought it himself and held it until his death, in 1888, when his heirs sold it to another white man.[43]

The great majority of African Americans who acquired land in Montgomery County, then, had to buy it themselves and had to do so at market prices. They often did so with the help of family members, friends, and white allies. Dianne Swan-Wright and Jacqueline Jones have both noted such practices in other parts of the postwar South, and this was certainly evident in Montgomery County.[44] The most common pattern was one in which members of a nuclear family—husbands, wives, and children—worked together to pay for the family's home or farm. Orville McNorton and his wife, Esther, for example, seem to have used their earnings as a railroad hand and a servant, respectively, to pay for the nine acres they bought in 1871 and were farming in 1880, with the help of their two oldest sons—William, age thirteen by then, and Stanley, age eleven. Even after their children had left home, parents and their adult offspring sometimes helped one another buy land. Susan Lester, for example, helped two of her sons buy land in Christiansburg during the 1870s. After being manumitted, in 1860, Lester had worked as a chambermaid on steamboats plying the Ohio River, and when she returned to Christiansburg in 1871, she used part of her savings to help her sons buy lots in town. Siblings and friends also pooled their efforts to make a purchase. Jerry Watson and his sister, Violet Watson James, bought twenty-five acres together in 1884, and in 1879 Richard Canaday and Anderson Jones, together, bought fifty acres near Big Spring.[45]

Most of these collaborative efforts involved just a few individuals buying a single, relatively modest tract of land, but at least one grew into a sort of land development collective. Scott Casper has documented the existence of such a collective in Fairfax County, where five African American men formed the Joint Stock Club of Gum Springs, bought two acres together, and resold it in smaller parcels to individuals. Three freedmen living in eastern Montgomery County—Israel and William Owens and David Burks—organized a similar activity on an even larger scale, though it was never formally organized in any way. The three principals were all native to the border region between Montgomery and Roanoke Counties and had known one another for years. Israel and William Owens were brothers and had both been slaves of Charles Thomas, a farmer in western Roanoke County. Their partner, David Burks, had been enslaved in eastern Montgomery County, near Lafayette, but had married another of Charles Thomas's slaves and had probably come to know the Owens while visiting his wife. By 1870, the three men and their families were all living outside Big Spring, where the men worked as farmhands. In March 1871, they jointly purchased 137 acres of land along Seneca Creek, just west of Big Spring, for a total of $1,243.50. They bought the land from Samuel McConkey and Archer White, two prominent members of the local white community, and each of the three signed three promissory notes that came payable over the next three years to cover his share of the debt. Each then exercised control over one-third of the land and began to resell portions of it to other African Americans at the same price per acre he had paid for it. Between 1872 and 1875, they sold at least eighty-five acres in smaller parcels to nine other men, including a number of friends and family members. In addition, David Burks sold or gave part of his land to his son, Wallace. Thus, by 1879, twelve men (plus William Owens's widow, Sallie) held shares of the Seneca Creek land ranging from less than an acre to almost thirty-six acres.[46]

Payments for the land, however, did not keep up with its distribution. By 1879, McConkey and White still owed money to the estate of James Barnett, from which they had originally purchased the land. They had not been able to redeem the promissory notes of David Burks and Israel Owens, however, because the latter had been unable to collect what they were due from the men to whom they had resold portions of the land. In an effort to settle this chain of obligations, the twelve men occupying the land along Seneca Creek agreed in 1879 "[to] convey unto John Barnett [administrator of James's estate] all of our entire crops of tobacco to be sold and the proceeds to be applied to the payment that is now due by Mc-Conkey to Barnett as balance on purchase." They also agreed to pay back taxes owed on the land, and when all these outstanding obligations had been paid, McConkey and White would transfer title and provide deeds to each of the twelve. Ultimately, the effort failed. In 1884, the Barnett estate filed a petition in chancery seeking to determine who owed how much and to whom for the land along Seneca Creek and how best to complete or cancel the sales of that land. This, in turn, led to a court-ordered auction at which all 137 acres was sold in May 1886.[47]

The story did have a happy ending, though. The winning bid at the auction came from Charles Schaeffer, the former agent of the Freedmen's Bureau in Montgomery County, who was still living in Christiansburg and was then serving as the pastor of two largely black churches, including the Big Spring Baptist Church. After buying the Seneca Creek land, Schaeffer sold at least one hundred acres of it back to eight of the men who had been living on it, or to their widows. Unfortunately, it is unclear from the deeds whether the men and women who bought their land back from Schaeffer actually had to pay twice for the land or if Schaeffer discounted the price in recognition of their earlier payments. Each paid about half the original price per acre, though, suggesting that Schaeffer did take into account what they had already paid.[48]

Few African Americans received as much support from white allies as those living along Seneca Creek did from Charles Schaeffer, but many did benefit from the willingness of white landowners to extend credit to African Americans and to wait years for full payment. Most of these loans were secured by the land itself. Buyers simply signed promissory notes to pay for the land over several years, and sellers could redeem the notes any time after they came due or sue to reclaim the land if the notes were not honored. Creditors often waited years, however, before seeking payment. As described above, Harvey Black waited six years before taking action against Abraham Vaughn and his partners, and the Barnett family waited more than a decade before demanding payment of the debts due them for land along Seneca Creek. Gordon and Nellie Mills, however, may have had the most patient creditor of all. Gordon Mills agreed in 1878 to buy thirty acres of land from Hamilton D. Wade for a total of $600, plus interest. He paid nothing at the time, but signed six bonds payable over six years, and the family took immediate possession of the land. Ten years later the Millses had paid just seventy-six dollars toward the price of the land, and Wade renegotiated the terms of the sale. He agreed to accept $400 for the deed and the six bonds Gordon had signed in 1878. Over the next three years, Mills paid Wade another forty dollars, but then he died, in 1891, and Wade agreed to restructure the deal again. He initially offered to take $300 for the land and bonds, but eventually settled on $200 dollars when ten of the thirty acres were carved off and sold to a neighbor, Judy Trussell. The sale had still not been completed, however, when Wade died, in 1908, and the Millses entered yet another round of negotiations with his estate's administrator. Finally, in 1910, Gordon Mills Jr. made the final payment on sixteen of the original thirty acres and secured a deed to the property—thirty-two years after his father and Hamilton Wade had first negotiated the sale.[49]

Even with patient creditors, however, buying land required hard work and persistence. Men often took second jobs to help pay for their families' land. Wallace Burks described himself as a farmer, but in the early 1890s, he went to work temporarily on the railroad to earn enough to pay his "land debt." "I wrented my little place out so that I can work out to meet this debt," he wrote in 1893; on the railroad, he earned twenty-two dollars a month after paying his board and promised his creditor "20 dollars a month until he is payed." Given the relatively modest earnings of many African American workers, however, buying land often demanded extraordinary persistence. Catherine and Norvell Curtis were working as a servant and a laundress when they bought her house and lot and took almost three years to pay it off. The account book of Rice D. Montague, a merchant in Christiansburg, also reveals the protracted efforts of black men there to buy land through a combination of cash and labor over several years. Henry Warrington, for example, began buying land from Montague in 1872, and over the next five years made a number of small payments in cash or through labor toward the purchase of three and a quarter acres.[50]

Sharecropping was another route employed by African Americans in Montgomery County to enter the ranks of landowners. As noted above, sharecropping had a long history in Montgomery and other Appalachian counties, and agreements often included elements that seem exploitive to modern observers. In 1876 and 1877, for example, John Lawson entered sharecropping agreements with William F. Tallant under which the two would divide equally the corn and fodder that Lawson raised on land belonging to Tallant. In addition, Tallant agreed to provide housing, firewood, and a garden plot for Lawson and his family, as masters had often done for their slaves, while Lawson and his sons agreed to work for Tallant "any time that Tallant wants [them]." The Lawsons were, however, to be paid for such extra work, and this helped to provide the means by which John Lawson became a landowner himself. In 1878, he bought a lot near Christiansburg and in 1880 was farming seven acres of his own land with his son, John.[51]

African Americans also showed creativity in their efforts to buy land. Aaron and Hanah Watson, for example, joined with Teeny Morton to buy a lot outside Blacksburg and then employed a tontine to establish the land's ultimate owner. The three may all have been slaves together and had certainly known one another as slaves. Aaron and Hanah Watson, who were husband and wife, had both been slaves of Giles D. Thomas, and Aaron Watson and Teeny Morton had both been members of the Methodist Church in Blacksburg. All three were still living in Blacksburg in 1876 when they pooled their resources to buy a half-acre lot in New Town, a community that was just emerging on what had been farm land adjacent to Blacksburg and the Virginia Agricultural and Mechanical College. In the purchase agreement, the three agreed "to associate themselves as equal owners" of the tract. They further stipulated, "It is the desire of all three of the parties first named above, that the one who shall live the longest, shall become the full owner of the aforementioned half acre of ground." After buying the land, neither Morton nor the Watsons occupied it until the early 1880s. In 1882, however, the lot was deeded to Hanah Watson, "at the request of . . . Aaron Watson," and by then it included a house that Aaron Watson had built. Evidently, Teeny Morton had died by 1882. Under the tontine one of the Mortons was certain to become the lot's eventual owner, so they built a house on it and decided that Hanah should be the owner of record.[52]

And like their white neighbors, some of the county's African American residents found that buying land required a good lawyer. In 1872, John Johnson bought five acres between Christiansburg and Shawsville from James Edmundson. Over the next several years, Johnson paid for the land in full and built a house on it, but the men had signed no contract for the sale, and Johnson received no deed before Edmundson died in 1881. Johnson believed, however, that Edmundson had kept a record of the sale and of his payments for the land, so he hired a lawyer and through him submitted a petition in chancery asking the court to order the administrator of Edmundson's estate to produce the papers and provide a deed. Ultimately, the administrator found and delivered a memorandum from James Edmundson showing that Johnson had paid for the land, and the court ordered the estate to provide Johnson a deed and to pay the costs of his suit.[53]

In these various ways, black ownership of land in Montgomery County increased significantly during the final decades of the nineteenth century, but the exact rate at which it did so is difficult to establish. This is partly a result of the fact that sellers often withheld deeds for the land they were selling until payment was complete. Occupancy, however, did not depend on a deed. Buyers might occupy a piece of land for years and act as if they owned it—build on it, farm it, even sell or bequeath it—before they actually became the owners of record. Moreover, they might never attain that final status. If they failed to complete the purchase, it might never appear in the deed books and they might never appear in the records as a landowner, in spite of having acted as de facto owners for years. Further complicating the quest for precision is the fact that racial mores in the county were still evolving. As was true of many other legal documents in the decades following Reconstruction, deeds in Montgomery County do not

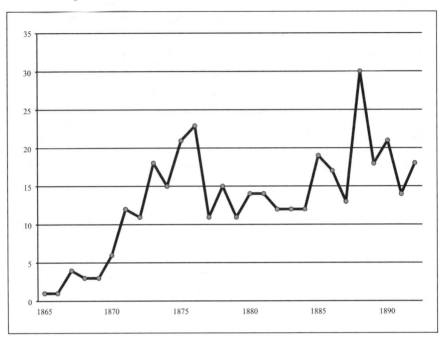

FIGURE 5. First-time black land purchases per year, 1865–1892

always identify African Americans by race. Nor do the land books, which record land holdings and the taxes assessed on them each year. Not until 1890 did Virginia require "White" and "Colored" land books; until then, assessors in Montgomery County sometimes indicated that a landowner was black, but not always and not consistently.[54] Deeds and tax records can sometimes be matched against marriage records, where race *was* carefully recorded, but only if the individual married in Montgomery County and did not share his or her name with another person of a different race.

Such challenges notwithstanding, figure 5 attempts to demonstrate the increasing incidence of black landownership in the county by tracking the number of African Americans purchasing land for the first time in any particular year. It probably underestimates the number of such purchases for the reasons explained above, but it still shows clearly that landownership among Montgomery County's African American residents rose significantly between 1870 and 1900. Moreover, it indicates that the increase occurred fairly steadily across those years. Writing about land acquisition by freedpeople in Virginia's tobacco belt, both Lynda Morgan and Jeffrey Kerr-Ritchie suggest that most of the freedpeople who acquired land in that region did so in the final two decades of the century. Morgan identified a few individuals who bought land during late 1860s and early 1870s but then concluded: "Landholdings that originated in postwar purchase appear to have originated primarily in the 1880s." Kerr-Ritchie, on the other hand, focuses almost exclusively on the 1890s in his discussion of land acquisition by African Americans. Similarly, while Loren Schweninger found that black landownership in Virginia rose significantly between 1870 and 1890, it rose much faster after 1890 than it had before.[55] In Montgomery County, however, black land acquisition began in earnest during the early 1870s. As figure 5 shows, the rate of black land acquisition in the county began rising sharply in 1870 and continued rising through 1876. It dropped in 1877 but then resumed rising at a lower rate through 1892, with two spikes in 1885 and 1888. The median number of first-time African American buyers was 13.5 per year during the 1870s and 14 per year during the 1880s, and by the end of 1892, at least 369 African Americans had purchased land in Montgomery County since 1865.

This does not, of course, reveal how many African Americans actually owned land at any given time because some of those who bought land resold it, divided it among heirs, or lost it to creditors. As a result, it is impossible to gauge the full extent of landownership in the county's African American community until the final decade of the century, and even then the picture remains confused. Montgomery County's "Colored" land book for 1893 is the first to have survived intact after the state began to segregate land tax records. It identifies 282 African American owners or co-owners of 267 parcels of land in Montgomery County. Thadeus Morgan and Lucy Leftwich, however, seem to have held land in two districts; so the total number of owners was actually 280. In his study of Virginia's tobacco counties, Jeffrey Kerr-Ritchie divided the total black population of each county by five to estimate the number of black "households" in that county. Using land books, he then calculated the percentage of "households" in each county that owned land.[56] By that method and using the county's 1890 population, an estimated 40.1 percent of Montgomery County's African American "households" owned land in 1893, which is squarely within the range Kerr-Ritchie found in tobacco counties. It is also very close to the rate of 42 percent shown in Montgomery County on the census of 1900, when the enumerator was directed to indicate whether "each head of family" owned or rented the property on which he or she lived. Thus, it seems reasonable to conclude that by the end of the nineteenth century,

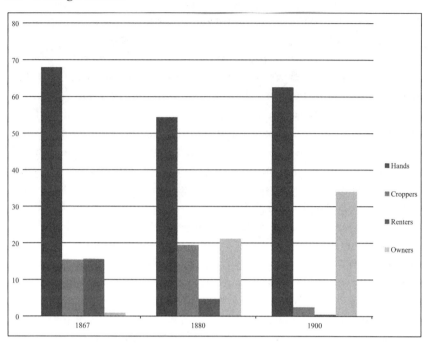

FIGURE 6. Percentages of African American men
engaged in agriculture by tenure

approximately 40 percent of African American families in Montgomery
County owned at least some land.[57]

Few of them owned much, though. Like freedpeople across the South,
those in Montgomery County generally held very small tracts of land.[58]
Allen and Charlotte Lewis did own two hundred acres, but that was extremely rare. The average black farmer in Montgomery County owned just
twenty-six acres in 1880, including on average fifteen improved acres. This
was far below the county average of 139 total acres and 68 improved. In
fact, among black farmers in the county that year, only the Lewises owned
as much as the county average. By 1893, the first year in which it is possible
to identify all of the county's black landowners, their average holding, including town lots, was just a little more than seven acres, and it continued
to shrink slowly as migration to town continued during the final years of
the nineteenth century.[59]

The rising number of African American landowners in Montgomery
County was most evident, perhaps, in the distribution of African American
workers engaged in agriculture. As figure 6 demonstrates, the percentage

of these workers who owned their own farms rose significantly between 1867 and 1900. Among the county's 493 African American men working on farms in 1867, 68 percent (336) worked as hired hands, 15.6 percent (77) leased farms, 15.4 percent (76) worked as sharecroppers, and less than 1 percent (4) owned their own farms.[60] Discrepancies between the population and agricultural schedules of the 1880 census make absolute precision impossible, but the best estimate indicates that of the 319 of the black men engaged in farming that year, 54.5 percent worked as hired hands, 21.3 percent owned their own farms, 19.1 percent worked for shares, and 5.1 percent paid cash rent for their land.[61] Discrepancies also exist on the 1900 census, but the best estimate suggests that farm laborers represented 62.6 percent of black men engaged in agriculture that year (132 of 211), up from the 54.5 percent seen in 1880. Owner operators (seventy-two), however, had also increased as a share of black agricultural workers—from 21.3 percent in 1880 to 34.1 percent in 1900. African American renters and sharecroppers, on the other hand, had nearly vanished from the county by 1900. Fewer than 3 percent of African Americans in the county engaged in agriculture that year (6 of 211) were sharecroppers and just one black farmer rented for cash.[62]

Like most farmers in Montgomery County, black farmers were generalists rather than specialists. Sharecroppers, renters, and owner-operators all raised a variety of crops and performed a variety of tasks during the course of the year. Nearly all grew corn, the mainstay of both people and livestock. About half grew wheat, tobacco, or both; these were mostly farmers in the Alleghany and Auburn districts of the county—east and south of Christiansburg—where some of the largest areas of relatively flat land lay. More than three-quarters of the county's African American farmers also kept hogs, which could largely fend for themselves before being slaughtered to provide meat. Cows were equally common on black farms, though often just one and probably for milk rather than meat. Conspicuously absent were sheep. The number of sheep in Montgomery County rose steadily and significantly between 1870 and 1900, and dozens of white farmers in the county kept them, usually in fairly small numbers, though a few had flocks in excess of one hundred head. Among black farmers, however, sheep were virtually non-existent. The 1880 agricultural schedule indicates just one of 145 black farmers in the county raised any sheep, and in 1900 just one of 528 black men listed on the personal property tax roll reported owning any.[63] A number of the county's African American landowners also complemented farming with logging. White landowners often retained the best land for themselves and sold rockier, uphill tracts to African Americans. These tracts were frequently wooded, though, and timber provided their owners an additional source of income. Barney Brown, for example, farmed thirty-eight acres on the western edge of the county, but he used logs and shingles to settle his store account with D. B. Bill.[64]

Ironically, even as more African Americans in Montgomery County were acquiring land of their own, agriculture was declining as a source of African American employment in the county. The transition was gradual and did not begin immediately, but the years after the Civil War did see a steady and significant decline in the percentage of African Americans in the county engaged in agriculture. Immediately after emancipation, the great majority of freedmen in the county had worked on farms; almost 78 percent were farmhands or independent farmers in 1867, and in 1870 just over 70 percent were. By 1880, however, this figure had dropped to less than 44 percent, a rate that matched quite closely the percentage found among African American men applying to marry between 1870 and 1879. This decline continued through the end of the nineteenth century. The percentage of grooms who identified themselves as farmers or farmhands fell to 31.3 percent between 1880 and 1889 and 28 percent between 1890 and 1899, while the 1900 census reported that 31.2 percent of African American men working in the county that year worked as farmers or farmhands. These figures are certainly not perfect; some men identified as preachers or railroad hands on the population schedule in 1880 also appear on the agricultural schedule that year, and some of those identified as laborers may have worked as agricultural laborers. The trend, however, is clear. Between 1865 and 1900 the percentage of African American men in Montgomery County who worked in agriculture declined significantly, from three-quarters of the total immediately after the abolition of slavery to a third at the opening of the twentieth century.[65]

In part, this shift away from agricultural employment reflects the tenuous nature of black farming in the county. Because the farms owned by African Americans were relatively small, they were often difficult to divide among several children without cutting them into pieces too small to be economically viable. Even the family of Allen and Charlotte Lewis, whose two hundred acres near Vickers was the largest African American landholding in the county, had trouble making this transition when eleven of the couple's thirteen children lived to be adults. Making matters worse

was the fact that land sold to African Americans in the county was often
located up narrow hollows or on rockier hillsides and was less well-suited
to farming than were the bottomlands found on many larger, white-owned
farms. Thus, as time went on and the generation of African Americans
who had been adults in 1865 passed their estates to their children, it became increasingly difficult for members of that next generation to survive
as independent farmers. At the same time, the demand for hired farm
workers in the county also seems to have fallen. The final two decades of
the nineteenth century saw declining crops of corn, wheat, and tobacco in
Montgomery County and growing herds of cattle and sheep. This probably
reduced the demand for labor on county farms, and the number of black
men working as farm hands declined, from 174 in 1880 to 132 in 1900.[66]

This shift away from agricultural employment among the county's African American workers reflected a widespread trend in the New South
and was accompanied by an increase in the number of black men working
in other sectors of the economy.[67] In Montgomery County, the greatest
number of nonfarm workers appeared in the category identified simply as
"laborer." These were the men who performed a range of physical activities
on construction sites and loading docks, at lime kilns and saw mills, and
elsewhere throughout the county. In 1870, they represented only about 5
percent of the county's African American male workers, but their number
grew quickly in the years that followed. By 1880, the number of laborers
on the census (260) still trailed the combined total of farmers and farmhands (336), but laborer was the largest single job category among the
county's African American men that year and included more than a third
of its black male workers. A similar pattern appeared on the 1900 census,
which showed 195 farmers or farm laborers and 185 laborers, with the
latter making up just under 30 percent of all black male workers. Marriage
records suggest the number of black laborers may have been even greater
than that. Between 1880 and 1889, 33.6 percent of black men requesting
marriage licenses identified themselves as laborers, and the figure reached
48 percent among those who married between 1890 and 1899.[68]

A significant number of the county's African American men also moved
into various forms of service as cooks, dishwashers, coachmen, hostlers,
servants, waiters, and related occupations. Their number grew gradually
between 1870 and 1900, as the county economy grew and diversified. Men
in these service occupations represented 6.7 percent of working African
American men in the county on the 1870 census, 8.8 percent a decade

later, and 9.5 percent in 1900. This growth was accompanied, however, by a change in the nature of men's domestic work. Until at least 1880, many of these men served as domestic servants who lived and worked in white households, and they were found throughout the county. Between 1880 and 1900, however, the number of men engaged in service declined sharply beyond the towns of Christiansburg, Blacksburg, and Radford, and in these towns, men engaged in service were more likely to work as waiters, cooks, or porters in restaurants or hotels than in private homes. As discussed below, domestic service increasingly became black women's work in the late nineteenth century. Black men in Montgomery County continued to fill service positions but were more likely to do so in public venues.[69]

Smaller numbers of black men also appeared in more specialized categories of nonfarm work, such as that associated with the railroad. From their beginnings during the 1830s, southern railroads had often employed black men—both free and slaves—as laborers and brakemen. This practice continued, and even accelerated, after the abolition of slavery. Section gangs, the men who maintained the roadbeds and realigned the track, were often entirely black under white supervision. James Dow, whose grandfather of the same name went to work for the Virginia and Tennessee Railroad in 1868, recalled watching members of a section gang from the Brake Branch neighborhood heading home after work when he was a child: "It was like watching a line of crows." African Americans also served as brakemen and firemen on many southern railroads, although white workers sometimes tried to keep them out of these positions, and as dining and sleeping cars became more widespread in the decades after the Civil War, growing numbers of black men worked in the kitchens, as waiters, and as sleeping car attendants. Some of these jobs kept men away from home for extended periods of time, many were physically demanding, and some were quite dangerous. Nevertheless, railroads were a major source of employment for black men throughout the South. Positions on sleeping cars or dining cars were among the most desirable jobs available to African Americans at the time, and even the more physically demanding, dangerous work as section hands or brakemen appealed to many black men because it often paid better than farming and the pay was more predictable.[70]

The 1870 census did not differentiate among "railroad hands" but showed that a total of forty-six African American men from Montgomery County (just over 6 percent of the total) worked for the railroad that year. Most if not all of these men probably worked in track maintenance. Over the next thirty years, the Virginia and Tennessee became part of the Atlantic, Mississippi, and Ohio Railroad (1870–81) and then the Norfolk and Western, but whatever its name, the railroad remained one of the most important nonfarm employers for African American men in the county. Census data show that rail workers increased from slightly more than 5 percent of the county's black male workforce in 1880 to 14 percent in 1900.[71] The number of railroad workers among men who applied for marriage licenses in Montgomery County was similarly high — 10 percent during the 1870s and 16 percent during the 1880s, though it dipped again, to 7.6 percent, during the final decade of the century.[72] The exact number of railroad workers among the county's African American men fluctuated from year to year, but it seems to have risen between 1870 and 1900 from approximately 5 percent to at least 10 percent, and for most of this time railroad work was the third most common job category for black men in the county, after farmer/farmhand and general laborer.

Surprisingly few black men in Montgomery County worked as coal miners during the final decades of the nineteenth century. Scholars such as Ronald Lewis and Joe Trotter have described the experiences of black miners in the nearby coalfields of West Virginia during the late nineteenth and early twentieth centuries.[73] There and elsewhere in the United States, the operators of coal mines often employed African Americans either as temporary strikebreakers or as regular workers, and as noted in chapter 1, men from Montgomery County often moved to West Virginia, Ohio, and Iowa after the Civil War to work in coal mines there. In Montgomery County, however, few black men worked in the mines before 1900. Coal production in the county did increase after the Civil War, but the industry remained a relatively small element in the local economy, employing just forty-seven men in 1880 and fifty-six in 1890.[74] According to the federal census, there were no black miners in the county in 1870, just five in 1880, and ten in 1900, and they never made up more than 1.5 percent of the county's black male workers in any of these years. Marriage records from the county include slightly more miners — 3 percent of African American grooms during the 1880s and 4.5 percent during the 1890s — but these were often men who lived and worked elsewhere. Between 1890 and 1899, for example, twenty-one African American men applying for marriage licenses in Montgomery County identified themselves as miners, but only ten of them actually lived in the county. Almost as many, nine of the twenty-one, reported living in West Virginia, while two others lived in Virginia counties southwest of Montgomery. Each of these men married a woman who was living in Montgomery County at the time and then probably returned to the communities in which they were working.

As they had since before the Civil War, skilled craftsmen remained a small but important element within Montgomery County's African American workforce during the decades following the abolition of slavery. Carpenters, masons, plasterers, blacksmiths, barbers, and shoemakers constituted a small economic elite in the county's African American community. Both census data and marriage records suggest they represented 6 to 8 percent of black male workers in the county between 1870 and 1900, though their number declined as a percentage of the workforce by the end of that period. Blacksmiths and carpenters were the most numerous members of this group and also the ones most widely distributed, geographically. All of the skilled trades, however, were more concentrated in towns such as Christiansburg and Blacksburg, and this pattern became even more evident by 1900. Some of the county's African American craftsmen, such as Zacharia Carr and Felix Johnson, learned their skills during the antebellum era; Carr, born a free person of color, had trained as a carpenter, while Johnson, a slave, had learned to lay brick. Both then continued to practice their trade after 1865 and helped to train a new generation of African American craftsmen in Montgomery County. John Grimes, for example, was a former slave from Wythe County who came to Christiansburg early in the 1870s and in 1874 entered an agreement with Felix Johnson to serve a three-year apprenticeship as a brick mason. Grimes went on to work as a mason and a plasterer in the county for at least forty years and became one of its largest African American property owners by the beginning of the twentieth century.[75]

The presence of black craftsmen such as John Grimes led to at least one instance of racial tension with their white competitors in the county. In May 1879, the *Christiansburg Messenger* reported without comment that a black builder had won the contract to build a house for James H. Lane, a professor of chemistry and natural philosophy at Virginia Mechanical and Agricultural College. A week later, however, the paper noted: "The mechanics are indignant, because a negro has been awarded the contract for building a professor's house." The issue may not have been simply the builder's race, though, because the *Messenger* noted that the white mechanics were "especially" angry that the contract had gone to a man who had "served in the Yankee army and came here from Tennessee." He was not just black; he was evidently unfamiliar to whites in Montgomery County and further suspect as a Union army veteran. He was probably seen as more threatening to the community's racial norms than a man familiar to the county's white residents. In the cases of men better known in the county and without the complication of military service, there is little evidence of such tension between black and white workers in Montgomery County. Minnis Headen, for example, had been a slave in Bedford County but had been married to a woman living in Christiansburg and by 1866 had moved to the county to join her. He lived in Christiansburg until at least 1885, operated a blacksmith shop on the west side of town, and included a number of whites among his customers. Not only is there no evidence that whites ever objected to his presence or activity in the community, in 1885 Headen entered an agreement with a prominent white businessman in Christiansburg, David W. Frizzell, to market an improved "striking hammer" for which Headen had obtained a patent and to share the profits.[76]

An even smaller number of black men in Montgomery County held professional positions in the decades after the Civil War. These were all ministers or teachers; there is no record of any African American lawyer or doctor in the county until well into the twentieth century. As described more fully in later chapters, African American churches and schools had both begun to operate in Montgomery County by early 1867, and the numbers of each increased significantly over the next thirty years. By the end of the century, more than a dozen black churches and almost twenty black schools had opened in the county, and as their numbers increased, so did the number of black ministers and teachers. The federal census identified three black ministers in the county in 1870, four in 1880, and nine in 1900. It also found one black man teaching in 1880 and eight in 1900. Black professionals appeared less frequently among the county's marriage records; between 1870 and 1899 just seven men who applied for marriage licenses in Montgomery County identified themselves as ministers (three) or teachers (four). For ministers, however, such numbers are somewhat misleading as they sometimes include men who were short-term residents of the county. Nearly all of the black men identified on the census as ministers, for example, were Methodists posted in the county for terms of one to three years by their regional conferences. Local men did serve as ministers, especially among the county's Baptists, but they were rarely identified as ministers on the census and usually pursued some other occupation that provided their livelihood. John Campbell and Felix Johnson, for example, were both ordained in the early 1870s and appeared regularly among ministers in the Colored Valley Baptist Association, but the census identifies Campbell as a carpenter and Johnson as a brick mason.[77]

Black ministers in Montgomery County, whether part time or full time, were always men, and that did not change during the nineteenth century. Teaching, however, was also open to women, and the gender distribution among black teachers in the county followed a distinctive pattern. When Montgomery County began to establish public schools, in 1871, the majority of its white teachers were male, though over the next thirty years the gender balance among white teachers in the county shifted decisively from a male majority to a female. Among African Americans, on the other hand, teachers were initially divided by gender fairly evenly. Few slaves or free people of color had enjoyed literacy before 1865, and immediately after emancipation economic pressure seems to have limited the time men and boys spent in schools operated by the Freedmen's Bureau. As a result, perhaps, black women entered the teaching profession as frequently as black men did in the early 1870s. During the course of 1870s and throughout the 1880s, however, black men increased as a percentage of teachers in the county. African American men seeking white-collar employment in Montgomery County had fewer options than their white counterparts, so teaching remained attractive to black men longer than it did to white men. The number of African American male teachers did eventually decline during the final decade of the century, but men remained about half of the county's black teachers into the early years of the twentieth century.[78]

Finally, a small number of black men operated bars, stores, or restaurants in Montgomery County after the Civil War. Only one, however, did so before 1890. John Campbell, not the carpenter/minister of the same name, operated a "Bar & Eating House" at the Big Spring train station between 1870 and 1873, though he seems to have done so intermittently. The local correspondent for R. G. Dun & Co. first mentioned Campbell in August 1870 but a year later reported that "[he] patronized his own bar too freely" and had gone out of business. Campbell seems to have reopened sometime between 1871 and 1873 but had closed for good by 1874.[79] After that, no African American is known to have operated any mercantile facility in Montgomery County for almost twenty years. Black men's success buying land within a few years of gaining their freedom suggests that they did have access to credit and an interest in economic success, but for men who had been adults when slavery ended, shopkeeping may not have seemed a viable economic opportunity. Before the Civil War, only one free person of color, William Campbell, had operated a store in the county, but his too had failed after just a few years. The postwar generation, however, had no such memories, and as they came of age, a small community of African American merchants appeared in the county. George W. Hopkins and Stephen Wysong opened a "soda fountain" in Big Spring about 1890; three years later, in 1893, Anderson Harvey received a license to operate a restaurant in Blacksburg, and two other African American men, Samuel Stuart and Hooper Dill, identified themselves as "merchants" when they applied for marriage licenses. Dill died just two years later, but Stuart operated a grocery store in Cambria for several decades. By 1900 he had been joined in the Cambria/Christiansburg area by two other grocers, James Briggs and James Clark, while two black restaurateurs, Peter Wade and James Davis, had opened in Blacksburg and Radford, respectively.[80]

Of course men were not the only ones who worked in Montgomery County. African American women often worked too, and many of them did so outside the home. This was especially true in the case of unmarried women. As noted in chapter 2, a significant number of black women in the county found themselves alone through choice, divorce, abandonment, or the death of their spouse. Each federal census between 1870 and 1900 found that about 45 percent of African American women in the county eighteen years and older were unmarried at the time of the census. Some of these were daughters still living with their parents or older widows living with their adult children, but about half were women living on their own. Moreover, many of these women had dependent children to support; each census between 1870 and 1900 found that 12 to 13 percent of African American women eighteen years or older in Montgomery County were unmarried with minor children.[81] Not all of these women worked outside the home. Charlotte Calloway, for example, lived on her own from 1870 until her death in 1893 and for half of that time raised a young niece, Olivia Smith, yet there is no evidence that Calloway worked for wages during those years.[82]

Most women living on their own, however, especially those with children, found such work essential. When, for example, Jackson Ford "banished" his wife, Julia, from their home, about 1880, she was "compelled to maintain herself by hiring herself as a labouring woman to the best white families," and Georgiana Twine "went out to service to earn a living for her-self and children" when her abusive husband refused to support them in 1893. County and town officials provided little public assistance to either white or black citizens in need during the nineteenth century and usually did so only for those with physical infirmities that kept them from work-ing.[83] As a result, most unmarried women living on their own worked for wages. Among women shown on the federal census as heads of household, 65 percent worked outside the home in 1880 and 70 percent did in 1900.[84]

Married women, on the other hand, were much less likely to work outside the home. As noted earlier, freedmen often wished to assert their manhood and authority over their families by discouraging their wives from working, and married freedwomen, themselves, were often anxious to demonstrate their new status by withdrawing from the paid labor force.[85] As early as 1867, fewer than half the married freedwomen in the county were working outside the home, and by 1870 the number had dropped even further. The 1870 census does not include relationships, and from surnames alone it is not always possible to distinguish men's wives from their sisters, daughters, or mothers. Among the black and mulatto women named on that census, however, 388 seem to have been married and living with their husbands at the time the census was taken, and of that number, just 39 (10.1 percent) were described with occupations other than "keeping house." In 1880 and 1900, census enumerators did indicate family relationships, and working wives remained rare. In 1880, just nine-teen married women (3 percent) worked outside the home, while in 1900 the number was thirty-seven (7 percent). Some of these women may have worked to augment their families' income. Hannah Price, for example, was a "washer woman" married to a laborer, and the couple had five children to support in 1880, plus Hannah's mother. At least one woman worked, however, so she could leave her husband. Phoebe Grimes was married to John Grimes, a successful mason and one of the wealthiest African Amer-ican men in the county at the turn of the twentieth century. Beginning about 1890, Phoebe declared, her husband began to exhibit "barbaric and inhuman cruelty" toward her, so she went to work as a teacher for more than a decade and used her earnings to purchase a lot, build a house on it, and move out on her own in 1903.[86] Cases like those of Hannah Price or Phoebe Grimes were unusual, though. After 1870, the great majority of married women in Montgomery County's African American community quickly moved to fill the role expected of wives and mothers in nineteenth century America and worked "keeping house."

Black women who did work outside the home found very limited opportunities in Montgomery County. A small number served as teachers. As described above, black men retained a significant presence in county classrooms until the twentieth century, but a growing number of women did too. Before 1885 it was only three or four per year, but by the late 1880s the number had risen to eight and fluctuated between eight and eleven through the turn of the century.[87] Equally small numbers of African American women worked as farmers, farmhands, or laborers, while even fewer found employment as dressmakers, weavers, or seamstresses. And one, Phoebe Grimes, operated a store, though only briefly. The overwhelming majority of African American women who worked outside the home performed some sort of domestic service. Each census between 1870 and 1900 found that at least 88 percent of the African American women in Montgomery County with an occupation other than "keeping house" worked as domestics—cooks, housekeepers, nurses, and servants—or washed laundry.

Within that consistency, however, women's work did change in the decades following the Civil War. Through 1880, at least, the most common occupations for black women were cook and servant; together these accounted for 57 percent of working women in 1870 and 71 percent in 1880. Many of these women, and their children, lived with the white families for whom they worked, and this became a common means of providing for unmarried African American women and their children in the aftermath of slavery. Jane Carter, for example, seems to have been a slave of Joseph Edie, a Christiansburg physician, until her emancipation in 1865. By then, Carter was thirty-one years old and, apparently, a widow, and after gaining her freedom she continued working as a servant for Dr. Edie until at least 1867. By 1870, however, she had gone to live and work with Edie's daughter, Mollie, and her husband, Dr. William F. Figgat, and a decade later was still with the widowed Mollie Figgat (figure 7). In 1888, Maggie Figgat, the daughter of William and Mollie, married William F. Henderson, a physician at the Virginia Mechanical and Agricultural College, and sometime before 1900 both Mollie Figgat and Jane Carter, still working as a servant, moved from Christiansburg to Blacksburg to live with the Hendersons. There Carter remained until her death, sometime between 1910 and 1920.[88]

FIGURE 7. In this 1886 photograph of a gathering in Christiansburg,
Jane Carter appears on the far right, apparently tending to the children.
(Courtesy of the Montgomery Museum and Lewis Miller Regional Art Center)

By the early twentieth century, however, the nature of black women's work in Montgomery County had begun to change. Census data indicate that cooks and servants still represented 43 percent of black women working outside the home, and more than half of these women still lived with the white families for whom they worked, but the single largest occupational category for African American women in 1900 was washwoman/laundress (37.5 percent of the those working outside the home), and just two of eighty-eight washwomen lived in white households. In a pattern similar to that found by Rebecca Sharpless, women in Montgomery County who had been adults under slavery seem to have been more willing than their daughters and granddaughters to continue living in the homes of their white employers, and by the turn of the twentieth century this generational change was making itself visible in the patterns of black women's work and lives.[89]

As Sharpless also found, black women's work became increasingly urban. For more than a decade after the Civil War, the percentage of Montgomery County's population that lived in its towns actually declined slightly, and during those years African American women working as cooks or servants were distributed fairly evenly throughout the county. Between 1880 and 1900, however, the county's urban population more than doubled as Blacksburg grew significantly and Radford explosively. And as the county's population grew more concentrated in towns, the demand for African American cooks and washwomen became even more concentrated. Auburn and Alleghany districts, the least urbanized portion of Montgomery County, still included 35.6 percent of the county's African American population in 1900 and 30.7 percent of its black *male* workers but only 11.2 percent of its black women working outside the home. Urban residence was especially common for female heads of household; while they made up 29.1 percent of African American households in the county in 1900, they were 36.6 percent of those in the more urban districts and just 17.6 percent in the more rural districts. Even women whose homes remained in those more rural districts sometimes found it necessary to seek work in town. When, for example, Georgiana Twine went to work to support her family in 1893, she traveled from Elliston to Christiansburg to find work as a domestic and returned home to visit her children just once a month.[90]

Economically, African American women were more than just workers, however; they were engaged in all aspects of the economy of Montgomery County. They were certainly not as economically visible as men; Virginia did not grant married women full rights as property owners until 1877, and even then centuries of tradition reduced women's role in economic matters.[91] And black women, of course, faced additional barriers as result of their race. Despite their gender and race, however, a number of African American women—both married and unmarried—participated fully in the postwar economy of Montgomery County. Deeds and mechanics' liens often identify those who borrowed or lent money to purchase land or build houses, deeds of trust describe secured loans for both real and personal property, and court records detail unpaid loans that led to legal action as well as the economic lives of couples suing for divorce. Smaller or less eventful activities seem to have gone unrecorded, but it is clear from the records that have survived that between 1865 and 1900 a significant number of African American women participated in the economy of Montgomery County as creditors, debtors, and property owners.

Martha Shaver, for example, was an unmarried African American woman who appeared in all three of these capacities. In 1871, she sold on credit eight head of cattle, two hogs, and a lot of tobacco—worth a total of $196.50—to Beverly Deaton, a white farmer for whom she had worked as a cook. The debt was still unpaid when Deaton died, and Shaver brought suit for repayment in 1874. Soon thereafter, in 1876, Shaver herself secured a loan when she bought a house and lot in Christiansburg from Thomas and William Spindle, two of the town's most successful merchants. The property cost $275, and Shaver paid most of the purchase price in cash. She also "deferred payment," however, of $41.66, for which she signed a promissory note that she subsequently redeemed in full, plus interest. Similarly, Caroline Campbell, also unmarried, built a house in 1878 on land she had owned since before the Civil War, and at least part of the construction cost was secured by a mechanic's lien filed by Joshua Webster, the builder she employed. Married women, too, obtained credit and purchased property in their own right. Lucinda Richardson, for example, had been married about a year when she purchased a lot in Christiansburg from Mary Mays, a white woman. Richardson bought the land on credit in 1890 and paid for it in small increments over the next year. Eventually, she paid a total of fifty dollars "from her separate estate" for the lot and another seventy dollars to have a house built on it.[92]

As these cases suggest, African American women were most visible in the economy of postwar Montgomery County as owners of real estate. Between 1865 and 1892, a total of 370 African Americans in the county are known to have purchased land, and 82 of them (22.2 percent) were women. Other women inherited land or received it as gifts, and by 1893 nearly a third of African American landowners in the county were women. That year entries in the county land book were divided into "White" and "Colored," and among the latter women made up 91 of the 280 owners and co-owners. It is also clear that a number of these women were quite determined to assert control over their property. Lucinda Richardson did so in the case cited above, and so did Bessie Banks. Banks and her father, Norbourn Banks, both signed a statement in 1880 that the land they were buying from Madison Smith was to be Bessie's, and several years later Bessie Banks testified in a suit brought by Smith's heirs that "the land in the bill mentioned was purchased for her sole benefit and was paid for with her money." Some of these black female landowners also made it clear that the land they owned was to remain in female hands. Catherine Curtis, for example, had four daughters and two sons when she died in 1888. She also owned a house and lot in Christiansburg that her son, Norvell, had helped her purchase twenty years earlier. In her will, Curtis specified that her daughters should repay their brother the money he had provided his mother but that the land itself was to remain with her daughters. And because her daughters were all married, she also made sure to stipulate that "their husbands have no interest in it & can't control it." Clearly, African American women in Montgomery County understood as well as African American men did that the ownership of property was an essential element in maintaining one's personal autonomy.[93]

The decades following the Civil War also saw significant changes in the distribution of wealth in Montgomery County's African American community. Initially, very few members of that community had any wealth to speak of. A handful of former free people of color owned land, houses, or modest personal property when slavery was abolished, but most of the county's freedmen were former slaves, who gained their freedom with nothing but their clothes and a few household goods. This was certainly evident in 1866, when the county's first postwar tax rolls were compiled. Former slaves were now subject to a capitation tax that Virginia levied on free males aged twenty-one years and older and to taxes on land and various categories of personal property—including livestock, household furniture, mechanics' tools, and farming implements.[94] Only about a dozen African Americans in the county owned land in 1866, and of 303 black men listed on the tax roll that year, only 18 were assessed any tax on personal property. Between 1866 and 1900, however, wealth became much more widespread in the county's African American community. As described above, the number of freedpeople in the county acquiring land began to increase significantly after 1870, and by the turn of the century perhaps 40 percent of black families in Montgomery County owned land. Personal property became even more widespread than land and did so even more rapidly. While just 6 percent of black men on the 1866 tax roll had been subject to property taxes, almost half were in 1870, and that figure continued rising over the next thirty years. It did not rise as rapidly after 1870 as it had before, but in 1880, 64.6 percent of African American men on the county's tax roll were assessed personal property taxes and in 1900, 68.4 percent.[95]

As property and wealth became more widespread among members of the county's African American community, the economic advantage initially enjoyed by former free people of color faded quite rapidly. Immediately after emancipation, former free people of color were significantly over-represented among African American property owners. The initial advantage enjoyed by former free people of color was especially evident in the ownership of land. By the end of 1866, about a dozen African Americans owned land in Montgomery County, and only one of them, Spencer Haden, had been a slave in 1865. Former slaves, however, rapidly improved their economic position relative to that of the former free people of color. By 1870, more than half of black landowners in the county, including the largest, were former slaves, and while John Campbell and Zacharia Carr were the two largest holders of taxable personal property among African Americans in the county, they were the only former free persons of color among the 25 largest African American property owners in the county that year. This trend continued in the decades that followed, and there was soon no discernable economic advantage to having been free before 1865.

And as members of the African American community became wealthier after 1870, economic stratification within that community also became more evident. By 1900, three distinct groups, marked by different levels of property ownership and different standards of living, had emerged within Montgomery County's African American population. The poorest of these groups is the most difficult either to measure or describe. Its members were often casual laborers, washwomen, people who worked odd jobs, or those with no jobs at all, and they rarely appear in land, tax, or probate records. One partial measure of this group's size is the percentage of African American men subject only to the capitation tax and shown on state tax rolls with no taxable personal property. This group shrank significantly between 1866, when it amounted to 94 percent of black men on the tax roll, and the end of the nineteenth century, but in 1900 it still included almost 32 percent of African American men on the tax roll for Montgomery County. Moreover, that figure certainly underestimates the actual level of poverty in the African American community because it misses poor women. Only men were subject to the capitation tax; thus the only women to appear on state tax rolls were those with taxable personal property, and this seems to have been a small percentage of unmarried, African American women. In 1900, for example, the census found more than 200 adult, African American women in Montgomery County who were single or widows, but only 14 were assessed taxes that year on any personal property. This suggests that black, female heads of household in

Montgomery County were even poorer as a group than their male counterparts, and because approximately one quarter of black households in
the county were headed by women, perhaps as many as half of the county's African American households had little or no taxable property by the
opening years of the twentieth century.

It seems that an equally large economic group in Montgomery County's
postwar African American community was those in the middle. They were
certainly not "middle class" in the sense that term is used today, or even as
white Americans would have used it in the late nineteenth century. They
were working class—small farmers, craftsmen, railroad workers, even
laborers—with modest holdings of real and personal property. The average black-owned farm in the county during these years was about 25 acres
(one-sixth of the county average) but because so many African American
landowners had house lots in or near a town, the average holding was less
than 10 acres. Holdings of personal property were similarly modest; the
mean assessment for African Americans on the 1900 personal property
roll was $23.91—one-tenth the mean among whites that year. Life for
these men and women was comfortable but simple. Joseph Dill, for example, worked as a laborer in Blacksburg and by the early 1880s lived with
his wife Rosa in "a good & comfortable log dwelling house with four rooms
& all necessary out buildings." When he died, in 1883, Dill's personal property included two bedsteads with mattresses and bedding, three tables,
six chairs, a rocking chair, a bookcase, "1 lot of old books," a wardrobe, a
cupboard, a clock, a framed picture, dishes and plates, and a cook stove—
appraised at a total value of $38.35. Barney Brown, who died in 1884, was
a farmer and timber cutter living near Snowville. His estate included more
tools and livestock than did Joseph Dill's—including a wagon, two plows,
a horse, and four head of cattle—but his household furnishings were com-
parable to Dill's: three bedsteads with all the bedding, a trundle bed, a
cupboard, four chairs, a table, a clock, and kitchen utensils, worth a total
of $41.75.[96]

Not all of Montgomery County's African American residents led such
modest lives, though. A small number did come to enjoy a genuine middle-
class lifestyle, and they represented the economic elite of the county's post–
Civil War African American community. Some of those in this middle-
class elite were the descendants of free people of color (figure 8). James
Carr, for example was the son of Zacharia Carr, who had been a free black
carpenter before the war. James first tried to buy land in 1876, from the

FIGURE 8. James and Harriett Carr late in the nineteenth
century. (Used with the permission of Lois C. Teele)

family that had owned his wife, Harriett, but fell behind in the payments
and eventually lost the land. In 1884, the family tried again. Harriett Carr
purchased land just outside of Christiansburg on which she and James
established a profitable farm and raised a family. James also served as a
deacon for Memorial Baptist Church, the oldest and largest black Baptist
church in the county. Most members of the county's black middle class,
however, were former slaves, such as Charlotte Calloway. Calloway was a
former slave who moved from Lynchburg to Christiansburg soon after the
Civil War. There she worked briefly as a seamstress before purchasing a
lot in town, building on it what was probably the largest African American
home in the county, and living there with her niece, Olivia Smith, until her
death in 1893. No image of Calloway's home is known to have survived,
but according to the inventory of her estate, the house contained at least
two rooms and a hall upstairs; a hall, a parlor, a pantry, and two other
rooms downstairs; and a kitchen and cellar in the basement. Its contents
included carpets and curtains throughout, oak and mahogany furniture,
an organ, more than a dozen pictures, two clocks, "2 figures under glass
cover," and a refrigerator in the kitchen. After Calloway's death, her house
sold for $2,350 and her personal property for $393.67—excluding that
distributed to her sisters or niece.[97]

In a final sign of her middle-class status, Charlotte Calloway was laid to rest in the first commercial cemetery in Montgomery County established "as a place to bury colored people." It stood on the crest of a hill overlooking downtown Christiansburg and adjacent to what had been the earliest Methodist cemetery in town. Calloway's niece and heir, Olivia Smith, bought a plot large enough for both of them and marked her aunt's grave with a professionally carved stone, two feet tall and decorated with a rose blossom. Three years later, the cemetery's developer fled his creditors and his wife by moving to Chicago, and in the wake of his default and divorce the county bought his largely empty cemetery "for the purposes of burying the poor of the county." It is unclear whether or not county officials ever actually used the land for that purpose, and if they did, the graves they laid out were never marked. Many of the stones in the old Methodist Burying Ground have also been destroyed over the years; so most of the hilltop stands vacant today. Charlotte Calloway's stone, however, remains — a quiet reminder of the economic success achieved by Montgomery County's African American community in the decades following the Civil War.[98]

4 SCHOOLS FOR THE BENEFIT OF OUR CHILDREN

IN FEBRUARY 1869, eleven-year-old Hart Wayland wrote a letter from Christiansburg that was printed in April by the *American Freedman,* a journal published monthly in New York by the American Freedman's Union Commission (AFUC) "for the benefit . . . of all who are interested in the work of education in the South." Little is known for certain about young Wayland's early years. He had been born a slave, though where remains a mystery, and by 1867 was living in Christiansburg with Jackson Burgess, a white horse trader who had moved to Montgomery County from Fayette County shortly after the Civil War began. In 1869, when Wayland wrote his letter, he was still living in Christiansburg and was attending a school there funded in part by the New York branch of the AFUC, which is why he addressed his letter to its journal. He wrote to thank the commission's supporters for the presents they had sent, probably for Christmas, and to show them how well he was doing in the school they helped to support. "I am in the third Reader, Geography, Arithmetic, Spelling, and History," he told them. Acknowledging his teacher, Lucy Eastman, whose salary was paid by the AFUC, Wayland wrote, "When Ms. Lucy came here I did not know anything and now don't you think I write pretty well?" He assured readers of the *American Freedman* that "the school is getting along very well" and invited them to visit: "We would be glad to see you."[1]

When Hart Wayland wrote that, he was one of several hundred African American students attending four new schools in Montgomery County. He and his classmates were pioneers, and the schools they attended were among the most visible and the most important signs of a new world that was emerging in the wake of slavery's abolition in the county. It was the start of what Hilary Green has called "Educational Reconstruction," and as Green found in Richmond, the process in Montgomery County extended over several decades and involved a variety of players. To be sure, freed-people in the county took an immediate and intense interest in expanding their educational opportunities; according to James Anderson, such attitudes provided "the foundation of the freedmen's educational movement." They did not do so alone, however. As Green has described in the case of Richmond, and as other scholars have found in much of the postwar South, the success of black schools in Montgomery County depended on the combined efforts of freedpeople, philanthropic societies, and both state and federal officials. Nor did success come easily, for as Anderson found, African Americans and their allies often disagreed among themselves over the proper course to follow.[2]

Until 1865, Hart Wayland and the county's other African American residents would have found it nearly impossible to secure an education. The possibly seditious effects of black literacy on slavery and public safety had long worried white Virginians, especially after Nat Turner's rebellion. Thus, in 1819, 1831, and 1849 the General Assembly had passed or re-passed increasingly stringent restrictions on any effort to educate slaves or free people of color. Schools for black Virginians were declared unlawful assemblies, and county officials were directed to shut them "forthwith."[3] In spite of such restrictions, a small number of blacks in Montgomery County still managed to gain an education before the Civil War. It was a very small number, though. When the Freedmen's Bureau conducted a census of the county's "colored population," during the summer of 1865, it found only five who could read among 826 freedpeople aged fifteen years or older. This census did omit those who had been free before the war, a third of whom had been at least partially literate in 1860. Nevertheless, the overall picture is clear: when slavery ended in Montgomery County, few of the county's black residents could read or write.[4]

Equally clear is the fact that freedpeople in the county wanted schools as quickly as possible. Literacy promised real freedom—spiritual, political, and economic—and freedpeople across the South sought it immediately for themselves and their children.[5] Thus, from the moment they arrived in Montgomery County, agents of the Freedmen's Bureau noted the demand for schools and teachers among its black residents. Immediately after the war, however, those residents were in no position to provide schools for themselves. As detailed in the preceding chapter, most of the county's black workers received only board and clothes for their labor immediately after their emancipation, which meant that few had any cash that could be used to rent facilities, hire teachers, or provide supplies. Moreover, as noted above, very few of the freedpeople in Montgomery County could read or write in 1865, which made it almost impossible for them to establish the sort of informal schools that emerged in Richmond immediately after the fighting stopped and in a number of other southern communities even earlier.[6]

Nor could the freedpeople in Montgomery County expect much help from their white neighbors. Even for whites, antebellum Virginia had provided little public support for primary education. Dozens of private schools and academies had served those who could afford to pay their tuition, but for those who could not, the only public support available had been the state's Literary Fund, which provided an annual stipend to each county that local commissioners used to cover the tuition of "indigent children" at common schools. Counties could request money from the Literary Fund to help build and operate public schools for all white children, but only if county residents agreed to pay most of the cost themselves through local taxes. A few Virginia counties established such systems before the Civil War, but Montgomery County was not among them.[7]

The destruction wrought by four years of war did nothing to change white Virginians' attitudes toward public education or education for African Americans. James Anderson and Ronald Butchart have documented the breadth and depth of southern whites' opposition to black education during Reconstruction. Opposition in Montgomery County never reached the level of "unrelenting terrorism" that Butchart found elsewhere in the South. It did not even generate the level of harassment and legal obstructionism that Hilary Green found in Richmond. It was widespread, however. Teachers and officials of the Freedmen's Bureau reported that white opinion toward the education of blacks in the county ranged from "indifference" through "unchristian" to "very unfavorable" and was especially hostile to "Northern fanatics, as they term teachers sent from the North." Major George Sherwood, then commanding the Freedmen's Bureau district that included Montgomery County, did point out in 1866 that several white residents of the county "have expressed themselves favourably towards the establishing of schools for freedpeople" but went on to explain that this simply meant "they will not throw any obstacles in the way of establishing the schools." He then concluded that "the sentiment of the public generally . . . is not opposed to schools but no disposition is manifested to contribute anything towards establishing schools for the benefit of freedmen by the whites."[8]

It is not surprising, then, that black education in Montgomery County began only after the arrival there of the Freedmen's Bureau. Even then, it took time. Until mid-1866, the bureau had neither a mandate to establish schools nor an effective presence in Montgomery County. Initially, the Freedmen's Bureau had no explicit directive to address education, and facing what seemed more pressing needs, its agents focused on emergency relief—providing clothing and rations for destitute freedpeople—and on labor relations—ensuring that free black workers continued to provide labor for southern landowners and received the wages they were owed. Only in July 1866, when Congress extended the bureau's existence indefinitely, was it granted explicit authority to establish schools for freedpeople. Over the next three years, education became a major focus of the bureau, but it still functioned more as a facilitator than as a primary provider. The bureau supplied buildings in which to house schools (or material with which to build them) and transportation for teachers from their homes to their teaching posts, but it relied on religious and philanthropic societies to recruit and pay the teachers and provide instructional material, and it depended on local populations to provide the teachers' room and board.[9]

Initially, black schooling In Montgomery County was further handicapped by the relative ineffectiveness of the local Freedmen's Bureau office. While Buel Carter, first superintendent of Virginia's Eighth District, had initially established his headquarters in Christiansburg, in September 1865 he relocated the office to Wytheville—forty-five miles farther west—and left Montgomery County with almost no bureau presence. Moreover, Carter seems to have been relatively ineffective as an agent. By mid-1866, however, conditions in the county had begun to change. In June, Carter was succeeded as superintendent of the Eighth District by Brevet Major George P. Sherwood, who proved more diligent than Carter had in promoting black schools. More important, in May of that year Charles Schaeffer assumed his post as an assistant superintendent specifically responsible for Montgomery, Giles, and Pulaski Counties and established his headquarters in Christiansburg. As noted earlier, Schaeffer was a devout Baptist whose prior work with the Philadelphia Tract Society had brought him into frequent contact with that city's large black community, and while working for the Freedmen's Bureau he proved a zealous advocate for black education.[10]

Because Schaeffer's arrival in Christiansburg coincided with the Freedmen's Bureau's increased emphasis on education, he was ordered almost immediately to conduct "a thorough inspection" of the district in order to determine where it was "practicable and desirable to establish schools." In Montgomery County, Schaeffer recommended that schools be established at Christiansburg and at Blacksburg, each of which, he estimated, would provide a hundred students for a day school. How to accomplish this goal, however remained unclear. There were no former Confederate facilities in either place that the Freedmen's Bureau could confiscate for use as school buildings, and many white landowners refused to sell land or rent buildings to use for black schools. Schaeffer had found an available lot in Blacksburg with a frame building that could be converted for school purposes and a lot in Christiansburg on which it would be possible to build, but to do so would require more than a thousand dollars. Schaeffer believed that the freedpeople would do everything they could to support the schools financially, but "the great majority of them," he noted, "receive scarcely sufficient wages, to supply them with shelter, clothing, and the necessaries of life." And support from the white community still seemed unlikely. "There is no interest taken whatever in the matter," Schaeffer reported.[11]

Buildings were not the only essential in short supply. Teachers were even harder to find. Part of the problem, of course, was the limited number of freedpeople available to serve as teachers. Bureau officials such as George Sherwood understood that "colored teachers [were] preferred by the freed people" but also recognized that few freedpeople in the county were qualified to teach "in consequence of [the] deficiency in their education." In some Virginia communities with larger African American populations, especially of those who had been free people of color before 1865, literate freedpeople were more common. In Richmond, for example, teachers sent by the New England Freedmen's Aid Society reported that "nearly every colored family in Richmond has one or more members who can read." This was not the case in Montgomery County, which had only a handful of literate freedpeople in 1865, and it is hardly surprising that Major Sherwood found it difficult to recruit teachers among the county's African American residents.[12]

An even greater problem, perhaps, was Charles Schaeffer's reluctance to employ black teachers. As the agent of the Freedmen's Bureau directly responsible for Montgomery County, Schaeffer played a key role in establishing black schools there, but like many of his peers Schaeffer considered white teachers better qualified than their African American counterparts and chose the former whenever he could, especially in the schools he considered most important.[13] For Montgomery County, he envisioned a system in which "teachers from the north are expected to take charge of important localities, while country places in some instances will be supplied with colored teachers from our established schools." In this way, he wrote, "country schools taught by colored teachers" would "prepare the way by teaching the more simple and primary branches of education" and then pass their students along to white teachers "better qualified to advance these pupils in the higher and more difficult branches of study." His surviving correspondence includes no explicit requests for white teachers, but the responses to letters he sent to philanthropic organizations that supplied teachers often include an acknowledgement of the organization's inability "to find a white teacher for you."[14] White teachers were the essential foundation of Schaeffer's model for a school system to serve Montgomery County's African American community, and he was determined to find what he regarded as the right material for that foundation. As a result, no school for African Americans opened in Montgomery County until 1867. When one finally did, it was a result of both black and white initiative and an element of chance.

In November of 1866, a delegation of freedmen from neighboring Pulaski County came to Schaeffer seeking a teacher. The men came from Neck Creek, a rural neighborhood in the northeastern portion of Pulaski County, some fifteen miles from Christiansburg. Freedpeople in the community had secured an acre of land from two white neighbors and were now in the process of building a schoolhouse on it. Construction was "nearly if not quite complete," the committee reported, and arrangements had been made to board a teacher at the home of one of the white families who had provided the land. The freedmen had come to Schaeffer to ask for the bureau's help with things they could not provide by themselves: a stove, books, and a teacher.[15] Even with its expanded responsibility for education, though, the Freedmen's Bureau still did not provide teachers. Rather, it had established relationships with a number of philanthropic or religious organizations that did. The bureau agreed to cover the cost of transportation for teachers from their homes to their schools but did not provide the teachers themselves. They were recruited and paid by the aid organizations and provided their room and board either by the organization that sent them or by the freedpeople themselves.[16]

Schaeffer, no doubt, explained this to the delegation from Neck Creek. He then forwarded their request to district headquarters in Wytheville for consideration "as early as practicable." Wytheville endorsed the request immediately and sent it to Richmond, and bureau officials there contacted the AFUC. The AFUC was an umbrella organization established in 1866 to reduce competition among a number of eastern and midwestern aid societies seeking to reconstruct the South. It never succeeded in that goal. Denominational loyalties and personal rivalries among its leaders led to a restructuring of the group within six months of its creation, and its ceased operations entirely in 1869. While it lasted, though, the AFUC employed an extensive network of agents to raise money, recruit teachers, and support their work throughout the South, and among the teachers it had recruited in 1866 was Lucy Eastman. Eastman was from Lisbon, a village in northern New York, and had just turned twenty in January of 1867, when the AFUC sent her to Virginia in response to the request from Neck Creek. On arriving in Christiansburg, however, she learned from Schaeffer that "some malicious persons" had attacked the schoolhouse at Neck Creek. They had not destroyed it, but construction had been set back and its opening delayed. Schaeffer was not going to let a teacher go to waste, and he quickly put together an alternative. In doing so, however, he ignored Neck Creek and focused on Christiansburg, which had always been his first choice for a school in his division.[17]

For a schoolhouse, Schaeffer turned to the town's African American community. Nancy Campbell, a free woman of color before emancipation, had purchased a lot northwest of the town square in 1857 and had built a small house there (figure 9). A decade later, she agreed to rent the Freedmen's Bureau one room of her house for a makeshift school. The room was small—just twelve by fourteen feet—and could only be heated by setting up a small stove and running its chimney out the window, but with the reluctance of whites to see a black school in their midst, Schaeffer wrote, "It was the only place we could secure for the purpose." The school did have local white supporters, though. James C. Taylor, a prominent lawyer in Christiansburg who had served in both the Confederate army and the state senate and was soon to become Virginia's attorney general, provided

FIGURE 9. The first school in Montgomery County open to African Americans (Christiansburg School No. 1) met here in Nancy Campbell's house. The woman in the doorway is probably the teacher, Lucy Eastman.

benches for the students, while Thomas Wilson, who kept hotels in and near Christiansburg, lent the school a table and chairs. It was hardly ideal, but it was a start, and on February 7, 1867, the first school for African Americans in Montgomery County opened its doors.[18]

Predictably, many whites in the county objected to the school's presence. Unlike their neighbors in Pulaski County, who had physically attacked the Neck Creek school, opponents of black schooling in Montgomery used sarcasm and the press. Just two days after the school opened in Christiansburg, the local newspaper there, the *Christiansburg Southwest*, responded with a brief article entitled "Light Shining into Dark Places." The article noted that the school was supported by "a 'Commission of Freedmen,' established in New York City" and that the school itself was located in "Campbell Town"—the first known appearance of a term used to describe the black section of Christiansburg through at least the 1950s. The author of the article and many of its white readers probably knew that Nancy Campbell was reputed to have been a prostitute in the 1850s and played on her name to link the school's supporters to the Pharisees. Putting the school in Campbell's house, noted the *Southwest,* clearly showed that its founders "belong to that numerous branch of Yankees known as 'the gnat strainers and camel (Campbell) swallowers.'"[19]

Schaeffer also reported that white employers initially threatened to dismiss any black workers who supported or attended the school, though he reported by late February that "this feeling [was] gradually subsiding." Resentment never vanished, however. In her monthly reports to the Freedmen's Bureau, Lucy Eastman described the public attitude toward her school as "Unchristian," "Unkind," and "very wicked," and a year after it opened Schaeffer still found that "[black] schools are denounced, and every effort made for their advancement, is looked upon with distrust." This is hardly surprising, given what Schaeffer and others had said of public opinion before the school opened and what scholars such as Butchart have found occurred elsewhere in the South. What is surprising is the relatively low level of animosity found in Montgomery County. White opposition to black schools there seems never to have gone beyond suspicion and resentment. Neither Schaeffer nor Eastman ever reported any physical attacks on the schools or teachers or the dismissal of any workers for seeking an education.[20]

Neither insults nor threats, however, deterred the freedpeople of Montgomery County. They had no newspaper through which to counter the *Southwest,* but they immediately and enthusiastically demonstrated their support for black education and their determination to have it. School No. 1, as it was officially designated, was overwhelmed almost immediately. Thirty students applied for admission when the school opened, and within three weeks their number had increased to seventy-two. More were waiting, but there was simply no room for them all in Nancy Campbell's small house. The school was already running two sessions each day—girls in the morning and boys in the afternoon—with every seat full, but according to Schaeffer, "double that number could be gathered in a few days had we a suitable location for holding night sessions and larger accommodations."[21]

Schaeffer began working almost immediately to provide such accommodations. Reports to his superiors invariably complained of the school's "dwarfish condition" and urged them to provide greater resources. He also sought private support. In March 1867, Schaeffer informed his new district superintendent, Captain William P. Austin, that a number of his friends in Philadelphia were raising money to purchase a lot and asked whether they could expect any help from the bureau in meeting the cost of building on it. He also wrote directly to the Reverend Ralza M. Manly, the bureau's superintendent of education for Virginia, explaining that the construction of a new schoolhouse in Christiansburg was of "the utmost importance" to the freedpeople there. Encouraged by Manly's response, Schaeffer submitted a detailed estimate for the construction of an eighteen-hundred-square-foot building for use as a school and offered to build, using his and his friends' money, a second story "for church purposes and religious worship."[22]

The cost of Schaeffer's plan—$800 for construction of the school alone—was far more than Manly was willing to provide. He was, however, sympathetic to Schaeffer's intentions and encouraged him to consider alternative plans, reminding the captain that "when we cannot do as we *would* we must *do as we can.*" Schaeffer responded with a second, "reduced" estimate. This one called for a smaller, one-story building with "an audience room for public worship," which he believed could be built and furnished for just $550. Adding the cost of a lot brought the total to $750, which Schaeffer proposed to split with the government. "If the Bureau will appropriate three hundred dollars ($300) of this amount," he offered, "I will either raise or give the balance myself." Manly agreed to this modified plan, and the bureau appropriated $300 for "repairs" to the Christiansburg facility.[23]

This left only the question of where to build the school. In earlier letters, Schaeffer had claimed that white landowners in Christiansburg were reluctant to provide land for a black school, and his biographer, Charles Harrison, wrote later that Schaeffer could only acquire a lot through the cooperation of a "Mr. W——," who agreed to buy the land himself and then sell it to Schaeffer. The story may be true, but the diary that Harrison used in writing his biography is no longer available, and the remaining sources are not nearly so dramatic. The mysterious "Mr. W——" was actually Hamilton D. Wade, who came from one of Christiansburg's most prominent families. Wade had served with distinction as a Confederate officer during the Civil War, but he had also been raised by an aunt, Mary Wade, who had demonstrated long-standing objections to slavery. She had emancipated several of her slaves during the decades before the Civil War, and when she died in 1864, her will directed that all her slaves be freed as soon as the war was over and assisted in leaving the state, as was then required by Virginia law, for "such non-slaveholding state or country as they may select." She also left a significant amount of land to Hamilton D. Wade, and it seems to have been part of this land that he sold to Schaeffer and on which Schaeffer had the new school built during the summer of 1867.[24]

The new building was a frame structure, thirty by forty feet, erected on the crest of a hill between the town of Christiansburg and the railroad depot north of town. It was smaller than Schaeffer had hoped, twelve hundred square feet rather than eighteen hundred, but he reported that it "seats comfortably 250 scholars." As Schaeffer had expected, the school's enrollment quickly rose to fill the increased capacity. By the end of 1867, it had reached two hundred students, who attended in shifts so that there was room for all. And to help with the increased enrollment a second teacher had arrived shortly after the new school was finished. The new teacher, Elizabeth Bosworth, was also a white Congregationalist from Lisbon, New York, and her salary, too, was paid by the AFUC. Her arrival brought to a close the opening phase of black education in Montgomery County. With a new building, two teachers, and little overt opposition from the white majority, black schooling was becoming an established feature of life in Christiansburg by 1868. And the town's African American community publicly celebrated that fact at the school's closing examinations ceremony in June.[25]

Of even greater significance is the fact that by the summer of 1868 black schooling was entering a new, more expansive, phase in the county. Initially, Schaeffer had focused all of his attention on the Christiansburg school. In fact, just a month after it opened, he apparently ignored a letter from Hercules Marrs, a freedman living west of Christiansburg, seeking help with a school in the Shellville neighborhood. As the Christiansburg school grew, however, so did the demand for schools from freedpeople like Marrs who understood the value of education and wanted it for their children. By the fall of 1868, Schaeffer noted, "The call from almost every quarter is for teachers to come among them, many of those living in the country justly fearing that those having the advantages in the towns will outstrip them entirely and that their children will never be able (I will give it in the language of an anxious parent) to catch up with them." At the same time, Schaeffer noted, white opposition to black schools had eased. This is not because county residents had come to see education as a right to which black citizens were entitled. Rather, they were coming to believe that a certain level of black education would enhance white lives. During the summer of 1867, Schaeffer reported that white employers claimed "the pupils are better servants"—that they were "more prompt and faithful in the performance of their duties"—and that "the prejudices and opposition which was at first manifested toward the [Christiansburg] school has entirely disappeared." White resentment did rise again later that year as a result of tension surrounding the election of delegates to the constitutional convention, but it seems to have declined again in 1868.[26]

Between 1868 and 1870, schools for freedpeople opened in Blacksburg, Alleghany Springs, Brush Creek, Wake Forest, and Lovely Mount.[27] Of these, only Blacksburg was among the locations initially proposed by Schaeffer for the establishment of a school. Neither Alleghany Springs, ten miles east of Christiansburg, nor Lovely Mount, ten miles west of Christiansburg, was even a village. They were rural neighborhoods, though they were fairly close to the villages of Shawsville and Central Depot, respectively, each of which was on the railroad. Brush Creek and Wake Forest were even more remote. The former was a rural neighborhood ten miles south of Christiansburg and, according to the teacher there, "rather out of the way," while Wake Forest, in the county's northwestern corner, lay far from any population center and accessible only by some of the roughest of roads in the county.[28]

Schaeffer's original plan had been to secure northern white teachers for "more important localities," and once schools were established in those locations to staff the schools in "country places" with freedpeople who had gained a rudimentary education at one of the schools staffed by white teachers. This plan hit an obstacle, however, when the freedpeople demonstrated a determination to realize their own vision of African American education. Black students in Christiansburg made clear that they preferred to continue their own education instead of leaving as quickly as possible to become teachers. "The pupils of the Christiansburg School, who are qualified to take charge of primary schools, cannot be persuaded to leave off their studies," Schaeffer wrote in October 1868. "Those who are well advanced in their studies wish to prepare themselves fully for the work of teaching, before engaging in it." Even if a sufficient number of students could be persuaded to become teachers, Schaeffer still needed books and supplies for their classrooms and money for their salaries. Expanding the number of African American schools, therefore, also depended upon expanding the sources that supported them. In 1868, the AFUC was still able to pay the salaries of Lucy Eastman and Elizabeth Bosworth in Christiansburg, but its resources were already shrinking. Expansion would be impossible without new sources of funding.[29]

Fortunately, just such a source had recently appeared in the Friends' Freedmen's Association (FFA). Quakers in and around Philadelphia had established the FFA in 1863, and by 1867 it was supporting more than a dozen schools for former slaves in Maryland, Virginia, and North Carolina. Soon after arriving in Christiansburg, in the summer of 1866, Schaeffer had contacted the FFA's Richmond agent, Sarah Smiley, in an effort to secure textbooks for a school begun by freedpeople in neighboring Giles County. Nothing initially came of this request, as Smiley was about to return north for the summer, but a year later, as the FFA considered opening its own school in Giles County, its Committee on Instruction wrote to ask Schaeffer if the freedpeople there could provide a building and board for a teacher if the Friends provided one.[30] This soon grew into a working relationship between Schaeffer and the FFA. In 1868, the association began sending books and supplies to Schaeffer for use in the schools of his division, and its directors opened negotiations with Schaeffer and with William P. Austin, superintendent of the Eighth District, about the provision of teachers for schools in southwestern Virginia. Those first FFA teachers went to schools outside Montgomery County, but early in 1869 the association's Committee on Instruction decided to provide a teacher for a new school opening in Alleghany Springs, and in 1870 it did so for Lovely Mount. It also assumed financial responsibility for two existing schools in the county: the Brush Creek School, in 1869, and Christiansburg's School No. 1, in 1870. By 1870, the Friends had become the single most important source of funding for black schools in Montgomery County, and their relationship with those schools would last more than sixty years.[31]

A second new source of external support for black schools in Montgomery County also appeared during the summer of 1868. This was the African Methodist Episcopal (AME) Church, a black denomination established by the Reverend Richard Allen in Philadelphia in 1816. Before the Civil War, the church had gradually expanded among African American communities in the North, where most denominations admitted blacks but treated them as second-class members. It was barred, however, from operating in slave states because its abolitionist views and its cadre of black preachers violated southern norms and laws. That changed once the Civil War began. As Union troops and emancipation advanced across the

Confederate states, the AME Church followed.[32] The church organized its first Virginia Conference in May of 1867, and within a month the Reverend John Wesley Diggs, an AME itinerant, visited Blacksburg to help black Methodists there establish a separate AME congregation. The following April, the Virginia Conference appointed William B. Derrick to the Blacksburg church, and a school opened there on July 6, 1868.[33]

The Blacksburg school seems to have been entirely an AME project. Schaeffer had been negotiating with the FFA to provide a teacher for Blacksburg during the spring of 1868, and its Executive Board had approved sending one, but the AME got there first, and no evidence has survived that Schaeffer or anyone else from the FFA or the Freedmen's Bureau played any role in securing a schoolhouse in Blacksburg or in recruiting its first teacher.[34] Indeed, William Derrick was one of many in the AME who opposed cooperation with whites and advocated black self-reliance in religion and education. In 1868, he told a meeting in nearby Wythe County that "he wanted nothing to do with the white man north nor the white man south" and claimed that he had told Schaeffer "to his face" that the Freedmen's Bureau "had not done any good in the South."[35] This may explain why no teacher from the Blacksburg school ever submitted a report to the bureau.[36] A year later, in the spring of 1869, the AME also established its second church and school in the county. The Virginia Conference appointed Richard J. Gassaway to a new congregation organized in Wake Forest, and in May he opened the Daniel A. Payne School. Like its counterpart in Blacksburg, the Payne School seems to have been entirely an AME project, though unlike William Derrick, Gassaway did submit monthly reports to the Freedmen's Bureau.[37]

Regardless of when or how they began, every school in Montgomery County open to blacks at this time faced the same financial challenges: buying, renting, or building a facility in which to operate; supporting a teacher; and providing adequate supplies to ensure its continued operation. Normally, the Freedmen's Bureau paid, or helped to pay, only the cost of renting or building a schoolhouse and of travel to Christiansburg for teachers recruited by one of the northern aid agencies. The bureau did not generally provide salaries for teachers. Its assistant commissioners, however, did sometimes have the authority to pay teachers, and Virginia's assistant commissioner, Colonel Orlando Brown, established a policy in 1869 under which his office would provide "a fair salary" for teachers "in rural localities [where] persons of the neighborhood competent to teach can be found, if the people will pay the board."[38] The AFUC and the FFA, on the other hand, did not fund school construction; they paid teachers' salaries (and sometimes their board) and provided supplies such as books and maps for use in the schools. And finally, both the AME Church and local black communities contributed in any way they could. As a result, every black school in Montgomery County was a joint venture among two or more groups, and the precise sources and levels of support varied from school to school and from time to time across the county.

The most well-supported school was always School No. 1, in Christiansburg—the county seat, the largest town in the county, and home to the local office of the Freedmen's Bureau. Black schooling there began in quarters rented by the bureau, with supplies provided by it and several different aid agencies, and with a teacher whose salary and board were paid by the AFUC, though students were asked to pay ten cents each week if they could. The school then moved to a new building that was paid for by the Freedmen's Bureau, Schaeffer himself, and other white supporters and was transferred soon after its completion to the trustees of the Christiansburg African Baptist Church. In this new building, the AFUC continued to pay the salary and board for two teachers, Lucy Eastman and Elizabeth Bosworth, until the AFUC folded in July 1869. The Presbyterian Committee of Home Missions then stepped in for a year and paid the salaries of Eastman and her sister, Mirriam, who replaced Bosworth for the 1869–70 school year. Finally, the FFA took over in 1870. It paid the two teachers' salaries and provided books and a variety of other supplies, though it expected the bureau or the local community to provide the teachers' board and fuel for the schoolhouse stove.[39]

At the other extreme was the Brush Creek School, located in a rural community south of Christiansburg. It began as a subscription effort organized by Thomas A. Faulkner, a white resident of the neighborhood. Faulkner announced in November of 1868 that he planned to open a school "for the benefit of the colored people of my neighborhood" at a cost of "one dollar per month for each scholler." The school's opening was delayed, however, because of the economic challenges facing black families at the time. Faulkner reported that older black children were still needed at home to help bring in the harvest. As for the younger children, Faulkner wrote: "They say they could send the small ones now but for want of shoes." When the school finally did open, in January 1869, it did so in the home of William Green, a freedman and father of two of the school's students, while Faulkner tried to find money with which to build a more suitable facility. "The col^d people say they cannot buy & build without sacrifice of what little they have," Faulkner wrote; so he asked the Freedmen's Bureau for help. The bureau did eventually contribute ten dollars toward the purchase of a lot but nothing toward the cost of construction, and the school remained at William Green's home until April, when classes stopped for the summer. When they resumed in November, classes were held in Faulkner's house, though by then members of the community were working to build a schoolhouse, which was completed by January 1870. The school's finances remained precarious, however. Faulkner hoped to collect the tuition in cash, but initially none of his thirty students paid in cash and few paid in full. Even when he agreed to take half the tuition in corn, all he got the first month was corn. "My family is now suffering for the necessaries of life," wrote Faulkner early in 1869, and if circumstances did not change, he feared he would have to give up teaching altogether. Little changed before April, but late that summer, the FFA agreed to "take up" Brush Creek School and began paying Faulkner's salary in November.[40]

Other schools in the county fell somewhere between these two extremes. In Blacksburg, the AME congregation used a former Presbyterian church for its school and meetinghouse. Elsewhere it is often impossible to glean from the surviving records any details of the school facilities. Reports filed by their teachers, however, indicate that all of these schoolhouses were owned by the freedpeople themselves. Like families in the Brush Creek community, African Americans throughout Montgomery County found or built spaces in which to hold classes. They also helped support the teachers who conducted those classes. At Alleghany Springs and Lovely Mount, the FFA provided the teachers' salaries, but community members provided their board. In Blacksburg and Wake Forest, where William Derrick and Richard Gassaway taught in their capacity as ministers in the AME Church, it is unclear if the Virginia Conference or the individual congregations paid their teachers' salaries, though students at Wake Forest were asked to pay fifty cents per month toward meeting the school's costs.[41]

The growing number of African American schools in the county also saw an increasingly diverse pool of teachers staffing them. Hilary Green found that in Richmond the expansion of schools established by the Freedmen's Bureau and by northern benevolent societies often led to white teachers replacing black ones during the late 1860s. Montgomery County, however, did not have the symbolic status of the Confederacy's former capital and found it harder to attract teachers. Those working there in the 1860s included some of the iconic Yankee schoolmarms—Lucy and Mirriam Eastman and Elizabeth Bosworth—but as scholars have found across the South, northern white women were actually a minority among the teachers in black schools.[42] The nine men or women known to have taught in Montgomery County's black schools between February 1867 and June 1870 included three white northern women, one black northern man, one foreign-born black man, one white southern man, one black southern man, and two black men of unknown origins. Thus, five of the nine were black, six of the nine were men, and at least two of the nine were southern.

Elizabeth Bosworth and the Eastman sisters came from New York. Bosworth was in her forties when she came to Christiansburg, so she may have had prior experience teaching. The Eastmans, however, were barely out of their teens and may never have left home before going south to teach.[43] William B. Derrick, who arrived in Blacksburg in 1868, was also an outsider, but hardly a Yankee. He had been born in Antigua in 1843, a decade after slavery ended there, and educated by Moravians at their Gracefield school. He went to sea in 1860 and sailed several times to the United States before joining the Union navy in 1861. After three years aboard USS *Minnesota*, he left the navy for the AME Church and was ordained in the spring of 1868, just before going to Blacksburg.[44] Thomas A. Faulkner, who taught at Brush Creek, had been born in Halifax County in 1830 and was a clerk there when Virginia voted to secede. He enlisted immediately to fight for the Confederacy and served in the Fourteenth Virginia Infantry until he was wounded, captured, paroled, and discharged during the spring and summer of 1862. He then returned to civilian life and moved to Montgomery County sometime between 1864 and 1868. He had never been a teacher before, but he had been a clerk, and his letters suggest that he was relatively literate.[45] Alexander Hopkins, who taught at Lovely Mount, was identified in a letter to *The Freedman's Friend* as "a native colored teacher." He was born in Montgomery County about 1842 and lived as a slave at Kentland, the plantation of James R. Kent, until his emancipation in 1865. It is impossible to say when or how Hopkins learned to read and write, but he was teaching by early 1870 and his monthly reports to the Freedmen's Bureau are in a strong, clean hand with no mistakes either in spelling or addition.[46]

Even with six schools operating in the county by 1870, the demand for black education greatly exceeded the number of seats available. The first state census of the county's school-age population, in 1871, found 1,062 African Americans between the ages of five and twenty-one, yet peak monthly enrollment in the county's black schools was less than five hundred.[47] Moreover, the 1870 federal census found 1,082 black adults in Montgomery County who could not read, and they, too, often tried to attend when they could. Each month, teachers were asked to report the number of students attending and the number who were older than sixteen. Not all the reports have survived, and none have from Blacksburg. Those reports that do survive show that in most months the great majority of those attending school were younger children. Winter weather prevented some young children from traveling to school but freed more older children and adults from farm work, so during the winter months students older than sixteen made up about a third of the school population. Fall and spring, on the other hand, saw older students drop to about 10 percent of those attending as farm work took precedence over school. The gender balance among students also varied across the county and shifted with the seasons and the time of day. In most of the county's schools, female students were a majority during the spring and fall, when men and boys were planting or harvesting. During the winter months, however, the reduced pace of farm work brought more older boys and men to school, and males sometimes made up 60 percent of enrollments in January and February. But in Christiansburg, where more black women lived, female students almost always outnumbered males and often by nearly two to one. This was only true during the day, however; night school in Christiansburg drew almost twice as many men as women.[48]

It is difficult to provide objective measures of the success of the schools established in Montgomery County, but it is clear that the image presented by Wilma Dunaway of black schools in Southwest Virginia during Reconstruction is much too bleak. First, schools open to black students in the region were more common than Dunaway reported. In *The African American Family in Slavery and Emancipation,* Dunaway wrote that she found just "twenty schools in the Appalachian counties of Tennessee and Virginia." Moreover, an accompanying map of "Black primary schools in the Mountain South, 1866–70" shows a Freedmen's Bureau school in just one county (Washington) west of Roanoke. Dunaway seems to have missed entirely the half dozen schools established in Montgomery County between 1867 and 1870, as well as at least twelve more schools in five other counties west of Roanoke. Her total of "twenty schools in the Appalachian counties of Tennessee and Virginia" seems impossible in light of the fact that in January 1869 the Freedmen's Bureau counted twenty-two schools just in Virginia's Eighth District—the region encompassing Southwest Virginia.[49]

Moreover, evidence from Montgomery County suggests that the operation of those schools was quite different and much more effective than Dunaway claimed. She maintained that most of the teachers at black schools in the Appalachian South were itinerants: "Educational personnel were usually responsible for a multi-county area, so most teachers operated short-term schools by riding a circuit of geographically scattered schools." This seems to be a result of her misreading the diary of Jacob Yoder, who was initially a teacher for the Freedmen's Bureau in Lynchburg but then became the superintendent of a district that included six counties outside Lynchburg. In the latter capacity, Yoder did ride from school to school, but he did so to observe the teachers assigned to those schools, not to conduct classes himself. Exactly the same situation prevailed in Montgomery County. Schaeffer often spent days traveling through the counties for which he was responsible, but this was to supervise, not to teach. Teachers in the county stayed at the schools to which they were assigned for the duration of the school year, and schools operated continuously during that time.[50]

Schools in Montgomery County generally opened in October and closed in June, though this too varied. When Thomas Faulkner opened the school at Brush Creek, for example, the term began in early November and ran only until the end of March. Once he began receiving support from the Friends, however, he taught through the end of June, as other schools did. The school day and week also varied. Most schools operated for six or seven hours each day for about twenty days each month. During the winter, though, when the number of students increased, Lucy Eastman reported longer class days in Christiansburg and classes at night. "I teach from half-past nine A.M., till five P.M., with five minutes' recess," she wrote in February 1869, "and then from seven till ten in the evening." In Wake Forest, on the other hand, Richard Gassaway taught fewer days some months because he also spent time "Prachin the gospel."[51]

What went on in early black schools such as those established in Montgomery County has also been subject to debate.[52] Admittedly, many of the county's black schools clearly worked to instill in their students the values of white middle-class northern Protestants. In his 1869 letter, for example,

Hart Wayland told readers of the *American Freedman*, "I am most always a good boy now, but used to be a bad boy. Miss Lucy [Eastman] prays for me, and I prays for myself."[53] It is also apparent, however, that students like Wayland acquired essential academic skills too. In June of 1868 a Miss Canon, from the Baptist Home Missionary Society, attended closing examinations at Christiansburg's School No. 1 and provided a glowing testimonial:

> The classes acquitted themselves with honor to themselves and their teachers. In Miss Boyworth's grade, a little boy, who had to stand on a chair in order to be seen, held his Second Reader in his little hand, and read correctly a part of the lesson which had been read incorrectly by a preceding scholar. . . . The more advanced classes also did splendidly, beginning by spelling, geography, and answering promptly every question put to them on every map through Africa, and reciting in concert the descriptive part. Equal quickness was exhibited in arithmetic; exercises were gone through by little children who had to stand on their toes to reach the blackboard; then the whole class saying together without one mistake, the multiplication table, after which spelling such words as "multiplication," "addition," "division," etc.

It was a wonderful performance, and Miss Canon was certainly impressed: "I mean no disparagement to others when I say, for the time engaged, this school is far in advance of any I have visited."[54]

Almost as soon as they were established, however, this first generation of African American schools in Montgomery County faced major challenges as both the Freedmen's Bureau and the AFUC reduced or suspended their activities in the county. Congressional support for the Freedmen's Bureau was waning by 1868. As a result, the bureau closed its office in Christiansburg and halted most of its legal and economic activities in the county at the end of December 1868. Schaeffer did stay on as the bureau's assistant superintendent of education, and the bureau did continue limited educational work until the end of June 1870, but its role was significantly reduced. That of the AFUC was even more reduced as it ceased operations entirely in July 1869. Fortunately, the Freedmen's Department of the Presbyterian Committee of Home Missions stepped in to provide funding for the 1869–70 school year. It paid the salaries of Lucy Eastman and her sister, Mirriam, who arrived to replace Elizabeth Bosworth that year, but the future of African American education in Montgomery County was growing increasingly uncertain.[55]

The AME Church was still sending ministers to Blacksburg and Wake Forest, and the ministers it sent continued to serve as teachers in the schools there. The FFA also continued to work with Schaeffer—its "Special Supt. In Virginia"—to provide books and supplies for schools in the county, to pay the salaries of teachers at several schools outside of Christiansburg, and to pay the cost of board and travel for those in Christiansburg, but by 1869 the Friends, too, faced mounting financial difficulties. Mary Shearman, actuary for the FFA, warned Schaeffer in November 1869 of the association's reduced circumstances. "Our treasury is now completely exhausted," she wrote; she hoped to replenish it somewhat at an upcoming public meeting but still, she cautioned, "Great economy will be necessary." She urged Schaeffer to impress this fact upon teachers in the county and "[to] encourage the freedmen to depend more upon themselves." Economy, however, was not enough, and freedmen in the county were still hard pressed to provide much financial support to the schools. As a result, during the spring and summer of 1870, the FFA began planning to close some of its "smaller schools" in Montgomery County when the new term commenced that fall. The Christiansburg school would remain open with teachers provided by the FFA, and the Friends would provide very limited support (five dollars per month) toward a new school on Crab Creek, just outside Christiansburg. Other schools in the county were less fortunate. Thomas Faulkner's school at Brush Creek lost its support and was forced to close, though the Friends hoped to resume their assistance and reopen it in the future. Schools at Alleghany Springs and Lovely Mount were to retain support if "a fair average attendance can be maintained at each," but in October Schaeffer was told to decide which of the two was "most needed at the present" and to close the other. During the course of the 1870–71 school year, Schaeffer and the FFA tried to prevent schools from closing by shifting funds and reducing payments, but it was clear the Friends would no longer be able to support many schools in the county.[56]

Even as Schaeffer and the FFA were scrambling to protect African American schools in Montgomery County, the educational landscape there was changing completely. Military Reconstruction, which began in 1867, had required most states in the former Confederacy to draft new constitutions before they could rejoin the Union, and when Virginians did so, advocates of universal education demanded that the new constitution require the establishment of public schools throughout the commonwealth. As a result, when the state's new constitution was ratified in 1869, it called for the establishment of "public free schools" in every county as quickly as possible, and in 1870 the assembly responded with enabling legislation to establish public schools in Virginia. For supporters of universal education, the law represented a great step forward; it was the first time Virginia had ever established a system of public education.[57]

For freedpeople, however, the new law included several troubling provisions. First, it required the creation of separate schools for black and white students. This was hardly surprising; white Virginians were accustomed to racial mixing in some venues, but educating children together was too much for most of them to accept. Schools established by the Freedmen's Bureau, for example, had been open to white children but few had attended. As Charles Schaeffer noted in Montgomery County, "poor whites" were "willing to mingle with negroes, at their homes, but when asked to avail themselves of their school advantages, you could not possibly induce one of them to be enrolled among them." More worrisome to freedpeople was the fact that all of the new public schools came under the authority of *appointed* local officials. Legislation establishing the public school system placed it under the supervision of a state board of education consisting of the governor, the superintendent of public instruction, and the attorney general—all of whom could be expected to be white conservatives. They, in turn, were empowered to appoint local school superintendents and boards of trustees in every county. It was a system designed to keep public schools safely in white hands. The enabling legislation did require that all public schools operate under "the same general regulations as to management, usefulness, and efficiency," but many African Americans questioned the commitment of white school boards and white superintendents to the well-being of black public schools and their students.[58]

In Montgomery County, local officials wasted little time in establishing public education. By November 1870, the county's newly appointed superintendent of schools had laid out four school districts for the county and directed the school trustees in each to meet and organize themselves as district boards. By February 1871, these boards had begun to establish schools and to hire teachers, and by April three of Montgomery County's existing African American schools had been "adopted by the state as free schools."[59] This transition raised a number of thorny issues concerning schools the FFA already helped to support in Montgomery County and exactly how they would function as public schools. Records for the county's school system during the nineteenth century are spotty, but they include no evidence that any African American ever served on any of the district school boards. Nor is there any memory in the local African American community of any black serving on such a board before the modern era. And it is absolutely clear that no African American ever served as superintendent of the county's schools. Not surprisingly, freedpeople in the county, who by then often owned several schools and the land on which they stood, worried they would lose control of them. At a meeting held in February 1871, the Executive Committee of the FFA noted: "The colored people [in Montgomery County] are distrustful, perhaps not without warrant, of the school commissioners, fearing that they wish only to get the schools into their own hands." The association appreciated this concern, and shortly thereafter its Committee on Instruction directed Schaeffer "to see that when the schools are made free such risk may be averted by written articles of agreement insuring continued possession to the Freedmen." No such agreements have yet been found, however. The Christiansburg school had already been deeded to trustees of the Christiansburg African Baptist Church, and it clearly remained church property after becoming a public school. For the other schools, however, it is impossible to say.[60]

Equally challenging were issues surrounding the salaries of teachers. Initially, the problem was that Montgomery County had established public schools before it actually had any funding for them, so it had no money with which to pay the teachers. The FFA guaranteed teachers at the schools it had been supporting in Christiansburg, Big Spring, and Lovely Mount that it would pay their salaries through the end of the 1870–71 school year, though it also decided that Thomas Faulkner, at Brush Creek, did not need aid from the association. Having responded to the teachers' concerns, the FFA then turned to its own financial needs. Some of its teachers received both a salary and board, and the Friends discovered that these teachers still expected their full allocation for board even if their salaries rose as public school teachers. Rebecca and Blanche Harris, a black mother and daughter from Ohio, had begun teaching in Christiansburg in October 1870 with monthly salaries of fifteen and twenty dollars, respectively. In addition, the FFA provided thirty dollars per month for their board. When Montgomery County "adopted" the school, in March 1871, it offered the Harrises monthly salaries of fifteen dollars each, and the FFA planned to use its own funds to maintain Blanche's at its original level. A month later, however, the school board decided that fifteen dollars per month was "inadequate" and raised it for each woman to twenty-five dollars. The Harrises hoped to enjoy the raise themselves, but the FFA's Committee of Instruction objected. It ruled that "they shd have just what they received before." The Friends had been paying thirty-five dollars in salary and thirty for board—a total of sixty-five dollars per month—and decided that "if the state pays of this $50 it of course leaves $15 to be paid by the Assoc." This was not negotiable. Mary Shearman, the FFA's actuary, wrote Schaeffer: "If this arrangement is not satisfactory to the teachers they are of course at liberty to act independently of the Assoc. & make such terms as they can with State." The Harrises finished out the year on the association's terms and were informed in June that they would likely be transferred in the fall to a school in North Carolina.[61]

By the end of the summer of 1871, the transition was complete, and schools in Montgomery County that had begun under the auspices of the AME Church, the Freedmen's Bureau, or northern benevolent societies had all become part of the public system. Public schools for African Americans in Montgomery County were never exclusively public, though. The Christiansburg school remained a public-private hybrid well into the twentieth century. The district school board provided nominal oversight of the school, but Charles Schaeffer, the Friends' Freedmen's Association, or a board of trustees they appointed actually directed it. As a result, it would be the only school in the county over which local blacks exercised any control after 1870. Similarly, while state and county funds provided salaries for the school's teachers, the FFA continued providing significant financial support to the Christiansburg school. In addition, Schaeffer himself continued to offer support, solicited money from others, and worked with members of the local African American community to raise additional funding through "school entertainment." He tried in 1873, for example, to raise money through performances of "Slave Songs" by "The Virginia Singers" in Philadelphia and other northern cities, though according to his biographer, "The undertaking was not financially successful." Full financial reports are rarely available before the early twentieth century, but those that have survived indicate that public money covered only about a third of the total cost of operating the school in Christiansburg.[62]

Only the Christiansburg school, however, enjoyed this level of private support. The establishment of public schools in Virginia and other southern states coincided with a decline in contributions to the FFA and a decision by the association to reduce its activities in the region. It did provide very modest support to the school at Alleghany Springs during the 1871–72 school year, but for the most part it followed a policy announced by its Executive Board in April 1871: "The purpose being to teach the largest number of freedpeople with diminished means, it has been our policy rather to give prominence to schools at the centres of population." In the case of Montgomery County that meant Christiansburg, and there is no evidence of FFA support for any other school in the county after June 1872. Other African American schools may have received limited financial support from the local community or, in the case of Blacksburg, from the AME Church, but after 1871 most of the money for African American education in the county outside of Christiansburg came from public coffers. Some local communities also seem to have offered sweat equity in the form of building schoolhouses for black children. Deeds from Matamoras, west of Blacksburg, and Vickers, west of Christiansburg, indicate that "colored" schoolhouses were already standing on lots purchased there by the district school boards in 1881 and 1884, and these may have been built by the residents in anticipation of public schools being established there.[63]

For African Americans, the most immediate and most significant result of the shift to public education in Montgomery County was the increased availability of a basic education for their children. Before 1871, only six schools in the county had ever been open to black students, and it is not clear that all six were ever open at the same time. By 1877, however, thirteen black schools were operating in the county. Because of financial and political turmoil occurring in Richmond at the time, several of the county's black schools closed in the late 1870s, but their number resumed climbing in 1880 and reached a total of twenty-one in 1885. That number declined slightly during the final years of the century, as the county's African American population declined, but there were still eighteen black schools in the county in 1900. Moreover, as figure 10 shows, these schools were widely distributed throughout the county. By 1885, there were at least four black schools in each of the county's four school districts, and though the number declined somewhat by 1900, there were still several schools for African American children in each district at the end of the century. Not surprisingly, black schools were never as common as white schools in the county, though the discrepancy did ease somewhat by the end of the century. Between 1871 and 1900, annual reports of the state superintendent of education often included the "school population"—those between the ages

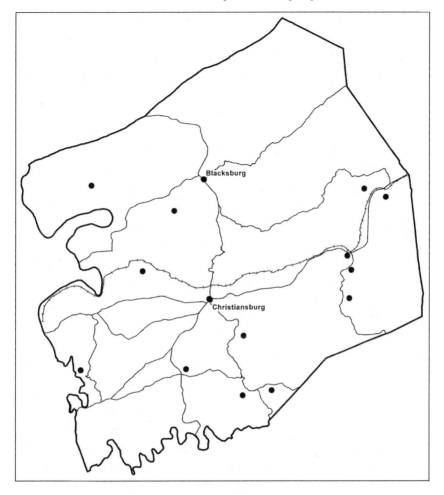

FIGURE 10. Selected black schools in Montgomery County, 1870–1900. The locations of several other schools cannot be determined precisely and are not included. (Base map by Matthew Layman)

of five and twenty-one—as well as the number of schools in each county. In Montgomery County, the ratio of school-aged African Americans to African American schools declined from more than 175:1 during the early 1870s to 85:1 in 1895. Even as it declined, however, this ratio was always at least 25 percent above that found in the white population and considerably higher in some years.[64]

The number of African American children attending these schools rose and fell as well, but the trend in the county between 1871 and 1900 was certainly one of increased participation. In 1871, the state reported total African American enrollment in Montgomery County was 272, which was just over a quarter of the black "school population." By 1880 total enrollment had reached 839, or 45.4 percent of the school population. Over the next twenty years, enrollment fluctuated more than school numbers did, topping nine hundred in 1882, 1888, and 1893 but falling to as low as five hundred in 1885. For most of this period, however, total enrollment fluctuated between 750 and 850 and the percentage enrolled between 45 and 55 percent. These figures, however, are somewhat misleading because total enrollment was always higher than average enrollment. As William Link has pointed out, Virginia did not require children to attend school until 1922, and many children in rural Virginia, both black and white, were essential sources of labor for their families. That, combined with harsh weather, transportation problems, and a simple desire to play hooky, meant that the monthly average attendance among African Americans in Montgomery County was generally only about 80 percent of total enrollment. This, in turn, means that in most months fewer than half of the county's African American children were actually in school at any particular time.[65]

Originally, public schools in Montgomery County seem to have met for nine or ten months each year. Teachers' contracts in the Christiansburg school district covered ten months during the 1871–72 school year, and the state superintendent's report for 1874 indicated that schools in the county remained open for nine or nine and a half months that year. Within a few years, however, the county cut back to five or six months in most of its schools, though Christiansburg continued to operate for seven or eight. And however long they were open, public schools in Montgomery County probably offered a very basic education. The legislation establishing public schools in Virginia had stipulated they were to teach "orthography, reading, writing, arithmetic, grammar, and geography" and barred other subjects "except as allowed by special regulations to be devised by the board of education." Link suggests that such curricular rigidity was actually rare during the nineteenth century, but he also found that few schools offered much beyond what the state required—if that. Education in rural Virginia generally involved rote memorization and "little more than basic literacy, a knowledge of arithmetic, and an elementary understanding of grammar" along with a strong dose of white, middle-class morality. Most of the schools in Montgomery County, both black and white, were also ungraded.

Regardless of pupils' ages or abilities, all came together in a single room with a single teacher, though he or she might work with different groups of students separately during the course of the day. As early as 1873, however, the county system did include at least one African American graded school—meaning different rooms and teachers for different cohorts of students—in Christiansburg. The state superintendent's report for 1888 also identified black graded schools in Blacksburg and Big Spring, though the latter schools do not appear in any other reports.[66]

Rising numbers of black students and black schools in Montgomery County also meant a rising number of black teachers. As described above, finding people who were willing and even minimally qualified to teach in black schools had been a major challenge when the Freedmen's Bureau began trying to establish schools for freedpeople in Montgomery County. Things had not changed significantly by 1871, when local school boards assumed the task of hiring teachers, so teachers in the county's first public schools for African Americans were also a mix of men and women, black and white, locals and outsiders. As Jane Dailey has noted, this was not unusual in Virginia during the 1870s, but it began to change fairly rapidly. By the late 1870s, Christiansburg seems to have been the only black school in Montgomery County with white or northern teachers. There, Charles Schaeffer and the Friends' Freedmen's Association retained the authority to recruit teachers, and, as described more fully below, they were often reluctant to recruit African Americans. While they did employ a few northern black teachers in Christiansburg, most of the teachers there before 1887 were white women from Ohio, Maine, Pennsylvania, and other northern states. Elsewhere in the county, however, it seems that teachers in black schools were usually black and local. The Brush Creek school had at least two white teachers between 1871 and 1877, but annual reports from the state superintendent indicate that by 1880 the numbers of black schools and black teachers in the county matched, except for those at Christiansburg. And after 1887, when Christiansburg shifted to black teachers, all the black schools in the county seem to have had black teachers.[67]

Only some of the African Americans who taught in Montgomery County's public schools before 1900 can be individually identified, but those who can be represent a range of backgrounds and abilities. Some were farmers or housewives who seem to have taught for just a year or two. Samuel W. Carr, for example, was farming in 1880 and a railroad laborer in 1900, but in 1887–88 he taught at the High Rock school. Three years earlier, in 1884–85, the incumbent there had been Sarah Jane Sweeney, who appeared as "keeping house" on the 1880 census. A growing number of the county's black teachers, however, were more professional. Some, such as Sandy Boston and Pheobe Grimes, had little formal training before they began teaching but continued to further their own education over the course of extended careers. Boston eventually graduated from the Hampton Institute, while Grimes participated in summer teachers' institutes conducted by the Virginia Normal and Collegiate Institute in Petersburg and later graduated from the Christiansburg Industrial Institute. Another small number of African American teachers in the county included educated men and women who made careers of teaching. Initially their numbers were quite small. Blanche and Elizabeth Harris, both Oberlin graduates, taught at Christiansburg and Big Spring, respectively, in 1870–71; their mother, Rebecca Harris also taught at Christiansburg that year; and George W. Milford, a graduate of Brown University, taught there in 1877–78. By the 1880s, however, teachers like these were becoming a bit more common. Amos Strother, another Hampton graduate, taught in the county, as did E. Otho Parker, a graduate of Philadelphia's Institute for Colored Youth. Trained black educators became especially prominent in Christiansburg; between 1888 and 1893 nearly all of the teachers there were graduates of the Institute for Colored Youth in Philadelphia, and beginning in 1893 most were graduates of the Tuskegee Institute.[68]

Partial records of teachers' pay have survived from just one of the county's four school districts—Christiansburg—and this limited evidence is mixed on the issue of pay equity among teachers in the district. Sometimes, it seems, they were paid on the basis of their qualifications, not their race or that of the students they were hired to teach, but not always. The district school board first entered into contracts with five teachers in March 1871. R. W. Douthat and A. M. Lucas, white men teaching at white schools, were to receive twenty dollars and fifteen dollars per month, respectively, plus an unspecified "supplementary amt." paid by the patrons of the school. Thomas Faulkner, a white man teaching at a black school, was to receive fifteen dollars per months from public funds and ten from the FFA. Blanche and Rebecca Harris were black women hired to teach in a black school, but Blanche was a college graduate, and both already had teaching experience. Initially, each was to receive fifteen dollars per month, but a month later the board decided that figure was "inadequate" and raised it to twenty-five. Over the next six years, the district employed no other black teachers, but it did operate a black school near Pilot. Records from these years indicate that district policy was to set teachers' pay according to the level of their certificates, and teachers at "Pilot col'd" during these years, who were white men, received the same salary as other teachers with similar certificates. Thomas Faulkner's salary was reduced for a month in 1872, but that was because average enrollment at the Pilot school fell below twenty that month. Surviving records from the 1880s and 1890s are less complete and do not indicate the levels of teachers' certificates, but they seem to show that black teachers in the district received less than their white counterparts during the 1880s and early 1890s. During the 1880s, white teachers in the district were paid between $100 and $125 per term, while black teachers earned between $70 and $100 dollars, and in 1893–94 whites earned $125 to $140 dollars and blacks $125. In both 1898 and 1899, however, the district seems to have offered greater pay equity. During those years, almost every teacher in the district received either twenty or twenty-five dollars per month (one received thirty and assistants got fifteen), and both black and white teachers received twenty and twenty-five in similar ratios. Moreover, this pattern continued into the early twentieth century, when the surviving records end.[69]

The Christiansburg district may have been unusual, though, because more of its black teachers had higher qualifications, more experience, or both. Between 1886 and 1895, annual reports by the state superintendent for public education provide information on average salaries by race and gender in each of Montgomery County's four school districts (plus the town of Radford after 1891). In Christiansburg the differences among white men, white women, black men, and black women varied significantly from year to year but showed no consistent pattern. In 1886, for example, black women were the lowest-paid group and received less than half the salary of white women. But a year later, black women had the highest average salary in the district and exceeded both white men and women by more than 25 percent. Elsewhere in the county, especially in the more rural districts, the situation was different. There black teachers almost always earned less than white teachers and often by significant margins. Unfortunately, little is known about these teachers. They were almost certainly younger, less qualified, and less experienced than their counterparts in Christiansburg and perhaps less than their rural white peers. This may explain much of the salary differential, but it is also possible that simple racial prejudice was also a factor. Given the existing evidence, it is impossible to say for sure.[70]

Black schools in Montgomery County sometimes had black principals as well. Scholars such as Jane Dailey and Hilary Green have shown that the issue of black principals was often a racial powder keg in Virginia, even when those principals had no authority over white teachers or students.[71] In Montgomery County, however, this seems not to have been a divisive public issue, perhaps because the number of black principals was never large and almost all were at the Christiansburg school, which to a significant degree operated outside of state control. The number of black principals was never large because almost no black schools in the county were "graded" during this era. Graded schools divided students by age or ability into different classes, had different teachers for the different classes, and included one teacher designated the principal. The great majority of Montgomery County's public schools, however, were ungraded; they were one-room facilities with a single teacher and students who were not formally divided by age or ability. During most of the period between 1870 and 1900, fewer than 10 percent of the county's white schools were graded, and among black schools they were rarer still. Except for 1888, only the Christiansburg school was graded. There Charles Schaeffer, the Friends, or the school's trustees chose the principal. As long as they employed mainly white teachers, principals were white, though after they shifted to black teachers, in 1887, the principal was always black too. Outside of Christiansburg, 1888 was the only year in which black graded schools are known to have operated. That year both Blacksburg and Big Spring also had a graded school for African Americans, and each had a black principal—Pheobe Grimes and Lucy Johnson, respectively.[72]

Postwar public education in Montgomery County was not simply divided into black and white, however. Among African American schools, Christiansburg was in a class by itself. Before the establishment of public schools in the county, Charles Schaeffer, and then the FFA, invested much more time, energy, and money in the Christiansburg school than in any other African American school in the county. The difference widened once public schools opened in the county because Christiansburg was the only one to continue receiving significant financial support from Schaeffer or the Friends. It was also where, in 1873, Schaeffer elected to establish the county's first (and only) black normal school for the training of teachers. Schaeffer and the Friends also continued to employ white northern teachers in Christiansburg long after most black schools in the county had black teachers. Well into the 1880s, Schaeffer and the FFA seem to have thought that only white teachers could maintain the educational standards to which they aspired for Christiansburg. In the words of Mary Shearman, actuary of the FFA: "It seems such a pity for that good school to be put under colored teachers." It is not surprising, then, that early in the 1880s Schaeffer began pushing the Friends to help him provide "still higher educational advantages" for students in Christiansburg. Doing so took nearly a decade and further distinguished the Christiansburg school from any other African American school in the county or region. At the same time, it also transformed the nature of the school as part of a debate that affected African American education throughout the United States.[73]

The process began in September 1880, when Schaeffer wrote a letter that was published in the *Friends' Review,* a Quaker journal published in Philadelphia. In it, he proudly described the varied and extensive educational and religious works in which he had been engaged in and around Christiansburg. It was not enough, though. Schaeffer ended his letter with a plea for money to help provide even greater educational opportunities in Christiansburg: "I want $5,000 next year to put up the buildings which are necessary, and am looking to our Heavenly Father to send the needed help." In this case, however, the Lord worked slowly. There is no evidence that any contributions came into the FFA following the publication of Schaeffer's letter, but Schaeffer and the black community around Christiansburg began raising funds on their own and collected nearly $1,000 by 1883. Inspired, or shamed, by this, the FFA took a leap of faith in April 1883. Confident that "with suitable appeals made to the Friends, the means will be forthcoming," members authorized the association's Executive Board to appropriate another thousand dollars toward the school's construction. The plan was to build "a commodious two story brick schoolhouse" divided into an assembly room and classrooms "fitted with educational appliances." This would not only provide room for newer and larger classrooms than the old school did but would also free up the school's two existing buildings for renovation as dormitories "for the use of well-grown lads and girls who may come from a distance to attend normal classes and prepare themselves for teachers." The association then issued a public appeal aimed at raising the money it had just instructed the board to spend.[74]

Directors of the FFA did, however, exercise caution. They decided that work on the new school should advance only as fast as fund-raising did, and when they authorized the start of construction they seem to have intended it to proceed in phases, as funds became available. Schaeffer, however, was confident the Lord would provide the necessary resources and was anxious to begin. Writing to the association's secretary in early 1885, he urged the board to have faith. By then he had already ordered "a large portion" of the building material and signed contracts for some of the work. "Please tell the Board to *aid us all they can,* and we will struggle through," he wrote. "In one way or other the Lord will provide." In the end Schaeffer prevailed. The board relented and in March directed him "to go forward with [the] new school building." That November a new two-story brick building was dedicated, but the board had been right to worry. The new school ended up costing much more than Schaeffer had predicted— more than $8,700. This left both Schaeffer and the association in debt and put them in the difficult position of trying to raise operating funds for the school and retire its debt, simultaneously. Both redoubled their efforts, though, as did the African American community in and around Christiansburg. By 1888, the debt had been reduced to just over $500, and it seems to have been paid in full by 1890.[75]

The construction of an impressive new building—soon dubbed the Hill School—was accompanied by an equally significant change in the structure and tenor of the school's administration. In July 1885, while the Hill School was still under construction, Schaeffer deeded the property on which it stood to a new board of trustees nominated by the FFA: Richard Wood and William Haines, both white Quakers living in Philadelphia and leaders of the FFA; James T. Carr and William Poindexter, both prominent members of the black community in Christiansburg and deacons of the African Baptist Church there; and Schaeffer himself. For the first time, African Americans in Montgomery County had a formal voice in the direction of the premier black school in the county. Until now, Schaeffer may have taken into consideration the wishes of the African American community, but he alone had directed the Christiansburg school. Under this new arrangement, he was simply one of five trustees, and two of the five were black. Moreover, the deed granted the FFA sole authority to nominate future members of the board, and by 1885 the Friends had become increasingly open to African American views concerning the sort of education their schools should offer. As a result, African Americans gained more and more influence over the nature and operation of the school, and in the years that followed it was caught up in the transformation that moved African American education toward a more technical or industrial model.[76]

Ironically, Schaeffer may have changed the school's governing structure in order to prevent just such a transformation. Under the terms of the deed, the school's trustees were bound to advance its stated goal "and none other," and that goal was explicitly defined as "the establishment, support and maintenance of an Institution of learning to be known as the Christiansburg Institute for the imparting of a liberal education to people of the colored race, under Christian influence." This is first recorded use of the name Christiansburg Institute, and it shows the school was clearly intended to advance the sort of liberal education that Schaeffer had advocated since his days with the Freedmen's Bureau. This had been a common approach in schools for freedmen during the years immediately after the Civil War, but by the 1870s many educators, both black and white, had begun calling for more technical or industrial training in black schools. Schaeffer had resisted that idea. Under his direction, the Christiansburg school had remained focused almost exclusively on literature, history, geography, mathematics, and other academic subjects, and it seems clear that Schaeffer intended for this to remain the focus of the Christiansburg Institute. If that was his intention, however, he failed, because almost immediately after its formal establishment, the Christiansburg Institute began shifting toward more vocational training.[77]

Central to this change was Philadelphia's Institute for Colored Youth and its principal, Fanny Jackson Coppin. The Institute for Colored Youth had first been established in 1837 with a bequest from Richard Humphreys, a Quaker silversmith who left $10,000 for "instructing the descendants of the African Race in school learning, in the various branches of the mechnik arts and trades and in Agriculture." After a brief experiment with a farm school, the institute had developed a program that emphasized classical, liberal education for black boys and girls and offered its students English grammar and literature, Greek, Latin, history, chemistry, and mathematics from basic arithmetic to geometry and trigonometry. After the Civil War, however, the institute had developed a more technical and industrial focus under the direction of Fanny Jackson Coppin. Coppin had been born a slave in Washington, D.C., but was purchased and emancipated by an aunt while still a young girl. She spent the rest of her childhood in New England, where she gained an education that enabled her to enroll at Oberlin College in 1860. There she acquired both a classical education and experience teaching in a night school established for African Americans in town during the Civil War, and on graduating she went to the Institute for Colored Youth to teach Latin, Greek, and mathematics. Four years later she became the school's principal, and in that role she immediately expanded the institute's normal school curriculum in order to train teachers for the growing number of African American schools in the United States. Then, in 1876, she attended the Centennial Exhibition in Philadelphia. There, in Coppin's words, "The foreign exhibits of work done in trade schools opened the eyes of the directors of public education in America as to the great lack existing in our own system of education," and by the early 1880s, she had begun calling for change at the Institute for Colored Youth and at other schools operated by the Friends.[78]

Many American educators had already adopted manual or industrial training as an element in African American education. It was, for example, central to the system of teacher training that Samuel C. Armstrong introduced at Hampton in 1868. To Armstrong, and others, the "chief difficulty" confronting freedpeople was not "ignorance"; it was "deficient character." He proposed to remedy both through a system that combined basic academic training with regular manual labor in order to "replace stupid drudgery with skilled hands . . . for the sake not only of self-support and intelligent labor, but also for the sake of character." Coppin, however, was not interested in basic manual training. Her concern lay in the fact that in Philadelphia and other northern communities it was nearly impossible for African Americans to gain access to skilled trades. "Here," she told an 1885 meeting in Philadelphia, "it is impossible for colored young men to become apprentices to learn blacksmithing, carpenter work, or that of any similar vocation." She envisioned the Institute for Colored Youth offering industrial and technical education that would lead its students into careers as skilled craftsmen, architects, and engineers. Neither Coppin nor the school's Quaker supporters had any plans to abandon classical education, though; they expected that to remain a central element in the institute's curriculum. Adding an industrial department to the institute was intended "to increase its benefits by going beyond the literary training which has been so successful hitherto." The white Quaker men on the school's board of directors were not prepared to go quite as far as Coppin wanted, but in 1885 they did announce that the Institute for Colored Youth would establish an industrial department to teach trades such as carpentry, plumbing, and bricklaying to young men and cooking, sewing, and other "household duties" to young women and, thus, to extend "the usefulness of the Institute."[79]

The changes wrought by Fanny Jackson Coppin at the Institute for Colored Youth also came to influence the Christiansburg Institute as its trustees grappled with the cost of its teaching corps. Under Schaeffer's direction, teachers in Christiansburg had been northerners who came south for the school term and then returned to their homes in Pennsylvania, Ohio, Maine, and other northern states. Most had been white women; only five African Americans are known to have taught in Christiansburg during the school's first twenty years: W. Robert Cooper (1870), Blanche and Rebecca Harris (1870–71), George Milford (1877–78), and Margaret Washington (1880–81). Bringing in northern teachers, however, involved the added expense of their travel, and as the FFA faced mounting financial pressure it became harder to maintain this practice. The Executive Committee had noted as early as 1879 that employing black graduates of the association's Danville School to teach in that area had "considerably reduced" expenses. "The cost of transportation was thus much lessened, while the efficiency of the schools was maintained." It was also becoming more difficult to find northern teachers who were willing to go south. It seems that one reason Margaret Washington taught in Christiansburg was that the FFA could not find a white teacher to send that year. By 1887 it had grown no easier to recruit willing candidates. Directors of the FFA reported that spring that "one of the changing phases of the work is the increasing difficulty of getting good Northern teachers for colored schools."[80]

In the face of such challenges, the FFA changed its recruitment process. Writing in May 1888 about the school year just ending, the chairman of the FFA's Executive Committee reported: "It has been thought wise during the past year to commit the Christiansburg School to a corps of colored teachers." Initially, it seemed the new teachers might come from the Hampton Normal School, which would reduce the cost of travel. The Executive Committee even reported in the spring of 1887 that "a correspondence has been opened with S. C. Armstrong at Hampton, and C. S. Schaeffer as to the advisability of replacing the white teachers at Christiansburg by graduates of Hampton." That plan, however, never came to fruition. Instead, the Friends turned to the Institute for Colored Youth, and from the fall of 1887 through the spring of 1893 all of the teachers in Christiansburg seem to have been graduates of that institution. There were four each year, two male and two female, with one of the men serving as "Principal Teacher" or simply "Principal." Annual reports of the FFA during these years contain nothing but praise for the transition. "The change from white to colored instructors has been satisfactory to the colored people," claimed the report for 1887–88, and other reports noted that Schaeffer too approved of the new teachers.[81]

These new teachers were not just graduates of the Institute for Colored Youth. After coming south they continued to work with Fanny Jackson Coppin to transform the Christiansburg Institute into something that more closely resembled their alma mater. Teachers from Christiansburg sometimes met with Coppin during the summer to discuss their progress; Samuel Comfort, then the principal at Christiansburg, returned to the Institute for Colored Youth over Christmas in 1891 to see "what I thought would be serviceable here," and Coppin herself visited Christiansburg in 1893. As a result, the Christiansburg Institute moved toward the model of the Institute for Colored Youth. Teachers at the Hill School, for example, established more structure at the school—"classifying" the students and assigning each to one of seven classes. They also adopted the Philadelphia school's policy of refraining from corporal punishment. More importantly, they began to expand the facilities and curriculum at Christiansburg to reflect those of their alma mater. The first known reference to a library in the Hill School came in 1889, and by then the curriculum had grown to include "Reading, Writing & Drawing, Spelling & Defining, Arithmetic, Geography, Grammar, Virginia History, U.S. History, Algebra, Physiology, Philosophy, Kitchen Garden Work, [and] Sewing." And in a marked departure from the goal laid out in the deed of trust establishing the Christiansburg Institute, they took the first steps toward more vocational education.[82]

For a decade, Fanny Jackson Coppin had been urging the Friends' Freedmen's Association to make vocational education a central element in the schools it supported, and that included Christiansburg. In 1891 Coppin wrote the directors of the FFA, "The best kind of training is that which ends in making the person helpful to himself and to others, and the colored people as a class being very poor ought to be taught how to make an honest living by capable service of some kind. It is my earnest hope that the Christiansburg school will aim to give first this kind of education." By the time Coppin wrote that, Christiansburg was already beginning to devote more attention to vocational training. Sewing lessons had begun for girls in 1888 and were already doing "some good." The purchase of photographic equipment in 1890 was also seen as "a step, albeit an easy and short one, towards a manual labor school." By 1892, cooking and carpentry classes had begun, discussions had begun about converting the basement of the old school building into "an industrial school," and the school's name, apparently, had become the Christiansburg *Industrial* Institute. No evidence marking a formal change in the name has yet come to light, but an 1891 program described ceremonies that spring as the first annual commencement of the Christiansburg Industrial Institute, and later catalogs of the Christiansburg Industrial Institute identify 1891 as the school's first graduating class.[83]

Students, their families, and the African American community in Christiansburg initially welcomed the addition of vocational training. Early in the process they held public meetings and organized a committee to explore converting the old schoolhouse into workshops, and they continued to hold fundraisers in an effort to collect money for expanding industrial training. Students themselves raised a quarter of the money needed to buy photographic equipment in 1890. "We cannot at this moment, state with accuracy, just how the gift of photographic equipment will affect us in our active life," they wrote, "but we believe it will give a different character and tone to the pupils of the Christiansburg Institute and will open up to us another avenue to honest livelihood." Charles Schaeffer, on the other hand, was less than enthusiastic about the school's new direction. The school was still teaching the academic subjects he had emphasized, but he begrudged any diversion of resources from liberal to industrial training and would only agree to the expansion of "manual instruction" if it could be done "without much expense."[84]

Opening the Hill School and adding more vocational education to its curriculum was accompanied by an expanded effort to provide facilities for boarding students who came from distances that made it impossible to commute each day. Virginia had established public primary schools for both black and white children in the state, and by 1890 there were dozens of black primary schools in Montgomery and the surrounding counties. Other than Christiansburg, however, there were no schools open to blacks in the region that offered higher education, normal school training, or industrial education. This made the Hill School a magnet for students from beyond Christiansburg and beyond Montgomery County. As early as 1890, its principal, William Polk, wrote that children from Radford, Pulaski, Pocahontas, and other locations hoped to attend the school. Polk worried, however, about where such students would live. When Schaeffer first proposed building a new brick school, he had also suggested converting one of the older wooden structures into a dormitory for boarding students, but he eventually concluded it would have to be torn down, as its roof leaked and its foundation had "given way." Having just spent almost $9,000 to build the school, though, neither he nor the FFA were in a position to fund the construction of a dormitory. Instead, school officials began renting houses in the neighborhood in which to board students attending the Hill School.[85]

In less than a decade, the Hill School had come to represent a new model of black education in Montgomery County, but even as this model was emerging, it gained a new champion and a new direction. In the late 1880s and early 1890s, Fanny Jackson Coppin had been the chief advocate of vocational education at Christiansburg, and graduates of the Institute for Colored Youth had been its initial architects. In 1892, however, the FFA's annual report spoke in glowing terms of the work being done by Booker T. Washington at "Tuskagee [*sic*] College." Washington was a graduate of the Hampton Institute and as the first principal of the Tuskegee Normal School for Colored Teachers set out to build a school that resembled his alma mater. Hampton and Tuskegee both focused heavily on teacher training, and while both included academic subjects in their curricula, they were best known for their emphasis on manual training. Unlike Fanny Jackson Coppin, however, neither Samuel C. Armstrong, at Hampton, nor Booker T. Washington, at Tuskegee, aspired to train students in architecture, engineering, or other more technical fields. Their view of industrial education placed more emphasis on building character while training teachers, farmers, and manual workers.[86]

During the 1880s, Washington worked tirelessly to spread the Hampton/Tuskegee philosophy of black education, and in 1895 his ideas garnered national attention after his speech at the Atlanta Cotton States and International Exposition. This was a philosophy that appealed to a growing number among Quaker supporters of the FFA, the Institute for Colored Youth, and the Christiansburg Institute. Many Quakers at the time were growing pessimistic about the future of African Americans and increasingly reluctant to support efforts such as those of the FFA. Conservative Quakers were still interested in elevating southern blacks, but not too high, and Washington's emphasis on "practical" education and training for African Americans struck a sympathetic chord among them. Washington often spoke in Philadelphia during the late 1880s, and it was after a lecture he gave at Bryn Mawr in 1892 that James E. Rhoads, president of the FFA, highlighted the progress Washington was making at Tuskegee and "earnestly pressed the continuance of the work." Another member of the FFA, J. Henry Scattergood, was even more emphatic. Scattergood later recalled that by the early 1890s the original aim of the FFA—providing "elementary education" for African Americans—had been met or taken over by public schools, and that the association faced a new "Negro problem." Educated southern blacks had "devoted their talents to unworthy objects." Many had "become debauched in politics and morals," and the only solution Scattergood saw was "the plan of industrial and agricultural education inaugurated at Hampton Institute by General Armstrong, and also developed at Tuskegee by Booker T. Washington."[87]

In 1893, this thinking led the FFA to appoint a protégé of Washington's, Hiram H. Thweatt, to serve as the principal in Christiansburg and to make the Christiansburg school more like Hampton and Tuskegee. The Executive Board of the FFA then opened negotiations with Washington himself in 1896 in hopes of securing his services as the school's supervisor. After visiting Christiansburg and convincing the board to commit another $2,000 to the conversion, Washington agreed to assume a supervisory role over the Christiansburg Industrial Institute, and the shift there to industrial training accelerated rapidly. The Friends clearly hoped Washington could do at Christiansburg what he had done at Tuskegee: "We sincerely wish we could see a Hampton, or a Tuskegee school in Christiansburg, with all the interest and enthusiasm of either." Washington was the school's supervisor, but actual control lay with its principal, and following Washington's appointment as supervisor, Hiram Thweatt was succeeded as principal by another Washington protégé, Charles L. Marshall, who brought with him a staff "thoroughly imbued with the Tuskegee idea."[88]

But "the Tuskegee idea" was not well received in Montgomery County's African American community. Members of that community had supported the move toward a school modeled on the Institute for Colored Youth. Enrollment held steady after Fanny Jackson Coppin began to influence the program in Christiansburg, and the FFA reported enthusiasm for the shift to black teachers and popular support for the start of vocational training. Those changes, however, did not undermine the academic character of the Christiansburg Institute; in fact, the library and new course offerings strengthened it. The Tuskegee model, on the other hand, seemed too industrial and not sufficiently academic to many black residents of Montgomery County. Other black leaders of the day often considered Washington's approach too servile and objected to introducing the Tuskegee model at other southern schools, and this seems to have been the reaction of many blacks in Montgomery County. Adding to the discontent in Christiansburg was the absence of support from Schaeffer for the Tuskegee model. He still commanded great respect among the county's African American residents, and while he did not actively oppose Washington, Marshall, or the FFA, he clearly believed their efforts were misguided. In Washington's words, "He does not oppose the school actively but he is not actively in favor of it." It was not just Schaeffer, though. According to Marshall, his plans faced "well-nigh insurmountable" opposition from local African Americans when he introduced them at Christiansburg. "The people seemed almost crazed that a Tuskegee graduate should be planning to engraft the Tuskegee Idea in that section," he wrote. In Marshall's opinion this was a result of people's "misunderstanding" of Washington and his philosophy, but the effect was real. Enrollment in Christiansburg dropped by more than a third between the 1893–94 academic year and that of 1896–97, a decline Marshall attributed to a widespread belief "that the Institute was to be an industrial school," and there were, apparently, no students graduated between 1894 and 1898.[89]

Marshall and his staff pressed on, though. A shop for a wheelwright opened in 1896, "a shanty for the blacksmiths" was erected in 1897, enrollment began to recover during the 1897–98 school year, and three students graduated that year. But there was little room on Zion Hill for further expansion. The Christiansburg Industrial Institute was still located in the Hill School, and it quickly became apparent that it would need more room for workshops and dormitories in order to pursue the Tuskegee model. In the thirty years since Charles Schaeffer first built a schoolhouse on an empty ridge above Christiansburg, dozens of black and white families had bought land in the neighborhood, and it had become a thriving commercial and residential neighborhood. There was simply no land available near the Hill School for the expansion envisioned by school leaders, so they looked outside of town and in 1898 began buying farmland just north of Christiansburg. Once again Marshall reported widespread opposition to the change among members of the local black community. "As soon as the fact became known that we had purchased a large tract of land and would endeavor to build a boarding and industrial school thereon," he wrote in

1905, "the members of the faculty at once became objects of scorn to almost the entire colored population." Moreover, the school's enrollment fell by 40 percent in a month and continued falling for the rest of the year.[90]

That proved the school's low point, though, and gradually it won back community support. Over the next decade, the FFA purchased more land outside of Christiansburg and began to establish on it a new facility that focused on agricultural, industrial, and teacher training. This campus served older students, many of whom came from beyond Montgomery County and boarded in dormitories, while the Hill School operated as its preparatory school and drew younger students, mainly from the Christiansburg area. Initially, many African Americans in the county saw this as a step backward. It seemed to represent a move away from the classical model of education emphasized by Schaeffer and Coppin that symbolized equality and greater opportunity and toward a more utilitarian model more appropriate to a subordinate people. But in keeping with the sentiment of the local black community, the Christiansburg Industrial Institute never abandoned liberal education. It continued to offer courses in a range of academic subjects at a higher level than was available at any other school in the region open to African Americans. As a result, it eventually won renewed trust and respect from Montgomery County's African American community and became one of its most important and cherished institutions.[91]

African American education in Montgomery County made great advances between 1865 and 1900. At the close of the Civil War, no school open to blacks had ever existed anywhere in the county, and few freedpeople could read, write, or perform basic arithmetic. Thirty years later, black public schools were operating throughout the county and had been for decades. These schools were often simple, underfunded, and open for less than half the year, and because attendance was voluntary, many black children attended them infrequently, if at all. Still, the county's black schools had a profound effect among the people they served. In 1895, black children in Montgomery County were almost as likely to be enrolled in school as white children were, and by the close of the century enrollment rates for the two races were identical: 58 percent in 1898 and 57 percent in 1899. This was one reason black literacy rates had risen significantly. They were still lower than white rates, but in 1895, 58 percent of black children between the ages of five and twenty-one were literate (compared to 68 percent of white children), and in 1900, almost two-thirds of the county's

African American residents over the age of ten could read or write. And though black children in Montgomery County still had fewer opportunities to study "higher branches," a small number of the county's African American residents used the education they received there as a base from which to continue their studies elsewhere. At least three went on to the Hampton Institute, two attended Shaw University, one studied at Morgan College, and at least six went to Wayland Seminary or the Richmond Theological Seminary or, after their merger, to Virginia Union University.[92]

This success was certainly not solely a result of efforts within the county's black community. Building an educational system for Montgomery County's African American community was, to use Hilary Green's phrase, "a collaborative effort." Freedpeople in the county began searching for educational opportunities as soon as they gained their freedom. They and their children then continued to work with a number of allies over the years: the Freedmen's Bureau, various northern benevolent societies—most notably the Friends' Freedmen's Association, and public school officials of both the county and state. Together they and their allies built and maintained a system that served not only to educate African Americans in Montgomery County but to help meld them into a community. Black teachers were prominent figures among the community's leaders and served as role models for their peers and for black children. Schoolhouses provided physical symbols of the local African American communities they served and spaces in which members of those communities met to socialize, to discuss politics, or to mark significant events in their collective lives. In Montgomery County, black schools had a great deal in common with another institution binding African American families and individuals into a community—black churches.

5 TEMPLES BUILT UNTO THE LORD

RICHARD TAYLOR DIED in February 1879. By then, according to the local newspaper, he was one of the most respected preachers in Montgomery County. Taylor had been born about 1800, and he and his family had been slaves on the farm of George Earhart, east of Blacksburg, until the fall of the Confederacy set them free. "Pious from early manhood," Taylor had become a devout Methodist and by the 1830s was serving as a lay minister to his local African American community. In spite of a state law passed in 1832 that banned preaching by slaves or free people of color, Taylor continued to preach through the close of the antebellum era. The *Messenger* reported that he was "especially eloquent in prayer" and with the permission of his master and the consent of the white community had preached "where-ever he felt called to go"—including the resort at Montgomery White Sulphur Springs. Following his emancipation, Taylor initially remained active in the Methodist Church, but according to Charles Schaeffer, he began to grow "much exercised in his mind on the subject of baptism." As a result, in 1869, Taylor joined the Baptists and for the final decade of his life served as pastor of the African Baptist Church in Christiansburg.[1]

The experience of Richard Taylor was, in some ways, quite different from that of any other African American living in Montgomery County during the nineteenth century. He was among the small number of men in his day—and perhaps the only black man—to warrant a newspaper obituary at his death, and his coffin was escorted to the cemetery by "one of the largest processions ever seen in this place [Christiansburg], composed of both colors." Taylor was, the paper noted, "listened to with profit by white and black alike." In other regards, however, Richard Taylor's experience typified those of other men and women of color in the county following the end of slavery. During and after Reconstruction, Taylor and other African Americans in Montgomery County moved out of the biracial religious communities in which they had participated before 1865 into a different and much more racially homogenous community. Martin Luther King famously described church services in the modern United States as "the most segregated hour of Christian America," and the *Messenger* notwithstanding, Richard Taylor helped to create that hour. In the years after the Civil War, he and other African Americans living in Montgomery County reoriented their spiritual lives and played a major role in the creation of distinctly black churches throughout the county, and these churches quickly took their place among the most important institutions in the county's African American community.[2]

Religion had been a key element in Montgomery County's African American community long before the Civil War. Both slaves and free people of color had frequently attended church services and been members of churches in antebellum Montgomery County. Because fully autonomous black churches were illegal in Virginia at that time, however, most of the religious activity that can be documented before 1865 was in white-controlled churches. More than 150 African Americans appeared among the members of Methodist, Presbyterian, or Baptist congregations in the county during the 1850s and early 1860s, and many others who were not members also attended services. In some parts of Virginia, including nearby Botetourt County, what were essentially independent black churches did sometimes operate under nominal white control. No such churches are known to have existed in Montgomery County, though there may have been at least one independent black congregation in the county. Tradition among today's members of St. Paul African Methodist Episcopal Church in Blacksburg is that the congregation was organized in 1857. Blacksburg's Methodist station included two churches, Blacksburg and Trinity, each of which had dozens of black members during the 1850s. Many of those black Methodists were enslaved on neighborhood farms, and at least some of them came together at events such as weddings and funerals. Thus, it is possible that they did organize an independent congregation of some kind before the Civil War, though no contemporary evidence that they did has survived.[3]

In the immediate aftermath of emancipation, little changed in the institutional landscape of religion Montgomery County. Freedpeople in Montgomery County continued to attend the same white-controlled churches they had as slaves, and Methodism remained the most common denominational affiliation among freedpeople in the county. Indeed, the number of black Methodists actually rose between 1865 and 1867. The Blacksburg church recorded fifteen black baptisms, of both children and adults, during the last six months of 1865, and eleven African Americans were admitted to the congregation as probationers in December 1865 and January 1866. In Christiansburg, Methodists established a new black Sunday school in 1866, and the minister there reported in April 1867 that "the attendance of the colored people has been very good, both at the Sunday afternoon preaching and with the white congregation." Indeed, when the Freedmen's Bureau conducted a census of the county's freedpeople during the summer of 1867, more than a quarter of those aged sixteen years or older reported a denominational affiliation, and almost three-quarters of those who did so identified themselves as Methodists. Most of the rest were Baptists, though a handful were Presbyterian, and two identified themselves as Catholic.[4]

Whatever their denominational affiliation, immediately after the Civil War Montgomery County's African American church members still worshipped in mixed-race congregations under white control. There is certainly evidence that groups of like-minded freedpeople sometimes met together to worship without a minister, but in terms of organized, denominational services, little changed in the first two years after the abolition of slavery. Until 1867, every Methodist congregation in Montgomery County, at least one of the two Presbyterian congregations, and almost half the Baptist meetings still included African American members, and no independent black congregation of any denomination can be documented there before the middle of 1867. In 1867, however, the religious patterns that had marked the antebellum county began to break down, and when they did, change came quickly and completely. By the early 1870s, every denomination in Montgomery County was almost entirely segregated by race, and Baptists had replaced Methodists as the largest denomination among the county's African American residents. These new patterns would mark black religious life in Montgomery County for the remainder of the nineteenth century and beyond.[5]

The separation of churches in Montgomery County along racial lines was the result of multiple forces. Throughout the South, freedpeople often wanted to withdraw from white congregations as quickly as possible. After years of subordinate status in churches that had never really accorded them "the privileges of membership" and years of listening to white ministers emphasize the virtues of loyalty and obedience among "servants" over those of brotherhood and charity, many freedpeople were anxious to control their own spiritual lives and to participate in churches that better addressed their particular wishes and needs. Others, however, worried that by themselves they lacked the resources necessary to support a fully satisfying religious life. They could meet anywhere, and they could sing and pray under the leadership of exhorters and lay preachers, but baptism and communion called for ministers, and properly ordained black ministers were exceedingly rare in the years immediately after emancipation. Whites, for their part, were similarly ambivalent. Many were anxious to end the mixing of races that had marked so many antebellum churches and were willing to tolerate African American members but only with totally separate meetings for the two races. Most whites were not anxious, however, to see fully independent black congregations. They considered any black organization—including black churches—a potential vehicle for the organization of black political power and the establishment of black control over white lives and property. Thus, they demanded that freedpeople acknowledge the "inferiority . . . submission and dependence . . . [that] Scriptures themselves declare to be unchangeable" and accept continued white oversight of their religious lives. This combination of hopes and fears among blacks and whites was evident across the religious spectrum in Montgomery County, though exactly how it played out varied among denominations and congregations.[6]

Among Methodists, race had long been a contentious issue, and by 1867 various branches of the faith reflected an array of different attitudes. Late in the eighteenth century and early in the nineteenth, black Methodists in northern cities such as Philadelphia and New York had rejected the segregationist polices of the Methodist Episcopal Church (MEC) and formed separate black Methodist denominations, including the African Methodist Episcopal (AME) Church and the African Methodist Episcopal Zion (AME Zion) Church. Later, white Methodists themselves split over the issue of slavery, leading to the emergence of the proslavery Methodist Episcopal Church, South (MECS). Methodists opposed to slavery then continued wrestling with the issue of race, and during the Civil War some black members of the church had pushed for separate black conferences within the MEC. In spite of opposition by other members to the idea of institutionalized racial segregation, the MEC adopted this policy and in 1864 established black conferences in Maryland, Virginia, and Washington, D.C. Meanwhile, both the AME and AME Zion churches took advantage of the war to expand into southern states that had barred them during the antebellum era—including Virginia, where the AME established a state conference in 1867. It was this new Virginia conference of the AME that sent John Wesley Diggs to be its first minister in Southwest Virginia and provided one of the factors triggering the separation of black and white Methodists in Montgomery County.[7]

At its first session, the Virginia Conference appointed Diggs to the Salem Mission, in Roanoke County, which he reached in May 1867. Within a month, he "heard of others in Blacksburg" and traveled there in early June. What brought Diggs to Blacksburg were probably echoes of discontent among black Methodists there. A significant number of freedpeople in and around Blacksburg, including Richard Taylor, were members of the Methodist Church in 1867 and had no doubt noticed some white members' growing uneasiness at worshipping with *free* African Americans. Robert Preston had taken the most dramatic stand when two of his former slaves, Thomas and Othello Fraction, tried to attend services at the Blacksburg church during the fall of 1866. According to Charles Schaeffer's report of the incident, Preston declared "that he was the proprietor there, and that they and him could not worship in the same church, nor live in the same town together and threatened to shoot them if they did not obey his order [to leave]." This was part of an ongoing struggle by Preston to assert his authority over the Fraction brothers, who had run away from his plantation during the war and joined the Union army, but it sent a clear message to other freedpeople in the congregation that their position in the church was just as vulnerable. Nor was Preston alone in sending a message to black Methodists. By the time Preston confronted the Fractions, the Blacksburg congregation had begun to segregate its records for the first time. Until late 1864, black and white baptisms were recorded together in a section of the church book labeled "Record of Baptisms." In June 1865, however, when Harriet Ronald was baptized, someone started a new page and amended it to read "Record of Colored Baptisms." Similarly, until 1864 black and white probationers were enrolled in the order in which they were admitted, regardless of race. That pattern had stopped, however, by the end of 1865, when someone wrote across the register "Whites & Blacks are separated—white list some pages ahead," labeled the next page "Colored Probationers," and began to list freedpeople separately.[8]

African American Methodists in the Blacksburg Station could no doubt sense the discomfort of their white brethren, and the arrival of John Wesley Diggs offered them the opportunity to do something about it. When Diggs reached Blacksburg, early in June 1867, he "gathered forty" freedpeople and began to establish the first independent African American church in Montgomery County. Unfortunately, there is no record of who Diggs gathered in Blacksburg. Certainly, some of them had been members of the Methodist Church there before Diggs arrived. That August, minutes of the quarterly meeting of the Blacksburg Station recorded, "Coloured members withdrawn," and among the five men identified in 1882 as trustees of the AME congregation in town, two had been members of the Blacksburg Methodist Church and a third was married to a woman who had been a member. Others may have belonged to another faith or may have been unchurched before 1867, but the AME's core in Blacksburg seems to have been freedpeople who left the white-controlled Methodist congregation there. And their departure seems to have been amicable. Not only did other members of the Blacksburg Station refrain from any criticism of the AME or of those who joined it, at their quarterly meeting in December 1867 they approved a resolution "[to] make an arrangement with the Baptists for occupying our house (in order to accommodate the African M.E. Church)." Not until the following spring did William B. Derrick arrive to serve as the first resident AME minister in Blacksburg, and not until 1881 did the congregation have a building of its own in which to meet, but by late 1867 the AME congregation in Blacksburg was functioning as an independent black institution.[9]

A new Methodist congregation may also have emerged in Christiansburg that year, but it affiliated with the MEC rather than the AME and appeared under more confusing circumstances. In contrast to the situation in Blacksburg, nothing clearly suggests a connection between the existing mixed-race Methodist congregation in Christiansburg and the new black church that came to be known as the Wesley Chapel or the "Colored Methodist Church." In April 1867, the minister in Christiansburg reported that black members' attendance was "very good," and a list dated 1867–68 identified twenty-seven "colored" members of the Christiansburg church. After that, the record is silent; there is no further reference to African American members either attending or withdrawing from congregations of the Christiansburg Station. A month earlier, however, minutes of the Washington Conference of the MEC had included Christiansburg among the places where preachers were stationed that year. The minutes did not actually identify a preacher (one was "to be supplied"), and Christiansburg was not included on a table detailing the number of members in each circuit or station of the conference; so it is unclear just what its inclusion in the minutes signified. Minutes of the 1868 conference also indicate that Christiansburg was "to be supplied" but also fail to report any specific number of members in the congregation. Finally, in 1869, conference minutes identified Charles Price as the minister in Christiansburg and reported forty-one members in the congregation there. This could mean that black residents of Christiansburg had gathered a church themselves in 1867 and approached the MEC for a minister, but this cannot be confirmed. Nor is it possible to say much about who might have gathered such a church, because just three early members of the Wesley Chapel can be identified by name. None of the three appear in the records of the Methodists' Christiansburg Station, and the two included on the 1867 census of freedpeople in the county both appear with no religious affiliation.[10]

Adding to the mystery of the Wesley Chapel's origins is its relationship with the larger community: whites in the county welcomed it, while at least some blacks did not. There is no evidence that white residents played any role in founding the Wesley Chapel. The new congregation belonged to the Washington Conference of the MEC, one of the black conferences established by northern Methodists in 1864. The Christiansburg and Blacksburg Stations, on the other hand, were among those from the Baltimore Conference of the MEC that belatedly joined the Methodist Episcopal Church, South, in 1866 in order to escape the "animus" of the MEC and to associate with churches "according with our own views." Soon after this happened, the MECS set out to establish its own black offshoot, known as the Colored Methodist Episcopal Church, in an effort to counter advances by the MEC, the AME, and other northern strains of Methodism. Wesley Chapel seems not to have arisen from this process, though. The existing Methodist congregation in Christiansburg did permit members of the Wesley Chapel to hold at least one service in its building, in 1873, but otherwise it offered no visible support to the new congregation. The town's white establishment, however, did. It welcomed the Wesley Chapel as an alternative to other, more disturbing black churches and provided it both moral and financial support in its early years.[11]

The emergence of independent black churches was clearly unsettling to many whites in Christiansburg, but black Baptist churches were especially worrisome because of the prominent role played in their formation by Charles Schaeffer, resident agent of the Freedmen's Bureau. Soon after the first black Baptist congregation was organized in Christiansburg, for example, the local newspaper described its members "worshipping Schaeffer and the departed spirits of Lincoln and John Brown, Radical Martyrs and Saints." In contrast, when the Wesley Chapel laid the cornerstone for its building in 1873, the *Messenger* celebrated the event and declared, "We are glad Captain Schaeffer and his Baptist friends will be constrained to divide their honors." According to the *Messenger*, white residents of the county also provided "substantial assistance" in raising money to build the new Methodist church, and "25 or 30 of our most respectable white citizens" attended its dedication service in 1874. Apparently, many whites in Christiansburg found any black Methodist congregation, even one associated with the MEC, preferable to a black Baptist congregation. Speaking for the white community, the *Messenger* described members of the Wesley Chapel as "well behaved" and "well governed" and promised that if the members put their faith in the Lord, "they will at all times receive the encouragement and assistance of the white citizens and their future [will] be a happy and prosperous one."[12]

The fact that the Wesley Chapel had such visible support from the white community may also explain why at least some of the county's African American residents opposed it. In 1870 and again in 1874 African Americans were charged with disrupting services at the Wesley Chapel, and at least one of those charged, Joseph Dill, was connected to the Blacksburg AME Church. Competition and conflict among different black churches was common in the postwar South, and members of the AME Church were often among those most zealous in their advocacy of black autonomy. This was certainly true of William B. Derrick, the AME minister in Blacksburg between 1868 and 1870. Derrick was outspoken in his contempt for the Freedmen's Bureau and in his belief that blacks should control their own destinies. If members of his congregation shared Derrick's view, they might well have seen the Wesley Chapel as a tool by which the white community hoped to maintain its influence over freedpeople, and that may have prompted them to disrupt its services.[13]

Both the AME Church in Blacksburg and the Wesley Chapel survived, though the latter suffered a financial setback during the1880s and lost its first church before reemerging as the Asbury Methodist Church in 1889. In addition, at least three other black Methodist congregations appeared in Montgomery County after the Civil War, though not all survived. In 1869, Virginia's AME conference sent Richard Gassaway to serve as a minister and teacher in Wake Forest. No evidence has survived to indicate what prompted this action. Freedpeople in Wake Forest may have requested it; William Derrick, in Blacksburg, may have suggested it; or members of the conference may have taken the initiative themselves. Whatever prompted it, Gassaway remained in Wake Forest for two years, and early in 1871 community members there purchased an acre of land on which to build an AME church. That spring, however, the church transferred Gassaway without replacing him, and no evidence has emerged that the AME ever reestablished a presence in Wake Forest.[14] Near Lovely Mount, in what would later become Radford, a handful of freedpeople reportedly began meeting in their homes in 1867 and eventually formed the Mount Olive Methodist Church. No written record of the church from before 1889 has yet been found, but it seems to have operated for years before its official organization and before constructing a sanctuary, which it had done by 1892.[15] Similarly, black Methodists in the community of Rough and Ready, southwest of Christiansburg, had certainly organized a congregation by 1881 and may have constructed a church by then. The congregation bought a tract of land in 1886 and soon built a church on it, but tradition among today's members is that the church they built replaced an older structure that stood nearby. Moreover, by then at least one African American couple had already married at the "Rough & Ready Church," and the congregation had already secured the services of a minister, Isaac L. Thomas, probably from the MEC.[16]

In the years after emancipation, however, Methodists were no longer the most important denomination among African Americans in Montgomery County. Baptists were. Between 1867 and 1875 at least eight Baptist churches were organized in the county, and their membership far exceeded that of any other denomination. This was not simply an extension of antebellum religious patterns in the county. Black Baptists had been relatively rare in Montgomery County before the Civil War. Baptists were certainly present in the county, and several of their congregations are known to have included black members during the 1850s and early 1860s. Most of the county's elite, however, were Methodists or Presbyterians, who permitted or required their slaves to worship with them. Baptist congregations were often poorer and were often located in more mountainous regions of the county, where there were fewer slaves or free people of color. As a result, they had relatively few black members. No countywide figures are available before 1867, but reports from two churches in 1851 and 1861–62 suggest that African Americans represented less than 20 percent of the county's Baptists at the time and numbered no more than a couple of dozen members in all. This is consistent with the total of thirty black Baptists in the county (11 percent of all Baptists there) reported by the Valley Baptist Association in 1867.[17]

Nor did this preexisting Baptist community attract newly freed African Americans by offering them greater autonomy than the Methodists did. William Montgomery has argued that the Baptists' emphasis on congregational autonomy was an important factor in the church's appeal to freedpeople after emancipation. This may have been true in other parts of the South, but there is little evidence of it in Montgomery County. After emancipation, the association to which Montgomery County Baptist congregations belonged made very clear its unwillingness to see genuinely independent black congregations any time soon. The Valley Baptist Association met for its annual session in August 1865, just four months after the war ended, and delegates there unanimously adopted resolutions calling for the establishment of "[colored] assemblies separate from those of white people" wherever it was "practicable" to do so and for the establishment of "colored churches" whenever it could be done "with propriety." Delegates also stipulated, however, that "for the present such churches can be represented in this body only by white delegates."[18]

This was very much in keeping with the racial hierarchy maintained by Virginia's antebellum Baptists. The Valley Baptist Association had included two "African" churches before the Civil War. As permitted under Virginia law, the Fincastle and Mill Creek churches were black congregations with white ministers under the "watchcare" of a white church. The association had made clear in 1865 its desire to maintain a similar arrangement in the future, and it acted on that desire in 1866, when the first postemancipation black congregation sought to join its ranks. During the months following the Civil War, a large number of freedpeople who had previously belonged to another Baptist congregation sought to join Enon Baptist Church, in Roanoke County, because their own congregation "had become entirely disorganized in consequence of the death or dispersion of all the white members and . . . the destruction of their house of worship." Enon Baptist Church already included about thirty black members, but its white members evidently balked at the idea of significantly increasing that number. According to the congregation's black members,

> As all new members of our race had to be recommended by us to the church before they could be rec^d, the white brethren thought it best that we should be formed into a church of our own and assume the entire responsibility of receiving or rejecting candidates for membership, they being, as a general rule, entire strangers to parties proposing to join. Moreover the discipline of the church could only be brought to bear on our colored brethren through the representations we might make. It was therefore thought best to turn over the whole matter to us.

Acting "under the advice of the white membership," black members of the congregation then constituted themselves into "a distinct and separate body to be known as Enon Colored Baptist Church," selected two white brethren to represent them, and applied for admission to the Valley Baptist Association.[19]

Faced with a situation that would certainly repeat itself in the future, delegates at the 1866 meeting of the association, all of whom were white, took time to consider their response. They tabled the application for a day, awaiting a report from the "committee on the Religious Instruction of the Colored people." When it came, the report made very clear that the Valley Baptist Association fully intended to keep black members in their place. "Whatever human law may enjoin, or infidel fanaticism may inculcate," it declared, "the line of demarcation [between the races] is too clearly drawn ever to be obliterated." Therefore, it continued, freedpeople should remain members of mixed-race congregations until their numbers justified the creation of "distinct churches and congregations." Once these black congregations appeared, the report's authors assumed that they would initially be too poor to afford their own facilities, so the report declared that white congregations should allow blacks to use their buildings "under proper restrictions" until they could build their own. The association should also do what it could to provide black ministers to these separate black churches and grant them representation in the association, but only through "white delegates chosen from among the membership of Churches connected with this body." Finally, the report recognized that it would certainly be desirable, someday, to establish "Colored Associations within the bounds of this Association," but this could not happen yet. "The congregating of colored persons in such large numbers as would, in all probability, attend such meetings, would constitute a most serious objection to such organizations," the report concluded. "Any neighborhood would object to an assemblage of the kind in their midst," and the "prejudices of race" would probably lead to "flagrant acts and excesses most injurious to the peace and good order of society." After "much discussion" the committee's report was unanimously adopted. Only then was Enon Colored Church admitted to the association.[20]

One reason the report was adopted unanimously may have been that neither of the existing black churches in the Valley Baptist Association sent delegates to the annual meeting that year. They were already meeting elsewhere to establish an alternative organization for black Baptists that helped set the stage for the church's transformation in Montgomery County. In August 1866, Jonathan P. Corron, a member of the American Baptist Home Mission Society serving the Fincastle African Baptist Church, took the lead in organizing four churches with some five hundred members into the Valley African Baptist Association. The response of white Baptists was clear and hostile, announcing in Christiansburg at the 1867 annual meeting of the Valley Baptist Association that "all colored organizations formerly under the supervision of the white membership of churches connected with this body, [shall] be stricken from the list of churches, they having been formed into distinct churches and connected themselves with another association composed wholly of colored membership." At the time this action was announced, the Valley Baptist Association still included one "colored" church, Enon, and a number of other congregations—including three in Montgomery County—with black members. By 1869, however, no "African" or "colored" congregations remained in the Valley Baptist Association, and by 1871 not a single congregation in the association reported any African American members.[21]

The emergence of a separate black Baptist association in Southwest Virginia and the response to it by its white brethren were certainly factors in the emergence of separate black Baptist congregations in Montgomery

County. Equally significant, however, was another event that also occurred in 1866: the arrival in Christiansburg of Charles Schaeffer. Schaeffer came, of course, as an officer of the Freedmen's Bureau, but he was also a devout Baptist who had worked during the 1850s proselytizing among black residents of Philadelphia as a member of that city's Tenth Baptist Church. In Christiansburg, he easily combined these roles and quickly became a major force behind the formation of numerous Baptist congregations in the county.[22]

The first to emerge did so officially in October 1867, though Schaeffer and fellow Baptists had been meeting informally for several months before that. In April, Schaeffer began planning to build a new schoolhouse in Christiansburg that included room for "church purposes and religious worship," and during the summer he oversaw its construction. He also contacted the minister at his own Tenth Baptist Church in Philadelphia, which sent hymn books, a communion service, and other church fixtures for the new congregation, and he contacted J. P. Corron in Fincastle to secure his assistance in organizing the church, which was vital because there were no ordained Baptists in Montgomery County willing to do so. By autumn everything was ready, and over three days in early October Schaeffer's "little band of disciples" was formally organized into the Christiansburg African Baptist Church. J. P. Corron and J. A. Davis, another Baptist missionary based at Liberty, Virginia, presided over the services with the help of two black preachers—John Jones, the African American minister at Fincastle, and a Brother Rose, who was probably at Liberty with Reverend Davis.[23]

This took place at a time when racial tension was rising in the county in connection with the election of delegates to the state's constitutional convention and freedmen's participation in the political process. Members of the African Baptist Church made no effort to hide their light, though. Instead, they and other African Americans in the county made their presence known in a very public but nonthreatening way. The congregation met in the new school/meeting house that Schaeffer and the Freedmen's Bureau had built on what became known as Zion Hill. At the foot of the hill was a small creek that formed a pool in which new converts could be baptized, and according to Schaeffer,

> After the services a procession was formed, headed by the ministry and followed by the church, her happy converts, Christians or other

denominations, and non-professors. The column was formed four abreast, and numbered from five to six hundred men, women, and children. As they marched down to the water, a distance of about half a mile, they all united in singing precious songs of Zion. And sweet melody mingled with praise and thanksgiving ascended to the Lord. On coming out of the water, we found a large collection of white citizens attracted thither to witness the baptism of those who had formerly been their slaves. . . . Our missionary, Brother Corron, then preached to a large assembly, giving them our views of the ordinance of baptism, and urging upon them the importance of repentance towards God and faith in the Lord Jesus Christ and obedience to His holy requirements.[24]

The services brought in seven additional Baptists, who had been "scattered as sheep having no shepherd," and nine people seeking baptism. Additional professions of faith continued in the days that followed, and within two weeks the African Baptist Church's 30 founding members had grown to 109, with more awaiting baptism. Founding members of the church included thirty scattered Baptists that Schaeffer found when he arrived in Montgomery County, but the church also drew members from other denominations and from among the unchurched. In its first two weeks, for example, the church received fourteen members from other churches and sixty-five through baptism. This same pattern is clearly evident among the small number of members who can be identified by name. Thirteen of the church's early trustees or deacons appear on the 1867 census of the county's freedpeople, which identifies the "sect" to which they belonged, and among them are one Baptist, four Methodists, and eight with no religious affiliation. The church's first resident minister was also a recent convert from Methodism. Richard Taylor had a been a Methodist lay preacher for almost forty years and as recently as 1867 had been a member of Trinity Church, part of the Blacksburg Station, but in February 1869 he was baptized and installed as the minister of the Christiansburg African Baptist Church, which he served until his death ten years later.[25]

This pattern, minus the material support provided to the Christiansburg church by Philadelphia Baptists, was soon repeated across the county. Between 1868 and 1875, seven new Baptist churches arose in Montgomery County: Alleghany Springs and Lovely Mount in 1869; Brush Creek (soon renamed High Rock), New Hope (located in the community of Vickers), and Big Spring in 1870; Cave Field in 1871, though it moved into Blacksburg two years later; and Wake Forest in 1874. In most cases Schaeffer, who was ordained in December 1869, and Richard Taylor or other representatives of the Christiansburg church went to meet with the people interested in establishing a congregation, preached, performed baptisms, and helped get the new congregation on its feet. In two cases, new churches were organized by members of an existing Baptist church in order to avoid traveling so far to worship. Schaeffer described founders of the church at Alleghany Springs as "a little colony" of the Christiansburg church, and the church at Big Spring then began as an offshoot of Alleghany Springs. In most cases, however, the founders were men and women seeking religion where none was available or seeking it in a form more appealing to them as African Americans.[26]

As had been the case in Christiansburg, few of those who joined the county's newer Baptist congregations had been Baptists before 1865. Membership lists have not survived for any of the county's independent black churches before the middle of the twentieth century. Surviving minutes of annual meetings held by the Colored Valley Baptist Association, as it renamed itself in 1870, do, however, include the names of delegates sent by these churches to the association's annual meetings plus the names of ministers and men from the county licensed to preach. These provide a limited sample of black Baptists in the county during the first decade after the Civil War. Among those from Baptist churches outside of Christiansburg between 1869 and 1875, twenty-three also appear on the 1867 census of freedpeople that asked their religious affiliation. Only three of these identified themselves as Baptist in 1867, though two or three others were married to Baptists. Six identified themselves as Methodist, four were married to Methodists or were the children of Methodists, and seven had no obvious connection to any denomination.[27]

More interesting, perhaps, is the fact that while all of the county's new Baptist congregations immediately joined the Colored Valley Baptist Association, not all of their members were initially black. In Christiansburg, Charles Schaeffer was among the founders of the African Baptist Church, and according to Schaeffer, those who first came together to express interest in forming churches at Brush Creek and New Hope included both blacks and whites. In the case of Brush Creek, at least, some of those whites actually joined. At the church's founding in 1870, Schaeffer baptized "three white and seven colored converts," and Thomas Faulkner, who was white, represented the church at several meetings of the Colored Valley Baptist Association during the 1870s. This modest interracial beginning did not spread, though, and outside of Christiansburg may not have lasted very long. No other black Baptist congregation reported any white members, and Thomas Faulkner seems to have died or left the county by 1880. After that, Charles Schaeffer and his family are the only whites known to have been members of any predominantly black church in Montgomery County during the nineteenth century.[28]

By 1875, Baptists were clearly the largest denomination among African Americans in Montgomery County. With eight churches and more than seven hundred members, they dwarfed every other black church in the county. Certainly the energy of Charles Schaeffer and his position with the Freedmen's Bureau were factors in the Baptists' success. Long after the Freedmen's Bureau closed and Schaeffer lost his official positions in the county, he remained in Christiansburg and worked to improve life for the county's African American residents. To be sure, he often did so in a patronizing manner. He seems always to have considered most African Americans as works in progress. In his eyes, they had come from a savage continent into a brutal institution that kept them ignorant and debased the institutions of marriage and family; after emancipation they needed to be brought into civilization by concerned white Christians such as himself. Despite this attitude, however, there can be no question that many in Montgomery County's black community loved and admired Schaeffer, and his influence was certainly a factor in the formation of Baptist churches in Montgomery and adjacent counties during the last third of the nineteenth century.[29]

Equally important, it seems, were the actions of the Colored Valley Baptist Association and its practice of employing local black ministers and preachers. At a time when freedpeople in Southwest Virginia had roles in very few institutions, the Colored Valley Baptist Association offered a rare opportunity for black men, and to a lesser extent black women, to take leadership positions in their community. Methodists, both AME and MEC, did employ black ministers in the county, but they sent in outsiders for relatively short terms. Baptists, on the other hand, immediately began to identify local men to fill their pulpits. Leaders of the Colored Valley Baptist Association kept their eyes open for men with potential and helped prepare them to become leaders in the church. Writing to his own spiritual mentor in Philadelphia in 1870, Charles Schaeffer, who served as secretary of the association, reported that among recent converts were several promising candidates: "The converts further embrace some of the first class among the colored communities in which they live, whose influence will be to strengthen and build up the cause. Some of them are men of good moral training, whose hearts are already interested on the subject of the ministry. These we have taken under special instruction, and hope soon to get one or more of them ready for admission to the Theological School at Richmond." At the time Schaeffer wrote that, six African American men from Montgomery County had already been ordained or licensed to preach by the Colored Valley Baptist Association, and others followed over the next several years. Moreover, at least three men from the county went to Wayland Seminary, in Washington, or to the Richmond Theological Seminary, both of which had been established by the American Baptist Home Mission Society to train black ministers. Except for Charles Schaeffer, who succeeded Richard Taylor as the minister in Christiansburg and also served the church in Big Spring, the ministers of black Baptist congregations in Montgomery County in the decades following emancipation all seem to have been members of the local black community, and many of them served their congregations for years.[30]

As mentioned above, the rise of black Baptists clearly disturbed some of Montgomery County's white residents, who characterized the church in Christiansburg as a wing of northern Republican radicalism. This reaction, however, seems to have been confined to Christiansburg for a relatively brief period in the late 1860s and early 1870s. As discussed more fully in chapter 6, African Americans in the county first gained and exercised the right to vote in the late 1860s, and debates about the proposed state constitution suggested that black voters could become a permanent and significant element in the county's political landscape. As a result, racial tension rose significantly in the county. The Ku Klux Klan made a brief appearance there in 1868, and its handbills and demonstrations left some freedpeople "afraid to attend their religious meetings and other gatherings."[31]

The new schoolhouse/church in Christiansburg built with "Yankee" money was an obvious target for white hostility. During its dedicatory celebrations, a large crowd of whites gathered "to witness the baptism of those who had formerly been their slaves," and Schaeffer was "filled with apprehension lest some violent outbreak should take place." None did, though shortly after the church opened, violence did erupt between blacks and whites in Christiansburg following the election of representatives to the constitutional convention. It never spread to the church, but in the weeks that followed, according to Schaeffer's biographer, "'rude fellows of the baser sort,' coming up from town, would surround the meeting-house, and by shouts, ridicule, and threats to burn the building seek to disperse the assembly." In response, members of the congregation reportedly brought their guns to services and stacked them in a corner "as a precautionary measure." Schaeffer also reported that threats had been made by opponents of the church to take the property on which it was built. The land belonged to Schaeffer at that point, and he did not explain how it could be taken, but he wanted to put it more securely "in such hands, as will secure it, for the objects for which it was intended." Unwilling to trust any white men in the county, he deeded the property to the church's black trustees in September 1868.[32]

Tension lingered into 1869, but gradually subsided. The *Messenger* was still happy to see the Baptists in Christiansburg face a Methodist rival when the Wesley Chapel began to build a church in 1873, but threats of violence had faded by then. Schaeffer's biographer credited the improvement to leaders of the white community listening outside while Schaeffer preached and concluding that "instead of embittering the colored people against them, as they supposed, he was only trying to do them good." Whether it was that or the general reduction in political tension as debate over the new constitution ended with a compromise and Virginia reentered the Union cannot be known, but white anxiety about black Baptists in Christiansburg had clearly eased by 1871. That summer the Colored Valley Baptist Association held its annual meeting in Christiansburg, and delegates from throughout the region descended on the town for five days of meetings and services. Not only is there no evidence of any opposition to the event, but members of the association were actually made to feel welcome. Three white churches in town opened their doors to black Baptists for Sunday services in their buildings, and the all-white Board of Supervisors voted to allow services in the county courthouse.[33]

By 1875, African American religion in Montgomery County had assumed the form it would retain into the twentieth century (figure 11). Congregations were black, and Baptist congregations predominated. This remained true through the final decades of the century, though the number of congregations continued to increase. By 1900, there were at least ten Baptist congregations in the county, as well as four Methodist (one

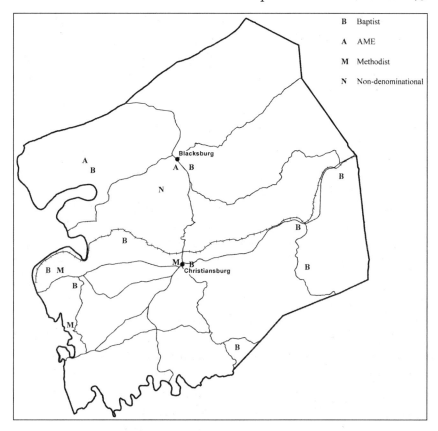

FIGURE 11. Black churches in Montgomery County, 1867–1900.
Not all of these operated during this entire period, and one church
cannot be located precisely. (Base map by Matthew Layman)

AME and three MEC), and two identified simply as "Colored" or "African,"
and members of the Schaeffer family are the only whites known to have
belonged to any of these congregations after 1875.[34]

Whatever their denominational affiliation, members of these congregations saw them as African American institutions and resisted efforts by
whites to influence them unless the members were certain those whites
could be trusted. Black Presbyterians, for example, had vanished from the
county by the early 1870s, but the church's annual "Report of the State
of Religion" still asked Presbyterian ministers to explain what they were
doing to serve African Americans in and around their congregations. In
Blacksburg, Presbyterians apparently did nothing for their black neigh-

bors during the 1870s and then tried to do something in 1881. As the minister explained, however, the attempt was not well received: "Our Pastor preached to the colored people a while once per month; they seemed pleased, attended well at first, but the last services [were] not so well attended. We think on account of the colored preacher thinking we were infringing upon their rights; therefore, services have been suspended for the present." They were never resumed.[35]

Many of the county's African American congregations also enlarged and improved their facilities during the final decades of the century, making black churches the most visible signs of the county's black communities. Many of these congregations had begun their independent existence meeting in private homes or, in the case of Baptists in Lovely Mount, in a store. When they did build proper sanctuaries, most of them were quite modest at first. While Baptists and Methodists in Christiansburg did build larger structures quite early, they had significant help in doing so. Baptists had been able to build a new frame structure thanks to financial support from the Freedmen's Bureau, Charles Schaeffer, and a number of his friends in Philadelphia, while members of the Wesley Chapel had received "substantial assistance" from the local white community in erecting "a substantial brick Edifice." These were exceptions, though, and most of the first African American churches in Montgomery County were very modest structures, often log with packed-earth floors. In some cases they were repurposed structures. The AME congregation in Blacksburg, for example, met for a decade in what had been the Union Hill Church—which the town's Presbyterians had outgrown and left in the late 1840s.[36]

During the final decades of the century, black congregations throughout the county built or expanded their facilities. Between 1880 and 1900, the AME Church in Blacksburg, Asbury Methodist in Christiansburg, Mount Olive Methodist in Radford, and Baptist congregations in Radford, Big Spring, Blacksburg, and Christiansburg all built or expanded their structures. Most of these were still relatively modest, but the new Baptist church in Christiansburg was one of the most impressive buildings in the county. The congregation had grown considerably since its first sanctuary was built, and that frame structure had not aged well. By 1880, members of the congregation were raising funds for a larger, brick church and, again, benefited greatly from Schaeffer's connection to the Tenth Baptist Church. Even then, it was a major challenge to raise the $11,000 the building ultimately cost, and work proceeded in fits and starts as money became

FIGURE 12. Memorial Baptist Church, Christiansburg, ca. 1900

available between 1883 and 1885. Finally, with gifts totaling $3,500 from a single Philadelphia donor in memory of her son, the work was completed, and early in 1886 the church was renamed Memorial Baptist Church in recognition of the donor's generosity. It was, and remains, an imposing structure (figure 12). Two stories of red brick, with a steeple, it stands on the crest of a ridge between Christiansburg and what was then Bangs, or Cambria, a smaller town that had grown up around the railroad station. Today, it is masked somewhat by trees that have grown taller over the years, but when it was built, Memorial Baptist Church was visible from any point in or near Christiansburg. It was, Schaeffer wrote, "a temple built unto the Lord upon the mountain top, attracting the notice of the people in all directions." It was a highly visible symbol of how far Montgomery County's African American community had come in the twenty years since slavery ended in the county.[37]

Black churches did not simply get bigger; they also developed auxiliary elements that broadened and strengthened their role in the African American community. Baptists, for example, were very active in the temperance/ prohibition movement. Within five years of its founding, the Colored Valley Baptist Association passed a resolution calling for "a Temperance Society in the bounds of every Church," and a number of congregations in Montgomery County responded by establishing organizations such as the Blue Ribbon Club in Christiansburg to support the passage of local temperance laws. In 1886, members of the Christiansburg club marched en masse from the church to the polls under banners proclaiming their cause and helped to pass a ban on alcohol in the county. The precise function of other church-related entities is less clear. Christiansburg Baptists also organized the Christian Union of the African Baptist Church in 1869, while Baptist women in Alleghany Springs organized the Sisters' Society, and members of the AME Church in Blacksburg organized the Good Samaritan Society. Exactly what any of these did remains a mystery, but each provided another thread linking the county's African American residents to one another and to a visible African American community. Black churches were also the first to establish cemeteries, other than family or plantation plots, open to African Americans. Most residents of the county, both black and white, still buried their dead in family plots, but between 1870 and 1900 black churches in Christiansburg, Big Spring, Shawsville, Lovely Mount, Brush Creek, and Rough and Ready each established a cemetery in which its members could remain together for eternity.[38]

Churches were not the only institutions by which African Americans in Montgomery County demonstrated their membership in a community larger than that of their families. As noted in chapter 1, black men in Christiansburg organized St. John's Lodge No. 35 of the Prince Hall Free and Accepted Masons in 1877; by 1891 men and women in town had established Zion Sons & Daughters Tabernacle No. 89 of the Grand United Order of Galilean Fishermen; and the opening years of the twentieth century saw lodges of the Independent Order of Odd Fellows operating in Blacksburg, Christiansburg, and, reportedly, Big Spring.[39] Churches were, however, the most visible element contributing to African Americans' sense of identity and purpose as a distinct community in postwar Montgomery County. They provided venues in which community members regularly gathered to socialize, to organize, to recognize their commonalities, and to provide one another moral, spiritual, emotional, and material support. And increasingly, they did so under African American leadership. Black ministers were among the most visible, best-known, and most respected members of the African American community in Montgomery County. They provided both formal and informal leadership for that community as it adjusted to the new world emerging during the critical years following the abolition of slavery, and their leadership was especially important because of the continuing challenges confronting the emergence of significant black political leadership in the county during those years.

6 GOVERNMENT AND POLITICS

IN THE SPRING OF 1879, Alexander Hopkins made history. In declaring himself a candidate for the office of Commissioner of the Revenue, Hopkins became the first African American to stand for election in Montgomery County since the end of military rule in Virginia. A native of the county, Hopkins had been born in 1842 at Kentland, the plantation of James R. Kent, and remained a slave there until April 1865. As a slave, Hopkins evidently worked as farmhand and continued doing so as a freedman, identifying himself on the 1866 cohabitation register as a "farmer" and on the 1870 federal census as a "farm laborer." By the spring of 1870, however, he was also teaching at the Lovely Mount school, one of those supported by the Friends' Freedmen's Association, and continued teaching in the county's new public school system until at least 1880. By 1870, Hopkins also belonged to the Lovely Mount Baptist Church. He was more than member, though; he represented the church at that year's meeting of the Colored Valley Baptist Association and soon became a leader among the county's Baptists too. By 1872 he was licensed to preach and was attending the Wayland Seminary, in Washington, D.C., to train for the ministry. Two years later he was serving as minister at the Alleghany Springs Baptist Church. During the 1870s, he also served Baptist congregations in Blacksburg and Wake Forest and by 1879 had become a familiar and trusted figure among the county's African American residents.[1]

Still, it was a huge step for any black man—however familiar or trusted he might have been in his own community—to stand for election to public office in Montgomery County at that time. Men like Hopkins had only been voting in the county for a little over a decade, and no man of color had ever held public office in the county. Indeed, only one is known ever to have run for office before Hopkins, and Minnis Headen had done it when federal troops were still available to protect him if necessary. Hopkins's decision to run was noteworthy enough to merit mention in the local newspaper, which rarely noted anything in the county's black community other than arrests. On May 2, 1879, the *Messenger*'s "Local Department" included a brief announcement entitled "Negro Candidate." The article neither endorsed nor criticized Hopkins; it simply informed the paper's readers that "Alex Hopkins, a colored school teacher has announced himself a candidate for Commissioner of Revenue, so we learn." Three weeks later, it was equally matter of fact in announcing results of the election. Hopkins's name and the number of votes he had received in each precinct were reported without comment just like those of the seven other, white, candidates. Alexander Hopkins did not win, but he did receive 329 votes and finished a respectable fourth in a contest in which the top two candidates were elected. Despite his creditable showing in the election that year, Hopkins seems never to have tried again, though he apparently remained active in county politics until at least 1889, three years before his death.[2]

Alexander Hopkins's run for office, public reaction to it, and the outcome of the voting were all parts of the evolving experience of African Americans in Montgomery County following the abolition of slavery. Like other aspects of African American life in the county, the relationship between African Americans and their local government and the place of African Americans in county politics underwent a series of changes, and these changes were not confined to the era traditionally defined as Reconstruction. They began in the decade immediately after the Civil War but continued to unfold through the beginning of the twentieth century. Sometimes things changed for the better, and sometimes they changed for the worse, but one fact remained constant: African Americans were part of the body politic, and their voices would be heard. As William Blair wrote of freedpeople's political experience during Reconstruction, "Freedpeople ensured a more complex dynamic as they employed a range of techniques to pressure authorities to live up at least partially to stated ideals."[3] By 1902, freedpeople in Montgomery County had certainly not gained full political or civic equality, but they had helped bring about movement in that direction. Some of the advances they made proved temporary and were partially or entirely reversed by the early twentieth century, but even these helped demonstrate to both black and white residents of the county what was possible and helped to establish a new normal from which to resume the process in later years.

Immediately after the collapse of the Confederacy, little changed in the government of Montgomery County. While federal troops occupied many parts of Virginia when the war ended or soon after its conclusion, none reached Montgomery County for almost three months. Local authority there remained entirely in the hands of officials elected or appointed under Virginia's Confederate government, and they continued to act as if nothing had changed when that government fell. In Christiansburg, the clerk of the court's office was functioning normally by April 20, 1865, and the county court opened its regular monthly meeting on May 1. And when they met, members of the court showed little change in their attitudes or behavior toward the county's African American residents. At their May session, justices ordered the formation of patrols in each district "for the purpose of suppressing riots and preventing lawless depredations"—as they often had during and before the war—and opened criminal proceedings against "'John,' a slave the property of William Pearl and 'Major,' a slave the property of William Byers."[4]

The structure of county politics finally began to change modestly in July, though its actions did not. In July, Captain Buel C. Carter arrived to administer Virginia's Eighth District of the Freedmen's Bureau. The bureau's original mandate was both broad and vague: "the control of all subjects relating to refugees and freedmen from rebel states." What that meant in practice, however, was often quite constrained. Agents could provide food, fuel, and clothing to freedpeople, but only to those in extreme need, and travel assistance to reunite families, but only to those deemed truly destitute by the agents. Efforts to guarantee the legal and civil rights of freedpeople were equally constrained. Agents tried to ensure that black workers were paid what they were due and that freedpeople were not killed or assaulted, but in Montgomery County the Freedmen's Bureau had no apparatus for independently enforcing its will. Civil government had never ceased to operate in this part of Virginia, so the bureau operated through that government. Moreover, bureau personnel could only protect those rights existing under current state laws, as neither the Fourteenth nor the Fifteenth amendment had yet been passed. They could not insist that freedpeople enjoy any additional rights or privileges beyond those provided by state laws and constitutions. The Freedmen's Bureau could not force local officials to enfranchise freedmen, place them on juries, or permit them to testify in all legal proceedings. To do so would have infringed on the authority of state government in ways that most Americans, including many of those in Congress who voted to establish the Freedmen's Bureau, would not tolerate.[5]

Captain Carter did order new elections for the county court, but they changed little. Freedmen could not participate in the voting, and almost half the incumbent justices were reelected. When the new court assembled in August, justices and other county officials did take oaths to support the Constitution of the United States and "the government of Virginia as restored by the convention which assembled at Wheeling on the 11th day of June 1861," but they then ignored Governor Pierpont's declaration that men who had served as local officials under the Confederate government were ineligible to serve in the restored county administrations. No one in Christiansburg seems even to have noted the declaration. In August 1865, the county court's order book did, for the first time, describe African Americans as "former slaves," but otherwise county government seems to have gone on much as it had before.[6]

The most significant arena in which freedpeople interacted with that government was the legal system. As Dylan Penningroth has pointed out, "For the first time in American history, ex-slaves had legal rights and could defend their property and family ties in court." The courtroom, however, was an arena in which black faces and black voices remained rare, and, initially at least, freedpeople remained highly vulnerable to abuse and exploitation by their white neighbors. This vulnerability was particularly evident when freedpeople were the victims of white abuse. Grand juries and magistrates, the two routes by which an individual could be indicted, were entirely in white hands still, so freedpeople with complaints against whites often found it difficult or impossible to obtain judicial relief. William Blair has described this as one of the greatest injustices facing freedpeople in Virginia, and it was, no doubt, one of the reasons that those in Montgomery County often turned to the Freedmen's Bureau for assistance during the first year of Reconstruction. Between August 1865 and January 1866, more than twenty of the county's freedmen and freedwomen filed complaints with the bureau after being cheated or abused by whites. Nine freedmen working for James R. Kent, for example, complained that "since he has got most of his work done he has ordered them to leave & will not pay them." Others, especially women, complained of physical abuse against themselves or their children. Pocahontas Dill, for example, alleged that Henry Fowlkes "struck her repeatedly," while Millie Clark complained that Fowlkes had whipped her daughter. The district's register of complaints ends in January 1866, but it is clear that freedpeople continued to face limited access to the courts at least through the middle of 1866; during his first two months in Christiansburg, Charles Schaeffer wrote at least twice to county magistrates about their refusal to honor requests for warrants from African Americans.[7]

By then, however, the Freedmen's Bureau was gaining what appears to have been a moderately effective alternative that could bypass the county court if necessary. Originally, freedpeople with complaints against whites who assaulted them, cheated them, or otherwise violated their rights or property could only register their complaint with the local agent. The agent might then contact the alleged offender and order him or her to appear and explain the situation to the agent, but in Montgomery County, at least, it is unclear that this ever happened. In July 1866, shortly after Schaeffer arrived, Congress extended and expanded the mandate of the Freedmen's Bureau and gave it the power to establish its own courts to hear cases involving the rights of freedpeople. Now Schaeffer backed his letters with the threat of legal action. In the months that followed, he wrote frequently to whites accused of assaulting freedpeople, threatening them, cheating them, evicting them, or otherwise abusing their rights and ordered them to the recognize the rights of freedpeople or face legal action. In August 1866, for example, he wrote to James Wilson, who was trying to evict George and Sarah Russell, to insist that Wilson follow proper legal procedures—giving the couple notice, in writing, and securing a verdict in his favor from the county court before moving to evict them. "Unless you proceed regularly according to the law," warned Schaeffer, "you are liable to be prosecuted for trespass, and to pay the full amount of damages which may result from it." On the bottom of the letter book copy he later wrote: "These instructions had the desired effect." This may not have been the ideal to which Schaeffer aspired, but it was often effective.[8]

Of course, freedpeople were also vulnerable to whites bringing charges against them and using the courts to harass and intimidate them. Robert Preston, for example, used the courts in an extended campaign against Thomas and Othello Fraction, freedmen he clearly saw as a threat to his own authority. Preston belonged to the most socially and politically powerful family in the county. As the son of a governor and a colonel in the militia and the Confederate army, he clearly believed that he was entitled to respect and a position of unquestioned authority. Thomas and Othello Fraction, on the other hand, were brothers whose extended family had long been enslaved by the Preston family. They had escaped during the war and joined the Union army, and Thomas had risen to the rank of sergeant in the Fortieth US Colored Infantry. After the brothers' escape, Preston let it be known that he would shoot them if they ever returned, and when Thomas Fraction learned of Preston's threat he felt obliged to respond that "they would not quietly submit to be fired upon." In February 1866 the brothers came back on furlough to visit their father, who still lived on Preston's land, and when Preston learned of their return, he gathered a number of family and friends and went looking for the Fractions "to do them bodily harm." Preston confronted the brothers outside their father's home, and when they defended themselves, he had them arrested. After several months in jail, however, they were released on orders from the military, which investigated the incident and took no action against either party.[9]

Later that year the brothers mustered out of the army and returned to live near their father in Montgomery County. When they did, Preston resumed his vendetta. As described in chapter 5, he confronted the Fractions when they attempted to enter the Methodist church in Blacksburg and threatened to shoot them if they tried it again. He also campaigned to have them "convicted and sent to the penitentiary" for defending themselves during their February confrontation with Preston and his friends. In September, a grand jury in Montgomery County handed down presentments against Thomas and Othello Fraction for attempted murder, and early in 1867 they were arrested and bound over for trial. Initially, they were also denied bail because, according to Schaeffer, the magistrate hearing their request was afraid to offend Preston. After two weeks in jail, however, they were released when a white neighbor was allowed to post bond for them. When their cases finally came to trial, in May, the charges were immediately dropped on the grounds that the military had already tried the case. After two failed attempts, Robert Preston seems to have given up trying to have the Fractions sent to prison, but that may simply have been because both brothers left the county soon after their second legal skirmish with him.[10]

The Fraction case clearly shows the ability of powerful white men in Montgomery County to use the legal system in an effort to intimidate freedpeople, even if they did not put them in prison. It also shows, as William Blair has argued, that even when freedpeople were not convicted, they often faced real injury at the hands of the legal system. Freedmen held without bail pending trial, for example, could not contribute to their families' support, which could lead to severe hardship. In Montgomery County, freedpeople were generally able to post bonds and avoid confinement while awaiting trial, but the danger was still quite real, as the Fractions' case demonstrated. When the brothers were arrested for the second time, delays in their initial examination threatened to postpone their trial for months "while their families are suffering, and their employers deprived of their labor."[11]

Arbitrary arrest and confinement were not the only legal abuses to which freedpeople were exposed. White county residents and officials also ignored basic legal rights of freedpeople, such as the necessity to secure proper warrants before searching their homes. It is impossible to say how often this occurred, but between June 1866 and February 1867, Schaeffer intervened in at least two cases of "illegal searching . . . of the premises of colored people in this county." One of these may have been a case of private citizens conducting a search, but at least one involved a magistrate. In June 1866, Schaeffer reprimanded a justice in Central Depot who had authorized an employer to search the homes of four freedmen when he had "no lawful authority to do so."[12]

Judicial proceedings were not the only contact between African Americans and local government in Montgomery County. Freedpeople also interacted with public officials in other contexts, and here too their experiences were mixed. This was certainly the case when it came to the official recognition of African American marriages. The register of marriages was the public record of who was legally married in the county, and registration could affect the legitimacy of one's children and the disposition of one's estate. Recording legal marriages was one of the duties of the clerk of the court, but until the final quarter of 1866, the clerk in Montgomery County often refused or neglected to record the marriages of freedpeople and, as a result, left them in legal limbo. Early in September 1865, Oscar Johnson and Nancy Duke became the first African American couple in Montgomery County known to have received an official license to marry. At least five black couples had married in the county since April of that year, but none of them had obtained a license to do so. Unfortunately, it is impossible to say whether or not any of those earlier couples had asked for a license and been denied one, so the fact Johnson and Duke obtained a license might or might not indicate a change in government relations with freedpeople. Even if it did represent a change in the official view, though, it did not mean that freedpeople were suddenly treated equally in even this one small way. After the wedding, the presiding minister completed his return, certifying that the marriage had taken place, but it was never entered in the register of marriages, as required by law. This could only have happened because the clerk of the court did not enter it. At least nine more black couples married before the end of 1865, and in at least two of these nine cases the couple obtained a license but their marriages were never recorded. Clearly, county officials were still coming to grips with the reality of black citizenship.[13]

Not until late 1866 did county officials fully accept their duty to record the marriages of freedpeople. Beginning in January of that year, black couples regularly began to secure licenses and ministers submitted their returns, but no black marriages were registered until September. Only in early September did the clerk begin to register the marriages of freedpeople fairly consistently, and not until December did he finally go back and register black marriages that had been licensed and performed between January and August. According to a marginal note in the register, these marriages had initially been "omitted" and were now, finally, entered. Officials of the Freedmen's Bureau often voiced concern about freedpeople's morality and their disregard for the sanctity of marriage. Late in 1867, for example, Charles Schaeffer complained to his superiors in Richmond that it was "a difficult matter to get the colored people to fully understand the binding obligation of their pledges to each other." Certainly some freedmen and freedwomen did ignore their marriage vows, but the record in Montgomery County shows that white officials often made it difficult for freedpeople to secure full legal recognition of those vows.[14]

The county was equally reluctant to consider freedpeople citizens when it came to poor relief. Like much of Virginia, Montgomery County offered only limited relief to its indigent citizens. It maintained a poorhouse, in which a modest number of children, the elderly, and invalids could be accommodated, and it provided "outdoor relief" in the form of reimbursement to those who cared for invalids in their homes. When Schaeffer arrived in Christiansburg to assume his duties as assistant superintendent of the Freedmen's Bureau, in May 1866, he initially reported that public officials there were caring for the county's poor "irrespective of color." Within three months, however, he learned from his own investigation that he had been "misinformed." According to Schaeffer, the president of the county's Overseers of the Poor had issued instructions "to pay no attention to the claims of indigent colored people." "Freedpeople were not to be supported in any way by that board of civil officers," the president had reportedly declared. As a result, according to Schaeffer, "there is no provision made whatever for the maintenance of the infirm indigent Freedmen."[15]

This certainly offended Schaeffer's sense of decency and his view of the rights of freedpeople, but it also threatened the budget of his office. Almost as soon as slavery had ended in the county, local planters had begun seeking to free themselves of the responsibility to care for elderly or disabled freedpeople who had been their slaves. The Freedmen's Bureau, however, was unwilling to assume the cost of caring for such people. It would provide only temporary relief—"to prevent starvation"—and expected public officials to accommodate freedpeople through the existing system. Having learned the real situation in Montgomery County, Schaeffer sent "a respectful communication" to the president of the Overseers of the Poor reminding him of the county's obligation. The president ignored Schaeffer's letter. Within a month, however, he had resigned, and his successor then took steps to modify the overseers' policy. By September 1866, Schaeffer could report that county officials really were caring for the poor "irrespective of race," and he repeated the claim in later reports. Other evidence confirms that by 1867 citizens caring for elderly or invalid freedpeople were receiving compensation from the county and that the county was paying medical and burial expenses for at least some indigent blacks. It is not clear if freedpeople entered the poorhouse that early, but they certainly had by the summer of 1868.[16]

County officials were much more willing to embrace equality when it came to freedmen meeting their obligations to the state. In this regard, if no other, they were often color-blind. They had no intention, for example, of excluding freedman from the tax rolls, and in October 1865 the county court ordered the Commissioners of the Revenue "to take a list of all the male tithables (white & black) in this county from 16 years and upwards." They did not, however, discriminate between black and white taxpayers. Throughout the 1850s, free men of color between the ages of twenty-one and fifty-five had paid a special "Free Negro tax" to support Liberian colonization. That had ended in 1861, and no such distinction appeared in the postemancipation tax regime. Freedmen were required to pay land taxes, personal property taxes, and a capitation tax, but the rates they paid were identical to those paid by white men. Public officials were also quick to add freedmen to the pool of labor used to maintain roads in the county. Montgomery County was divided into dozens of road districts with a supervisor for each, and district supervisors were responsible for summoning men to maintain or build roads as a form of public service. In one way, this system perpetuated the mentality of the plantation; calls often ordered a landowner, almost always white at this time, to appear with "his hands," many of whom were, no doubt, freedmen. In another way, however, roadwork was sometimes color-blind. In 1866, for example, twenty-seven individual white men and three black men were ordered to maintain Center Street in Christiansburg. All of the freedmen were identified as "Col^d" and two by only their first name and that of their employer (e.g., "Anthony (Col^d) at Pugh's"), but in theory each of the men named was subject to the same expectations. Unfortunately, what actually happened on Center Street remains a mystery. Did black and white men work side by side? Did the freedmen do more work or harder work? It is impossible to say.[17]

Relations between freedpeople in Montgomery County and their government changed fundamentally in 1867 when Congress passed the Reconstruction Acts. Under the first of these acts, Virginia and most other "Rebel States" came under military authority until their citizens approved new state constitutions in which the right to vote was not restricted on the basis of race or previous condition of servitude and until they ratified the proposed Fourteenth Amendment to the US Constitution. Moreover, voting for delegates to the state conventions that would act on these requirements was to be open to any man, regardless of race, who had not been disenfranchised for "participation in the rebellion." And until Virginia met these requirements, all levels of government in the state were considered "provisional" and subject to "the paramount authority of the United States" to alter, abolish, or control them at any time. After nearly two years of working within the confines of Virginia law, federal officials had the authority to make radical changes in the status quo, beginning with the franchise.[18]

Military officials in Richmond immediately issued orders directing local agents of the Freedmen's Bureau "[to] inform all Freedmen entitled to be registered, of the necessity for, and the time and place of registration, and of the time and place of voting" and laying out the process by which registration was to be carried out. Charles Schaeffer, president of

Montgomery County's Board of Registration, and C. A. Chipley, its registrar, then traveled to each of the county's four magisterial districts and with the registering officer of the district constituted a board to identify and register eligible voters living in that district. All of the board members were white, but six eligible voters in each district—three black and three white—were appointed to challenge men who might not meet the requirements to vote. White residents may not have welcomed the idea of freedmen registering to vote and participating in the process of approving voters, but they saw this as the lesser of several possible evils. Waller Staples, a prominent Christiansburg attorney and former member of the Confederate Congress, pointed out in a letter to the *Southwest* that previous opposition to the proposed Fourteenth Amendment had led to "the more exacting laws now presented" and continued opposition to the Reconstruction Acts might lead to "confiscation and perhaps worse." For this reason, he urged county residents to accept the registration of black voters as "the only means of restoring peace and tranquility." It is impossible to say how widely Staples's view was shared in the county, but the registration of freedmen there did proceed smoothly. "I do not know of a single instance where they were deterred from registering as voters," Schaeffer declared, and by the end of June he was able to report that "every effort has been made to circulate among them necessary information, and I feel fully persuaded that most if not all the males over 21 years of age, will be found enrolled upon the lists prepared by the Boards of Registration."[19]

Schaeffer proved quite accurate in his estimate. Freedmen in the county responded enthusiastically to the opportunity to register as voters, and 566 had done so by the end of October. It is unclear exactly how many eligible freedmen there were in the county at the time, but 566 was certainly a very high percentage of that total. A census taken earlier that year found 522 African American men aged twenty-one years or older, and the 1870 census found approximately 600; thus, the 566 registered black voters in October 1867 probably did represent, as Schaeffer had predicted, "most if not all the males over 21 years of age." This also meant that in 1867 freedmen in Montgomery County were slightly overrepresented in the county's electorate. African Americans made up a little less than 23 percent of the county's 1870 population, but they made up nearly 27 percent of registered voters in the fall of 1867. This may have been the result of some white men in the county having been barred from registering due to their "participation in the rebellion," but it does not change the fact that when freedmen in Montgomery County were finally afforded the opportunity to gain a key attribute of freedom, they seized it with both hands.[20]

While the registration of black voters in Montgomery County proceeded with relatively few problems, voting was another matter. In addition to ordering the registration of black voters, military authorities in Richmond also called for elections to a convention that was to draft a new state constitution. The prospect of freedmen actually voting and of voting independently proved far more unsettling to the county's white residents. Adding to the anxiety was a concern among whites that their vote might fracture along class lines or on the basis of wartime allegiances. Such divisions were quite common in the Appalachian South after the Civil War, and Captain William P. Austin, who was then responsible for the Freedmen's Bureau district in which Montgomery County was located, wrote that lingering wartime divisions among white residents of the district still resonated. During the war, he reported, "Poor Whites" had often supported the Union and been persecuted for their loyalty. "Since the war," he continued, "they are treated with the utmost contempt . . . and every effort is made to prevent the Blacks from uniting with them." According to Austin,

> The interests of these are one and the same. They both want such laws as will give equal rights, to all. They both want free schools, and an equitable system of taxation they want the way clear to improvement, wealth, & prosperity. And if they unite they will be greatly benefited. . . . If the Unionists and the Freedmen cooperate they can hardly fail, of having their interests represented in future legislative assemblies so as to secure for them better enjoyment of their rights and privileges than they can expect, if they do not cooperate.

The result, he observed, was that "the Anti-Union Elements are determined either by fair means or by unfair to bring the blacks over to vote with them so as to assure the control of affairs."[21]

Voting for delegates to the convention was scheduled for late October, and in the months preceding the election it became increasingly clear to many whites in the county that they would not be able to control black voters. Freedmen in Montgomery County were not just registering to vote, they were *organizing,* and they were organizing to advance *their* interests in opposition to those of white voters. "They appear to have no faith or confidence in the teachings of those who have heretofore been their oppressors," observed Austin, "while the greatest confidence is placed in the teachings of those to whom they look as the authors of their liberty and the defenders of their rights."[22] The most visible symbol of this independent black political activity in Montgomery County was the Union League, part of a national network established to support the federal government and the Republican Party. In May 1867, a black organizer named F. A. Brown arrived from Baltimore to make the case for the Union League in Montgomery County. Speaking to a racially mixed audience at the courthouse in Christiansburg, Brown called on freedpeople to unite behind the Republican Party "for the furtherance of the cause of freedom, and to obtain for themselves their just rights under the law." He also urged them to join the Union League. According to Schaeffer, some three hundred people joined the Union League chapter organized after Brown's speech, and whites in the county immediately saw this as a serious threat to their control. The *Southwest,* for example, claimed that members of the Union League deliberately misled freedmen into believing the Republican Party advocated the confiscation and redistribution of white-owned land: "These men talk to simple-minded negroes about a division of land and thus keep them in a constant state of excitement and idleness." In response, white landowners began using their economic position to punish freedmen who joined the Union League.[23]

Leading the campaign to intimidate black voters, Schaeffer thought, was Waller Preston, a nephew of the Fractions' nemesis, Robert T. Preston. Daniel Crawford, a freedman, had a contract to work for Waller Preston for all of 1867, but in early June he appeared in Schaeffer's office to report that he had been "dismissed . . . for having on the Saturday previous, connected himself with the Union League." Schaeffer reported Crawford's dismissal to his commander in Wytheville, who passed the report on to his superiors in Richmond. Within days the office of the judge advocate there responded that, under the commanding general's orders, "for the purpose of protecting individuals in their rights and property," Preston's actions "present a proper claim for breach of contract," and Schaeffer should seek damages on behalf of Daniel Crawford. Schaeffer first ordered Preston to appear before him for "an investigation of the facts." When Preston failed to appear, and through a third party allegedly declared "that he would not report to no D——Yankee" and that Schaeffer "might go to H—— and K—— his A——," he was ordered to appear before Schaeffer in the latter's role as military commissioner. There Preston was found guilty of discharging

Crawford "on account of political opinion," ordered to pay Crawford damages, and required to post a bond of $500 "not to interfere with col^d citizens for joining the Union League." Within a month, though, Preston had resumed his efforts to intimidate freedmen. When he caught two black children trespassing on his land, he whipped them because their father, Taylor McNorton, had joined the league. He also refused to mill corn for another freedman, Andrew Oliver, "who previous to his joining the Union League was on the best of terms with said Preston." In each of these cases Preston was also ordered to pay damages and in that of McNorton to post bond to keep the peace. It is unclear that he ever did.[24]

Despite the actions of men such as Preston, freedmen in Montgomery County remained politically active during the months preceding the election of delegates to the constitutional convention. They continued to join the Union League and, according to Schaeffer, "seem[ed] to take a great interest in the politics of the country." Moreover, they remained solidly Republican. A month before the election Schaeffer reported, "The colored men are almost a unit in sustaining the National Republican nominee for the state convention." Part of the Republicans' appeal to freedmen in Montgomery County was, undoubtedly, the national party's connection to the Union, to emancipation, and to Radical Reconstruction. But their local candidate, Adam Flanagan, probably also appealed to African Americans in the county. Flanagan seems never to have owned slaves, and though he voted for secession in the 1861 referendum and served in the home guard in 1863, he was widely reported to have been loyal to the Union during the war and to have deserted the home guard and fled to the Union-controlled Kanawha Valley in order to avoid service in the regular Confederate army. More recently, in 1866, he had named his new son Ulyses G. Flanagan and seven months before the election had offered freedpeople in his neighborhood a building in which to establish a school for their children.[25]

The election itself went relatively smoothly. Schaeffer did report two "disturbances" in the county, but only one of these had racial overtones, and it does not seem to have influenced the voting. According to Schaeffer, "a disturbance of the peace occurred at Christiansburg between white and colored, which for a short time had the appearance of a general riot, but was promptly suppressed by the power invested in me as Military Commissioner." Otherwise, voting in the county seems to have gone smoothly and quietly, and freedmen demonstrated both their eagerness to participate and their strong support for the Republican candidate. Of the 566 freedmen registered to vote in Montgomery County, 506 cast votes. This was the first time in the county's history that nonwhites had been eligible to vote, and few freedmen missed the opportunity to demonstrate publicly their new political status. Turnout among black voters in the county was almost 90 percent and far exceeded the figure of just under 66 percent recorded among white voters. African Americans' support for the Republican candidate was even more overwhelming than their turnout; of the 506 freedmen who cast votes, 504 voted Republican. Freedmen did not, however, decide the election in Montgomery County. White men represented a significant majority of voters in the county that fall, and as Captain Austin had noted, they were still divided by class and wartime allegiance. In fact, a majority of Montgomery County's white voters (626 out of 1,011) also voted for the Republican candidate.[26]

The election may have gone smoothly, but it was soon followed by increased resentment among conservatives in the county's the white community. Just days after the election, Schaeffer noted:

> Very generally, the whites are not on as good terms with the Freedmen as represented in former reports. This is the result of large numbers of the Freedmen having connected themselves with the Union League, and voting for the Republican candidate for the convention. I have received Information from numerous sources that there will be a general dismissal from service, at the termination of the present contract year. Parties who now have Freedmen in their employ, who politically are in opposition to what they term their interests, will discharge them immediately on the termination of their present term of service—and further have concluded not to employ or hire, in future any colored man, who is opposed to them politically.

Indeed, Schaeffer believed that only the threat of "military interposition" had prevented "a general dismissal" of African American workers immediately after the election. For the time being, he remained confident that he could deal with the threat by holding employers to the contracts they had negotiated for 1867. When those contracts expired, however, he had heard from several sources there would be a widespread dismissal of freedmen and an effort to replace them with white workers. There was, he noted, "a deep seated, bitter and intense hatred toward the colored man with the open declaration, that in the future, his place is to be occupied by white men."27

Among freedpeople, reported Schaeffer, there was "considerable anxiety" about the economic threat facing them. More worrisome to Schaeffer, though, was the danger that the increasingly angry rhetoric would lead to violence: "The united action of the Freedmen at the recent election, in supporting the Republican candidate, in opposition to what was announced as the *white man's candidate* has had the effect to bring down upon their heads the wrath, indignation and mistrust of many of those who were in sympathy with the conservative movement, and which eventually I fear will lead to serious complications and perhaps end in blood." Schaeffer declared repeatedly and emphatically during the fall that freedmen in the county were giving "no cause for offense" and were certainly not contemplating violence. Nevertheless, he reported that whites had begun spreading rumors of freedmen "preparing for actual conflict, by securing arms & ammunition and combining together—for the overthrow of the whites." The *Southwest,* wrote Schaeffer, had even published a call to whites in the county to respond to the threat: "Arm yourselves and your families 'to the teeth' that you may be prepared for the worst. Be vigilant and the complete extermination of their race will be the result of an uprising of the ungrateful, fiendish Blacks."28

Racial tension in Montgomery County continued to rise during the winter and spring of 1868 as the state convention drafted and then released a proposed constitution that would grant African American men the right to vote and serve on juries for the first time while disenfranchising many former Confederate military and political figures. In Christiansburg, the *Southwest* denounced this "Mongrel Constitution": "See how it tramples upon the white man, and elevates the black! Can white men of common decency hesitate longer to rally with the 'WHITE MAN'S PARTY' and work with might and main for the defeat of this infamous instrument, that the blessed land of our nativity may be rescued from ignorant negroes and contemptible scoundrels and traitors." The paper also printed the full text of the draft constitution in order to "[expose] the glaring imperfections and impurities of this infamous instrument and to insure its rejection by the intelligent people of Montgomery and the other counties through which the Southwest circulates." Potential voters in the county, both black and white, then spent several months debating the draft in anticipation of a referendum on its adoption scheduled for later that year, and with these debates came increased pressure on freedmen to "renounce their present political sentiments."[29]

Economically, the threat to dismiss black workers entirely quickly evaporated. As William Cohen has noted, white employers in many parts of the South might have longed to replace black workers with white, but it was simply not practical. Economic pressure did continue, however, through the winter and spring of 1868. According to Schaeffer, white landowners in Montgomery County hoped to intimidate freedmen into voting against the proposed constitution by refusing them long-term employment until after the referendum. "There seems to be a disposition on the part of the whites not to enter into written contract with these people, until after the Election," he noted in January, "hoping thereby to influence their vote." Two months later he warned, "Their object no doubt is to control as far as possible, their vote at the coming election—either by expulsion from their service, if they do not vote to suit them, or through liberal offers of steady employment and prompt pay, in cases where they comply with the wishes of their Employers." Finally, with the draft constitution circulating and public attention turning to the referendum, Schaeffer declared, "Every effort possible is now being made to influence their vote against the adoption of the Constitution recently framed by the convention." Indeed, he was convinced that "quite a number of freedmen" in the county had already been discharged on account of their "political sentiments" and was frustrated that he could not prove it: "In every case it has been made to appear, that some other cause than those of a political nature has led to their expulsion . . . and although we feel confident, that it was on account of their political sentiments, yet no direct proof could be brought to bear, to establish the fact."[30]

The spring of 1868 and the debate over the proposed constitution also saw the only reports during the Reconstruction era of Ku Klux Klan activity in Montgomery County. Most of this activity was in print. Members of the Klan or their supporters posted handbills around the county announcing meetings that may or may not have actually taken place. Meanwhile, the *Southwest* printed a poem entitled "Death's Brigade," which described the vengeance of "the pale Brigade" and in which every stanza ended with "Ku-Klux." It also published articles lauding the Klan and calling on its members to reverse "the demoralizing effects of the late war." Reports of actual Klan activity, however, were rare. The Freedmen's Bureau did report some activity in Roanoke County, just east of Montgomery, but the only evidence from Montgomery County appears in a letter from Blacksburg printed in the *Southwest*. It detailed an April incident in which three black men were reportedly lured to a cemetery outside of town by a strange light and startled when "several white robed objects, with lights extended, slowly rose, amid the most dreadful moans and ratling of bones, to the height of fifteen feet." The startled men escaped, and no other action by the Klan was reported in the county. In the end, Schaeffer noted, "Some have been intimidated and afraid to attend their religious meetings and other gatherings, but most of them consider it only a scare and act accordingly."[31]

Neither economic pressure nor Ku Klux Klan activity deterred African Americans in Montgomery County from continued public support of the Republican Party and of the proposed state constitution. Schaeffer reported at the end of April that "the mass of the colored people seem to stand firm to the principles of the republican party," and just three days later many of them attended a meeting in Christiansburg of county Republicans. There they joined in adopting a public statement asserting that all men were entitled to "equality of all rights, civil and political" and endorsing "all measures instituted, or enacted by Congress, either for the expergation of official abuses, the punishment of political offenses or the radical reconstruction of, and future peaceful preservation of the Union." An unknown number of freedmen also served on a mixed-race committee that nominated county delegates to the Republicans' state nominating convention. Reportedly, black Republicans also took steps that day to ease the worst fears of Conservatives in the county. They had already shown some restraint in response to white concerns; according to Schaeffer, they had refused for this reason to celebrate publicly after Adam Flanagan's election to the constitutional convention. Now, according to the *Southwest*, "the colored people of Montgomery county" adopted a resolution in response to Conservative claims that they sought "political supremacy." If the paper's report is accurate, African Americans at the rally acknowledged that "we, in our present uneducated condition are incompetent to discharge the duties devolving upon persons holding high and important trusts" and called for the election of "intelligent and educated men who will faithfully represent us and our interest." They did not, of course, suggest a willingness to forgo political office permanently but may have hoped that white fears would ease in the future.[32]

Two days later, Conservatives in the county held their own "Grand Rally of White Men" and over the course of the summer speakers denounced radicalism, Republicans, and the proposed constitution. They and editors of the *Southwest* continued their campaign to convince white residents of the county that the fate of their community hung in the balance. "Let every White Man, who respects himself, his family or his State," proclaimed the *Southwest*, "register, and thereby arm himself with a vote to defeat Radicalism and Negro Supremacy." None of it, however, weakened African Americans' determination to bring about change. According to Schaeffer, the pressure simply made freedmen "more united," and he continued to assert that most African Americans in the county "will stand up to their Republican principles." In late July, just after a date was announced for the referendum on the proposed constitution, he reiterated the strength of freedmen's support for the convention's draft: "The colored people are anxious to secure for themselves, the advantages to be derived from its adoption, and also to show that they will not waver in what they conceive to be their duty, though it may cause them to suffer temporary loss, and bring down upon their heads, the wrath of those who are in opposition to Congressional reconstruction." In the end, though, neither side prevailed immediately. Shortly before the August date set for the referendum, General John M. Schofield, commander of Military District Number One, blocked it, and no vote on the constitution was held until July 1869, at which time a separate vote was held on the features most objectionable to Conservatives—a test oath and the ban on ex-Confederates voting. In the meantime, freedmen in Montgomery County would bide their time. Schaeffer reported in August that they wished "to remain quiet spectators of the contest, until the time shall come for them to act."[33]

When voting finally did take place, in July 1869, the new constitution was approved both statewide and in Montgomery County without the test oath or the disenfranchisement of former Confederates. Unfortunately, few records have survived of either the campaign or the voting in Montgomery County. There was, however, at least one episode in Christiansburg that suggests racial tension remained high. In a letter to her daughter, Mary Sullivan reported that six weeks before the election Governor Henry H. Wells came to Christiansburg and delivered a speech in which he urged freedmen "to let the plow rot in the furrow the grass forget to grow the grain rot in the field rather than be kept from the poles." Even worse, according to Sullivan, Wells told them, "If needs be whet there [*sic*] daggers and use them." Later that evening a black man reportedly struck Rice D.

Montague, a prominent political and legal figure in town. In response, "the white men and boys flew to his rescue with clubs and anything they could get in their hands and made the negroes fly."[34]

Adding to the tension that summer may have been the fact that for the first time in the county's history, the name of a black man appeared on the ballot: Minnis Headen was one of five candidates vying for a seat in the House of Delegates. Headen, a former slave about forty years old at the time, was a blacksmith living in Christiansburg. Two years earlier, Charles Schaeffer had described him as "one of the best colored men in the state" and placed him first on his list of freedmen in the county "in whom both races have confidence." Few whites, however, seem to have been willing to vote for him. In a letter to his sister, Arthur Sullivan complained that more than two hundred white men in the county had voted for Henry Wells, the Radical candidate for governor. If that number is accurate, then Wells must have received some 500 votes from freedmen, which suggests that Headen's 473 votes probably came exclusively from black voters. It was not enough to win, though, even with the white vote split four ways. Headen did finish second, but the African American population of Montgomery County was just too small to carry the day.[35]

Beyond voting, Military Reconstruction seems to have had a limited effect on the relationship between African Americans in Montgomery County and government there. It did not lead to freedpeople gaining any new rights other than the right to vote, though it did lead to their enjoying a bit more fully some of the rights they had already begun to enjoy by 1868. In terms of recognizing and recording marriages, levying taxes, and administering poor relief, county officials seem to have been treating African Americans as citizens by late 1867 and early 1868 and continued to do so under military supervision. Couples who married went through exactly the same steps, the age of consent was identical regardless of race, and black ministers were accepted by county officials and authorized to perform marriages. Tax rates were also identical, and by 1868 African Americans were not only receiving outdoor poor relief but were also admitted to the county poorhouse. It is certainly possible, indeed likely, that freedpeople in Montgomery County had a harder time securing public assistance than whites did, but they were eligible, and a number did receive it. It also seems that county officials may sometimes have tried to hold African American orphans to a different standard than whites. In October 1868, the county court ordered the Overseers of the Poor to bind Ann Spotts, an eight-year-old black girl, to Thomas D. Childress, a white man, until she turned twenty-one. Four months later, however, the court modified its order and directed the Overseers to bind Spotts "according to the law," which bound female orphans until age eighteen.[36]

Military Reconstruction also saw a growing number of African Americans participate in the judicial system. Some did so unwillingly, as defendants charged with crimes or liability for debts, but others came into court as plaintiffs. They came in cases pitting black against white as well as black against black. There were certainly still cases of blacks being charged with crimes against whites, most often theft or refusing to vacate a property, but there were also frequent instances in which one African American brought charges against another or in which the commonwealth charged one freedperson with an offense against another. There were also a number of instances in which whites were charged with theft or assault against blacks, and in one instance, it seems, a white man was indicted for raping a young African American woman. All of these scenarios occurred, but because criminal records are often incomplete and because the race of the contending parties cannot always be identified, it is impossible to say which variants were most common.[37]

While African Americans' experience in Montgomery County's judicial system did improve somewhat under Military Reconstruction, it remained far from perfect. There were still no black justices or attorneys, blacks were still excluded from juries, and though freedmen did appear as witnesses, surviving records are too fragmentary to say with certainty that they did or did not appear as witnesses in cases in which neither the plaintiff nor the defendant was black. Many freedmen did, at least, have adequate legal representation when they went to court. Nothing suggests that white lawyers were unwilling to accept black clients if the latter could afford to retain them, and in a number of cases the county provided attorneys—including some of the most respected practitioners in the county—for freedmen who could not afford one themselves. And the results of legal actions followed no particular pattern. African American parties sometimes won and sometimes lost, regardless of the other parties' race, and if they appealed, as some did, some won their appeals and some did not. Racial differences may have surfaced in sentencing, however. When Monroe Wilson (or Calloway) was convicted of horse theft, for example, Schaeffer complained to his superiors that because Wilson was an accomplice rather than the principal, the twelve-year sentence he received was "too severe."

He was told, however, he could do nothing about it because the trial had been "fair and impartial." Schaeffer also worried that cases brought by black plaintiffs often dragged out longer than they should have; cases were continued, he wrote, "from one week to another, and from one term of the court to another, causing loss of time and expenses to those who have not the time or money to prosecute properly their cause."[38]

Modest as these changes were under Military Reconstruction, even they were still superficial. Whites in Montgomery County may have acted in ways that extended somewhat greater civil and legal rights to African Americans in the county, but they did so reluctantly and certainly did not believe that blacks were entitled to equal treatment before the law. William Austin, writing from Wytheville and describing the Freedmen's Bureau district to which Montgomery County belonged, told his superiors in Richmond that white officials and residents in the district acted out of fear, rather than conviction:

> Were it not for the fear the people have of the Military authorities a Union or colored man could feel no certainty of getting justice before the courts. This is not so much the fault of the Judges as of the Magistrates and Jurors who have no sympathy with any who took part in the war and who cannot divest themselves of old prejudices against the Negroes. This is particularly the case where the defendants are Whites and the Blacks are prosecutors. Since the Military authorities are supreme the people know that they are closely watched and that any failure on the part of civil officers to do their duty will result in suspension or removal from office, they are now careful in their treatment of all persons with whom they have to deal. This gives rise to the report that "justice is impartially administered" while if carefully examined in all its bearings it could only be said to be administered "nominally."

In a subsequent report he was even more pointed. Speaking of the magistrates who represented the lowest level of the judiciary, Austin concluded: "They do not admit the colored man as entitled to equal rights with the white man and a majority of them do not admit him as entitled to any rights white men are bound to respect."[39]

By 1870, however, whites in Montgomery County had little to fear if they ignored the rights of African Americans. The Freedmen's Bureau no longer played any role in the county beyond advancing African American education, and that too was coming to a close. Moreover, in January of that year Virginia was readmitted to the Union and emerged from military supervision. The state's own constitution did now permit blacks to vote, hold political office, and serve on juries, and it declared that all citizens possessed "equal civil and political rights and public privileges." Moreover, the recently adopted Fourteenth Amendment to the US Constitution was intended to guarantee all citizens—including African Americans—"equal protection of the laws." None of these protections, however, had yet been tested, and it remained to be seen just how strictly or loosely they would be interpreted and enforced. This process of defining "equal" in Virginia extended into the early years of the twentieth century, and while the long-term trend was to restrict and to very nearly eliminate African American rights and political power in Virginia, it was not a steady process. As Steven Hahn has noted, "The formulas and constituencies of support for Jim Crow were not easily or quickly found, and in an atmosphere of contention over policy and power, black communities remained politically mobilized and alert to new openings, arrangements, and alliances."[40]

The opening move in defining the limits of black political power in Virginia came with the state's restoration to the Union. In 1869, more moderate elements from both the Conservative and Republican camps combined to steer a course that would satisfy Congress without changing Virginia too radically. Their compromise of "universal suffrage and universal amnesty" promised to preserve the franchise for both freedmen and rebels and led to the election of a Conservative governor and legislature. This new government rapidly negotiated Virginia's restoration to the Union and then, over the next several years, employed a variety of legal and constitutional changes to reduce steadily the number of African Americans who could vote and the political influence of those who still could.[41]

The Conservative government also acted to settle the state's finances through legislation to repay its prewar debt. To do so, it issued new bonds and permitted bondholders to use the coupons on their bonds, instead of cash, to pay their state taxes. This led to a steep drop in tax revenue during the 1870s, to which the Conservatives responded with sharply increased taxes and draconian cuts to public schools. This in turn led to growing opposition from a variety of white groups—including urban workers and small farmers—and the emergence of a movement known as the Readjusters, which advocated a partial repudiation of the state's debt in order to preserve public education and restore state finances to a sustainable footing. This division among white voters left both Readjusters and their opponents seeking political allies, and one target of their attention was African Americans. They had demands that had little to do with the debt or state finances, including the removal of taxpaying as a requirement for voting, the elimination of whipping as a punishment for theft and of petit larceny as grounds for disenfranchisement, and a repeal of the state's ban on interracial marriage. White Readjusters and black Republicans never agreed on all of these issues, but they found enough common ground in the early 1880s to gain control of the General Assembly and bring about some of the changes African Americans wanted, including the elimination of taxpaying as requirement to vote.[42]

The prospect of African Americans gaining political power through their alliance with Readjusters concentrated the minds of white Virginians. Conservatives, renamed Democrats in 1883, launched a bitter, racially motivated campaign to regain control through elections to the General Assembly that year and succeeded. They then initiated what they described as reforms to reduce corruption in the electoral process, reforms that had the effect of guaranteeing continued white Democratic control. In 1884, the assembly passed legislation that, essentially, put the choice of local election officials into Democratic hands. A decade later, in 1894, the Walton Act mandated the use of secret written ballots under procedures that made it virtually impossible for an illiterate voter to make a meaningful choice. Finally, in 1901–2, a state convention dominated by Democrats drafted a new state constitution that included both literacy and taxpaying requirements and disenfranchised the vast majority of Virginia's African American men when it took effect, in July 1902.[43]

The ebb and flow of black voting rights seen across Virginia between 1870 and 1902 was also evident in Montgomery County. There, for example, the Conservatives' return to power in 1869 and their subsequent efforts to reduce black electoral strength significantly reduced the number of African American voters between 1870 and 1880. Voter rolls for the final decades of the nineteenth century have not survived in the county, so it is impossible to be precise about just how many black men lost the right to vote or when they lost it, but it seems that amending the state constitution in 1876 to require payment of the capitation tax in order to vote cut the number of black voters in the county by about half. It is clear from newspaper reports and records of the Freedmen's Bureau that more than 550 African American men had registered to vote by October 1867,

and that "nearly if not all entitled to register have done so." By 1880, however, the situation had changed significantly. A tally of registered voters
in the county dating from 1880 or 1881 shows a total of just 380 African
Americans. This number is consistent with the total of 338 "Col'd Repub'n"
voters reported by the chairman of the county's Readjuster Party in 1882,
though the chairman's count omitted "2 or 3 small precincts of minor importance." Although the county's black population had risen by more than
70 percent since 1867, the number of registered black voters had fallen
by at least a quarter, to under four hundred, and represented only about
half of the black men aged 21 and over in the county. And while African
Americans still made up a quarter of the county's total population in 1880,
they were only about 17 percent of its registered voters.[44]

Further reducing the political influence of African Americans in Montgomery County was the fact that not all of those who were registered to
vote in 1880 were actually eligible to vote. The count of "registered voters"
in 1880–81, for example, notes that only 286 of the 380 "registered" black
voters were "qualified." While Virginians amended the state constitution in
1876 to bar voting by men who had not paid their capitation tax, the legislature did not modify the statute governing the registration of voters. Men
who otherwise met the requirements for voting could register but were
not considered eligible to vote if they had not paid their tax. In Montgomery County, African American men were almost twice as likely as white
men to be registered but ineligible (25 percent for blacks compared to 13
percent for whites); as a result, blacks made up 17 percent of the county's
registered voters in 1880–81 but only 14 percent of its eligible voters. It
was possible for third parties to pay the taxes for ineligible voters. In many
parts of Virginia, the Readjusters did this for men they believed would
vote their way, and they certainly considered this approach in Montgomery County. In October 1882, the Readjusters' chairman in Montgomery
County, Frank Palmer, wrote the party's leader, William Mahone, seeking
help with potential voters' back taxes. He informed Mahone that "a large
majority of the delinquents are of *our party*" and concluded: "Hope you
will be able to help us in this respect." Mahone's response is unknown, but
by then the need for such assistance was vanishing.[45]

Elections in 1881 had given Readjusters control of the state legislature,
and in 1882 they secured a repeal of the constitutional amendment linking taxes and voting. This led immediately to a significant increase in the
number of black voters in Montgomery County. Their position was not

as strong as it had been in 1867, but it did improve markedly. Prior to the election of 1883, canvassers for the Readjusters identified every voter in the county by name, race, and how he was likely to vote. The number of African American voters, 591, showed an increase of 55 percent compared to registered voters in 1880–81 and a rise of more than 100 percent compared to eligible voters that year. Black voters were still a minority in Montgomery County. Even in precincts with the greatest concentrations of black voters, Long Shop and Big Spring, they were only about a third of the total, and countywide African Americans represented just under 21 percent of the total electorate in 1883. This was, however, very close to their share of males aged twenty-one and over, according to the 1880 census, and a significant increase since 1880.[46]

The increase in black voters may have been short lived, though, and was a major factor in Democratic efforts to reverse it. In the election of 1883, Democrats used the rise in black voting that followed repeal of the tax requirement and claims that it would lead to "Negro Rule" to scare white voters into turning out and supporting them. The campaign that year saw an intense focus on race that peaked with the infamous "Danville Circular" and reports of the "Danville Riot." Democrats in Danville published a pamphlet describing the "injustice and humiliation" to which whites in town had been subjected as result of Readjuster rule, and days before the election a confrontation over who would yield to whom on a sidewalk led to gunfire, several deaths, and reports of a "riot" or "massacre." According to the Readjusters' chairman in Montgomery County, both the circular and reports of violence were major factors in the election there. Writing from Blacksburg shortly after the election, C. A. Heermans claimed that "the last of the campaign was carried out by the Funders [i.e., Democrats] almost entirely as a race issue." Democrats circulated copies of the Danville Circular throughout Montgomery County during the final week of the campaign and "made passionate appeals to the white people to rescue their brothers of the east from the terrible consequences of negro rule." Heermans reported that "people were told there would be mixed marriages and that their children should set in mixed schools and that white lady teachers would have to be examined by negro trustees before they could teach if the Readjusters succeeded." Then, the weekend before the election, word arrived of "the Danville Massacre (Riot they called it)" and quickly spread through the county, helped by "extra copies of the Lynchburg *News* with exaggerated accounts." None of this led to racial violence in Montgomery County, and Heermans did not report any "overt act of intimidation" on polling day. He was certain, however, that fear of violence did deter a number of the Readjusters' supporters from voting, and while he did not mention the race of any voters put off by the threat of violence, it seems likely that African American voters were among them.[47]

Fear of "Negro Rule" proved an effective campaign strategy, and Democrats won the 1883 election both in Montgomery County and in Virginia. They then set out to reduce African American political power without flagrantly violating the Fourteenth or Fifteenth Amendment and without disenfranchising too many white voters. In 1884 the General Assembly enacted legislation putting control of local elections in the hands of appointed (and generally Democratic) officials, and in 1894 it mandated the use of secret written ballots and stipulated that only an appointed constable could provide assistance with the ballot for electors who were "physically or educationally unable to vote." Because neither of these measures affected who could register to vote, the number of potential African American voters in Montgomery County should not have changed between 1883 and 1902. This is impossible to confirm, however, as none of the county's voter lists for that period are known to have survived. Even if they had survived, however, and even if they showed no decline in the number of black men registered to vote, this would not mean there was no decline in black political influence. The right to vote was hollow if election officials could block it simply by challenging a voter's registration or if a voter could not read the ballot or follow correctly the exacting rules for marking it.[48]

It is impossible to say how effective the written ballot was at reducing the number of African American voters in Montgomery County, but evidence has survived that Democratic election officers in the county did use their positions to prevent at least some African Americans from voting during the late 1880s. William Mahone, by then a leading figure in Virginia's Republican Party, routinely asked his network of political informants around the state to report electoral fraud or intimidation, and a number of reports from Montgomery County describe both. After the election in 1889, for example, the Republican precinct captain in Radford reported to the state party executive that forty-eight black Republicans were barred from voting there because "they were told their names were not on the books." Two others were barred for having lived outside the precinct during the months preceding the election," and another two "by the dilatory proceedings of the officers of the election." He then concluded that blacks in Radford who had been able to vote had voted almost solidly Democratic because "when they were known to be Republicans or when Democrats couldn't coerce them into voting for them they would harass them with their challenges that had no foundation whatever for the purpose of scaring weak kned Republicans away from the polls." In another unidentified precinct in the county, twenty-two black Republicans were barred from voting for similar reasons that election day.[49]

It is also possible to show, at least partially, exactly how effective white Virginians finally were at stripping the county's African Americans of their right to vote. By 1900, Democratic leaders in the state had decided to end the "problem" of black voting once and for all, even if doing so also disenfranchised a significant number of poor white men. Thus, the state constitution adopted in 1902 was drafted specifically to reduce the number of black voters and employed both taxes and a literacy requirement to accomplish this goal. Jane Dailey has written that, statewide, the impact of the new constitution on black voting was "immediate and catastrophic." That certainly describes the change in Montgomery County. Lists of "colored voters" for 1902 or 1903 have survived from five of the county's twelve precincts and show the near total elimination of African Americans from the county electorate by then. In 1883, these five precincts had included a total of 194 registered black voters; in 1902–3, they had just 16—a decline of 92 percent. Naturally, African Americans' share of the total electorate plummeted too. In Blacksburg, for example, African American voters had represented 16.5 percent of registered voters in 1883, while in 1903 they were just 2 percent. Demographics alone had always made African Americans a minority in Montgomery County politics, but the constitution of 1902 made them, for all practical purposes, politically invisible.[50]

Not surprisingly, African Americans also held very few government positions in Montgomery County between 1870 and 1902. Steven Hahn has estimated that "blacks had their best opportunities to hold local office in counties where at least 40 percent of the population was black, and their best opportunity to hold a number of offices where at least 60 percent of the population was black." In Montgomery County, though, African Americans were never more than a quarter of the county's population, and while increasing residential separation in the county did create a number of largely black neighborhoods, there were no majority black precincts or districts. Electoral victory always depended on support from white allies, and they were never able or willing to provide enough support. Republicans faded as a political force in Appalachian Virginia by the late 1870s; during the 1880s, Readjusters were rarely willing to put black men on the ballot in white-majority counties, such as Montgomery, because doing so would cost them more in lost white support than they could gain in black; and by the 1890s whites of all political stripes had come together to elim-inate blacks from Virginia politics. It is not surprising that little evidence has survived of any black public officials in Montgomery County during these years.[51]

No black man was elected to any public office in Montgomery County during the nineteenth century. As described earlier, Alexander Hopkins ran for Commissioner of the Revenue in 1879, finishing fourth among the eight candidates, but he seems to have been the only African American who even tried between 1870 and 1902. And black men were almost never appointed to government positions. As a United States senator from 1881 to 1887, William Mahone used his power over post office appointments to build a bi-racial political machine in many parts of Virginia, but he seems to have recommended no African Americans for positions in Montgomery County.[52] One black man, Lewis Haden, was deputized in 1874 to exe-cute a bench warrant on another black man, Henry Taylor, whom Haden had accused of stealing a pair of boots from him. The only other known instance of black men wielding any state power in Montgomery County came during an outbreak of smallpox in 1883. In an effort to stop the spread of the disease, county supervisors authorized the creation of quar-antine lines with guards to enforce them, and among those hired as guards were several African American men. Even district road supervisors, men responsible for the maintenance of public roads in neighborhoods of the county, and road viewers, men delegated to decide where proposed new roads might run, seem to have been drawn overwhelmingly from the white community, even when the roads in question served black neighborhoods. In one instance, in 1891, a mixed panel of three whites and two blacks was assigned to lay out the Seneca Road, which ran through a largely African American community, but that was a rare exception to the rule of white men filling government positions in Montgomery County.[53]

Blacks in Montgomery County enjoyed a greater presence and voice in the judicial system between 1870 and 1902 than they did in politics, though control of the county's legal system remained almost as firmly in white hands as the political system did. All of the judges, all of the justices of the peace (also known as magistrates), the sheriff, and all of the constables in the county during these years were white. This was not because blacks were formally barred from any of these positions; technically, all of them were open to any qualified individual, and race was not a qualification. Judges, however, were elected by the General Assembly, while justices of the peace, constables, and sheriffs were elected by county residents, and because white Democrats generally held majorities in both the state and in Montgomery County during these years, these positions generally went to them. And because judges in Montgomery County were usually white Democrats, jurors in the county were generally white too. Virginia law permitted any eligible voter between the ages of twenty-one and sixty to serve as a juror, so until 1902 a significant number of the county's African American men were eligible to serve as jurors. But the law also gave judges the authority to shape the pool of potential jurors. Each year, the presiding judge of each county court was to draw up a list of those voters "he shall think well qualified to serve as jurors" and create a master list from which potential jurors were drawn by lot before each session of the court. Any county judge, then, had the option to include African Americans among potential jurors, but most chose not to, and for most of this period all of the jurors in Montgomery County—both grand and petit—were white. Between late 1880 and mid-1884, however, blacks did serve on a third of the county's grand juries and on least one petit jury.[54]

When a coalition of Readjusters and Republicans gained control of Virginia's General Assembly in 1879, one of the goals of black Republicans was to expand the African American presence in local government—including service on juries. This they accomplished in part by electing judges who were willing to include blacks among potential jurors, and one of these judges was Charles H. Miller in Montgomery County. Miller was a lawyer and farmer from Blacksburg, who described himself as a Readjuster "doing my duty to the party." The assembly elected him county judge in January 1880, and he ascended the bench in March of that year. Until that time, no black man is known to have served on any jury in Montgomery County, but between December 1880 and July 1884 at least twenty-one African American men served on grand juries convened in the county, and at least ten of thirty grand juries convened during that period included at least one black member. None of these juries was all black or even a majority black; at most, African Americans made up a third of any particular panel and usually an even smaller share. In one sense, this pattern is hardly surprising. Once a judge had drawn up a list of potential jurors for the year, those called for any particular grand jury were to be chosen at random from that list, so it is not surprising that the number of African Americans on any particular grand jury would vary. And because African Americans made up about 20 percent of registered voters in Montgomery County between 1880 and 1884, it is not surprising that they never constituted more than a third of the members of any grand jury. If jurors were called randomly, however, it is surprising that two-thirds of grand juries during this time included no black men at all. This suggests that Judge Miller may have decided not to rely on chance alone and chose to exercise personal control over the frequency with which black men might sit on grand juries. He did not, however, make any effort to ensure that grand juries including African Americans could only indict African Americans; mixed-race grand juries in Montgomery County brought bills against both black and white individuals.[55]

Petit juries were a different matter. Black service on these was much more rare and much more circumscribed, suggesting that Miller may have believed that black petit jurors might appear more threatening to the county's white majority. Grand juries brought indictments, which meant there was reason to believe that an individual might have committed a crime. He or she still had to stand trial before a white judge with extensive power over the proceedings and be found guilty by a jury before facing any punishment. Petit juries, on the other hand, were the bodies that rendered a verdict, and while their verdicts could be appealed or set aside, they were often final and often led directly to fines or imprisonment. This may explain why it was not until December 1882, two years after the first known mixed-race grand jury sat in Montgomery County, that black men there served on a petit jury for the first time. And when they did, it was under quite different circumstances. In the case of *Commonwealth v. Palmer,* both the defendant and the victim were black, and the jury that heard the case was probably all black. Ten of its twelve members can be identified with certainty as members of the county's African American community, and one of the others, Thomas Mars, bore the surname of a black family that had been in the county since the early nineteenth century. Once again, it seems, Judge Miller intervened in the selection of potential jurors. When African Americans made up only about 20 percent of the registered voters in Montgomery County, the odds of choosing by lot a pool of potential jurors that included at least ten African Americans among its sixteen members (defendants in felony cases could challenge up to four potential jurors and Palmer did) were remote.[56]

It seems that Judge Miller may have bypassed the statutory procedure and created an all-black pool from which the jury in this case was selected. He may have done so as an experiment to gauge public sentiment before repeating the experience. Perhaps the judge hoped that a black jury would render a verdict with which the public agreed and demonstrate to skeptical whites that black jurors could be trusted—at least in matters involving other African Americans. If that was his hope, it was not realized. Malcolm Palmer had been charged with attacking John Toliver with a razor "to wound, maim, kill and murder him," and after hearing evidence in the case the largely (or entirely) black jury failed to reach a verdict. Three months later, with a substitute judge presiding, an all-white jury found Palmer guilty of a lesser charge, "unlawfully cutting John Toliver," and sentenced him to six months in the county jail.[57] Miller may then have decided that the experiment had not gone well enough to repeat. Mixed-race grand juries continued for another eighteen months, but no other petit jury in the county is known to have included African Americans until the mid-twentieth century.[58] Even when a later defendant's counsel requested a black jury, Judge Miller refused. Martha Gray was alleged to be a white woman, and when she married a black man in 1883, she was charged with violating Virginia's antimiscegenation statute. When she came to trial in June 1884, her counsel asked Judge Miller "to summon a negro jury," but he refused "and ordered a white *venire* [jury pool] to be summoned." That jury deadlocked, but another—also white—eventually convicted Gray and sentenced her to two years in prison.[59]

Judge Miller's refusal to provide a black jury pool for Martha Gray's trial may also have been a response to political changes in Richmond. The coalition of Readjusters and Republicans that had controlled the General Assembly for several years had been defeated in 1883, and by mid-1884 Democrats were firmly in control again. Not only were Democrats in control, they apparently used that control to intimidate Miller into abandoning his effort to include African Americans in the jury system. In November 1884, the House of Delegates announced its intention to impeach Judge Miller for corruption involving the sale of liquor licenses and for behavior both on and off the bench "such that all respect for, and confidence in his court is destroyed." Ultimately, the proceedings were suspended. The Committee on Courts of Justice reported that the distance witnesses would have to travel and the brief time remaining in the legislative session made it "impractical" to proceed and recommended postponement until the next session. The case never resumed, however, and Miller served out his term on the bench, though he was not reelected. He also seems to have been sufficiently intimidated and not to have permitted any more black jurors during his tenure in office. Between March 1880 and July 1884, Miller had called thirty-three grand juries, and at least ten of them had included African Americans. Between August 1884 and December 1885, however, he convened another twelve grand juries, and every one seems to have been all white.[60]

Between 1870 and 1902, then, the courtrooms of Montgomery County were dominated by white men. All of the judges were white, all of the lawyers were white, and with very few exceptions all of the jurors were white. In spite of this imbalance, the legal system during this period was not hopelessly stacked against African Americans. This is not to say that it was entirely fair. African Americans seem to have been arrested and convicted more often than their share of the county's population would warrant, though given the lack of complete records and the difficulty of determining racial identity, it is impossible to say for sure. They were certainly jailed more. For a brief period in 1896–97 monthly censuses of the county's jail population have survived in the court order books. They indicate that blacks made up a majority (56 percent) of inmates, while on 1900 census they represented less than 18 percent of the county's population. African Americans also suffered judicial whippings far more often than whites did. Between 1870 and 1882, when the General Assembly barred whipping as a punishment for any crime in Virginia, more than a dozen African American men in Montgomery County suffered public whippings while, perhaps, two white men did. Court personnel also acted at times as if they held blacks and whites to different standards. In 1885, for example, a county magistrate accepted a plea from Thomas Simpkins, a white man, "for assaulting (not intending to maim or disfigure, but mearly to chastize one Harvey Fields) (Col)." Simpkins was fined $2.50.[61]

African Americans in Montgomery County were also more likely to be the targets of official concern about immorality. During the 1870s, grand juries in the county periodically indicted unmarried couples for "lewd & lascivious association & cohabitation." There seems to have been no clear pattern regarding the timing of such charges or the identity of the couples indicted. It seems that every now and then county officials simply decided to make examples of a handful of couples in order to send a message: get married or face the consequences. The tactic was not confined to non-whites; both black couples and white couples were indicted. Blacks and mulattos, however, were targeted more frequently and more vigorously than whites were. African Americans made up just under a quarter of the county's population at the time, but more than half of those indicted for illegal cohabitation were black or mulatto. Moreover, in the cases of couples who did not marry after being indicted, charges against white couples were more often dropped than were those against nonwhites.[62]

In spite of such reminders that justice was not blind, courts in Montgomery County certainly granted African Americans greater equality than the political system did. At least some African Americans charged with crimes seem to have enjoyed the same rights that whites did, though given lacunae in the surviving records it impossible to say precisely how common or unusual this was. Magistrates did, for example, sometimes issue search warrants for the homes, barns, or wagons of African Americans, though illegal searches may also have occurred. Some black defendants had attorneys to represent them, though not all apparently, and it is not possible to say whether or not the county ever provided counsel for indigent defendants. Accused African Americans were also granted bail pending trial, negotiated plea deals, called witnesses—both black and white—in their defense, and sometimes submitted appeals when they lost in court. And a number of cases suggest that black defendants were afforded legitimate opportunities to prove their innocence and that their testimony was sometimes taken seriously by magistrates and jurors. In 1879, for example, Norborn Allen, a white laborer, accused Silas Robinson, a black laborer, of stealing a counterpane and several tablecloths. On Allen's complaint, a magistrate issued a warrant to search Robinson's wagon, where a counterpane and two tablecloths were found. When the magistrate examined Robinson, however, the latter was able to explain the items' presence to the magistrate's satisfaction, and he was released without being charged.[63] It is impossible to show that no miscarriages of justice took place between 1870 and 1902, and it seems highly unlikely that none did, but the surviving court records clearly show that blacks charged with crimes—up to and including murder—against both blacks and whites were sometimes convicted and sometimes found innocent.

Nor has any evidence survived of extralegal action against African

Americans in Montgomery County between 1870 and 1902. As noted above, immediately after the Civil War, freedmen who had served in the Union army had sometimes been beaten by whites in the county, and the Ku Klux Klan had been active there for several months in 1868. After 1870, however, whites in the county seem to have felt that their domination of the political and legal systems was sufficient to maintain control. In many parts of the South, including Virginia, the final decades of the nineteenth century saw the beginning of what Ashraf Rushdy has called "the age of lynching" and a marked increase in the number of African Americans murdered by white mobs, often for crimes allegedly committed against whites. Lynchings were not as common in Virginia as they were in states farther south, but they did occur fairly often during these years, and they occurred in Southwest Virginia more often than anywhere else in the state. According to Fitzhugh Brundage, between 1880 and 1900 nineteen African Americans were lynched in Southwest Virginia, including two in Roanoke. No lynching is known or reported to have taken place in Montgomery County during these years, however, and the only known instance in which county residents reported that such an attack was imminent was against two white men accused of raping a white woman in 1889. The relative calm in Montgomery County seems to support Brundage's view that racially motivated lynchings in the region were most common in areas such as Roanoke with small black populations into which relatively large numbers of African Americans suddenly moved during the final decades of the nineteenth century. In the case of Montgomery County, there was no such increase; in fact, the county's African American population began to decline about 1885 and continued declining through the end of the century, which may have contributed to the absence of lynchings there.[64]

In the decades following Military Reconstruction, however, Montgomery County's black residents were not simply the objects of legal action by their white neighbors. They also used the courts themselves and brought a variety of legal actions, both civil and criminal, against both whites and other African Americans. They often used the legal system, for example, to protect and advance their economic interests. They did so most frequently by bringing suits in common law against their debtors, as Felix Johnson, a black brick mason, did against James Edmundson, a wealthy and prominent white neighbor in 1870 or as the Christiansburg blacksmith, Minnis Headen, did against Jesse Noell, a hotel owner in town, in 1882. African Americans also used the chancery court to protect their property.

John Johnson, for example, had purchased five acres of land from James Edmundson in 1872 and had paid for it in full by 1877, but he had still not received a deed for the land when Edmundson died in 1881. Later that year, therefore, Johnson successfully petitioned the chancery court to order the administrator of Edmundson's estate to deliver a memorandum in the papers of the deceased that Edmundson had signed confirming the sale and Johnson's payment in full. Blacks even learned to exploit loopholes in the legal system to protect their economic interests. James Brown was a young blacksmith in Cambria who bought a lot there in 1881. Three years later, he sold the lot to his wife for one dollar shortly before a white creditor, William McClanahan Montague, brought suit against him to secure payment on three notes Brown had signed to buy another lot adjacent to the first. This seems to have been a deliberate effort on Brown's part to put the land beyond his creditor's reach, which is certainly what Montague thought: "Complainant avers that said deed was made to hinder & delay & defraud him in the collection of his claim."[65]

For African American women seeking to protect their economic interests in a society dominated by men, chancery courts proved particularly important because they were courts of equity. This function was most evident perhaps in divorce proceedings. Between 1870 and 1900, at least forty-five African American couples began divorce proceedings in Montgomery County, and in nineteen of these cases the wife initiated the process. Some of these women were married to men like Julius Twine, who owned no property, worked infrequently, and when he did work "spent his earnings in riotous living." Cases such as these involved no financial settlement. Georgiana Twine was already supporting her family through her work as a cook and sought no property, child support, or alimony from her husband because he had none to give. In other cases, however, where wives depended on their husbands' wages or the husband had significant property, women used divorce proceedings to protect their economic interests and those of their children. When Lucy Fuqua petitioned the court for a divorce from her husband, Thomas, the couple had three young children, and Thomas was working as a fireman on the Atlantic, Mississippi, and Ohio Railroad for a salary of forty-one dollars per month. Fuqua owned no real estate, but Lucy asked the court to provide "a sufficient amount to be paid to your oratrix to maintain her and said children" from her husband's wages. This the court did, ordering the railroad to garnish Thomas Fuqua's wages and pay Lucy twelve dollars per month. George and Belle Hopkins, on the other hand, had no children, but George, a schoolteacher, had full or partial interests in several properties in the county when he ran off to Ohio with one of his students. Through chancery, Belle secured a divorce plus costs and $200 in alimony, and the court ordered the sale of George Hopkins's property in order to cover the cost of the judgment. In all, nearly half of the divorce proceedings initiated by black women in Montgomery County between 1870 and 1900 included a financial element in the wife's favor as part of the final decree—costs, alimony, or both.[66]

Black women in Montgomery County also used the chancery court to secure their dower rights. Under Virginia law, widows were entitled to a dower share of one-third of the real estate owned by their husbands at the time of their death, but in some cases it took court action to secure that right. Lucy Lynch, for example, had been married to Charles Lynch, who owned a house on a half-acre lot near Cambria when he died in 1890. Lucy may not have understood her dower right at the time Charles died, or she may have been intimidated by her father-in-law and chosen not to exercise it. Seven years later, however, the remarried widow, now Lucy Ford, petitioned the chancery court to compel her former father-in-law, George Lynch, to provide an accounting of the "rents and profits" he had earned on the property of Charles Lynch since the latter's death and to provide his widow "her share of the rents received." Ultimately, the court found for Lucy Lynch Ford and ordered the property's sale in order to pay her the dower to which she was legally entitled.[67]

African Americans also used the legal system in less adversarial ways to protect their economic interests. Virginia, like most states, afforded its citizens a number of legal mechanisms by which to protect their interests and property. Certain craftsmen, for example, could file mechanics' liens to enforce payments due them for their work, and a number of black workers in Montgomery County employed such liens in an effort to ensure payment for their work. Joshua Webster, for example, was a house builder in the Christiansburg-Cambria area, and during the 1880s and 1890s he went frequently to the county clerk's office to file mechanic's liens on homes he had built in order to establish a claim against the property in the event he was not paid fully for his work. Virginia also offered its citizens the opportunity to shelter a portion of their property from seizure in many cases of debt action. The state constitution and state law provided that any householder or head of family could exempt up to $2,000 worth of real and personal property from levy or seizure due against most forms of debt. In an era when it often seems that everyone was suing everyone for nonpayment of debts, this "homestead exemption" was a valuable legal right, but only about a hundred Montgomery County residents are known to have taken advantage of it between 1871 and 1900. That number includes at least thirteen African Americans. Zacharia Carr, for example, filed an exemption almost immediately, in June 1872, enumerating the crops he was raising on rented land, livestock, farming equipment, his carpenter's tools, and household furniture, all worth an estimated total of $667.25. Like Carr, most of the African Americans filing homestead exemptions in Montgomery County were artisans or landowners, who may have had more to protect and may have been better able to afford the fee for recording a public document, but they also included John Bratton, a farm worker who exempted his tobacco crop, his household furniture, and a single pig—worth a total of one hundred dollars.[68]

African Americans in Montgomery County also used the legal system in response to criminal matters. In a majority of instances, this seems to have been against other members of the black community, though a significant minority of criminal complaints were made against white defendants. Some charges, generally more serious crimes such as rape and theft, were brought by grand juries in the name of the commonwealth. It is often unclear how these matters came to the attention of county officials, but presumably it was a report from the victim to a magistrate or constable. In less serious cases black victims often went directly to a magistrate, and that single official could take action against the accused. In 1872, for example, Granville Saunders went before Henry W. Cox, a county magistrate, to complain that Joseph Edie, a white man, had whipped two black teenagers, Fanny Schaeffer and Jenny Bannister. Cox ordered Edie's arrest, and after hearing from a number of black and white witnesses, including the victims, he ordered Edie to post bond "to keep the peace and be of good behavior for six months"—a common outcome in such cases.[69]

Members of the African American community also used the courts to resolve what seem to have been relatively minor disputes that they could, perhaps, have handled among themselves or through community institutions such as the church. In the spring of 1882, for example, a conflict between two neighbors in Christiansburg, Edwin Campbell, age thirteen, and Minnis Headen Jr., age twenty, escalated into mutual criminal charges against the two. In late April, Campbell allegedly threw rocks at Headen's house and horse, and Headen responded by beating the boy. Four days later, Campbell's grandmother went before a local magistrate to complain about Headen's action, and shortly afterward Headen complained to the same magistrate about Campbell's rock throwing. Each of the accused was then brought before the magistrate for trial; Headen was fined $2.50, plus costs, for beating Campbell, while Campbell was ordered to post a bond to guarantee his good behavior for six months. This might indicate how comfortable African Americans in Montgomery County felt approaching the legal system, though it could also be a sign of their desperation: when all else fails, try the courts. In either case, it is yet another indication that the county's black residents saw themselves, and to some extent were seen by others, as members of the body politic.[70]

This was also evident in a small number of other ways in which nineteenth-century Virginians interacted with their governments. Like their white neighbors, African Americans were sometimes exempted from taxes on the basis of "infirmities"; they were compensated for land taken for public use, such as the construction of roads or sidewalks; and they were provided modest poor relief, either in the county poorhouse or through outdoor relief. And while county officials tried repeatedly to avoid providing any poor relief outside the poorhouse, this seems to have been more a sign of their stinginess than racism. One area in which it does seem that African Americans received less from county government than might be expected was in road construction. Any landowner or community could approach county officials to request a new road or an improvement to an existing road. Based on the surviving records, requests from African Americans were relatively rare and often met with opposition, either from white landowners whose property would be affected or from county officials reluctant to spend public money. In 1885, for example, the Board of Supervisors refused to authorize an expenditure of $150 to open a road from Brake Branch, a largely black community, to the Roanoke County line and recommended that "[it] be opened with hands on Brake road."[71]

In a variety of ways, large and small, African American residents of Montgomery County tried to assume the public roles to which they felt entitled as free men and women in the decades following their release from slavery. Clearly, they did not entirely succeed. In important ways they were actually less equal by 1902 than they had been in the decades immediately after the Civil War. In the process, however, they demonstrated a keen understanding of both the legal and political systems of the county and state, a desire to participate in them, and the ability to do so when they had the opportunity. These attributes did not disappear when African Americans lost the right to vote or to sit on juries. Members of the county's African American community remembered what they, their parents, or their grandparents had done before and prepared for the day when those opportunities would return. It would be, however, a long wait. Almost a century passed before another African American stood for election in Montgomery County, and not until 2000, when Penny Franklin won a seat on the county school board, was any African American elected to public office in the county.[72]

CONCLUSION

On a warm summer day in 1909, Booker T. Washington spoke before a crowd of several thousand black and white residents of Southwest Virginia. It was one stop on a weeklong tour of Virginia and West Virginia during which the "Great Negro Educator" was scheduled to deliver some two dozen "educational addresses." This address, however, was special because it was delivered at the Christiansburg Industrial Institute. Washington had been the school's superintendent since 1896 and in that role had helped shape the broad contours of its educational program along the lines he had made famous at the Tuskegee Institute. Washington rarely came to Christiansburg, though, which is what made this visit so special. This was the first time in more than a decade that he had been to campus and seen what had been accomplished there.[1]

Realizing Washington's vision for the school had actually been the responsibility of its principal, and since 1906 that task had fallen to Edgar A. Long. A Tuskegee graduate himself, Long had come to Christiansburg in 1897 and taught science, agriculture, and printing at the institute before succeeding Charles L. Marshall as its principal. He was a prominent and highly visible member of Montgomery County's black community, and it is not surprising that he was among the dignitaries who introduced Washington that day. In his remarks, Long emphasized the extraordinary success of Montgomery County's African American community. It was a county, he noted, "where the jail is empty and the schoolhouse is full" and where "nine out of every ten colored men . . . own their own homes." Washington then took the stage and opened his remarks by continuing the theme begun by Edgar Long, acknowledging the "industry, thrift, intelligence, and refinement that were apparent every where in this community."[2]

What Long and Washington described that day was the result of a long, slow, and uneven process. African Americans in Montgomery County had struggled for almost fifty years to remake the world in which they or their parents had been born and to create the new one seen by Long and Washington in 1909. They had begun as former slaves—with little formal education, few economic resources, and little experience organizing or administering any public institution. They had sometimes enjoyed support from friends and government, but they had done much of the work themselves. In the face of skeptical if not hostile, neighbors they had established families, communities, and institutions that helped them exercise greater control over their personal and spiritual lives, enjoy more fully the fruits of their labor, and begin to participate as citizens in the state and nation that they and their ancestors had helped to build.

They had also benefited from the particular history of Montgomery County. Because the railroad arrived there during the 1850s, slavery had been well established in the county before the outbreak of the Civil War, especially in comparison to many other parts of southern Appalachia. It had not, however, had time to develop into the all-encompassing institution that it was in the tobacco or cotton kingdoms farther east or south. As a result, when slavery ended in Montgomery County, its African American population had been large enough to support many of the institutions essential to the maintenance of a viable community but not large enough to trigger widespread fear among its white residents of "black domination." To be sure, racism and racial discrimination ran through every element of life in Montgomery County between the end of the Civil War and the dawn of the twentieth century. African Americans there endured a range of indignities and restrictions—both formal and informal—on their personal, political, social, and economic lives. But the racism evident in Montgomery County during these years was less virulent and less violent than that found in many other parts of the South. And in spite of those indignities and restrictions, African Americans in the county had begun to make lives for themselves and their children.

The progress they made during those years was neither even nor constant. Blacks in Montgomery County gained significant control over their families—marrying when they chose, ending those unions when they chose, and raising their children as they saw fit. They also saw real, if limited, economic success. Many remained poor in 1909, but as Edgar Long pointed out, some among them had reached middling status, and all had come far from the days when most had owned nothing. They fought for and supported schools in which they and their children made great advances toward the skills needed to function in a world of numbers and written documents, and one of their schools, the Christiansburg Industrial Institute, emerged among the elite of southern black educational establishments. They also gained control over their spiritual lives and enjoyed a vibrant religious community in which they worshipped their God in ways that seemed appropriate to them. And though they never enjoyed the full benefits of citizenship and equal rights under the law, they did exercise some of its prerogatives some of the time.

Ironically, by the time Booker T. Washington celebrated their success, it had stalled. By 1909 life was growing harder for African Americans in Montgomery County. Economically, they faced a number of challenges. Many still worked in agriculture at a time when farmers throughout the southern Appalachians, whatever their race, were finding it harder and harder to compete with more productive competitors in other regions of the country. Several hundred African American families in the county had managed to buy their own land by 1909, but it was often inferior land along the rockier, steeper ridges. This made it even harder for them to support their families through farming. Moreover, the holdings of first-generation black landowners were often too small to divide among their children without further reducing their economic potential. It was also growing harder for black men to support a family working on someone else's land. The late nineteenth and early twentieth centuries in Montgomery County saw declines in the production of crops such as tobacco and wheat and increasing numbers of livestock, especially sheep, that required fewer workers. Beyond farming, however, there were still few economic opportunities for African Americans in Montgomery County. Industrial development there was limited to coal mining and railroading, neither of which provided many opportunities for black workers. Coal was still a minor element in the local economy, dwarfed by the larger operations in West Virginia, and one that hired very few black workers. The Norfolk and Western Railroad was still hiring black men, but mainly outside of Montgomery County, in towns such as Roanoke that had large shops and maintenance divisions.

Politically, their situation was even worse. By the early twentieth century white Virginians had virtually eliminated African Americans from the political and legal systems of Virginia. The constitution of 1902 had drastically reduced the number of black voters through a poll tax and a literacy requirement. African Americans had never been numerous enough in Montgomery County to influence significantly or by themselves the outcome of elections in the county, but they had been able to participate and demonstrate publicly their status as free men. After 1902, even that modest ambition became impossible for most black men in the county to realize. And because they were no longer eligible to vote, African Americans were even less likely to serve as jurors after 1902. By then, no black man had served on a jury in the county in almost twenty years, but as long as they had been voters, they had still been legally eligible for such service. That too disappeared with the new constitution.

And socially, it seems that relations between black and white residents of Montgomery County had become less familiar by the early twentieth century. Schools and churches, of course, had been segregated since the 1870s, either by law or by custom. By the end of the century, however, the races were also more likely to live apart. In towns such as Christiansburg and Blacksburg, African American residents tended to settle in black neighborhoods, such as Campbell Town and New Town. Elsewhere in the county, they often lived in majority black neighborhoods such as Wake Forest, Piney Woods, and Brake Branch. Less visible, but more significant perhaps, was a change in the tone of race relations in the county. John Randolph was a boy in 1892, when his father began teaching at the Virginia Agricultural and Mechanical College. Writing later, he recalled the growing divide between blacks and whites in Blacksburg at that time. "As the older people of both races died or moved and were replaced by strangers," Randolph wrote, "living side by side became less pleasant."[3]

The problem may have been particularly acute in Blacksburg because, as Randolph explained, "some of our students were from the mountains, where strange negroes were apt to get shot." The issue of "strange negroes," however, was not confined to Blacksburg. Though African American migration into Montgomery County had actually slowed by the time Randolph arrived, the 1870s and early 1880s had seen a significant influx of black migrants from adjacent or nearby counties such as Floyd and Franklin. But in another, more important sense, being a "strange negro" had nothing to do with one's origins. To white residents of Montgomery County, it seems, all African Americans were becoming increasingly "strange" by the turn of the century. Slavery had brought black and white southerners into close and frequent contact. As a result, they had known one another as *individuals*, not just as racial categories. White southerners had often believed that blacks, *in general*, were lazy, dishonest, ignorant, and potentially treacherous because this permitted them to rationalize the system of race-based slavery on which their way of life depended. At the same time, however, their personal experiences with *individual* men and women of color had often convinced them that those particular people were diligent, honest, intelligent, and loyal. This led to a situation in which the state drafted laws and policies to address the danger of African Americans in general, while individual citizens often ignored those laws in the local context of particular slaves or free people of color.[4]

Immediately after the Civil War, such attitudes were still readily apparent in Montgomery County. In 1867, for example, the *Southwest*, which often published harsh racist comments, printed a letter from Andrew Fulton, who lived in nearby Wythe County. Writing to express his support for extending the vote to black men, Fulton wrote of freedpeople: "They have raised our children, they have grown up with them, they stood by us in the cruel war which has just passed away, they protected our property in our absence from home, and we never ought to forget or be insensible of such acts of friendship."[5]

This attitude was also evident in 1879, when the *Messenger* published a glowing obituary for Richard Taylor and described the crowd following his coffin to the cemetery as "one of the largest processions ever seen in this place" and noted that it was "composed of both colors." According to the *Messenger*, businesses throughout Christiansburg closed for the funeral and bells in white churches tolled to mark Taylor's passing; the paper noted, "We could but feel the respect even the world has for virtue and goodness, despite color and lack of education."[6]

Patronizing as such comments were, they demonstrated a degree of familiarity and comfort with African Americans that was fading by the end of the century. A new generation of whites in Montgomery County lived in a world in which blacks attended separate churches and schools, in which fewer blacks lived in white homes, and in which fewer blacks worked with whites as closely as they had before 1865. Steven Hahn has argued that this "'thickening' of African-American civic and associational life" and the emergence of "black neighborhoods and enclaves" offered southern blacks "some semblance of safety" from southern whites.[7] That was, no doubt, true; it may also, however, have contributed to a growing estrangement between the races. To white residents of Montgomery County, it seems, African Americans became strangers to be feared rather than familiar people entitled to a modicum of trust, and that attitude contributed to a harsher form of racism and to increased restrictions on black freedom. This in turn contributed to the decision of more African Americans to leave Montgomery County in search greater opportunities and less pervasive oppression.

This process had begun by the mid-1880s and accelerated thereafter. Some of those who left went to West Virginia, Pennsylvania, Ohio, or Iowa to work in coal mines. Others moved to cities such as Chicago, Cleveland, Philadelphia, Baltimore, New York, and Washington. By 1910, the county's African American population was barely half of what it had been in 1880, and it continued falling through the middle of the twentieth century. It did not, however, vanish. Mary and Tom Brown, James and Fanny Dow, Thadeus and Amanda Morgan, Gordon and Nellie Mills, and James and Harriet Carr all saw some of their children leave the county, but others remained, and a century later, each of these families is still present in Montgomery County. Others are too: Eaveses, Shermans, Wades, Clarks, Briggses, and more. Together they worked to preserve the community and the institutions their parents and grandparents had established. The first half of the twentieth century was an era of relentless pressure on African Americans in Virginia. Having been pushed almost entirely out of political life, they were subjected to a broad array of Jim Crow laws that sought to isolate them and render them second-class citizens in public life. As that process unfolded, the families, churches, schools, and economic institutions established in the decades immediately after emancipation helped provide an alternative community from which Montgomery County's black residents gained support in the face of an often hostile and oppressive world around them.

In the decades after their emancipation, African Americans in Montgomery County worked to establish and maintain families and communities within a society that continued to restrict them politically, economically, and socially. These African American institutions operated *in* the dominant white society around them, but were rarely *part* of it. They intersected that dominant society at many points, but at others they remained separate and virtually unknown. They provided, however, essential systems of support—emotional, psychological, physical, and economic—and helped their members survive and function in a world that often refused to recognize legally their humanity or their society. These institutions served to provide essential connections and support and helped to ensure that Montgomery County's African American community survived through the dark days of Jim Crow and into the twenty-first century.

NOTES

SHORT TITLES AND ABBREVIATIONS

BRFAL-ACVA   Records of the Assistant Commissioner for the State of
Virginia, Bureau of Refugees, Freedmen, and Abandoned
Lands, 1865–1869, microfilm publication 1048, record group
105, National Archives, Washington, D.C.

BRFAL-EDVA   Records of the Superintendent of Education for the State of
Virginia, Bureau of Refugees, Freedmen, and Abandoned
Lands, 1865–1870, microfilm publication 1053, record group
105, National Archives, Washington, D.C.

BRFAL-FOVA   Records of the Field Offices for the State of Virginia, Bureau
of Refugees, Freedmen, and Abandoned Lands, 1865–1872,
microfilm publication 1913, record group 105, National
Archives, Washington, D.C.

Cocke Papers   Charles Lewis Cocke Papers, Wyndham Robertson Library,
Special Collections, Hollins University, Roanoke, Va.

Cornell   Division of Rare and Manuscript Collections, Carl A. Kroch
Library, Cornell University, Ithaca, New York

1865 Census   "Census Return of the Colored Population of Montgomery
Co., State of Va. August 1865," reel 198, Records of the Field
Offices for the State of Virginia, Bureau of Refugees, Freed-
men, and Abandoned Lands, 1865–1872, microfilm publica-
tion 1913, record group 105, National Archives, Washington,
D.C.

1867 Census   "Census Returns of Colored Population of Montgomery
County, State of Virginia" [1867], reel 68, Records of the

	Field Offices for the State of Virginia, Bureau of Refugees, Freedmen, and Abandoned Lands, 1865–1872, microfilm publication 1913, record group 105, National Archives, Washington, D.C.
FFA	Friends Freedmen's Association Records, 1863–1982, RG 4/024, Friends Historical Library, Swarthmore College, Swarthmore, Pa.
LOV	Library of Virginia, Richmond, Va.
Mahone Papers	William Mahone Papers, David M. Rubenstein Rare Book & Manuscript Library, Duke University, Durham, N.C.
MCCH	Montgomery County Clerk of the Circuit Court's Office, Christiansburg, Va.
MC Cohabitation	"Register of Colored Persons of Montgomery County, State of Virginia, Cohabiting Together as Husband and Wife on 27th February, 1866," Montgomery County Clerk of the Circuit Court's Office, Christiansburg, Va.
MCM	Montgomery Museum and Lewis Miller Regional Art Center, Christiansburg, Va.
MCPS	Montgomery County Public Schools, Christiansburg, Va.
Pardons	Case Files of Applications from Former Confederates for Presidential Pardons, microfilm publication 1003, record group 94, National Archives, Washington, D.C.
SCCD	Barred and Disallowed Case Files of the Southern Claims Commission, 1871–1880, microfilm publication 1407, record group 233, National Archives, Washington, D.C.
SCCV	Southern Claims Commission Approved Claims, 1871–1880: Virginia, microfilm publication 2094, record group 217, National Archives, Washington, D.C.
USCT	Compiled Military Service Records of Volunteer Union Soldiers Belonging to the 36th through the 40th Infantry Units, Organized for Service with the United States Colored Troops, microfilm publication 1993, record group 94, National Archives, Washington, D.C.
VBHS	Virginia Baptist Historical Society, Richmond, Va.
VHS	Virginia Historical Society, Richmond, Va.
VT	Special Collections, Newman Library, Virginia Tech, Blacksburg, Va.

INTRODUCTION

1. Examples of this traditional historiography include Johnston, *A History of Middle New River Settlements;* Crush, *The Montgomery County Story;* Kegley and Kegley, *Early Adventurers on Western Waters;* P. Johnson, *The New River Early Settlement.*

2. Gutman, *The Black Family*, 547n13.

3. Litwack, *Been in the Storm So Long;* Ayers, *The Promise of the New South;* Litwack, *Trouble in Mind.*

4. Gutman, *The Black Family;* J. Jones, *Labor of Love, Labor of Sorrow;* Cohen, *At Freedom's Edge;* Hahn, *A Nation under Our Feet.*

5. Alexander, *North Carolina Faces the Freedmen;* Morgan, *Emancipation in Virginia's Tobacco Belt;* Penningroth, *The Claims of Kinfolk;* O'Donovan, *Becoming Free in the Cotton South.*

6. Kerr-Ritchie, *Freedpeople in the Tobacco South;* Holt, *Making Freedom Pay;* Dailey, *Before Jim Crow;* Green, *Educational Reconstruction.*

7. McKinney, *Southern Mountain Republicans;* Turner and Cabbell, *Blacks in Appalachia;* Lewis, *Black Coal Miners in America;* Inscoe, *Mountain Masters;* Trotter, *Coal, Class, and Labor;* Noe, *Southwest Virginia's Railroad;* Dew, *Bond of Iron;* Dunaway, *The First American Frontier;* Inscoe and McKinney, *The Heart of Confederate Appalachia;* Inscoe, *Appalachians and Race;* Crawford, *Ashe County's Civil War;* Dunaway, *Slavery in the American Mountain South;* Dunaway, *The African-American Family;* Sarris, *A Separate Civil War;* Inscoe, *Race, War, and Remembrance;* Slap, *Reconstructing Appalachia;* Nash, *Reconstruction's Ragged Edge.*

PROLOGUE

1. "[Recollections of] Janie Milton," John Nicolay Papers, Ms 87–027, box 1, folder 38, VT; MC Cohabitation.

2. Testimony of Charles Hunter in file of Edmund Otey, Roanoke County, Va., SCCD; file of William Moon (sometimes Moore), Montgomery County, SCCV; Ash, *A Year in the South*, 158; Dunaway, *The African-American Family*, 212–19; "[Recollections of] Janie Milton," John Nicolay Papers, Ms 87–027, box 1, folder 38, VT.

3. *Lynchburg Daily Virginian*, Mar. 5, 1855.

4. Lindon, *Virginia's Montgomery County*, 163–69; Noe, *Southwest Virginia's Railroad*, 11–52; Dunaway, *The First American Frontier*, 123–55, 195–248.

5. Lindon, *Virginia's Montgomery County*, 188–92; Noe, *Southwest Virginia's Railroad*, 67–84; Clement Daniel Fishburne Diary, 37, Mss 4069, Albert and Shirley Small Special Collections Library, University of Virginia Library, Charlottesville, Va.

6. 1850 and 1860 censuses (slave and agriculture schedules).

7. E. Hergesheimer, "Map of Virginia Showing the Distribution of Its Slave Population from the Census of 1860," C. B. Graham, lithographer (Washington, D.C.: Henry S. Graham, 1861), LOV.

8. 1860 census (population and slave schedules); Dusinberre, *Strategies for Survival*, 51. Slave owners located with land records and "Map of Montgomery County Virginia" [1864], Hotchkiss Map Collection, Library of Congress, Geography and Map Division.

9. 1860 census (population and slaves schedules); Lindon, *Virginia's Montgomery County*, 59–60, 103–4.

10. [Elizabeth A. L. Payne], "A Brief Outline of My Life," folder 50, Isaac White

Papers, Ms 97–013, VT; May 1, 1865, Order Book Co. Court Com. Law & Chancy. 1859–1868, MCCH.

11. J. Smith, "Virginia during Reconstruction," 1–14; Lowe, *Republicans and Reconstruction in Virginia*, 10–35.

12. In Montgomery County, seven of the nineteen justices elected in August 1864 were reelected in July 1865. See, for example, pardon application of Rice D. Montague, Pardons; Tripp, *Yankee Town, Southern City*, 167; Kanode, *Christiansburg*, 147–60; Aug. 1 and Aug. 7, 1865, Order Book Co. Court Com. Law & Chancy. 1859–1868, MCCH.

13. *Records of the Field Offices for the State of Virginia*, 1–5; Randall M. Miller, "The Freedmen's Bureau and Reconstruction: An Overview," in Cimbala and Miller, *The Freedmen's Bureau and Reconstruction*, xiii–xxxii.

14. *Records of the Field Offices for the State of Virginia*, 1–5; obituary for Orlando Brown, *Proceedings of the Connecticut Medical Society*, 484–85; Thompson, *Thirteenth Regiment of New Hampshire Volunteer Infantry in the War of the Rebellion*, 613–14; Carter to Brown, July 31, Aug. 9, and Aug. 29, 1865, reel 38, BRFAL-ACVA; Brown to Curtis, Sept. 18, 1865, reel 1, BRFAL-ACVA; Special Order 72, May 1, 1866, reel 193, BRFAL-FOVA; Special Order 9, May 23, 1866, reel 193, BRFAL-FOVA; Harrison, *Consecrated Life*. The organization of the Freedmen's Bureau changed slightly in 1867, when "districts" were designated "sub-districts" and what had been subdistricts became "divisions" (*Records of the Field Offices for the State of Virginia*, 3).

15. Henry Fowlkes to "My Dearly Beloved Children," Oct. 12, 1865, Henry M. Fowlkes Letters, Ms 80–004, VT; Foner and Walker, *Proceedings of the Black State Conventions*, 2:271.

1. People and Communities

1. "Veterans—Colored Division," *Norfolk and Western Magazine* 8, no. 3 (1930): 166–67; 1867 Census; marriage licenses, 1876: 133, MCCH; 1870, 1880, 1900, 1910, 1920, and 1930 censuses (population schedules); Lindon, *Virginia's Montgomery County*, 274; personal communication, James Dow, 2011.

2. "Veterans—Colored Division," *Norfolk and Western Magazine*, 8, no. 3 (1930); 1870, 1880, 1900, 1910, 1920, and 1930 censuses (population schedules); personal communication, James Dow, 2011.

3. Inscoe and McKinney, *The Heart of Confederate Appalachia*, 208–31; Jaime Amanda Martinez, "The Slave Market in Civil War Virginia," in Ayers, Gallagher, and Torget, *Crucible of the Civil War*, 106–35 (especially 125–26); Schaeffer to Austin, Nov. 15, 1867, reel 67, BRFAL-FOVA; 1860 census (population schedule); *Calendar of Wills in West Virginia;* 1865 Census.

4. Thorp, "Soldiers, Servants, and Very Interested Bystanders."

5. 1865 Census; 1860 census (population schedule).

6. David, Alfred, and Andrew Moore and Joseph Nelson, for example, were all identified as "freedmen" in a labor agreement they reached in August with William and David Edmundson, but none of the four is included on the 1865 census ("Agree-

ment made and entered into this 14th August 1865 . . . ," sec. 31, Mss1 Ed598 a, 1,079–1,085, Edmundson Family Papers, VHS).

7. 1867 Census; censuses 1870–1900 (population schedules); *Virginia School Report.*

8. McKinney, *Southern Mountain Republicans,* 134–35; Kerr-Ritchie, *Freedpeople in the Tobacco South,* 241. For purposes of consistency, in discussing the county's population in 1900 I have retained the population living in Radford, which became an independent city in 1892. If its residents are subtracted, the county's black population had declined to 2,925 in 1900.

9. Hahn, *A Nation under Our Feet,* 364–65.

10. For more on the desire of freedmen and of the Freedmen's Bureau to reunite families, see Gutman, *The Black Family,* 363–431; Litwack, *Been in the Storm So Long,* 229–47; Dunaway, *The African-American Family,* 257–67; Penningroth, *The Claims of Kinfolk,* 163–86; Farmer-Kaiser, *Freedwomen and the Freedmen's Bureau,* 96–140; H. Williams, *Help Me to Find My People,* 145–53; Sternhell, *Routes of War,* 167–79.

11. MC Cohabitation.

12. Order Book Co. Court Comm. Law & Chancy. 1859–1868, 87, MCCH; deposition of Susan Lester, *Mary Vaughn v. R. Carrington Vaughn,* Chancery 1952, MCCH.

13. Gutman, *The Black Family,* 363–431; Dunaway, *The African-American Family,* 257–61; Sternhell, *Routes of War,* 169–70; H. Williams, *Help Me to Find My People; Christian Recorder,* June 24, 1871; Woodroof to Schaeffer, Aug. 13, 1866, reel 68, BRFAL-FOVA; deposition of Susan Lester, *Mary Vaughn v. R. Carrington Vaughn,* Chancery 1952, MCCH.

14. Expenditures for "Uniting Families", "Complaints Wytheville Va 8th Dist." [Aug. 1865–Jan. 1866], reel 193, BRFAL-FOVA; Schaeffer to Remington, Dec. 3, 1866, reel 67, BRFAL-FOVA; Remington to Schaeffer, Dec. 10, 1866, reel 193, BRFAL-FOVA; 1867 Census; Woodell to Hunt, Aug. 27, 1866, reel 68, BRFAL-FOVA; Poor to Schaeffer, Oct. 19, 1866, reel 68, BRFAL-FOVA; Schaeffer to Callahan, Oct. 21, 1866, reel 67, BRFAL-FOVA; Schaeffer to Woodell, Oct. 21 and Oct. 30, 1866, reel 67, BRFAL-FOVA; Woodell to Schaeffer, Oct. 31, 1866, reel 68, BRFAL-FOVA; Sherwood to Schaeffer, July 21, 1866, reel 68, BRFAL-FOVA.

15. MC Cohabitation; Wedin, "A Summary of 19th Century Smithfield, Part I," 79–95.

16. Cohen, *At Freedom's Edge,* 51–55; Kerr-Ritchie, *Freedpeople in the Tobacco South,* 93–101.

17. 1860, 1870, and 1880 censuses (agricultural schedules). For more on white reluctance to rent or sell land to freedpeople, see Litwack, *Been in the Storm So Long,* 407–8; Schweninger, *Black Property Owners in the South,* 143–76; Morgan, *Emancipation in Virginia's Tobacco Belt,* 192–93; O'Donovan, *Becoming Free in the Cotton South,* 111–61.

18. *Stanger v. Linkous et al.,* Chancery 804, MCCH.

19. Marriage licenses, MCCH; *Henderson v. Henderson,* Chancery 1763, MCCH.

20. Ronald L. Lewis, "Railroads, Deforestation, and the Transformation of

Agriculture in West Virginia Back Counties, 1880–1920," in Pudup, Billings, and Waller, *Appalachia in the Making,* 297–320 (quotation on 297). See also McKinney, *Southern Mountain Republicans,* 124–41; Dotson, *Roanoke, Virginia,* 1–82; Ken Fones-Wolf, "A House Redivided: From Sectionalism to Political Economy in West Virginia," in Slap, *Reconstructing Appalachia,* 237–68; Nash, *Reconstruction's Ragged Edge,* 149–77.

21. Lindon, *Virginia's Montgomery County,* 220, 340–54; marriage licenses, MCCH.

22. *Christiansburg Messenger,* Feb. 20, 1880; Lindon, *Virginia's Montgomery County,* 366–68; Lewis, *Black Coal Miners in America,* 121–42; Trotter, *Coal, Class, and Color,* 9–38; Schwieder, Hraba, and Schwieder, *Buxton,* 22–23, 183; transcript of interview with Frank Bannister conducted by Clyde Kessler in 1982 in Cain, "Wake Forest," 149; Dotson, *Roanoke, Virginia,* 66–68, 105–12; E. Johnson, *Radford Then and Now,* 20; Killen, *Radford's Early Black Residents.*

23. Cohen, *At Freedom's Edge,* 107; account of "William Campbell, free negro," Virginia, vol. 28, p. 527, R. G. Dun & Co. Collection, Baker Library Historical Collections, Harvard Business School, Cambridge, Mass.; *Fickey v. Campbell,* Common Law A-2873, MCCH; Scharf, *The Chronicles of Baltimore,* 598.

24. Woodward, *The Strange Career of Jim Crow;* McKinney, *Southern Mountain Republicans;* Dailey, *Before Jim Crow;* Hahn, *A Nation under Our Feet.*

25. Schaeffer to Brown, July 25, 1866, reel 59, BRFAL-ACVA; Schaeffer to Brown, Aug. 25, 1866, and Oct. 27, 1867, reel 67, BRFAL-FOVA; Schaeffer to Remington, Feb. 14, 1867, reel 67, BRFAL-FOVA; Schaeffer to Mallery, June 25, 1867, reel 67, BRFAL-FOVA; Schaeffer to Coulter, Apr. 30, 1868, reel 67, BRFAL-FOVA; deposition of Othello Fraction, Oct. 21, 1895, in Isabella Fraction, widow's pension application no. 577,695, service of Thomas Fraction (private, Co. H, Fortieth US Colored Infantry), Civil War and Later Pension Files, Department of Veterans Affairs, record group 15, National Archives, Washington, DC.; *Christiansburg Southwest,* Apr. 25, May 2, and May 9, 1868.

26. American Colonization Society, *The African Repository* 42 (1866): 40; Schaeffer to Coppinger, July 31, 1867, American Colonization Society Records, Incoming Correspondence, 1819–1917, Domestic Letters, 1823–1912, reel 100, Library of Congress (accessed through https://www.Fold3.com). For more on postemancipation emigration to Liberia, see Cohen, *At Freedom's Edge,* 138–67; Hahn, *A Nation under Our Feet,* 320–45, 364–65; Clegg, *The Price of Liberty,* 249–70; *F. C. Kessler's Admr. v. George Clare's Heirs,* Chancery 908, MCCH.

27. McKinney, *Southern Mountain Republicans,* 134. For a fuller discussion of race in Virginia at this time, see Maddex, *The Virginia Conservatives,* 184–203; Pincus, *The Virginia Supreme Court;* Dailey, *Before Jim Crow,* 15–47.

28. Lewis, *Black Coal Miners in America,* 121; Schwieder, Hraba, and Schwieder, *Buxton,* 220.

29. George Washington Hopkins to "Dear Wife," June 29, 1892, in *Hopkins v. Hopkins,* Chancery 1453, MCCH; George Washington to Fannie Washington, Feb. 22, 1899, in *Washington v. Washington,* Chancery 1735, MCCH; "'Nigger Bill' (William

McNorton)", box 5, folder 5, Neil Fullerton Research Collection, Montana Historical
Society, Research Center Archives, Helena; marriage license of William McNorton
and Ella Harra, May 29, 1900, Missoula County Court House, Missoula, Montana,
https://familysearch.org. See also Gutman, *The Black Family*, 432–60; Cohen,
At Freedom's Edge, 78–108, 248–98; Kerr-Ritchie, *Freedpeople in the Tobacco South*,
240–45.

30. 1865 Census; 1867 Census; MC Cohabitation; Ash, *A Year in the South*, 158;
O'Donovan, *Becoming Free in the Cotton South*, 112–16; Dunaway, *The African-
American Family*, 212–26; "Complaints Wytheville Va 8th Dist." [Aug. 1865–Jan.
1866], reel 193, BRFAL-FOVA.

31. For a fuller discussion of postwar migration by freedpeople and the economic
challenges this involved, see Cohen, *At Freedom's Edge*, 44–197.

32. "[Recollections of] Janie Milton", box 1, folder 38, John Nicolay Papers, Ms
87–027, VT.

33. Reiff, Dahlin, and Scott, "Rural Push and Urban Pull"; Kerr-Ritchie, *Freedpeople in the Tobacco South*, 236–39; Fields, *Slavery and Freedom on the Middle
Ground*, 194–206.

34. 1860, 1870, 1880, and 1900 censuses (population schedules). The figure 26.4
percent in 1900 includes 456 African Americans living in Radford, which had become
an independent city in 1892. If they are omitted, then 14.9 percent of the county's
black population was "urban" (i.e., lived in Christiansburg, Cambria, or Blacksburg) in
1900.

35. Kanode, *Christiansburg*, 13–18, 34; Lindon, *Virginia's Montgomery County*,
265–67, 274–76.

36. Deed Book S: 92, MCCH. The racial geography of Christiansburg is evident
through a comparison of land sales to locations plotted on "Gray's New Map of
Christiansburg, Montgomery County, Virginia" [ca. 1880], folder D-7, Historical Map
Collection, VT. Description of Calloway's neighborhood from flyer in *Archer Phlegar,
Trst. v. Wm. C. Hagan et al.*, Chancery 583, MCCH.

37. 1860, 1870, 1880, and 1900 censuses (population schedules).

38. *Christian Recorder*, May 2 and Dec. 12, 1868; Butt, *History of African Methodism*, 71; Deed Book W: 190, MCCH; *Minutes of the (Colored) Valley Baptist Association . . . 1873;* Schaeffer to Austin, July 28, 1868, roll 67, BRFAL-FOVA; *Virginia
School Report;* Dunay, *Blacksburg*, 102; censuses of 1880 and 1900 (population
schedules).

39. Wallenstein, *Virginia Tech*, 47–52; *Stanger v. Linkous et al.*, Chancery 804,
MCCH; Deed Book X: 45, MCCH; censuses of 1880 and 1900 (population schedules);
MC Cohabitation.

40. Deed Book 27: 109, MCCH; *Wade v. Mills*, Chancery 2347, MCCH. Scott
Casper found a similar pattern among black landowners in Fairfax County (Scott E.
Casper, "Out of Mount Vernon's Shadow: Black Landowners in George Washington's
Neighborhood, 1870-1930," in Reid and Bennett, *Beyond Forty Acres and a Mule*,
39–62.)

41. Cain, "Wake Forest," 13–31 (Wake Forest story from Sonny Johnson's recollec-

tions, 25); "Map of Montgomery County Virginia" [1864], Hotchkiss Map Collection, Library of Congress, Geography and Map Division; *Christian Recorder,* May 22, 1869; school teachers' reports, reels 17 and 19, BRFAL-EDVA.

42. Arthur Sullivan to Lake Sullivan, July 25, 1869, Box Doc 3047, folder 2, Sullivan Family Papers, accession number 2014.32.02, MCM; *Richmond Daily Dispatch,* July 12, 1869; Deed Book Z: 210, MCCH; US Patents 325,342 (1885) and 350,363 (1886); *Christiansburg Messenger,* May 2, 1879; Abstract of Votes, May 24, 1879, file drawer #1, MCCH; *Minutes of the (Colored) Valley Baptist Association . . . 1873.*

43. Harrison, *Consecrated Life,* 173–75; 1860 census (population schedule); *Minutes of the (Colored) Valley Baptist Association . . . 1873;* Schaeffer to Brown, Mar. 15, 1867, in Linda Killen, *Freedmen's Bureau,* 16–18. For a more extended discussion of black leaders in Virginia at this time, see Lowe, "The Freedmen's Bureau and Local Black Leadership," and Lowe, "Local Black Leaders during Reconstruction in Virginia."

44. Berlin, Reidy, and Rowland, *Freedom's Soldiers,* 47–50; Thorp, "Soldiers, Servants, and Very Interested Bystanders."

45. Harrison, *Consecrated Life,* 171, 284; *Christiansburg Messenger,* July 10, 1874; Genovese, *Roll, Jordan, Roll,* 475–76; *Christiansburg Southwest,* Jan. 2, 1869; marriage licenses, MCCH.

2. Families in Freedom

1. Marriage license issued Dec. 19, 1865, and included among licenses for that year filed in MCCH but not recorded in the Register of Marriages and not numbered; MC Cohabitation; 1865 Census.

2. "Register of Deaths 1873, 1876, 1889, 1891" (these are loose sheets that provide a fragmentary record of deaths in Montgomery County during these years), MCCH; 1880 and 1900 censuses (population schedules); marriage licenses, 1879: 45, and 1884: 4, MCCH; *Morgan v. Morgan,* Chancery 835, MCCH; Will Book 13: 5, MCCH.

3. Gutman, *The Black Family,* especially 3–326; Escott, *Slavery Remembered;* Manfra and Dykstra, "Serial Marriage"; Burton, *In My Father's House,* 148–202; Malone, *Sweet Chariot;* Stevenson, *Life in Black and White,* 159–319; Schwalm, *A Hard Fight for We;* Dunaway, *The African-American Family,* 51–178; Pargas, *The Quarters and the Fields.*

4. Neither chap. 107, "Of Free Negroes," nor chap. 108, "Of Marriages, Births, and Deaths," of the *Code of Virginia* makes any mention of slave or free black marriages, though chap. 108 does provide for the registration of births and deaths of both slaves and free blacks. Chap. 109, "Of Divorces," declares interracial marriages "absolutely void, without any decree of divorce, or other legal process" (*Code of Virginia* [1860], 529).

5. 1850 census (population schedule); Court Order Book 32: 291, MCCH; Will Book 9: 345, MCCH.

6. Gutman, *The Black Family,* 363–431; Litwack, *Been in the Storm So Long,*

229–47; Bardaglio, *Reconstructing the Household,* 129–36; Regosin, *Freedom's Promise;* Nash, *Reconstruction's Ragged Edge,* 47–48.

7. Gutman, *The Black Family,* 417; MC Cohabitation; Register of Marriages, MCCH; *Code of Virginia* (1860), chap. 108, as amended by chap. 20, Mar. 15, 1861 (*Acts of the General Assembly . . . 1861*).

8. Marriage license of Oscar Johnson and Nancy Duke, issued Sept. 1, 1865, and included among licenses for that year filed in MCCH but not recorded in the Register of Marriages and not numbered; "Record of Marriages" in Record of Baptisms, 1859–1878, box 5, Whisner Memorial Methodist Church Records, Ms 64–003, VT; Marriage Licenses, 1865, MCCH; Register of Marriages, MCCH; MC Cohabitation; *Acts of the General Assembly . . . 1865–66,* chap. 18 (passed Feb. 27, 1866), 85–86.

9. Woodroof to Schaeffer, Aug. 13, 1866, reel 68, BRFAL-FOVA; 1865 Census; MC Cohabitation.

10. Carter to Brown, Sept. 9, 1865, reel 38, BRFAL-ACVA; Schaeffer to Mallery, May 25 and June 25, 1867, reel 67, BRFAL-FOVA; Schaeffer to Brown, Nov. 30, 1867, reel 67, BRFAL-FOVA. For a fuller discussion of the Freedmen's Bureau's attitude and actions regarding black families, see Gutman, *The Black Family,* 420–25; Litwack, *Been in the Storm So Long,* 229–47; Mitchell, *Raising Freedom's Child,* 143–87; Farmer-Kaiser, *Freedwomen and the Freedmen's Bureau,* 64–95; Nash, *Reconstruction's Ragged Edge,* 92–96.

11. Schaeffer to Bureau Officer in Charge of Spotsylvania Co., Apr. 18, 1868, reel 68, BRFAL-FOVA; Holladay to Sears, May 7, 1868, reel 68, BRFAL-FOVA; Sears to [?], May 11, 1868, reel 68, BRFAL-FOVA. For a fuller discussion of multiple spouses, see Litwack, *Been in the Storm So Long,* 241–42; Gutman, *The Black Family,* 418–25.

12. Mitchell, *Raising Freedom's Child,* 143–87; Farmer-Kaiser, *Freedwomen and the Freedmen's Bureau,* 64–95; Schaeffer to Remington, Dec. 15, 1866, reel 67, BRFAL-FOVA; Remington to Schaeffer, Dec. 17, 1866, reel 67, BRFAL-FOVA; Schaeffer to O'Neill, July 25, 1866, reel 67, BRFAL-FOVA; Schaeffer to Clark, Sept. 8, 1866, reel 67, BRFAL-FOVA.

13. 1865 Census; MC Cohabitation. Many of those on the census are identified by first name only. Some families can be identified, however, by the use of surnames on the census or by the presence of distinctive names found together on the census and on other documents in which they are identified as a family.

14. *Acts of the General Assembly . . . 1865–66,* chap. 18 (passed Feb. 27, 1866), 85–86; R. Washington, "Sealing the Sacred Bonds of Holy Matrimony"; Manfra and Dykstra, "Serial Marriage." Freedmen's Bureau officials in different states responded in a variety of ways to situations like that found in Virginia, though North Carolina seems to be the only other state in which cohabitation registers as detailed as those found in Virginia were created. See Alexander, *North Carolina Faces the Freedmen,* 58–66, and "Cohabitation Records" at https://www.familysearch.org/learn/wiki/en/Cohabitation_Records.

15. Litwack, *Been in the Storm So Long,* 242–43; Gutman, *The Black Family,* 418–25; Escott, *Slavery Remembered,* 44; Dunaway, *The African-American Family,*

261; Penningroth, *The Claims of Kinfolk,* 181–82; Schaeffer to Brown, Sept. 25, 1866, reel 67, BRFAL-FOVA.

16. Schaeffer to Robe, Sept. 11, 1867, reel 67, BRFAL-FOVA; Schaeffer to Brown, Nov. 30, 1867, reel 68, BRFAL-FOVA.

17. Schaeffer to Robe, Sept. 11, 1867, reel 67, BRFAL-FOVA; Penningroth, *The Claims of Kinfolk,* 111–30.

18. Schaeffer to Robe, Sept. 11, 1867, reel 67, BRFAL-FOVA; Schaeffer to Brown, Nov. 30, 1867, reel 68, BRFAL-FOVA; Order Book Co. Court Comm. Law & Chancy., 1859–1868, entries for Nov. 4 and Nov. 5, 1867, MCCH; *Commonwealth v. Saunders,* Criminal A-736, MCCH.

19. Order Book Co. Court Comm. Law & Chancy., 1859–1868, entries for Nov. 4, 5, and 6, 1867, MCCH; Order Book Com. Law & Chancy., 1868–1870, 67–68, MCCH.

20. Litwack, *Been in the Storm So Long,* 247–48. See also Regosin, *Freedom's Promise,* 54–78.

21. Gutman, *The Black Family,* 230–44; Genovese, *Roll, Jordan, Roll,* 443–50.

22. Scholars such as Leon Litwack (*Been in the Storm So Long,* 247–51) and Herbert Gutman (*The Black Family,* 245–56) have argued that many freedpeople rejected the names of their former owners and chose names that reflected their own histories or values. Still, the idea remains strong among many people that most African Americans adopted the names of their former owners; see, for example, Jackson, *My Father's Name.*

23. 1867 Census. In a few cases, families that appear separated on the 1867 census were probably not. Biddie Jones, for example, appears among the *J*s on the census while her children appear among the *B*s, as they went by Bolden, their father's surname. They all identified William Montague as their employer, though, and seem to have lived together with him (see 1870 and 1880 censuses [population schedules] and the marriage license of Nannie Bolden [1880: 5, MCCH]).

24. Thorp, "Cohabitation Registers."

25. The census enumerator did fail to provide any indication of marital status in the cases of twenty-three adults (1.9 percent of the total adult population).

26. In some Virginia counties, agents of the Freedmen's Bureau prepared a companion document to the cohabitation register known as the "Register of Children of Colored Persons . . . Whose Parents Had Ceased to Cohabit on 27th February, 1866, Which the Father Registers to Be His." These included columns in which to enter the residence of both the mother and father of each child registered and often reveal that the mother had died or been sold outside the county. In other cases, however, both parents were still living in the same county, which suggests that the couple had chosen to separate. No such register for Montgomery County has yet to come to light, but at least one example of a voluntary separation involving a woman in Montgomery County appears on the register from Floyd County, adjacent to Montgomery. Joe and Milly Crockett had both been enslaved in Floyd County and had at least two children while living together, but by 1866, when Floyd County's cohabitation register was compiled, the couple had split. The register of persons who had ceased to cohabit shows that Joe and the couple's son, Joe, were still living in Floyd County, while Milly

and their daughter, Amanda, had moved to Montgomery County (Thorp, "Cohabitation Registers"; "Register of Colored Persons in Floyd County, State of Virginia, Whose Parents Had Ceased to Cohabit on 27th February 1866, Which the Father Recognizes to Be His," Cohabitation Registers Digital Collection, LOV [http://www.virginiamemory.com]).

27. Marriage licenses, 1876: 29, MCCH.

28. 1867 census.

29. See, for example, Litwack, *Been in the Storm So Long*, 237–38; Fuke, "Planters, Apprentices, and Forced Labor"; Farmer-Kaiser, *Freedwomen and the Freedmen's Bureau*, 97–118; Zipf, *Labor of Innocents*, 40–105.

30. "Record of Indentures," reel 199, BRFAL-FOVA; Schaeffer to O'Neil, July 25, 1866, reel 67, BRFAL-FOVA; O'Neil to Schaeffer, July 28, 1866, reel 68, BRFAL-FOVA; Sherwood to Schaeffer, Aug. 10 and Aug. 30, 1866, reel 193, BRFAL-FOVA; Elizabeth Clark to "The Office of the Freedmen's Bureau Christiansburg," Sept. 8, 1866, reel 68, BRFAL-FOVA; Schaeffer to Remington, Dec. 15, 1866, reel 68, BRFAL-FOVA.

31. Marriage licenses, 1879: 67, MCCH.

32. Catherine Jones has explored the tension between "social obligation" and "material interest" in the matter of who was willing to take in black children too young to work toward their own upkeep and also concluded that it is simply not possible to generalize about the motives of those who adopted these children. See C. Jones, "Ties That Bind, Bonds That Break."

33. *Acts of the General Assembly . . . 1865–66*, chap. 18 (passed Feb. 27, 1866), 85–86. In describing the cohabitation register to his superiors, Schaeffer explicitly distinguished between "children" and "illegitimate offspring" (see Schaeffer to Brown, Sept. 25, 1866, reel 67, BRFAL-FOVA), though on the 1867 census he seems to have used a less explicit series of dots to identify children who were illegitimate according to the 1866 statute.

34. *Leftwich et al. v. Wm. Pattersons' admr. et al.*, Chancery 1772, MCCH.

35. Pincus, *The Virginia Supreme Court*, 63–69; *Commonwealth v. Lewis Brown*, Criminal No. 16, MCCH.

36. See, for example, Gutman, *The Black Family*, 363–431; Escott, *Slavery Remembered*, 169–71; Litwack, *Been in the Storm So Long*, 229–47; Manfra and Dykstra, "Serial Marriage"; Dunaway, *The African-American Family*, 257–67.

37. Population calculated from schedules of the censuses of 1880 and 1900; marriages calculated from licenses in MCCH. A similar pattern appears in approximate rates of marriage for the three decades following Reconstruction in Montgomery County. Using three-year rolling averages of the number marriages and the mean of the populations reported on the censuses bracketing a particular decade suggests that Montgomery County blacks married at a rate of about 12 per 1,000 during the 1870s and about 7.5 per 1,000 during the 1880s and 1890s, except for a jump in the five years around 1890, when the rate rose to about 10.7 per 1,000.

38. Thorp, "Cohabitation Registers"; MC Cohabitation. Ages at marriage extracted from marriage licenses and Register of Marriages, MCCH.

39. Of the forty-five cases that definitely involved African Americans, thirty-seven led to a final decree of divorce, five were dismissed, and three left partial records from which it is impossible to determine the outcome. In Montgomery County at this time divorce proceedings were heard in chancery, and the records of these cases are filed among the chancery records in the MCCH.

40. *Beverly v. Beverly,* Chancery 701, MCCH; *Cephas v. Cephas,* Chancery 1131, MCCH; *Leftwich v. Leftwich,* Chancery 331, MCCH.

41. See, for example, Gutman, *The Black Family,* 165–68; Litwack, *Been in the Storm So Long,* 229–47; J. Jones, *Labor of Love, Labor of Sorrow,* 58–68; Morgan, *Emancipation in Virginia's Tobacco Belt,* 142, 177; Holt, *Making Freedom Pay,* 10; Litwack, *Trouble in Mind,* 123–27; Farmer-Kaiser, *Freedwomen and the Freedmen's Bureau,* 64–65.

42. 1867 Census; 1870, 1880, and 1900 censuses (population schedules); *Scott v. Scott,* Chancery 1055, MCCH.

43. *Walker v. Walker,* Chancery 765-A, MCCH; *Briggs v. Briggs,* Chancery 1606, MCCH; *Twine v. Twine,* Chancery 1423, MCCH; marriage licenses, 1879: 42 (Twine) and 1882: 60 (Briggs), MCCH. Dylan Penningroth also notes that following emancipation, it became increasingly difficult for African Americans who were not part of an individual's family to intervene in his or her marital relations (*The Claims of Kinfolk,* 183).

44. MC Cohabitation; 1870 and 1880 censuses (population schedules); *Armstrong et al. v. Armstrong et al.,* Chancery 349, MCCH; *Fuqua v. Fuqua,* Chancery 512, MCCH; *Radford v. Radford,* Chancery 448, MCCH; *Payne v. Payne,* Chancery 429, MCCH; *Jones v. Jones,* Chancery 452, MCCH; *Wm. Lewis et al. v. Charlotte Lewis,* Chancery 3449, MCCH; *Morgan v. Morgan,* Chancery 835, MCCH; Deed Book U: 55–56, MCCH.

45. Daniel Mitchell had returned by the summer of 1874, when he provided a deposition in *Payne v. Payne,* Chancery 429, MCCH; he apparently died before 1880, though, when his wife, Maria, appears as a widow on the census. *Wm. Lewis et al. v. Charlotte Lewis,* Chancery 3449, MCCH; *Jones v. Jones,* Chancery 452, MCCH; *Morgan v. Morgan,* Chancery 835, MCCH; *Armstrong v. Armstrong,* Chancery 349, MCCH; *Mason v. Mason,* Chancery 901, MCCH.

46. 1867 Census; 1870, 1880, and 1900 censuses (population schedules); Will Book 12: 400, MCCH.

47. *Twine v. Twine,* Chancery 1423, MCCH.

3. LABOR, LAND, AND MAKING A LIVING

1. MC Cohabitation; 1867 Census. Ellen Mills appears as both Nelly and Nellie on various censuses over the years, but the only document known to have come from her immediate family—the will of her son James T. Mills—identifies her as Nellie (Will Book 13: 57, MCCH).

2. 1867 Census; Schaeffer to Austin, May 18, 1867, reel 67, BRFAL-FOVA; Austin to Schaeffer, May 21, 1867, reel 68, BRFAL-FOVA; *Jones & Son v. Mills,* Common

Law A-6817, MCCH; *Wade v. Mills Admir.,* Chancery 2347, MCCH; Deed Book T: 256, Deed Book Z: 181 and 253, Deed Book 26: 466: Deed Book 61: 405, MCCH.

3. Carter to [Brown], Aug. 14 (quotation) and Aug. 28, 1865, reel 38, BRFAL-ACVA; "[Recollections of] Janie Milton," box 1, folder 38, John Nicolay Papers, Ms 87–027, VT; Woodroof to Schaeffer, Aug. 13, 1866, reel 68, BRFAL-FOVA.

4. Cohen, *At Freedom's Edge,* 109–37; Kerr-Ritchie, *Freedpeople in the Tobacco South,* 31–34; O'Donovan, *Becoming Free in the Cotton South,* 121–32.

5. Statement of Archer A. Phleger in a deed conveying land to Robert Carter, Deed Book 47: 492–93, MCCH; American Colonization Society, *The African Repository* 42 (1866): 40 and 157; Schaeffer to Brown, Aug. 25, 1866, reel 67, BRFAL-FOVA; Etzler to "Agt. Freedmen's Bureau," Mar. 8, 1867, reel 68, BRFAL-FOVA.

6. Montgomery County Property Tax, 1863, Department of Taxation, Personal Property Tax Books, LOV. The 1860 census identified nine free black landowners, though not all of these can be found in the county's land records.

7. Notice sent by Schaeffer to freedmen in Giles and Pulaski Counties, Aug. 4, 1866, reel 67, BRFAL-FOVA; Schaeffer to Sherwood, Aug. 4, 1866, reel 67, BRFAL-FOVA; Schaeffer to Brown, Aug. 25 and Sept. 25, 1866, reel 67, BRFAL-FOVA. See also Cohen, *At Freedom's Edge,* 51–53.

8. For a discussion of the paradoxical attitudes toward free people of color in antebellum Virginia, see Ely, *Israel on the Appomattox;* Von Daacke, *Freedom Has a Face;* for a postemancipation example of white Virginians responding to blacks who were "strangers," see "Amanda: Colored Daughter of Virginia," box 1, folder 30, James Robbins Randolph Papers, Ms 1971–001, VT.

9. "Complaints Wytheville, Va. 8th Dist." [Aug. 1865–Jan. 1866], reel 193, BRFAL-FOVA; Schaeffer to Stanley, July 10, 1866, reel 67, BRFAL-FOVA; 1865 Census; [Elizabeth A. L. Payne], "A Brief Outline of my Life," folder 50, Isaac White Papers, Ms 97–013, VT; *Lynchburg Virginian,* July 29, 1865.

10. Carter to Brown, Aug. 18, 1865, reel 38, BRFAL-ACVA; 1865 Census; MC Cohabitation. The 1865 census also includes a small number of "infirm" adults who were not employed that summer.

11. 1865 Census. Susan O'Donovan found a similar reliance on board and shares in parts of southwest Georgia in the immediate aftermath of emancipation (*Becoming Free in the Cotton South,* 126–28).

12. 1865 Census (in fourteen cases, the method of compensation was not reported, and three freedpeople were self-employed); agreement with Andrew Hicks, Jan. 1, 1866, sec. 31, Edmundson Family Papers, Mss1 Ed598 a 1,079–1,085, VHS. See also agreement between Sam Hayden and Wm. R. Pepper in "Complaints Wytheville, Va. 8th Dist." [Aug. 1865–Jan. 1866], reel 193, BRFAL-FOVA.

13. Circular No. 11, July 12, 1865, reel 68, BRFAL-FOVA; "Complaints Wytheville, Va. 8th Dist." [Aug. 1865–Jan. 1866], reel 193, BRFAL-FOVA; agreement with David Moore, Alfred Moore, Andrew Moore, and Joseph A. Nelson [Aug. 14, 1865], sec. 31, Edmundson Family Papers, Mss1 Ed598 a 1,079–1,085, VHS; MC Cohabitation.

14. Order Book Co. Court Com. Law & Chancy. 1859–1868, entry for May 1, 1865, MCCH. This pattern is also evident in Litwack, *Been in the Storm So Long,* 336–86;

Cohen, *At Freedom's Edge*, 23–43; Kerr-Ritchie, *Freedpeople in the Tobacco South*, 40–54; O'Donovan, *Becoming Free in the Cotton South*, 111–21.

15. Dunaway, *The First American Frontier*, 87–121; Nash, *Reconstruction's Ragged Edge*, 40–43; agreement between Henry Edmundson and Andy Howard, Jan. 1844, sec. 9, Mss1 Ed598 a 669–672, Edmundson Family Papers, VHS.

16. Circular No. 11, July 12, 1865, reel 68, BRFAL-FOVA; "Complaints Wytheville, Va. 8th Dist." [Aug. 1865–Jan. 1866], reel 193, BRFAL-FOVA; Carter to Brown, Aug. 9 and Aug. 28, 1865, reel 38, BRFAL-ACVA.

17. Woodroof to Schaeffer, Aug. 13, 1866, reel 68, BRFAL-FOVA; Schaeffer to Brown, July 25, Sept. 25, Nov. 25, and Dec. 25, 1866, reel 67, BRFAL-FOVA; "An Act to Regulate Contracts for Labor Between White and Colored Persons . . . ," *Acts of the General Assembly . . . 1865–66*, chap. 15 (Feb. 20, 1865), 83.

18. Farmer-Kaiser, *Freedwomen and the Freedmen's Bureau*, 64–65.

19. 1867 Census.

20. Ibid.; 1865 Census.

21. 1867 Census; MC Cohabitation.

22. Schaeffer to Brown, Feb. 25, 1867, reel 67, BRFAL-FOVA; Etzler to "Agt. Freedmens Bureau," Mar. 8, 1867, reel 68, BRFAL-FOVA; Schaeffer to Mallery, June 25, 1867, reel 67, BRFAL-FOVA. The 1867 census records forms of compensation for 1,056 freedpeople, though some individuals are shown with two forms—lease and shares, for example. It also reports an occupation for 1,092 individuals, though not all of these are shown with a form of compensation. The 894 wage earners represent 81 percent of the 1,092 employed. Twelve of those shown receiving "wages," however, are shown with no employer—suggesting they were self-employed and receiving wages from their customers. Excluding them from wage earners would reduce the number to 882, which is 80.7 percent of those shown with an occupation.

23. Kerr-Ritchie, *Freedpeople in the Tobacco South*, 49–52; 1865 Census; 1867 Census.

24. Dunaway, *The First American Frontier*, 98–104; account book of David Edmundson, 1849–1865, sec. 24, Mss1 Ed598 a, 962, Edmundson Family Papers, VHS.

25. Litwack, *Been in the Storm So Long*, 447; Morgan, *Emancipation in Virginia's Tobacco Belt*, 187–96; Kerr-Ritchie, *Freedpeople in the Tobacco South*, 49–69; Nash, *Reconstruction's Ragged Edge*, 40–43; Schaeffer to Brown, Dec. 25, 1866, reel 67, BRFAL-FOVA.

26. Morgan, *Emancipation in Virginia's Tobacco Belt*, 188.

27. Agreement between W. R. and D. Edmundson and James Taylor, 1868, sec. 31, Mss1 Ed598 a 1,079–1,085, Edmundson Family Papers, VHS. Taylor appears on the 1870 census as a white man.

28. 1867 Census; Schaeffer to Austin, June 4, 1867, reel 67, BRFAL-FOVA.

29. Schaeffer to Mallery, May 25, 1867, reel 67, BRFAL-FOVA; Austin to Schaeffer, June 5, 1867, reel 68, BRFAL-FOVA.

30. Deed Books P: 249, Q: 368 and 386, R:358, 403, 480, and 568, S: 181, U: 417, W: 284, MCCH; *Kessler v. Clare's Heirs*, Chancery 908, MCCH; *Curtis v. Miller*, Chancery 1461, MCCH.

31. Carter to Brown, Aug. 28, 1865, reel 38, BRFAL-ACVA; Schaeffer to Coulter, June 30, 1868, reel 67, BRFAL-FOVA; Montgomery County Property Tax, 1867, Department of Taxation, Personal Property Tax Books, LOV.

32. *Haney v. Currin* and *Saunders v. Currin,* Chancery 717, MCCH; "Assessment of Real Estate in Christiansburg, Virginia," filed in Minutes of the Trustees of the Town of Christiansburg, 1854–1861, MCCH; Deed Book R: 403, MCCH; Deed Book S: 46, MCCH.

33. White to Schaeffer, June 24, 1868, reel 67, BRFAL-FOVA; Thomas to Schaeffer, Nov. 22, 1868, reel 67, BRFAL-FOVA.

34. For examples of sales that were never completed and deeds never transferred, see *Black v. Vaughn et al.,* Chancery 632, MCCH; *Lane v. Read,* Chancery 848, MCCH; *Sowder v. Brown et al.,* Chancery 905, MCCH; *Atkinson v. Doss,* Chancery 927, MCCH. Robert Beverly's purchase of twenty-five acres on Crab Creek in 1868 is in Unrecorded Deeds & Powr. Atty, MCCH; Catherine Curtis's purchase of a town lot in Christiansburg was eventually recorded in Deed Book Y: 193 and was dated 1883 but can be properly dated to 1867 through evidence in *Curtis v. Miller et al.* and *Curtis v. Curtis' Heirs,* Chancery 1461, MCCH.

35. MC Cohabitation; 1867 Census; Deed Book R: 358, 403, 480, 568, and 588, MCCH; Deed Book S: 46, 92, 181, and 332, MCCH; Deed Book Y:193, MCCH; Deed Book Z: 471, MCCH; "Allen Fizor & wife to Ro. Beverly (Col[d])" [May 2, 1868], Unrecorded Deeds & Power Atty., MCCH.

36. Deed Book R: 358, 568, and 588, MCCH; Deed Book S: 46 and 181, MCCH; *Hammet v. Hayden,* Common Law A-6017, MCCH; list of notes due to James P. Hammet, "James P. Hammet Miscellaneous, 1866–1868, n.d.," box 79, folder 5, J. Hoge Tyler Family Collection, Ms 67–002, VT; *Curtis v. Miller* and *Curtis v. Curtis' Heirs,* Chancery 1461, MCCH; Kanode, *Christiansburg,* 110, 140–41; 1867 Census; "Allen Fizor & wife to Ro. Beverly (Col[d])" [May 2, 1868], Unrecorded Deeds & Power Atty., MCCH; *Phleger Trst. v. Hagan et al.,* Chancery 583, MCCH.

37. Deed Book R: 445, MCCH; Linda Killen, "'Taylor Made' in Montgomery County, Virginia," unpublished manuscript in Killen Material, archives of the Christiansburg Institute Alumni Association, Christiansburg, Va. For examples of such gifts in later decades, see Deed Book U: 165 and 243, MCCH; Deed Book 45: 115, MCCH; Deed Book 47: 292 and 446, MCCH.

38. History of the Wake Forest community, folder 38, John Nicolay Papers, Ms 87–027, VT; "Sonny Johnson—1982," in Cain, "Wake Forest," 131–43; *Christian Recorder,* May 29, 1869; reports from the Daniel A. Payne School, Oct. 1869–June 1870, reels 17 and 19, BRFAL-EDVA; James Randal Kent Papers, Ms 87–031, VT; Deed Book T: 256, MCCH; Deed Book 30: 327, MCCH; personal communication, Mary Mills, 2012; *Jones & Son v. Mills,* Common Law A-6817, MCCH.

39. Litwack, *Been in the Storm So Long,* 399–408; Schweninger, *Black Property Owners in the South,* 143–61; Kerr-Ritchie, *Freedpeople in the Tobacco South,* 210–11.

40. *Mary Vaughn v. R. Carrington Vaughn,* Chancery 1952, MCCH.

41. The increase in Montgomery County between 1870 and 1900 was just under 2,000 percent. Schweninger calculated the increases in farm ownership and nonfarm

home ownership separately and did not provide the latter for 1900. Black farm ownership, however, rose almost 3,000 percent in Virginia between 1879 and 1900 (Schweninger, *Black Property Owners in the South,* 174, 180).

42. Deed Book T: 130, MCCH; Deed Book U: 165 and 243, MCCH; Deed Book 30: 327, MCCH; Deed Book 41: 270, MCCH; Deed Book 45: 115, MCCH; Deed Book 47: 446 and 492 (includes statement from Phleger), MCCH.

43. Harvey Black to Alex Black, Oct. 11, 1879, included in *Black v. Vaughn et al.,* Chancery 632, MCCH; Black, *The Civil War Letters of Harvey Black,* 29, 152n51; Will Book 12: 352, MCCH.

44. Deed Book S: 92, MCCH; *Phleger Trst. v. Wm. C. Hagan et al.,* Chancery 583, MCCH; Swann-Wright, *A Way Out of No Way,* 69–89; J. Jones, *Labor of Love, Labor of Sorrow,* 58–68, 101–2.

45. *Curtis v. Miller et al.* and *Curtis v. Curtis' Heirs,* Chancery 1461, MCCH; *Vaughn v. Vaughn,* Chancery 1952, MCCH; *Lane v. Read,* Chancery 848, MCCH; Deed Book V: 160, 256, and 400, MCCH; Deed Book W: 127, MCCH; Deed Book 27: 109, MCCH; marriage licenses 1875: 55 and 1889: 87, MCCII.

46. MC Cohabitation; "Roanoke County (Va.) Register of Colored Persons Cohabiting Together as Husband and Wife, 27th February 1866," http://www.virginiamemory.com/; 1870 census (population schedule); *Barnett et al. v. Burks et al.,* Chancery 1012, MCCH.

47. *Barnett et al. v. Burks et al.,* Chancery 1012, MCCH.

48. Ibid.; Harrison, *Consecrated Life,* 254–71; Deed Book 27: 219–21, 261–62, and 292–94, MCCH.

49. *Wade v. Mills Adminr.,* Chancery 2347, MCCH; Deed Book 61: 405, MCCH.

50. *Morgan v. Morgan,* Chancery 835, MCCH; Burks to "Mr. Junckings," Apr. 2, 1893, in *Brown v. Burks,* Chancery 1475, MCCH; *Curtis v. Miller et al.* and *Curtis v. Curtis' Heirs,* Chancery 1461, MCCH; "Store Account Book of Rice D. Montague, 1867–70," 88.09.01, MCM.

51. Deed Book U: 86 and 283, MCCH; Deed Book Z: 181 and 253, MCCH; Deed Book 26: 4 and 466, MCCH; 1880 census (population and agricultural schedules); *Wade v. Mills Admir.,* Chancery 2347, MCCH. Sharon Ann Holt found that "dual tenure" of the sort seen in the Millses' case—owning land and still renting or sharecropping—was fairly common among black farmers in Granville County, North Carolina, during the 1870s and 1880s (*Making Freedom Pay,* 84–88).

52. MC Cohabitation; Record of Baptisms, 1859–1878, box 5, Whisner Memorial Methodist Church Records, Ms 64–003, VT; 1870 and 1880 censuses (population schedules); Deed Book U: 195, MCCH; Deed Book X: 45, MCCH.

53. *Johnson v. Edmundson,* Chancery 768, MCCH.

54. *Acts and Joint Resolutions Passed by the General Assembly . . . 1889–'90,* chap. 92 (Feb. 22, 1890), 73–74.

55. Morgan, *Emancipation in Virginia's Tobacco Belt,* 207, 281–82n30; Kerr-Ritchie, *Freedpeople in the Tobacco South,* 209–45; Schweninger, *Black Property Owners in the South,* 174.

56. Kerr-Ritchie, *Freedpeople in the Tobacco South,* 213–15. Any effort to combine

tax records with census data to measure African American landowners as a percentage of the larger black population is complicated by the uncertainty surrounding what constitutes a family or household. Unrelated individuals often lived together, and some black families—especially those headed by women—continued to live in white households. In addition, the loss of the 1890 population schedules means that such details are simply not available for that census.

57. This is also close to the rate of "one out of three" Schweninger found for black farm owners in the Upper South in 1890 (*Black Property Owners in the South*, 176).

58. Kerr-Ritchie, *Freedpeople in the Tobacco South*, 220–21; Ayers, *The Promise of the New South*, 208–10.

59. 1880 census (agricultural schedule); Land Book, 1893, MCCH.

60. It is impossible to distinguish among different forms of tenure in 1870 because on the agricultural schedule that year the census enumerators in Montgomery County seem to have collected information only from owner-operators. Thus, it is possible to identify eight or nine men who seem to have farmed their own land (eight are identified as "farmers," while Robert Austin's occupation is given as "raises tobacco"); sharecroppers and renters, however, cannot be identified.

61. In 1880, the population schedule identifies a total of 174 black men as "works on farm" and 162 as "farmers," but only 145 of the latter appear on the agricultural schedule: 68 owners, 61 sharecroppers, 15 paying their rent in cash, and 1 unknown. Estimates in the text are based on a total of 319: 174 hands from the population schedule and 145 farmers from the agricultural schedule.

62. A total of 195 black men in the county identified themselves on the 1900 population schedule as farm laborers (132) or farmers (63), but the schedule also indicates that 79 black farmers owned or rented land in the county that year. Unfortunately, it is impossible to compare these numbers to those on the 1900 agricultural schedule because the latter were evidently destroyed in 1912 on the grounds that they served no immediate need and had "no permanent value or historical interest." ("Letter from the Acting Secretary of Commerce and Labor [to the Speaker of the House of Representatives]," Jan. 15, 1912, *House Documents*, no. 460). Estimates in the text are based on a total of 211: 132 hands, 72 owners, and 7 renters/sharecroppers.

63. Lindon, *Virginia's Montgomery County*, 220; 1880 census (agricultural schedule); 1900 Personal Property Tax Record, Department of Taxation, Personal Property Tax Books, LOV. Steven Nash describes efforts to introduce large-scale sheep farming in western North Carolina during the 1880s but provides no information on African American participation in the effort (*Reconstruction's Ragged Edge*, 165–68).

64. *M. Harvey Smith v. Barney Brown's Heirs*, Chancery 1053, MCCH.

65. 1867 Census; 1870, 1880, and 1900 censuses (population and agricultural schedules); marriage licenses, MCCH.

66. *Wm. Lewis et al. v. Charlotte Lewis et al.*, Chancery 3449, MCCH; Lindon, *Virginia's Montgomery County*, 213–20; 1880 and 1900 censuses (population schedules).

67. Ayers, *The Promise of the New South*, 149–52; Kerr-Ritchie, *Freedpeople in the Tobacco South*, 233–44.

68. Marriage licenses, MCCH.

69. 1870, 1880, 1900 censuses (population schedules).

70. Arnesen, *Brotherhoods of Color,* 10–39; Kornweibel, *Railroads in the African American Experience,* 39–57, 63–103, 113–59; personal communication, James Dow, 2013.

71. The total for 1900 excludes thirty-five black railroad workers who seem to have been part of a transient crew located in the county at the time of the census. Six black men in the Alleghany District were identified on the population schedule as "R.R. hands" and shown as living with their families; they were clearly resident members of the community. The thirty-five transients, each also identified as "R.R. hand," appear together in two distinct groups. In the column concerning each man's relationship to the "head of family" for his group, the enumerator wrote "messmate," and in the margin of the sheet, next to the household number, he wrote: "In tents furnished by the R.R. Co." (1900 census, population schedule, Enumeration District 62, sheets 17 and 18).

72. Marriage licenses, MCCH.

73. Lewis, *Black Coal Miners in America;* Trotter, *Coal, Class, and Color.* See also Gutman, "Reconstruction in Ohio"; Keiser, "Black Strikebreakers and Racism in Illinois, 1865–1900"; Schwieder, Hraba, and Schwieder, *Buxton.*

74. Lindon, *Virginia's Montgomery County,* 351–54.

75. MC Cohabitation; 1870, 1880, and 1900 censuses (population schedules); agreement between John Grimes and Felix Johnson, Unrecorded Deeds & Power Atty., MCCH; *Jno. Grimes v. Pheobe Grimes,* Chancery 2084, MCCH.

76. *Christiansburg Messenger,* May 9 and May 16, 1879; Wallenstein, *Virginia Tech,* 48; MC Cohabitation; "Gray's New Map of Christiansburg" (ca. 1880), folder D-7, Historical Map Collection, VT; *Headin v. Noell,* Common Law A-9661, MCCH; United States Patent no. 325,342 (Sept. 1, 1885) (accessed at http://www.google.com/patents/US325342); agreement between Minnis Headen and D. W. Frizzell, Deed Book Z: 210, MCCH.

77. Minutes of the Valley African Baptist Association and the Colored Valley Baptist Association of Virginia between 1869 and 1875 were published but are now exceedingly rare. They can be found in "Minutes, Baptist Association, Valley, 1841 to 1881," VBHS.

78. For details concerning the number, race, and gender of teachers in Montgomery County's public schools, see *Virginia School Report.* For details of the number and gender of students in schools operated by the Freedmen's Bureau in Montgomery County, see Thorp, "The Beginnings of African American Education."

79. Virginia, vol. 28, p. 538, R. G. Dun & Co. Collection, Baker Library Historical Collections, Harvard Business School, Cambridge, Mass..

80. 1880, 1900, and 1910 censuses (population schedules); marriage licenses, 1893: 27 and 31, MCCH; *Curtis v. Hopkins,* Chancery 1859, MCCH; Blacksburg Council Minutes, July 7, 1893, Office of the Town Manager, Blacksburg, Va.

81. Unmarried black women eighteen and older in 1870: 341 of 729 (93 of 105 heads of household); 1880: 466 of 1,054 (242 heads of household); 1900: 437 of 918 (288 heads of household). Unmarried black women with children in 1867: 15.6

percent (97 of 622); 1870: 13.0 percent (95 of 729); 1880: 12.3 percent (130 of 1054); 1900: 12.9 percent (118 of 918).

82. 1870 and 1880 censuses (population schedules); Will Book 12: 400, MCCH.

83. Receipts, 1867, 1868, and 1869, box 1, folder 6, John Nicolay Papers, Ms 87–207, VT; Supr.'s Book No. 1: 52, 101, 122, and 147, MCCH; Blacksburg Council Minutes, Dec. 7 and Dec. 22, 1877, and Aug. 15, 1881, Office of the Town Manager, Blacksburg, Va.; recommendation from G. Kabrich to the Montgomery County Board of Supervisors, Aug. 6, 1881, and account for Frank Moon, May 23, 1882, box 1, folder 8, Charles W. Crush Collection, Ms 84–180, VT.

84. *Ford v. Ford*, Chancery 797, MCCH; *Twine v. Twine*, Chancery 1423, MCCH; 1880 and 1900 censuses (population schedules).

85. Litwack, *Been in the Storm So Long*, 244–45; Farmer-Kaiser, *Freedwomen and the Freedmen's Bureau*, 64–71.

86. 1880 census (population schedule); *Grimes v. Grimes*, Chancery 2084, MCCH.

87. *Virginia School Report.*

88. 1867 Census; 1870, 1880, 1900, and 1910 censuses (population schedules). Jane Carter appears on the 1867 census of freedpeople as servant of Dr. Edie (1867 Census). Unusually, the census offers no clue of her marital status, nor has any marriage license for her come to light. Carter did, however, identify herself as a widow on the 1910 census.

89. Sharpless, *Cooking in Other Women's Kitchens*, 90–91.

90. Ibid.; *Twine v. Twine*, Chancery 1423, MCCH.

91. Gianakos, "Virginia and the Married Women's Property Acts"; Tarter, "When Kind and Thrifty Husbands Are Not Enough."

92. *Shaver v. Deaton's Admr.*, Common Law A-6456, MCCH; *Shafer v. Spindle*, Chancery 1236, MCCH; Deed Book V: 170, MCCH; *Richardson v. Richardson*, Chancery 1812, MCCH.

93. *Richardson v. Richardson*, Chancery 1812, MCCH; *M. V. Smith's Admr. v. Bessie Banks et al.*, Chancery 1353, MCCH; *Curtis v. Miller*, Chancery 1461, MCCH; Will Book 12: 302, MCCH.

94. In 1866 taxable property included livestock, carriages and coaches, watches and clocks, pianos, plate and jewelry, household furniture, grain and tobacco except for that produced by the taxpayer, and a variety of financial instruments. Other classes of property, including tools and farming equipment, were added in later years (Department of Taxation, Personal Property Tax Books, LOV).

95. Department of Taxation, Personal Property Tax Books, LOV. See also Snavely, *The Taxation of Negroes in Virginia.*

96. Lindon, *Virginia's Montgomery County*, 215–16; Will Book 12: 18, 48, and 108, MCCH; *Dill v. Vaughn*, Chancery 1279, MCCH; *W. Harvey Smith v. Barney Brown's Heirs*, Chancery 1053, MCCH.

97. *Sowder v. Brown et al.*, Chancery 905, MCCH; Poole and Poole, *Voices from Eastern Montgomery County*, 217, 498; Deed Book 26: 368, MCCH; personal communication, Lois Carter Teel, 2012; marriage licenses, 1884: 38, MCCH; Will Book 12: 400, MCCH; Will Book F1: 255, MCCH; "Statement of Account of Archer A. Phlegar,

Exr. of Charlotte Calloway," Nov. 16, 1898, in *Charlotte Calloway Exor. v. Oliva G. Smith*, Chancery 1727, MCCH.

98. Deed Book 42: 40, MCCH; Deed Book 47: 351, MCCH; *Washington v. Washington*, Chancery 1735, MCCH; *Saunders v. Washington*, Chancery 1909, MCCH.

4. Schools for the Benefit of Our Children

1. *American Freedman*, Apr. 1869; 1867 Census. The 1867 census reported that Hart Wayland lived with John Burgess. No one by that name appears on the 1870 census, though, and it should probably be Jackson Burgess, who moved to Christiansburg from Fayette County in 1862 (censuses for 1860 [Fayette County] and 1870 [Montgomery County] and the files of Jackson Burgess and J. Burgess, reel 121, Confederate Papers Relating to Citizens or Business Firms, microfilm publication 346, record group 109, National Archives, Washington, D.C.).

2. Green, *Educational Reconstruction;* Anderson, *The Education of Blacks in the South*, 5. See also Butchart, *Northern Schools, Southern Blacks;* Butchart, *Schooling the Freed People;* Dailey, *Before Jim Crow*, 15–47, 77–102; Litwack, *Trouble in Mind*, 52–113.

3. McColley, *Slavery and Jeffersonian Virginia*, 70–71; H. Williams, *Self-Taught*, 208–9.

4. 1860 census (population schedule); 1865 Census.

5. Anderson, *The Education of Blacks in the South*, 4–32; Butchart, *Northern Schools, Southern Blacks;* Butchart, *Schooling the Freed People*, 8–14; D. Williams, *I Freed Myself*, 211–13; Green, "Educational Reconstruction," 13–57.

6. 1865 Census; Anderson, *The Education of Blacks in the South*, 5–8; Butchart, *Schooling the Freed People*, 4–7; Green, "Educational Reconstruction," 16–17.

7. Mullins, "A History of the Literary Fund," 23–33.

8. Anderson, *The Education of Blacks in the South*, 20–25; Butchart, *Schooling the Freed People*, 156; Green, "Educational Reconstruction," 38–43. For Montgomery County, see comments in the teachers' monthly reports filed in reels 15–20, BRFAL-EDVA, and, especially, Schaeffer to Sherwood, Oct. 25, 1866, reel 67, BRFAL-FOVA, and Sherwood to Brown, Oct. 31, 1866, reel 14, BRFAL-EDVA.

9. Peirce, *The Freedmen's Bureau;* Cimbala and Miller, *The Freedmen's Bureau and Reconstruction*, ix–xxxii; Butchart, *Northern Schools, Southern Blacks*, 97–114; Richard Paul Fuke, "Land, Lumber, and Learning: The Freedmen's Bureau, Education and the Black Community in Post-Emancipation Maryland," in Cimbala and Miller, *The Freedmen's Bureau and Reconstruction*, 288–314.

10. Carter to Brown, July 31, Sept. 13, and Sept. 20, 1865, and Apr. 30, 1866, reel 38, BRFAL-ACVA; "Consolidated Report of Schools [in Virginia]", Mar. 1866, reel 11, BRFAL-EDVA; letters and telegrams sent, reel 1, BRFAL-ACVA; [Sherwood] to Brown, June 30, 1864 [1866], reel 12, BRFAL-EDVA; Harrison, *Consecrated Life*, 5–84; Butchart, *Northern Schools, Southern Blacks*, 97–114; Schaeffer to Sherwood, Oct. 25, 1866, reel 67, BRFAL-FOVA.

11. Circular No. 23, July 18, 1866, reel 14, BRFAL-EDVA; Schaeffer to Sherwood, Oct. 25, 1866, reel 67, BRFAL-FOVA.

12. Carter to Brown, Aug. 29, 1865, reel 38, BRFAL-ACVA; Sherwood to Brown, Oct. 31, 1866, reel 14, BRFAL-EDVA; Green, "Educational Reconstruction," 18; 1865 Census.

13. Such attitudes were not unusual among white advocates of education for freedpeople. See, for example, Litwack, *Been in the Storm So Long,* 452–53; Anderson, *The Education of Blacks in the South,* 38–42; Green, "Educational Reconstruction," 27–29.

14. Schaeffer to Coulter, June 30 and Oct. 31, 1868, reel, 67, BRFAL-FOVA; Schaeffer to Brown, Mar. 30, 1868, reel 67, BRFAL-FOVA; Remington to Schaeffer, Nov. 17, 1880, ser. 7, Correspondence, FFA; Haines to Schaeffer, Sept. 22, 1884, ser. 7, Correspondence, FFA.

15. Schaeffer to Sherwood, Nov. 25, 1866, reel 67, BRFAL-FOVA.

16. Morris, *Reading, 'Riting, and Reconstruction,* 1–53; Horst, *Education for Manhood.* General Howard's Circular 2, May 19, 1865, is included in Printed Circulars Issued by the American Freedman's Union Commission, 4672, Cornell.

17. Schaeffer to Sherwood, Nov. 25, 1866, reel 67, BRFAL-FOVA; Schaeffer to Brown, Nov. 26, 1866, Endorsements Sent, June 1866–Aug. 1867, reel 195, BRFAL-FOVA; Schaeffer to Remington, Feb. 16, 1867, reel 67, BRFAL-FOVA; Minute Book of the Executive Committee of the American Freedman's Union Commission, 4601, Cornell; American Freedman's Union Commission, Commission Book, 1867–68, 4601, Cornell; Butchart, *Northern Schools, Southern Blacks,* 77–95.

18. *Huff v. Campbell,* Common Law A-4814, MCCH; Schaeffer to Remington, Feb. 16, Feb. 22, and Feb. 25, 1867, reel 67, BRFAL-FOVA; Sherwood to Austin, Apr. 22, 1867, reel 67, BRFAL-FOVA; and Kanode, *Christiansburg,* 139–40, 251.

19. "Light Shining into Dark Places," *Christiansburg Southwest,* Feb. 9, 1867, clipping included among papers of the district office in Wytheville, reel 197, BRFAL-FOVA; minutes of the Quarterly Meeting, July 21, 1856, Records of Quarterly Meetings, Apr. 21, 1855, to Jan. 16, 1888, St. Paul Methodist Church, Christiansburg. African American residents of Christiansburg who grew up under segregation recall that during the 1950s the black section of town was known as Campbell Town.

20. Schaeffer to Remington, Feb. 25, 1867, reel 67, BRFAL-FOVA; Teachers' Monthly School Reports, reel 15, BRFAL-EDVA; Butchart, *Schooling the Freed People,* 153–78. Dunaway asserts that "white animosity probably accounted for the scarcity of black schools in the [Appalachian] region" but provides little evidence from Virginia to support that claim (*The African-American Family,* 252).

21. Schaeffer to Remington, Feb. 25, 1867, reel 67, BRFAL-FOVA.

22. Schaeffer to Mallery, Apr. 25, 1867, reel 67, BRFAL-FOVA; Schaeffer to Austin, Mar. 11, 1867, reel 67, BRFAL-FOVA; Schaeffer to Manly, Mar. 26 and Apr. 30, 1867, reel 67, BRFAL-FOVA.

23. Schaeffer to Manly, May 7, 1867, reel 67, BRFAL-FOVA; Austin to Schaeffer, May 14, 1867, reel 68, BRFAL-FOVA.

24. Harrison, *Consecrated Life*, 133–34; Will Book 8: 1 and 464, MCCH; Will Book 9: 276, MCCH; Will Book CC 1: 136, MCCH; Deed Book R: 444, MCCH; "Statement of Expenses . . . 30 Sept. 1867," reel 197, BRFAL-FOVA.

25. "Asst. Sub-Assistant Commissioner's Monthly Report on Education of Freedmen and Refugees in 3rd & 4th Divisions 8th Sub District of Virginia," Jan. and Feb. 1868, reel 13, BRFAL-EDVA; Schaeffer to Brown, Dec. 31, 1867, reel 67, BRFAL-FOVA; American Freedman's Union Commission, Commission Book, 1867–68, 4601, Cornell; "[Letter] From Miss P. Canon," *American Freedman*, July and Aug. 1868.

26. Marrs to Schaeffer, Mar. 8, 1867, reel 68, BRFAL-FOVA; Schaeffer to Coulter, Oct. 31, 1868, reel 67, BRFAL-FOVA; Schaeffer to Mallery, July 27, 1867, reel 67, BRFAL-FOVA; Schaeffer to Manley, July 18, 1867, reel 67, BRFAL-FOVA; Schaeffer to Brown, Jan. 31, 1868, reel 67, BRFAL-FOVA; Schaeffer to Coulter, Nov. 30, 1868, reel 67, BRFAL-FOVA.

27. These six are the only full-time schools that operated fairly consistently in the county. Schaeffer did, however, refer to a school near McDonald's Mill during the spring and summer of 1867 (Schaeffer to Mallery, May 25, June 25, and July 25, 1867, reel 67, BRFAL-FOVA) and to one at Peppers Ferry that fall (Schaeffer to Brown, Nov. 30, 1867, reel 67, BRFAL-FOVA). In fact, he wrote to his superiors in Richmond, "Schools are constantly being started in different locations, but owing to the incapacity of teachers and other circumstances working against their interest, they do not remain in operation very long" (Schaeffer to Brown, Nov. 30, 1867, reel 67, BRFAL-FOVA). "Sunday schools" also operated at a number of locations in the county. Their name suggests, however, that they met only on Sundays, and it is unclear from the surviving evidence whether they emphasized literacy, theology, or both (Schaeffer to Thomas, Feb. 2, 1869, reel 196, BRFAL-FOVA).

28. Faulkner to Thomas, Feb. 15, 1869, reel 196, BRFAL-FOVA.

29. Schaeffer to Coulter, June 30, 1868, reel 67, BRFAL-FOVA; Schaeffer to Thomas, Oct. 31, 1868, reel 67, BRFAL-FOVA; American Freedman's Union Commission, Commission Book, 1867–68, 4601, Cornell.

30. Butchart, *Northern Schools, Southern Blacks*, 93–95; list of schools, May 1867, ser. 5, Statistics of Schools, FFA; Schaeffer to "Mrs. S. F. Smily," July 19, 1866, reel 67, BRFAL-FOVA; Smiley to Schaeffer, Aug. 9, 1866, reel 68, BRFAL-FOVA; Minutes of the Committee on Instruction, Sept. 17 and Oct. 15, 1867, ser. 3, Instruction Committee, FFA; Shearman to Schaeffer, Sept. 20, 1867, ser. 7, Correspondence, FFA.

31. Shearman to Schaeffer, May 19, 1868, ser. 7, Correspondence, FFA; Minutes of the Committee on Instruction, Apr. 28, 1868, Jan. 25, 1869, and June 30, Aug. 15, and Nov. 7, 1870, ser. 3, Instruction Committee, FFA.

32. C. Smith, *A History of the African Methodist Episcopal Church*, 13–82; Walker, *A Rock in a Weary Land*, 46–81.

33. Butt, *History of African Methodism*, 34; Donald, "Growth and Independence of Methodist Congregations"; *Christian Recorder*, May 25 and June 22, 1867, and May 2, 1868; Schaeffer to Austin, July 28, 1868, reel 67, BRFAL-FOVA.

34. Shearman to Schaeffer, May 25, June 17, and Aug. 31, 1868, ser. 7, Correspondence, FFA; Minutes of the Executive Board, June 9, 1868, ser. 2, Executive Board, FFA.

35. C. Smith, *History of the African Methodist Episcopal Church*, 86; Woolwine and others to Thomas, Feb. 16, 1869, reel 196, BRFAL-FOVA; Walker, *A Rock in a Weary Land*, 82–107; Fairclough, *A Class of Their Own*, 72–75.

36. Schaeffer to Austin, July 28, 1868, reel 67, BRFAL-FOVA; Asst. Sub-Assistant Commissioner's (or Agent's) Monthly Report, Aug. 1868, reel 197, BRFAL-FOVA. Schaeffer, however, did inform his superiors of the school's opening and included it in his own reports for the division, though he mistakenly identified its teacher as "John Derrick."

37. *Christian Recorder*, May 22, 1869; Teacher's Monthly School Report, Oct. 28, 1869, reel 17, BRFAL-EDVA.

38. Peirce, *The Freedmen's Bureau*, 76–77; Thomas to Brown, Feb. 22, 1869, reel 196, BRFAL-FOVA.

39. Schaeffer to Remington, Feb. 25, 1867, reel 67, BRFAL-FOVA; Schaeffer to Thomas, Sept. 8, 1868, reel 67, BRFAL-FOVA; Deed Book S: 12–13, MCCH; American Freedman's Union Commission, Commission Book, 1867–68, 4601, Cornell; *American Freedman*, Apr. 1869; *Second Annual Report of the Freedmen's Department of the Presbyterian Committee of Home Missions*, 13, 20; Shearman to Schaeffer, Aug. 17, 1870, ser. 7, Correspondence, FFA.

40. Faulkner to Schaeffer, Nov. 2 and Nov. 14, 1868, reel 68, BRFAL-FOVA; Faulkner to Thomas, Jan. 25 and Feb. 15, 1869, reel 196, BRFAL-FOVA; Teachers' Monthly School Reports, Feb.–Mar. 1869, reel 15, BRFAL-EDVA; Teachers' Monthly School Reports, Nov. 1869–Apr. 1870, reels 18 and 19, BRFAL-EDVA; Faulkner to Manly, Nov. 26, 1869, reel 17, BRFAL-EDVA; Deed Book S: 131, MCCH; Shearman to Schaeffer, Sept. 28, 1869, ser. 7, Correspondence, FFA; Shearman to Faulkner, Nov. 19, 1869, ser. 7, Correspondence, FFA.

41. Smyth, *A History of Blacksburg Presbyterian Church*, 4; Teachers' Monthly School Reports, reels 15–20, BRFAL-EDVA.

42. Green, "Educational Reconstruction," 27–28, 90–91; D. Williams, *Self-Taught*, 99; Butchart, *Schooling the Freed People*, 179–83.

43. American Freedman's Union Commission, Commission Book, 1867–68, 4601, Cornell; 1860 census (population schedule), Saint Lawrence County, New York.

44. Simmons, *Men of Mark*, 88–96; *Christian Recorder*, May 2, 1868.

45. Faulkner to Schaeffer, Nov. 2, 1868, reel 68, BRFAL-FOVA; Crews and Parrish, *14th Virginia Infantry*, 103; Faulkner to Thomas, Jan. 25, 1869, reel 196, BRFAL-FOVA.

46. *Philadelphia Freedman's Friend*, Feb. 1871, 1; MC Cohabitation; Teachers' Monthly School Reports, reels 19 and 20, BRFAL-EDVA.

47. *Virginia School Report* (1871), 201. Adding the highest monthly attendance shown on the teachers' reports (reels 15–20, BRFAL-EDVA) provides a total of 357, though in no single month was the number actually that high. The reports do not include Blacksburg, for which the only known enrollment figure is sixty-five for the month of September 1869 (*Christian Recorder*, Sept. 25, 1869).

48. *Statistics of the Population of the United States . . . from the Original Returns of the Ninth Census*, 1:432; Teachers' Monthly School Reports, reels 15–20, BRFAL-EDVA; Schaeffer to Brown, Nov. 30, 1867, reel 67, BRFAL-FOVA.

49. Dunaway, *The African-American Family*, 252–53; Sub-Assistant Commissioner's (or Agent's) Monthly Report, Jan. 1869, reel 12, BRFAL-EDVA.

50. Dunaway, *The African-American Family*, 253–54; Horst, *The Fire of Liberty in Their Hearts*, xxiii, 138–78.

51. Teachers' Monthly School Reports, reels 15–20, BRFAL-EDVA; Minutes of the Committee on Instruction, June 13, 1870, ser. 3, Instruction Committee, FFA; Shearman to Schaeffer, June 3, 1870, ser. 7, Correspondence, FFA; *American Freedman*, Apr. 1869..

52. Morris, *Reading, 'Riting, and Reconstruction*, 149–73; Butchart, *Teaching the Freedpeople*, 120–30; Mitchell, *Raising Freedom's Child*, 129–33.

53. *American Freedman*, Apr. 1869.

54. *American Freedman*, July and Aug. 1868.

55. Peirce, *The Freedmen's Bureau*, 69–74; Morris, *Reading, 'Riting, and Reconstruction*, 243; Harrison, *Consecrated Life*, 119–31; Manly to Schaeffer, June 17 and Aug. 11, 1869, in Harrison, *Consecrated Life*, 124–26; *American Freedman* July 1869; *Second Annual Report of the Freedmen's Department of the Presbyterian Committee of Home Missions*, 13, 20.

56. Butt, *History of African Methodism*, 48; Teachers' Monthly School Reports, Oct. and Nov. 1869 and June 1870, reel 17, BRFAL-EDVA; "Letter from Bishop Wayman," *Christian Recorder*, Sept. 25, 1869; Harrison, *Consecrated Life*, 131; Shearman to Schaeffer, Nov. 10, 1869, ser. 7, Correspondence, FFA; Minutes of the Committee on Instruction, Dec. 20, 1869, June 13, Aug. 15, Aug, 23, and Nov. 7, 1870, ser. 3, Instruction Committee, FFA; Shearman to Schaeffer, Oct. 29 and Oct. 31, 1870, ser. 7, Correspondence, FFA; Shearman to Faulkner, Nov. 29, 1870, ser. 7, Correspondence, FFA.

57. Link, *A Hard Country and Lonely Place*, 16–21; Lowe, *Republicans and Reconstruction in Virginia*, 138–39; Dailey, *Before Jim Crow*, 19–21; Green, "Educational Reconstruction," 104–5; *Acts of the General Assembly . . . 1869-'70*, chap. 259 (July 11, 1870), 402–17.

58. *Acts of the General Assembly . . . 1869-'70*, chap. 259 (July 11, 1870), 402–17; Schaeffer to Brown, Jan. 31, 1868, reel 67, BRFAL-FOVA; Dailey, *Before Jim Crow*, 20–21; Green, "Educational Reconstruction," 105–20.

59. "School Districts," Will Book 10: 428, MCCH; Christiansburg District School Board Minutes, Nov. 7, 1870, Feb. 14, Mar. 7, and Mar. 26, 1871, MCPS; Executive Board Minutes, Apr. 11, 1871, ser. 2, Executive Board, FFA. Minutes of the Christiansburg district school board between 1870 and 1913 are also available on microfilm in the Library of Virginia but are mistakenly included in a group identified as Montgomery County School Board Minutes, which actually includes both minutes from the district school board between 1870 and 1913 and those from the county board between 1904 and 1935.

60. Executive Board Minutes, Feb. 21, 1871, ser. 2, Executive Board, FFA; Minutes of the Committee on Instruction, Mar. 13, 1871, ser. 3, Instruction Committee, FFA; Deed Book S: 12, MCCH.

61. Shearman to Schaeffer, Oct. 19, 1870, and Jan. 23, Jan. 25, Apr. 4, May 11, and

June 22, 1871, ser. 7, Correspondence, FFA; Minutes of the Committee on Instruction, Apr. 11, 1871, ser. 3, Instruction Committee, FFA; Christiansburg District School Board Minutes, Mar. 25 and Apr. 13, 1871, MCPS.

62. *Philadelphia Inquirer,* Dec. 18 and Dec. 19, 1873; Harrison, *Consecrated Life,* 136; Schaeffer to Wistar, Apr. 13, 1889, and May 13, 1890, ser. 8, Correspondence, FFA.

63. "Report of the Executive Board to the Friends' Association of Philadelphia and the Vicinity, for the Relief of Colored Freedmen," Apr. 11, 1871, included in Minutes of the Executive Board, ser. 2, Executive Board, FFA; Minutes of the Executive Board, June 13, 1871, ser. 2, Executive Board, FFA; Shearman to Schaeffer, Oct. 3, 1871, and May 14 and June 7, 1872, ser. 7, Correspondence, FFA; Deed Book X: 82, MCCH; Deed Book Y: 96, MCCH. The *Christian Recorder* reported on Nov. 22, 1883, that J. C. Williams, the AME pastor in Blacksburg, had been elected "principal" of the public school there, but it is unclear just what that meant or who was paying Williams's salary. The AME had stopped sending ministers to Wake Forest in 1871 (*Christian Recorder,* Apr. 9 and Dec. 10, 1870, and May 6, 1871).

64. *Virginia School Report;* Heatwole, *A History of Education in Virginia,* 226–27; Wynes, *Race Relations in Virginia,* 16–23.

65. *Virginia School Report.;* Link, *A Hard Country and a Lonely Place,* 52–57, 137.

66. Christiansburg District School Board Minutes, Sept. 18, Sept. 25, and Oct. 9, 1871, MCPS; "List of Contracts with Teachers for 1872 & 73," "List of Contracts with Teachers for 1875 x 6," and "Contracts with Teachers, for 1876 & 7," included in Christiansburg District School Board Minutes, MCPS; *Virginia School Report;* [?] to Arey, Feb. 12, 1884, ser. 7, Correspondence, FFA; Haines to Schaeffer, Aug. 18, 1884, ser. 7, Correspondence, FFA; Polk to "Respected Board of Managers," Mar. 4, 1889, ser. 8, Correspondence, FFA; Comfort to Wistar, Feb. 23, 1891, ser. 8, Correspondence, FFA; Schaeffer to Wistar, Mar. 6, 1891, ser. 8, Correspondence, FFA; *Acts of the General Assembly . . . 1869-'70,* chap. 259 (July 11, 1870), 414; Link, *A Hard Country and a Lonely Place,* 64–70.

67. Dailey, *Before Jim Crow,* 70–76; *Virginia School Report.* Individual teachers can be identified in only one of the county's four school districts—Christiansburg (Christiansburg School District No. 1, [Ledger] 1883–1884 to 1899, MCPS).

68. Teachers' names appear in correspondence between Schaeffer and the Friends' Freedmen's Association in the records of the Christiansburg District School Board and in a single countywide payroll dating from 1871 (Ledger Mont. County 1872–1883, MCCH). For their personal details, see 1870, 1880, and 1900 censuses; *Grimes v. Grimes,* Chancery 2084, MCCH; *The Twenty-Sixth Annual Catalogue,* 32 (original in the holdings of the Christiansburg Institute Alumni Association, Christiansburg, Va.; also available at Virginia Tech Imagebase [http://imagebase.lib.vt.edu/browse.php]); alumni files of Blanche and Frankie Harris, Oberlin College Archives, Oberlin, Ohio; Blanche Harris to James Monroe, Mar. 25, 1871, Correspondence, May 1870–Apr. 1871, James Monroe Papers, Oberlin College Archives, Oberlin, Ohio; [S. Armstrong], *Twenty-Two Years' Work,* 34–35, 152; Swain, "Christiansburg Institute," 50, 81–82; "Brown's Early African-American Alumni," http://library.brown.edu/cds/pollard

/earlyalumni.html; Coppin, *Reminiscences of School Life,* 162–63, 184, 188; Comfort to Wistar, Feb. 28, 1891, ser. 8, Correspondence, FFA; profile of Hiram H. Thweatt, *Colored American,* Nov. 10, 1900, http://chroniclingamerica.loc.gov/.

69. Christiansburg District School Board Minutes, 1871–1898 and 1898–1913, MCPS; Christiansburg School District No. 1, Ledger, 1883–1884 to 1899, MCPS. In 1898, seven whites were each paid twenty-five dollars and nine were paid twenty dollars, while among blacks, four received twenty-five dollars each and two received twenty dollars. In 1899, five white teachers each received twenty-five dollars and eight received twenty dollars, while three black teachers each received twenty-five dollars and one received twenty dollars.

70. *Virginia School Report.*

71. Dailey, *Before Jim Crow,* 103–31; Green, "Educational Reconstruction," 325–34.

72. Link, *A Hard Country and a Lonely Place,* 3–72; *Virginia School Report.*

73. Minutes of the Committee on Instruction, Mar. 10, June 3, and July 14, 1873, ser. 3, Instruction Committee, FFA; Shearman to Schaeffer, Mar. 12, June 5, July 16, and Sept. 30, 1873, ser. 7, Correspondence, FFA; Harrison, *Consecrated Life,* 136–37; "Are the Freedmen Rising?," *Friends' Review* 34 (1880–81): 99–101.

74. "Are the Freedmen Rising?," *Friends' Review* 34 (1880–81): 99–101; report of the annual meeting, *Friends' Review* 36 (1882–83): 586; "An Appeal by the Friends' Freedmen's Association on Behalf of the New Schoolhouse at Christiansburg," *Friends' Review* 36 (1882–83): 681.

75. Haines to Schaeffer, Oct. 26, 1885, ser. 7, Correspondence, FFA; Schaeffer to Wister, Feb. 13, 1885, printed in Harrison, *Consecrated Life,* 141–42; Swain, "Christiansburg Institute," 61; "Friends' Freedmen's Association of Philadelphia," *Friends' Review* 39 (1885–86): 631; "Report of the Executive Board to the Friends' Freedmen's Association . . . for 1887–1888," *Friends' Review* 41 (1887–88): 629. The last known reference to debt for the new school is in Schaeffer to Wister, Mar. 15, 1889, ser. 8, Correspondence, FFA.

76. Deed Book Z: 51, MCCH.

77. Ibid.; Butchart, *Schooling the Freed People,* 120–52; Anderson, *The Education of Blacks in the South,* 4–78.

78. Perkins, "Heed Life's Demands"; Perkins, *Fanny Jackson Coppin,* 168–225; Coppin, *Reminiscences of School Life,* 23; "Friends' Freedmen's Association of Philadelphia," *Friends' Review* 37 (1883–84): 615.

79. Anderson, *The Education of Blacks in the South,* 31–78; [S. Armstrong], *Twenty-Two Years' Work,* 6; "Work among the Freedmen," *Friends' Review* 38 (1884–85): 717–18; "Industrial Education of the Colored People," *Friends' Review* 38 (1884–85): 521; Perkins, *Fanny Jackson Coppin,* 168–210.

80. "Friends' Freedmen's Association," *Friends' Review* 32 (1878–79): 635; "Friends' Freedmen's Association of Philadelphia," *Friends' Review* 40 (1886–87): 636; letter from Schaeffer, Oct, 4, 1881, *Philadelphia Freedman's Friend,* Nov. 1881; Remington to Schaeffer, Nov. 17, 1880, ser. 7, Correspondence, FFA.

81. "Report of the Executive Board," *Friends' Review* 41 (1887–88): 629; "Friends'

Freedmen's Association of Philadelphia," *Friends' Review* 40 (1886–87): 636; "Friends' Freedmen's Association of Philadelphia," *Friends' Review* 42 (1888–89): 618.

82. Coppin to "Kind Manager," Aug. 5, 1891, ser. 8, Correspondence, FFA; Comfort to Wistar, Jan. 7, 1892, ser. 8, Correspondence, FFA; "The Thirtieth Annual Report of the Executive Committee," *Friends' Review* 46 (1892–93): 635; Polk to "Respected Board of Managers," Nov. 9 and Dec. 3, 1888, and Jan. 2, 1889, ser. 6, School Reports, FFA.

83. Coppin to "Kind Manager," Aug. 5, 1891, ser. 8, Correspondence, FFA; Comfort to Wistar, Feb. 23 and Nov. 3, 1891, and Mar. 1, 1892, ser. 8, Correspondence, FFA; Polk to Haines, Oct. 6, 1888, ser. 6, School Reports, FFA; "The 27th Annual Report of the Friends' Freedmen's Association of Philadelphia," *Friends' Review* 43 (1889–90): 651; "Annual Report of the Executive Committee," *Friends' Review* 45 (1891–92): 635; Swain, "Christiansburg Institute," 71; *The Twenty-Sixth Annual Catalogue,* 32.

84. Schaeffer to Wistar, Nov. 12, 1891, ser. 8, Correspondence, FFA; Comfort to Wistar, Mar. 28, 1892, ser. 8, Correspondence, FFA; "Annual Report of the Executive Committee," *Friends' Review* 45 (1891–92): 635; "The 27th Annual Report of the Friends' Freedmen's Association of Philadelphia," *Friends' Review* 43 (1889–90): 651. It is ironic that Schaeffer's biographer, Charles Harrison, seemed to suggest that Schaeffer was not opposed to industrial education at Christiansburg and objected only to the fact that the FFA was so tentative about it (*Consecrated Life,* 144).

85. Polk to Wistar, June 7, 1890, ser. 8, Correspondence, FFA; Comfort to Wistar, Nov. 3, 1891, ser. 8, Correspondence, FFA; Schaeffer to Wistar, Nov. 12, 1891, ser. 8, Correspondence, FFA; "An Appeal by the Friends' Freedmen's Association on Behalf of the New Schoolhouse at Christiansburg," *Friends' Review* 36 (1882–83): 681; *Curtis v. Hopkins,* Chancery 1859, MCCH; *Grimes v. Grimes,* Chancery 2084, MCCH.

86. Anderson, *The Education of Blacks in the South,* 64–78, 102–9; Perkins, *Fanny Jackson Coppin,* 225.

87. Anderson, *The Education of Blacks in the South,* 73–78; Swain, "Christiansburg Institute," 80–91; "Friends' Freedmen's Association of Philadelphia," *Friends' Review* 45 (1891–92): 647; Perkins, *Fanny Jackson Coppin,* 222–25; Scattergood, "Work of the Friends' Freedmen's Association."

88. Profile of Hiram H. Thweatt, *Colored American,* Nov. 10, 1900, http:// chroniclingamerica.loc.gov/; Morris to Washington, Feb. 6, 1896, in B. Washington, *The Booker T. Washington Papers,* 4:109; Minutes of the Executive Board, Feb. 5 and Apr. 29, 1896, ser. 2, Executive Board, FFA; Charles L. Marshall, "The Evolution of a Shoemaker," in B. Washington, *Tuskegee & Its People,* 338–54.

89. Anderson, *The Education of Blacks in the South,* 62–65, 102–9; Harrison, *Consecrated Life,* 146–47; Swain, "Christiansburg Institute," 80–107; Washington to Morris, Mar. 30, 1896, in B. Washington, *The Booker T. Washington Papers,* 4:150–52; Marshall, "The Evolution of a Shoemaker," in B. Washington, *Tuskegee & Its People,* 344; "Report of the Friends' Freedmen's Association for the Year 1893–94," *Friends' Review* 47 (1893–94): 434–36; Minutes of the Executive Board, Jan. 11, 1898, ser. 2, Executive Board, FFA; *The Twenty-Sixth Annual Catalogue,* 32–33.

90. Minutes of the Executive Board, Sept. 22, 1896, Apr. 26 and Nov. 16, 1897, ser.

2, Executive Board, FFA; *The Twenty-Sixth Annual Catalogue*, 32; Marshall, "The Evolution of a Shoemaker," in B. Washington, *Tuskegee & Its People*, 349; Deed Book 46: 273 and 275, MCCH.

91. Deed Book 48:547, MCCH; Swain, "Christiansburg Institute," 108–258; Smith and DeHart, *Christiansburg Institute*, 25–73.

92. *Virginia School Report;* 1900 census (population schedule); [S. Armstrong], *Twenty-Two Years' Work*, 49, 287; Comfort to Wistar, Nov. 3, 1891, ser. 8, Correspondence, FFA; "Statement of Account of Archer A. Phlegar, Exr. Of Charlotte Calloway," Nov. 16, 1898, in *Charlotte Calloway's Exor. v. Olivia G. Smith*, Chancery 1727, MCCH; Harrison, *Consecrated Life*, 325; Minutes, Baptist Association, Valley, 1841 to 1881, VBHS; *Richmond Planet*, Dec. 6, 1902.

5. Temples Built unto the Lord

1. "An act to amend an act entitled, 'an act reducing into one the several acts concerning slaves, free negroes and mulattoes, and for other purposes,'" *Acts Passed at a General Assembly of the Commonwealth of Virginia* [1832], chap. 22, 20–22; "Record for the Classes Severally," Record of Baptisms, 1859–1878, box 5, Whisner Memorial Methodist Church Records, Ms 64–003, VT; "Another Old Landmark Gone," *Christiansburg Messenger*, Feb. 7, 1879; diary of Charles Schaeffer, Feb. 15, 1869, quoted in Harrison, *Consecrated Life*, 173–74.

2. "Another Old Landmark Gone," *Christiansburg Messenger*, Feb. 7, 1879; "Communism's Challenge to Christianity," in King, *The Papers of Martin Luther King*, 6:146–50.

3. Whitt, "'Free Indeed!,'" especially 2836–66; *Leftwich et al. v. Pattersons' Admr.*, Chancery 1772, MCCH.

4. Record of Baptisms, 1859–1878, box 5, Whisner Memorial Methodist Church Records, Ms 64–003, VT; Apr. 3, 1866, and Apr. 22, 1867, Records of Quarterly Meetings, Apr. 21, 1855, to Jan. 16, 1888, St. Paul Methodist Church, Christiansburg; 1867 Census.

5. Record of Baptisms, 1859–1878, box 5, Whisner Memorial Methodist Church Records, Ms 64–003, VT; Register of Christiansburg Station, Roanoke District, Baltimore Conf. M.E. Church, South, St. Paul Methodist Church, Christiansburg; Records of the Church Session [1827–1869], Christiansburg Presbyterian Church, Christiansburg; Minutes, Baptist Association, Valley, 1841 to 1881, VBHS.

6. Montgomery, *Under Their Own Vine and Fig Tree*, 97–141; Stowell, *Rebuilding Zion*, 80–99; Register of Christiansburg Station, St. Paul Methodist Church, Christiansburg; Records of the Church Session, [1827–1869], Christiansburg Presbyterian Church; "Report on Religious Instruction of Colored People," *Minutes of the Valley Baptist Association Session of 1866*, 7–9.

7. Walker, *A Rock in a Weary Land*, 82–107; Montgomery, *Under Their Own Vine and Fig Tree*, 97–141; Raboteau, *Canaan Land*, 23–24; Melton, *A Will to Choose*, 63–124, 251–59; Richey, Rowe, and Smith, *The Methodist Experience in America*, 1:143–46, 217–18, 257–59; Butt, *History of African Methodism*, 32–38.

8. *Christian Recorder,* May 18, May 25, and June 22, 1867; Schaeffer to Brown, Feb. 25, 1867, reel 67, BRFAL-FOVA; Record of Baptisms, 1859–1878, box 5, Whisner Memorial Methodist Church Records, Ms 64–003, VT.

9. Donald, "Growth and Independence of Methodist Congregations"; *Christian Recorder,* June 22, 1867, and May 2, 1868; marriage licenses, 1867: 68, MCCH; Deed Book 28: 62, MCCH; Quarterly Meeting, Aug. 13, 1867, and Quarterly Meeting, Dec. 4, 1867, Recording Stewards Book, 1859–1880, box 3, folder 6, Whisner Memorial Methodist Church Records, Ms 64–003, VT. The AME church also sent a minister/ teacher to Wake Forest in 1869. He remained for two years, and residents purchased an acre of land on which to build a church, but it failed to take root and vanished from AME records by 1873 (*Christian Recorder,* May 22, 1869, Apr. 9, 1870, Dec. 10, 1870, May 6, 1871, Oct. 26, 1872, and Nov. 13, 1873; Deed Book S: 474, MCCH).

10. Records of Quarterly Meetings, Apr. 21, 1855, to Jan. 16, 1888, and Register of Christiansburg Station, St. Paul Methodist Church, Christiansburg; Deed Book S: 289, MCCH; Deed Book U: 95 and 359, MCCH; Com. Law Orders No. 5: 261, MCCH; *Minutes of the Annual Conferences of the Methodist Episcopal Church for the Year 1867,* 20–22; *Minutes of the Annual Conferences of the Methodist Episcopal Church for the Year 1868,* 44–47; *Minutes of the Annual Conferences of the Methodist Episcopal Church for the Year 1869,* 84–87; 1867 Census.

11. J. Armstrong, "The Baltimore Conference"; Register of Christiansburg Station, St. Paul Methodist Church, Christiansburg; *Christiansburg Messenger,* Aug. 22, 1873; Walker, *A Rock in a Weary Land,* 82–107; Montgomery, *Under Their Own Vine and Fig Tree,* 97–141; Melton, *A Will to Choose,* 261–81; Richey, Rowe, and Smith, *The Methodist Experience in America,* 1:217–18, 257–58.

12. *Christiansburg Southwest,* May 2, 1868; *Christiansburg Messenger,* Aug. 22, 1873, and July 31, 1874.

13. It is impossible to say whether or not Dill was a member of the AME Church when he interrupted services at the Wesley Chapel, but by 1882 he was one of its trustees. Criminal A-747, A-751, A-798, A-799, and A-802, MCCH; Deed Book 28: 62, MCCH; Montgomery, *Under Their Own Vine and Fig Tree,* 97–141; Richey, Rowe, and Smith, *The Methodist Experience in America,* 1:257–61; Woolwine and others to Thomas, Feb. 16, 1869, reel 196, BRFAL-FOVA.

14. *Christian Recorder,* May 22, 1869, Apr. 9, 1870, Dec. 10, 1870, and May 6, 1871; Deed Book S: 474, MCCH. When J. P. Campbell toured AME churches in Southwest Virginia in 1872, he made no mention of Wake Forest, which suggests that the congregation had vanished by then (*Christian Recorder,* Oct. 1, 1872).

15. Today it is the New Mt. Olive United Methodist Church. [Jordan], "Pride and Preservation," 46; Deed Book 40: 591, MCCH; Mechanics Liens, 1887: 122, MCCH.

16. Rough and Ready Church is known today as Mt. Airy United Methodist. Deed Book 41: 563, MCCH; marriage licenses, 1881: 126, MCCH; *Commonwealth v. John & Gran Day,* Criminal Papers, envelope 40, MCCH; personal communication, Cora Pack, 2012; "10-Member Church Works to Survive," *Roanoke Times,* Sept. 2, 2003. The 1886 deed conveying land for the church identifies its minister as Isaac L. Thomas; a minister of that name served the MEC's Asbury Church in Washington,

D.C., from 1896 to 1902 (Smythe, *Asbury United Methodist Church (Washington, D.C) Records,* iii, http://archives.nypl.org/scm/20849), and the 1900 federal census shows that he and his wife were both from Maryland but had a son born in Virginia in 1885.

17. North Fork reported sixty white and seven black members in 1851, while Blacksburg had twenty-three white and four black members in 1861–62. The seven county churches belonging to the Valley Baptist Association in 1867 included 245 white and 30 black members (Minutes, Baptist Association, Valley, 1841 to 1881, VBHS). Schaeffer's biographer also reported that soon after his arrival in the county he found "thirty persons who professed to hold the views of Baptists" (Harrison, *Consecrated Life,* 156–57). The number may actually have been higher, though. The 1867 census of freedpeople in the county found eighty-four people who identified as Baptists; this number is well above that reported by the Valley Association but still only a third of the number who identified themselves as Methodists on the census ("Census Returns of Blacks in Montgomery County State of Virginia" [1867], reel 68, BRFAL-FOVA).

18. *Minutes of the Valley Baptist Association Session of 1865.*

19. Montgomery, *Under Their Own Vine and Fig Tree,* 105–9; Whitt, "'Free Indeed,'" 2854–55, 2859; [Botetourt Heritage Book Committee], *Botetourt County, Virginia, Heritage Book,* 51; Enon Colored Baptist Church to the Valley Baptist Association, July 1866, Valley Association—Specific Congregations 1 (2) A–L, Writings (Series IV)—Baptist Associations & Organizations, Cocke Papers.

20. *Minutes of the Valley Baptist Association Session of 1866,* 6–9.

21. *Fortieth Annual Report of the American Home Mission Society,* 122; *Minutes of the (Colored) Valley Baptist Association of Virginia . . . 1874; Minutes of the Valley Baptist Association . . . 1867; Minutes of the Valley Baptist Association, . . . 1869; Minutes of the Valley Baptist Association . . . 1871.* Enon Colored Church seems to have been "advised" by the Valley Baptist Association to "withdraw from us and join an association of its own color." (See undated resolution in Specific Congregations 1 (2) A–L, Writings (Series IV)—Baptist Associations & Organizations, Cocke Papers).

22. Harrison, *Consecrated Life,* 31–75, 156–57.

23. Schaeffer to Kennard, Oct. 14, 1867, in Harrison, *Consecrated Life,* 157–61; Schaeffer to Manley, Apr. 30, 1867, reel 67, BRFAL-FOVA; Schaeffer to Brown, Oct. 27, 1867, reel 67, BRFAL-FOVA; *Fortieth Annual Report of the American Home Mission Society,* 122. It is impossible to say exactly when informal Baptist gatherings began in Christiansburg. Members of Schaeffer Memorial Baptist Church, as the Christiansburg congregation is known today, celebrated the 150th anniversary of their church's informal beginnings in Oct. 2016. Schaeffer's monthly reports, however, as well as internal evidence from the document itself indicate that the census that alerted him to the presence of Baptists in Montgomery County was not taken until early 1867 (Harrison, *Consecrated Life,* 156–57; Schaeffer to Mallery, Apr. 25, 1867, reel 67, BRFAL-FOVA; 1867 Census). Lindon, *Virginia's Montgomery County* (536) also claims that Baptists in Wake Forest organized a church in 1866 and cites Swain's "Christiansburg Institute" as the source of this information. I can find no such claim

in Swain's work, though, nor any other evidence of a Baptist congregation in Wake Forest that early.

24. Schaeffer to Kennard, Oct. 14, 1867, in Harrison, *Consecrated Life*, 157–61.

25. Ibid., 157–61, 173; Deed Book S: 12, MCCH; Deed Book Z: 464, MCCH; Kanode, *Christiansburg*, 73; 1867 Census; Colored Members, Trinity, 1866, Record of Baptisms, 1859–1878, box 5, Whisner Memorial Methodist Church Records, Ms 64–003, VT; *Christiansburg Messenger,* Feb. 7, 1879.

26. Minutes, Baptist Association, Valley, 1841 to 1881, VBHS; Harrison, *Consecrated Life*, 148–207.

27. Minutes, Baptist Association, Valley, 1841 to 1881, VBHS; 1867 Census.

28. Minutes, Baptist Association, Valley, 1841 to 1881, VBHS; Harrison, *Consecrated Life*, 197, 203–6.

29. Schaeffer's attitude toward blacks is evident throughout his correspondence with the Freedmen's Bureau and the Friends' Freedmen's Association and in the portions of his diary printed in Harrison's *Consecrated Life.* Harrison's book also includes, however, some of the tributes offered at Schaeffer's death, which clearly demonstrate the esteem and affection for him felt by many of the county's black residents.

30. Minutes, Baptist Association, Valley, 1841 to 1881, VBHS; Schaeffer to Kennard, Nov. 25, 1870, in Harrison, *Consecrated Life*, 213–14; Montgomery, *Under Their Own Vine and Fig Tree*, 241. AME ministers are identified in Butt, *History of African Methodism;* MEC ministers are identified in minutes of the annual conferences published by the church each year. Baptist women, of course, could not preach or be ordained at this time, but as early as 1875, and probably earlier, women's organizations such as the Sisters' Society at Alleghany Springs were operating among black Baptists in the county (*Minutes of the [Colored] Valley Baptist Association of Virginia . . . 1875*).

31. Schaeffer to Coulter, Apr. 30, 1868, reel 67, BRFAL-FOVA; *Christiansburg Southwest,* Apr. 28, May 2, and May 9, 1868.

32. Harrison, *Consecrated Life*, 157–64; Schaeffer to Brown, Oct. 27, 1867, reel 67, BRFAL-FOVA; Schaeffer to Thomas, Sept. 8, 1868, reel 67, BRFAL-FOVA; Deed Book S: 12, MCCH.

33. *Christiansburg Messenger,* Aug. 22, 1873; Harrison, *Consecrated Life*, 163–64; *Minutes of the Colored Valley Baptist Association of Virginia . . . 1871;* Supr's. Book No. 1: 15, MCCH.

34. The "Alleghany Colored Church" purchased land in 1878 (Deed Book Y: 407, MCCH) and a marriage was celebrated at "Matamoras African Church" in 1881 (marriage licenses, 1881: 78, MCCH).

35. Records of the Session of the Blacksburg Church (quotation from Sept. 4, 1881), Blacksburg Presbyterian Church, Blacksburg, Va.

36. [Jordan], "Pride and Preservation," 46; *Christiansburg Messenger,* July 31, 1874; Dunay, *Blacksburg*, 102, 148; Harrison, *Consecrated Life*, 132–34, 260.

37. "From S. S. Missionary by G. W. Otinger," *Christian Recorder,* Mar. 17, 1881; Mechanics Liens, 1887: 69, 122, 125, and 141, MCCH; [Jordan], "Pride and Preservation," 46; Harrison, *Consecrated Life*, 254–72.

38. *Minutes of the Colored Valley Baptist Association . . . 1870;* Harrison, *Consecrated Life,* 181–85; *Minutes of the (Colored) Valley Baptist Association of Virginia . . . 1875;* Acct. 669 [Christian Union of the Christiansburg African Baptist Church], Freedmans Bank of Richmond (Dec. 1869), "United States, Freedmans Bank Records, 1865–1874," https://familysearch.org (originals in Records of the Comptroller of the Currency, Record Group 101, National Archives, Washington, D.C.); Deed Book 42: 421, MCCH. Information on black cemeteries in Montgomery County from Deed Book U: 60, MCCH; [Jordan], "Pride and Preservation," 33–36; and personal visits. For more on the role and nature of cemeteries in Virginia's African American communities, see Rainville, *Hidden History.*

39. Personal communication, James Dow, 2011; Deed Book 39: 202, MCCH; Common Law A-10639 and Common Law 152, MCCH; *Grimes v. Grimes,* Chancery 2084, MCCH; Blacksburg [Virginia] Odd Fellows Lodge Records, 1910–30, Ms 88–009, VT.

6. Government and Politics

1. MC Cohabitation; 1870 census; Teachers' Monthly School Reports, Mar.–June, 1870, reel 19, BRFAL-EDVA; "A Voice from the Freedmen," *Philadelphia Freedman's Friend* 1, no. 26 (Feb. 1871): 4; the annual *Minutes of the Colored Valley Baptist Association . . .* from 1869 to 1875 are available in Minutes, Baptist Association, Valley, 1841 to 1881, VBHS.

2. Arthur Sullivan to Lake Sullivan, July 25, 1869, Box Doc 3047, folder 2, Sullivan Family Papers, accession number 2014.32.02, MCM; *Richmond Daily Dispatch,* July 12, 1869; *Christiansburg Messenger,* May 2 and May 23, 1879; Abstract of Votes for Sheriff, Commonwealth Attorney, Treasurer & Commissioner of the Revenue, cast in Montgomery County Virginia at the General Election held the fourth Thursday in May A.D. 1879, drawer 1, MCCH; Order Book Co. Court No. 10: 440, MCCH; Canvassing, Black Ministers, 1889, box 190, Mahone Papers.

3. Blair, "Justice versus Law and Order," 158.

4. May 1, 1865, Order Book Co. Court Com. Law & Chancy. 1859–1868, MCCH.

5. Foner, *Reconstruction,* 68–70, 142–53.

6. Order Book Co. Court Com. Law & Chancy. 1859–1868, MCCH.

7. Penningroth, *The Claims of Kinfolk,* 111–30; Blair, "Justice versus Law and Order"; Complaints Wytheville, VA. 8th Dist. [Aug. 1865–Jan. 1866], reel 193, BRFAL-FOVA; Schaeffer to Snidow, June 30, 1866, reel 67, BRFAL-FOVA; Schaeffer to Evans, July 30, 1866, reel 67, BRFAL-FOVA; Schaeffer to Brown, Aug. 25, 1866, reel 67, BRFAL-FOVA.

8. Complaints Wytheville, VA. 8th Dist. [Aug. 1865–Jan. 1866], reel 193, BRFAL-FOVA; Peirce, *The Freedmen's Bureau,* 55–74, 144–45; Cimbala and Miller, *The Freedmen's Bureau and Reconstruction,* xxvi; Schaeffer to Wilson, Aug. 3, 1866, reel 67, BRFAL-FOVA.

9. Service record of Thomas Fraction, reel 105, USCT; Schaeffer to Remington, Feb. 14, 1867, reel 67, BRFAL-FOVA.

10. Schaeffer to Remington, Feb. 14 and Feb. 16, 1867, reel 67, BRFAL-FOVA;

Schaeffer to Brown, Feb. 25, 1867, reel 67, BRFAL-FOVA; Schaeffer to Austin, May 6, 1867, reel 67, BRFAL-FOVA; Schaeffer to Mallery, May 25, 1867, reel 67, BRFAL-FOVA; *Commonwealth v. Othello Fraction,* Criminal A-711, MCCH; *Commonwealth v. Thomas Fraction,* Criminal A-716, MCCH; Order Book Cir. Court No. 4, 427, MCCH; Order Book Co. Court Comm. Law & Chancy, 1859–1868, May 6, 1867, MCCH.

11. Blair, "Justice versus Law and Order"; Schaeffer to Remington, Feb. 14, 1867, reel 67, BRFAL-FOVA.

12. Schaeffer to Akers, June 11 and June 12, 1866, reel 67, BRFAL-FOVA; Schaeffer to Furrow and Carver, Feb. 8, 1867, reel 67, BRFAL-FOVA.

13. Marriage licenses and Register of Marriages, MCCH.

14. Marriage licenses and Register of Marriages, MCCH; Schaeffer to Brown, Nov. 30, 1867, reel 67, BRFAL-FOVA. The timing of this change in the clerk's behavior suggests that it may have been the result of pressure from Charles Schaeffer, the newly arrived agent of the Freedmen's Bureau.

15. John A. Nicolay, "Virginia Poverty: Paupers and the Almshouse, an Examination of Montgomery County's Response to Poverty 1790–1860," Vertical Research Files, MCM; John Nicolay Papers, Ms 87–207, VT; Schaeffer to Brown, Aug. 25, 1866, reel 67, BRFAL-FOVA.

16. Schaeffer to Brown, Aug. 25 and Sept. 25, 1866, reel 67, BRFAL-FOVA; receipts for outdoor relief, medical, and burial costs, box 1, folder 6, John Nicolay Papers, Ms 87–207, VT; Order Book Com. Law & Chancy. 1868–1870: 77, MCCH.

17. Order Book Co. Court Com. Law & Chancy. 1859–1868: Oct. 2, 1865, and Oct. 2, 1866, MCCH; Christiansburg Minute Book, Feb. 10, 1857, MCCH; Russell, *The Free Negro in Virginia,* 112–16; Snavely, *The Taxation of Negroes in Virginia,* 13–15.

18. "An Act to provide for the more efficient Government of the Rebel States," chap. 153, 39th Cong.

19. General Order 28, Headquarters First Military District, State of Virginia, Mar. 13, 1867, *Executive Documents Printed by Order of the House of Representatives . . . 1867–'68,* vol. 2, part 1, 254–57; Circular No. 9, May 1, 1867, Head Quarters Assistant Commissioner, State of Virginia, https://www.archives.gov/exhibits/civil-war/preview/endings-and-beginnings/; Certificate of C. A. Chipley, *Documents of the Constitutional Convention of the State of Virginia,* 30–34; *Christiansburg Southwest,* Apr. 13 and May 11, 1867; Schaeffer to Mallery, June 25 and July 27, 1867, reel 67, BRFAL-FOVA. Schaeffer did report "interference" by Waller Preston, but it was for freedmen associating with the Union League rather than for their registering to vote (Schaeffer to Austin, June 12, 1867, reel 67, BRFAL-FOVA).

20. Schaeffer to Mallery, June 25, 1867, reel 67, BRFAL-FOVA; *Lynchburg Virginian,* Oct. 25, 1867; 1867 Census; 1870 census (population schedule). The First Reconstruction Act barred from voting those who were guilty of "participation in the rebellion," but it is unclear if any men in Montgomery County were actually barred from registering.

21. Austin to Mallery, May 31, 1867, reel 194, BRFAL-FOVA. For more on postwar divisions among the white residents of southern Appalachian communities, see Crawford, *Ashe County's Civil War,* 148–75; Sarris, *A Separate Civil War,* 144–80; Mar-

shall, *Creating a Confederate Kentucky,* 55–80; T. R. C. Hutton, "UnReconstructed Appalachia: The Persistence of War in Appalachia," in Slap, *Reconstructing Appalachia,* 71–104; Nash, *Reconstruction's Ragged Edge,* 54–88.

22. Austin to Mallery, May 31, 1867, reel 194, BRFAL-FOVA.

23. Mjagkij, *Organizing Black America,* 663–64; Lowe, *Republicans and Reconstruction,* 112–13; Foner, *Reconstruction,* 283–86; Hahn, *A Nation under Our Feet,* 177–264; Schaeffer to Austin, May 21 and June 12, 1867, reel 67, BRFAL-FOVA; *Christiansburg Southwest,* May 11, 1867.

24. Schaeffer to Austin, June 12, 1867, reel 67, BRFAL-FOVA; Mallery to Austin, June 17, 1867, reel 1, BRFAL-ACVA; Schaeffer to Mallery, Aug. 25, 1867, reel 67, BRFAL-FOVA; Austin to Mallery, Aug. 31, 1867, reel 60, BRFAL-ACVA; Schaeffer to Mallery, Sept. 25. 1867, reel 60, BRFAL-ACVA; Robe to Schaeffer, Oct. 12, 1867, reel 195, BRFAL-FOVA; Schaeffer to Brown, Nov. 30 and Dec. 31, 1867, reel 60, BRFAL-ACVA.

25. Schaeffer to Mallery, Aug. 25 and Sept. 25, 1867, reel 67, BRFAL-FOVA; *Documents of the Constitutional Convention of the State of Virginia,* 29–36; 1870 census (population schedule); Marrs to Schaeffer, Mar. 8, 1867, reel 68, BRFAL-FOVA.

26. Schaeffer to Brown, Oct. 27, 1867, reel 67, BRFAL-FOVA; *Lynchburg Virginian,* Oct. 25, 1867; *Christiansburg Southwest,* Nov. 2, 1867; J. Smith, "Virginia during Reconstruction," 55–57.

27. Schaeffer to Brown, Oct. 27 and Nov. 30, 1867, reel 67, BRFAL-FOVA.

28. Schaeffer to Brown, Oct. 27 and Nov. 30, 1867, reel 67, BRFAL-FOVA.

29. *Christiansburg Southwest,* Apr. 25 and May 2, 1868; Schaeffer to Brown, Feb. 29, 1868, reel 67, BRFAL-FOVA.

30. Cohen, *At Freedom's Edge,* 38–41; Schaeffer to Brown, Jan. 31, Feb. 29, Mar. 30, Apr. 30, May 31, June 30, and July 31, 1868, reel 67, BRFAL-FOVA.

31. J. Smith, "Virginia during Reconstruction," 62–103; Maddex, *The Virginia Conservatives,* 57–60; *Christiansburg Southwest,* Apr. 25, May 2 and May 9, 1868; Schaeffer to Coulter Apr. 30, 1868, reel 67, BRFAL-FOVA; Report of Outrages commencing January 1st 1868, reel 59, BRFAL-ACVA.

32. Schaeffer to Brown, Nov. 30, 1867, reel 67, BRFAL-FOVA; Schaeffer to Coulter, Apr. 30, 1868, reel 67, BRFAL-FOVA; *Christiansburg Southwest,* May 9, 1868.

33. *Christiansburg Southwest,* May 9, May 16, and July 25, 1868; Schaeffer to Coulter, June 30, July 31, and Aug. 31, 1868, reel 67, BRFAL-FOVA; J. Smith, "Virginia during Reconstruction," 128–30, 147–57; Maddex, *The Virginia Conservatives,* 67–85.

34. Mary Sullivan to Lake Sullivan, June 9, 1869, Box Doc 3047, folder 2, Sullivan Family Papers, accession number 2014.32.02, MCM.

35. MC Cohabitation; Schaeffer to Brown, Mar. 15, 1867, reel 67, BRFAL-FOVA; Arthur Sullivan to Lake Sullivan, July 25, 1869, Box Doc 3047, folder 2, Sullivan Family Papers, accession number 2014.32.02, MCM; *Richmond Daily Dispatch,* July 12, 1869.

36. Order Book Com. Law & Chancy., 1868–1870: 109 and 150, MCCH; *Code of Virginia* (1860), chap. 126.

37. Evidence of African Americans' experience with the judicial system under Military Reconstruction can be found among loose Criminal Papers, MCCH; the Criminal A-XXX series, MCCH; Court Order Books, MCCH; and, in a few instances, in *Christiansburg Southwest.*

38. Schaeffer to Austin, June 10, 1868, reel 68, BRFAL-FOVA; Schaeffer to Brown, Oct. 27, 1867, reel 67, BRFAL-FOVA.

39. Austin to Mallery, July 31 and Aug. 31, 1867, reel 60, BRFAL-ACVA.

40. Hahn, *A Nation under Our Feet,* 367.

41. Wynes, *Race Relations in Virginia,* 6–15; Maddex, *Virginia Conservatives,* 67–120; Dailey, *Before Jim Crow,* 15–47.

42. Dailey, *Before Jim Crow,* 15–102.

43. Wynes, *Race Relations in Virginia,* 39–67; Dailey, *Before Jim Crow,* 155–69; Hahn, *A Nation under Our Feet,* 400–11; Perman, *Struggle for Mastery,* 20.

44. Wynes, *Race Relations in Virginia,* 12–15; Maddex, *Virginia Conservatives,* 197–98; "Joint Resolutions agreeing to amendments to the Constitution of Virginia, in reference to the Elective Franchise and Qualifications for Office, and concerning the Legislative Department," in *Acts and Joint Resolutions Passed by the General Assembly . . . 1875–6,* chap. 87 (Feb. 22, 1876), 82–87; Schaeffer to Mallery, July 27, 1867, reel 67, BRFAL-FOVA; *Lynchburg Virginian,* Oct. 25, 1867; Number of Registered Voters in the County of Montgomery, Canvassing: Aug.1880–Oct. 1881, box 187, Mahone Papers; Palmer to Mahone, Oct. 7, 1882, box 188, folder 1, Canvassing 1882, Mahone Papers.

45. Number of Registered Voters in the County of Montgomery, Canvassing: Aug. 1880–Oct. 1881, box 187, Mahone Papers; Palmer to Mahone, Oct. 7, 1882, box 188, folder 1, Canvassing 1882, Mahone Papers; McKinney, *Southern Mountain Republicans,* 103; Dailey, *Before Jim Crow,* 62. In spite of the constitutional amendment, the statute governing voter registration ("An Act to Provide for a General Registration of Voters" in *Acts and Joint Resolutions Passed by the General Assembly . . . 1869–70,* chap. 46 [Apr. 12, 1870], 55–59) continued to govern voter registration.

46. List of Voters/Montgomery Co Va., Sept. 15–2[?], 1883, Canvassing 1883 Sept. ?–Oct., box 189, Mahone Papers.

47. Dailey, *Before Jim Crow,* 103–31; Heermans to Mahone, Dec. 17, 1883, Elections Frauds, Dec. 14–23, 1883, box 192, Mahone Papers. The text of the Danville Circular is available at http://www.virginiamemory.com/docs/hires/Staunton _Vindicator_HR.pdf.

48. Dailey, *Before Jim Crow,* 155–69; "An Act to provide for the method of voting by ballot," *Acts and Joint Resolutions Passed by the General Assembly . . . 1893–94,* chap. 746, 862–67.

49. Report from Radford Precinct and report from an unspecified Montgomery County precinct, in Elections Frauds, 1889, folder 4, Mahone Papers. See also Ellett to Mahone, Nov. 6, 1889, and Wilson to Mahone, Nov. 6, 1889, in Elections Frauds, 1889, folder 3, Mahone Papers.

50. Wynes, *Race Relations in Virginia,* 51–67; Dailey, *Before Jim Crow,* 162–65; Supr's Book No. 3: 288–90, MCCH. Rolls of "colored voters" for Alleghany Springs

(1902 and 1903), Auburn (1902), Blacksburg (1903), Grayson's Mill (1902), Harmon's (1902), and Long Shop (1902) have survived in List of Voters 1902 through 1903, MCCH.

51. Hahn, *A Nation under Our Feet,* 219, 401–2; McKinney, *Southern Mountain Republicans,* 50–64, 138.

52. Hahn, *A Nation under Our Feet,* 376–84; boxes 180–86, Mahone Papers.

53. *Commonwealth v. Henry Taylor,* Criminal Papers, drawer 30, envelope 182, MCCH; Supr's Book No. 1: 131–33, MCCH; Order Book Co. Court No. 10: 107, MCCH.

54. Pincus, *The Virginia Supreme Court,* 22–27; Howard, *Commentaries on the Constitution of Virginia,* 2:698–99; Dailey, *Before Jim Crow,* 48–76; *Code of Virginia* (1873), chap. 158; Order Book County Court 1875–80 and Order Book Co. Court No. 3, MCCH.

55. *Journal of the Senate of the Commonwealth of Virginia . . . 1879,* 105; marriage licenses, 1859: 9, MCCH; Order Book County Court 1875–80, MCCH; Order Book Co. Court No. 3, MCCH; 1870 and 1880 censuses (population schedules); index of incoming correspondence, 1882 index, 2: 208, box 169, Mahone Papers.

56. *Commonwealth v. Malcolm Palmer,* Criminal Papers, No. 141, drawer 30, MCCH; Order Book Co. Court No. 3: 211–12, MCCH. The statutes governing jury selection in 1882 seem to have been *Code of Virginia* (1873), chaps. 158 and 202.

57. *Commonwealth v. Malcolm Palmer,* Criminal Papers, No. 141, drawer 30, MCCH; Order Book Co. Court No. 3: 211–12, 217–18, 235, MCCH.

58. There *may* have been a single black member of a petit jury in June 1883, but both white and black voters named Floyd Dobbins lived in Montgomery County at the time, and it is impossible to be certain which served on this jury (Order Book Co. Court No. 3: 264, MCCH).

59. Order Book Co. Court No. 3: 418–20, 422, and 552. Virginia's Supreme Court subsequently overturned the convictions of Gray and her husband, Isaac Jones, on the grounds that the state had offered no evidence to prove Isaac Jones met the legal definition of a "negro" and "must be presumed not to be a negro until he is proved to be such" (*Jones v. the Commonwealth* and *Gray v. the Commonwealth,* Supreme Court of Virginia, 80 Va 538).

60. Dailey, *Before Jim Crow,* 132–54; *Journal of the House of Delegates . . . for the Extra Session of 1884,* 208–10 and 248; Order Book County Court 1875–80, MCCH; Order Book Co. Court No. 3, MCCH; Order Book Co. Court 1885, MCCH. Miller may have exacted some satisfaction as he left office, though. At the first session of the county court under his successor, George Junkin, it seems that a single black man, John Grimes, served on the grand jury, probably on the basis of a summons issued by Miller before stepping down (Order Book Co. Court 1885: 56 and 60, MCCH).

61. County Court Order Book 11: 435–585, MCCH; County Court Order Book, 1897–1901: 3, MCCH; *Commonwealth v. Thomas Simpkins,* Criminal Papers, drawer 30, envelope 166, MCCH. Evidence of whippings appears in Montgomery County Criminal Papers, MCCH; Council Minutes from the Town of Blacksburg (Office of the Town Manager, Blacksburg, Va.), and *Christiansburg Messenger.* Jacob Akers,

who was whipped in 1875, was white (*Commonwealth v. Jacob Akers,* Criminal A-812, MCCH; *Christiansburg Messenger,* July 2, 1875), and the James Stovall whipped in 1873 was probably James Stover, a white carpenter (*Commonwealth v. Stovall,* Criminal Papers, drawer 30, envelope 188, MCCH). For more on African American opposition to whipping, see Wynes, *Race Relations in Virginia,* 22–28, and Dailey, *Before Jim Crow,* 54–55.

62. Order Book Co. Court 1871–1875: 254, 313, 340, 344, 345, 348, 349, 359, 369, and 371, MCCH; Order Book County Court 1875–1880: 58, 73, 369, and 376, MCCH.

63. Criminal Papers, drawer 30, envelope 163, MCCH.

64. Rushdy, *American Lynching,* 69–93; Brundage, *Lynching in the New South,* 140–60, 281–83; Rand Dotson, "Race and Violence in Urbanizing Appalachia: The Roanoke Riot of 1893," in Stewart, *Blood in the Hills,* 237–71; Order Book Co. Court 1888: 281, MCCH; *Lynchburg Daily Virginian,* Dec. 8, 1889. The *Richmond Dispatch* did report in 1898 that two black men, Chris Wade and Garland Taylor, who had been charged with or convicted of assaulting white women in Montgomery County, had been moved from Christiansburg to Roanoke "to prevent the enraged citizens from meting out summary justice." County records do confirm that Chris Wade, who had been charged with rape, and Garfield Taylor, who was awaiting transfer to the state penitentiary, were transferred to the Roanoke city jail but say only that the move was made "for reasons satisfactory to the judge." Wade was returned to the county two weeks later, tried without incident, and sentenced to eight years in prison (Order Book Co. Court 1897–1901: 99,104, and 112, MCCH; *Richmond Dispatch,* Mar. 16, 1898).

65. 1871–72–73 Summons, envelope no. 132-C, MCCH; *Headin v. Noell,* Common Law A-9661, MCCH; *Johnson v. Edmundson,* Chancery 768, MCCH; *Montague v. Brown,* Chancery 1041, MCCH.

66. *Twine v. Twine,* Chancery 1423, MCCH; *Fuqua v. Fuqua,* Chancery 512, MCCH; *Hopkins v. Hopkins,* Chancery 1423, MCCH. Two cases initiated before 1900 were not settled until 1902, and in another case the final outcome is unclear.

67. *Ford v. Lynch,* Chancery 1927, MCCH. The statute governing a widow's dower right was *Code of Virginia* (1873), chap. 106.

68. Constitution of Virginia (1870), Art. 11; *Code of Virginia* (1873), chaps. 115 and 183. In Montgomery County, both mechanic's liens and homestead exemptions were entered into the deed books at this time; see, for example, Deed Books V: 170 and 465 (Webster), S: 563 (Carr), and U: 26 (Bratton), MCCH.

69. *Commonwealth v. J. A. Eddie* [*sic*], box 1, folder 21, John Nicolay Papers, Ms 87-027, VT.

70. *Commonwealth v. Edwin Cambel* [*sic*] and *Commonwealth v. Minnis Headen, Jr.,* Criminal Papers, drawer 29, envelopes 21 and 76, MCCH.

71. Evidence of the relationship between African Americans and county and town government is scattered throughout: Order Book Co. Court 1871–1875, Order Book County Court 1875–1880, Order Book Co. Court No. 3 [1880–85], Order Book Co. Court 1885, Order Book Co. Court 1888, Order Book Co. Court No. 10 [1890–96], County Court Order Book 11, Order Book Co. Court 1897–1901, Supr's Book No. 1 (quotation from 176), Supr's Book No. 3, and Road Book 1873–1889, all in MCCH;

Blacksburg Council Minutes, Office of the Town Manager, Blacksburg, Va.; box 1, John Nicolay Papers, Ms 87–027, VT; box 1, Charles W. Crush Collection, Ms 84–180, VT.

72. According to N. L. Bishop, "A classmate and close friend, Anthony C. Price, ran for town council or Mayor in about 1973 or 1974 while a student at V[irginia] T[ech]. Later, Mr. Burrell Morgan ran for town council in the early 1980s I think it was" (personal communication, 2014).

Conclusion

1. "A Handbill Announcing Washington's Tour of Virginia" and "An Address by William Taylor Burwell Williams on Washington's Tour of Virginia," in B. Washington, *The Booker T. Washington Papers,* 10:128, 143–49; Swain, "Christiansburg Institute," 77–138.

2. "An Address by William Taylor Burwell Williams on Washington's Tour of Virginia," in B. Washington, *The Booker T. Washington Papers,* 10:143–49; Swain, "Christiansburg Institute," 131–33.

3. "Amanda: Colored Daughter of Virginia," box 1, folder 30, James Robbins Randolph Papers, Ms 1971–001, VT.

4. For a fuller discussion of this phenomena, see Ely, *Israel on the Appomattox,* and Von Daacke, *Freedom Has a Face.*

5. *Christiansburg Southwest,* Apr. 13, 1867.

6. *Christiansburg Messenger,* Feb. 7, 1879.

7. Hahn, *A Nation under Our Feet,* 459–61.

BIBLIOGRAPHY

Primary Sources

Archival Collections
Blacksburg Presbyterian Church, Blacksburg, Va.
    Records of the Session of the Blacksburg Church
Christiansburg Presbyterian Church, Christiansburg, Va.
    Records of the Church Session [1827–1869]
Christiansburg Institute Alumni Association, Christiansburg, Va.
    Catalogs
    Killen Material
Cornell University, Carl A. Kroch Library, Rare and Manuscript Collections, Ithaca, N.Y.
    Anti-Slavery Collection
Duke University, David M. Rubenstein Rare Book & Manuscript Library, Durham, N.C.
    William Mahone Papers
Friends Historical Library, Swarthmore College, Swarthmore, Pa.
    Friends Freedmen's Association Records
Harvard Business School, Baker Library Historical Collections, Cambridge, Mass.
    R. G. Dun & Co. Collection
Hollins University, Wyndham Robertson Library, Special Collections, Roanoke, Va.
    Charles Lewis Cocke Papers
Library of Congress, Washington, D.C.
    American Colonization Society Records
    Hotchkiss Map Collection
Library of Virginia, Richmond, Va.
    Cohabitation Registers Digital Collection
    Department of Taxation, Personal Property Tax Books

Montana Historical Society, Research Center Archives, Helena, Mont.
    Neil Fullerton Research Collection
Montgomery County Courthouse, Clerk of the Circuit Court's Office, Christians-
    burg, Va.
    Births
    Cohabitation Register
    Common Law
    Criminal Papers
    Court of Chancery
    Deaths
    Deed Books
    Elections
    Indentures
    Ledger, 1872–1883
    Marriage Licenses
    Marriage Registers
    Mechanics Liens
    Minutes of the Trustees of the Town of Christiansburg
    Land Books
    Order Books
    Road Books
    Supervisors' Books
    Unrecorded Deeds
    Will Books
    Wills
Montgomery County School Board, Christiansburg, Va.
    Christiansburg District School Board Minutes, 1870–1904
    Ledger, Christiansburg School District, 1883–1899
Montgomery Museum and Lewis Miller Regional Art Center, Christiansburg, Va.
    Ledger of Dr. W. A. Wilson of Christiansburg
    Recollections of Nora Caper Haymaker
    Store Account Book of Rice D. Montague, 1867–1870
    Sullivan Family Papers
    Vertical Research Files
National Archives, Washington, D.C.
    Civil War and Later Pension Files, Department of Veterans Affairs (RG 15)
    Confederate Papers Relating to Citizens or Business Firms (RG 109)
    Records of the Bureau of Refugees, Freedmen, and Abandoned Lands (RG 105)
    Records of the Colored Troops Division (RG 94)
    Records of the Comptroller of the Currency (RG 101)
    Southern Claims Commission—allowed (RG 217) and disallowed (RG 233)
    U.S. Census, 1850, Population, Slaves, and Agriculture Schedules
    U.S. Census, 1860, Population, Slaves, Manufacturing, and Agriculture
        Schedules

U.S. Census, 1870, Population and Agriculture Schedules
U.S. Census, 1880, Population and Agriculture Schedules
U.S. Census, 1890, Special Census (Veterans)
U.S. Census, 1900, Population Schedule
Oberlin College Archives, Oberlin, Ohio
   Alumni Records
   Lawson—Merrill Papers
   James Monroe Papers
Office of the Town Manager, Blacksburg, Va.
   Council Minutes
St. Paul Methodist Church, Christiansburg, Va.
   Records of Quarterly Meetings
   Register of the Christiansburg Station
University of Virginia, Albert and Shirley Small Special Collections Library, Charlottesville, Va.
   Clement Daniel Fishburne Diary
   Map of Cambria, Va.
Virginia Baptist Historical Society, Richmond, Va.
   Minutes, Baptist Association, Valley, 1841–1881
Virginia Historical Society, Richmond, Va.
   Edmundson Family Papers
Virginia Tech, Newman Library, Special Collections, Blacksburg, Va.
   Brown Family Papers
   Charles W. Crush Collection
   Historical Map Collection
   Henry M. Fowlkes Letters
   James Randall Kent Papers
   John Nicolay Papers
   Odd Fellows Lodge Records
   James Robbins Randolph Papers
   J. Hoge Tyler Family Collection
   Whisner Memorial Methodist Church Records
   Isaac White Papers

CONTEMPORARY NEWSPAPERS AND JOURNALS
African Repository and Colonial Journal
American Freedman
Christian Recorder
Colored American
Richmond Daily Dispatch
Philadelphia Freedman's Friend
Friends' Review
Christiansburg Messenger
Philadelphia Inquirer

Richmond Planet
Roanoke Times
Christiansburg Southwest
Lynchburg Virginian

PUBLISHED OFFICIAL RECORDS

Acts and Joint Resolutions Passed by the General Assembly of the State of Virginia at the Session of 1875-6. Richmond: R. F. Walker, 1876.

Acts and Joint Resolutions Passed by the General Assembly of the State of Virginia during the Session of 1889-'90. Richmond: 1890.

Acts and Joint Resolutions Passed by the General Assembly of the State of Virginia during the Session of 1893-94. Richmond: J. H. O'Bannon, 1894.

Acts of the General Assembly of the State of Virginia Passed at the Session of 1869-'70. Richmond: James E. Goode, 1870.

Acts of the General Assembly of the State of Virginia Passed in 1861, in the Eighty-Fifth Year of the Commonwealth. Richmond: William F. Ritchie, 1861.

Acts of the General Assembly of the State of Virginia Passed in 1865-66, in the Eighty-Ninth Year of the Commonwealth. Richmond: Allegre and Goode, 1866.

Acts Passed at a General Assembly of the Commonwealth of Virginia, Begun and Held at the Capitol, in the City of Richmond. Richmond: Thomas Ritchie, 1832.

Calendar of Wills in West Virginia, No. 49. Upshur County. Charleston: West Virginia Historical Records Survey, 1941.

Code of Virginia. Richmond: Ritchie and Dunnavant, 1860.

Code of Virginia. Richmond: James E. Goode, 1873.

Documents of the Constitutional Convention of the State of Virginia. Richmond, 1867.

Executive Documents Printed by Order of the House of Representatives during the Second Session of the Fortieth Congress, 1867-'68. 20 vols. Washington, D.C.: Government Printing Office, 1868.

House Documents. Vol. 143, *62nd Congress, 2d Session.* Washington, D.C.: Government Printing Office, 1912.

Journal of the House of Delegates of the Commonwealth of Virginia for the Extra Session of 1884. Richmond: Superintendent of Public Printing, 1884.

Journal of the Senate of the Commonwealth of Virginia Begun and Held at the Capitol ... on Wednesday, December 3, 1879. Richmond: R. E. Frayser, 1879.

Statistics of the Population of the United States ... from the Original Returns of the Ninth Census, June 1, 1870, The. 3 vols. Washington, D.C.: Government Printing Office, 1872.

Virginia School Report: Annual Report of the Superintendent of Public Instruction of the Commonwealth of Virginia. Richmond: Superintendent of Public Printing, 1871-1917.

OTHER SOURCES

Alexander, Roberta Sue. *North Carolina Faces the Freedmen: Race Relations during Presidential Reconstruction.* Durham, N.C.: Duke University Press, 1985.

Anderson, James D. *The Education of Blacks in the South, 1860–1935*. Chapel Hill: University of North Carolina Press, 1988.

Armstrong, James Edward. *The Baltimore Conference: 1844–1866*. N.p., n.d. Originally published in *Methodist Review*, M.E. Church, South, September–October 1895 (reprinted n.p., n.d).

[Armstrong, Samuel C.] *Twenty-Two Years' Work of the Hampton Normal and Agricultural Institute at Hampton, Virginia*. Hampton, Va.: Normal School Press, 1893.

Arnesen, Eric. *Brotherhoods of Color: Black Railroad Workers and the Struggle for Equality*. Cambridge, Mass.: Harvard University Press, 2001.

Ash, Stephen V. *A Year in the South: Four Lives in 1865*. New York: Palgrave Macmillan, 2002.

Ayers, Edward L. *The Promise of the New South: Life after Reconstruction*. New York: Oxford University Press, 1992.

Ayers, Edward L., Gary W. Gallagher, and Andrew J. Torget, eds. *Crucible of the Civil War: Virginia from Secession to Commemoration*. Charlottesville: University of Virginia Press, 2006.

Bardaglio, Peter W. *Reconstructing the Household: Families, Sex, and the Law in the Nineteenth-Century South*. Chapel Hill: University of North Carolina Press, 1995.

Berlin, Ira, Joseph P. Reidy, and Leslie S. Rowland, eds. *Freedom's Soldiers: The Black Military Experience in the Civil War*. Cambridge: Cambridge University Press, 1998.

Black, Harvey. *The Civil War Letters of Dr. Harvey Black: A Surgeon with Stonewall Jackson*. Edited by Glenn L. McMullen, Baltimore: Butternut and Blue, 1995.

Blair, William A. "Justice versus Law and Order: The Battles over the Reconstruction of Virginia's Minor Judiciary, 1865–1870." *Virginia Magazine of History and Biography* 103 (1995): 157–80.

[Botetourt Heritage Book Committee]. *Botetourt County, Virginia, Heritage Book, 1770–2000*. N.p.: Walsworth, n.d.

Brundage, W. Fitzhugh. *Lynching in the New South: Georgia and Virginia, 1880–1930*. Urbana: University of Illinois Press, 1993.

Burton, Orville Vernon. *In My Father's House Are Many Mansions: Family and Community in Edgefield, South Carolina*. Chapel Hill: University of North Carolina Press, 1985.

Butchart, Ronald E. *Northern Schools, Southern Blacks, and Reconstruction: Freedmen's Education, 1862–1875*. Westport, Conn.: Greenwood, 1980.

———. *Schooling the Freed People: Teaching, Learning, and the Struggle for Black Freedom*. Chapel Hill: University of North Carolina Press, 2010.

Butt, Israel L. *History of African Methodism in Virginia, or Four Decades in the Old Dominion*. Hampton, Va.: Hampton Institute Press, 1908.

Cain, Morgan. "Wake Forest: Voices That Tell of a Faith Community." Unpublished manuscript, 2008.

Cimbala, Paul, and Randall Miller, eds. *The Freedmen's Bureau and Reconstruction: Reconsiderations*. New York: Fordham University Press, 1999.

Clegg, Claude A., III. *The Price of Liberty: African Americans in the Making of Liberia.* Chapel Hill: University of North Carolina Press, 2004.

Cohen, William. *At Freedom's Edge: Black Mobility and the Southern White Quest for Racial Control, 1861–1915.* Baton Rouge: Louisiana State University Press, 1991.

Cooke, Michael C. "Race Relations in Montgomery County, Virginia, 1870–1990." *Journal of the Appalachian Studies Association* 4 (1992): 94–104.

Coppin, Fanny Jackson. *Reminiscences of School Life, and Hints on Teaching.* Philadelphia: AME Book Concern, 1913.

Crawford, Martin. *Ashe County's Civil War: Community and Society in the Appalachian South.* Charlottesville: University Press of Virginia, 2001.

Crews, Edward R., and Timothy A. Parrish. *14th Virginia Infantry.* Lynchburg, Va.: H. E. Howard, 1995.

Crush, Charles W. *The Montgomery County Story, 1776–1957.* N.p., 1957.

Dailey, Jane. *Before Jim Crow: The Politics of Race in Postemancipation Virginia.* Chapel Hill: University of North Carolina Press, 2000.

Dailey, Jane, Glenda Elizabeth Gilmore, and Bryant Simon, eds. *Jumpin' Jim Crow: Southern Politics from Civil War to Civil Rights.* Princeton, N.J.: Princeton University Press, 2000.

Dew, Charles B. *Bond of Iron: Master and Slave at Buffalo Forge.* New York: W. W. Norton, 1994.

Dickenson, Richard B. "1867 Freedmens Bureau Census Extract." *Appalachian Notes* 13 (1989): 1–10, 48–57, 86–95.

———. *Entitled! Free Papers in Appalachia Concerning Antebellum Freeborn Negroes and Emancipated Blacks, Montgomery County, Virginia.* Washington, D.C.: National Genealogical Society, 1981.

———. "Some Freedman Identities, Part I." *Virginia Appalachian Notes* 2 (1978): 105–115.

———. "Some Freedman Identities, Part II." *Virginia Appalachian Notes* 3 (1979): 5–14.

———. "Some Freedman Identities, Part III." *Virginia Appalachian Notes* 3 (1979): 47–50.

Donald, Christopher Ross. "Growth and Independence of Methodist Congregations in Blacksburg, Virginia." *Smithfield Review* 10 (2006): 49–76.

Dotson, Rand. *Roanoke, Virginia, 1882–1912: Magic City of the New South.* Knoxville: University of Tennessee Press, 2007.

Dunaway, Wilma A. *The African-American Family in Slavery and Emancipation.* Cambridge: Cambridge University Press, 2003.

———. *The First American Frontier: Transition to Capitalism in Southern Appalachia.* Chapel Hill: University of North Carolina Press, 1996.

———. *Slavery in the American Mountain South.* Cambridge: Cambridge University Press, 2003.

Dunay, Donna. *Blacksburg: Understanding a Virginia Town, Town Architecture.* Blacksburg: Town of Blacksburg, College of Architecture and Urban Studies, and Extension Division, Virginia Polytechnic Institute and State University, 1986.

Dusinberre, William. *Strategies for Survival: Recollections of Bondage in Antebellum Virginia*. Charlottesville: University of Virginia Press, 2009.

Ely, Melvin Patrick. *Israel on the Appomattox: A Southern Experiment in Black Freedom from the 1790s through the Civil War*. New York: Alfred A. Knopf, 2004.

Escott, Paul D. *Slavery Remembered: A Record of Twentieth-Century Slave Narratives*. Chapel Hill: University of North Carolina Press, 1979.

Fairclough, Adam. *A Class of Their Own: Black Teachers in the Segregated South*. Cambridge, Mass.: Belknap Press of Harvard University Press, 2007.

Farmer-Kaiser, Mary. *Freedwomen and the Freedmen's Bureau: Race, Gender, & Public Policy in the Age of Emancipation*. New York: Fordham University Press, 2010.

Fields, Barbara. *Slavery and Freedom on the Middle Ground: Maryland during the Nineteenth Century*. New Haven, Conn.: Yale University Press, 1985.

Foner, Eric. *Reconstruction: America's Unfinished Revolution, 1863–1877*. New York: Harper and Row, 1988.

Foner, Philip S., and George E. Walker, eds. *Proceedings of the Black State Conventions, 1840–1865*. 2 vols. Philadelphia: Temple University Press, 1979–80.

Fortieth Annual Report of the American Home Mission Society. New York: American Baptist Home Mission Rooms, 1872.

Fuke, Richard Paul. "Planters, Apprentices, and Forced Labor: The Black Family Under Pressure in Post-Emancipation Maryland." *Agricultural History* 62, no. 4 (1988): 57–74.

Genovese, Eugene D. *Roll, Jordan, Roll: The World the Slaves Made*. New York: Pantheon Books, 1972.

Gianakos, Cynthia. "Virginia and the Married Women's Property Acts." MA thesis, University of Virginia, 1982.

Givens, Lula Porterfield. *Christiansburg, Montgomery County, Virginia: In the Heart of the Alleghenies*. Pulaski, Va.: Edmonds, 1981.

Glymph, Thavolia. *Out of the House of Bondage: The Transformation of the Plantation Household*. Cambridge: Cambridge University Press, 2008.

Green, Hilary Nicole. "Educational Reconstruction: African American Education in the Urban South, 1865–1890." PhD diss., University of North Carolina, 2010.

———. *Educational Reconstruction: African American Schools in the Urban South, 1865–1890*. New York: Fordham University Press, 2016.

Gutman, Herbert G. *The Black Family in Slavery and Freedom, 1750–1925*. New York: Pantheon Books, 1976.

———. "Reconstruction in Ohio: Negroes in the Hocking Valley Coal Mines in 1873 and 1874." *Labor History* 3 (1962): 243–64.

Hahn, Steven. *A Nation under Our Feet: Black Political Struggles in the Rural South from Slavery to the Great Migration*. Cambridge, Mass.: Harvard University Press, 2003.

Harrison, Charles H. *The Story of a Consecrated Life*. Philadelphia: J. B. Lippincott, 1900.

Heatwole, Cornelius J. *A History of Education in Virginia*. New York: Macmillan, 1916.

Holt, Sharon Ann. *Making Freedom Pay: North Carolina Freedpeople Working for Themselves, 1865–1900*. Athens: University of Georgia Press, 2000.

Horst, Samuel L. *Education for Manhood: The Education of Blacks in Virginia during the Civil War*. Lanham, Md.: University Press of America, 1987.

———, ed. *The Fire of Liberty in Their Hearts: The Diary of Jacob E. Yoder of the Freedmen's Bureau School, Lynchburg, Virginia*. Richmond: Library of Virginia, 1996.

Howard, A. E. Dick. *Commentaries on the Constitution of Virginia*. 2 vols. Charlottesville: University Press of Virginia, 1974.

Inscoe, John, ed. *Appalachians and Race: The Mountain South from Slavery to Segregation*. Lexington: University Press of Kentucky, 2001.

———. *Mountain Masters: Slavery and the Sectional Crisis in Western North Carolina*. Knoxville: University of Tennessee Press, 1989.

———. *Race, War, and Remembrance in the Appalachian South*. Lexington: University Press of Kentucky, 2008.

Inscoe, John, and Gordon McKinney. *The Heart of Confederate Appalachia: Western North Carolina in the Civil War*. Chapel Hill: University of North Carolina Press, 2000.

Jackson, Lawrence P. *My Father's Name: A Black Virginia Family after the Civil War*. Chicago: University of Chicago Press, 2012.

Johnson, Elmer D., ed. *Radford Then and Now: A Pictorial History*. Radford: American Revolution Bicentennial Commission of Radford, Va., 1975.

Johnson, Patricia Givens. *The New River Early Settlement*. N.p., 1983.

Johnston, David E. *A History of Middle New River Settlements and Contiguous Territory*. Huntington, W. Va.: Standard, 1906.

Jones, Catherine. "Ties That Bind, Bonds That Break: Children in the Reorganization of Households in Postemancipation Virginia." *Journal of Southern History* 76 (2010): 71–106.

Jones, Jacqueline A. *Labor of Love, Labor of Sorrow: Black Women, Work, and the Family from Slavery to the Present*. New York: Basic Books, 1985.

[Jordan, Kathryn, ed.]. "Pride and Preservation: A 'Sharing Our History' Community Project, Mountain View Cemetery." Radford, Va.: Center for Experiential Learning and Career Service, Radford University, n.d.

Kanode, Roy Wyete. *Christiansburg, Virginia: Small Town America at Its Finest*. Kingsport, Tenn.: Inove Graphics, 2005.

Kegley, Mary B., and F. B. Kegley. *Early Adventurers on Western Waters: The New River of Virginia in Pioneer Days, 1745–1800*. 2 vols. Orange, Va.: Green, 1980–82.

Keiser, John H. "Black Strikebreakers and Racism in Illinois, 1865–1900." *Illinois State Historical Society Journal* 65 (1972): 313–26.

Kerr-Ritchie, Jeffrey R. *Freedpeople in the Tobacco South: Virginia, 1860–1890*. Chapel Hill: University of North Carolina Press, 1999.

Killen, Linda, ed. *Freedmen's Bureau: The Reports of Charles S. Schaeffer from the Vir-*

ginia Counties of Montgomery and Pulaski, with Additional Information on the Counties of Floyd, Giles, Craig, Wythe, and Roanoke, 1866–1868. Self-published, n.d.

——. *Radford's Early Black Residents, 1880–1925.* Belspring, Va., n.d.

King, Martin Luther, Jr. *The Papers of Martin Luther King. Vol. 6, Advocate of Social Gospel.* Edited by Clayborne Carson, Susan Carson, Susan Englander, Troy Jackson, and Gerald L. Smith. Berkeley: University of California Press, 2007.

Kornweibel, Theodore, Jr. *Railroads in the African American Experience: A Photographic Journey.* Baltimore: Johns Hopkins University Press, 2010.

Lewis, Ronald L. *Black Coal Miners in America: Race, Class, and Community Conflict, 1780–1980.* Lexington: University Press of Kentucky, 1987.

Lindon, Mary Elizabeth, ed. *Virginia's Montgomery County.* Christiansburg, Va.: Montgomery Museum and Lewis Miller Regional Art Center, 2009.

Link, William A. *A Hard Country and Lonely Place: Schooling, Society, and Reform in Rural Virginia, 1870–1920.* Chapel Hill: University of North Carolina Press, 1986.

Litwack, Leon. *Been in the Storm So Long: The Aftermath of Slavery.* New York: Alfred A. Knopf, 1981.

——. *Trouble in Mind: Black Southerners in the Age of Jim Crow.* New York: Alfred A. Knopf, 1998.

Lowe, Richard G. "The Freedmen's Bureau and Local Black Leadership." *Journal of American History* 80 (Dec. 1993): 989–98.

——. "Local Black Leaders during Reconstruction in Virginia." *Virginia Magazine of History and Biography* 103 (1995): 181–206.

——. *Republicans and Reconstruction in Virginia, 1856–70.* Charlottesville: University Press of Virginia, 1991.

Maddex, Jack P., Jr. *The Virginia Conservatives, 1867–1879: A Study in Reconstruction Politics.* Chapel Hill: University of North Carolina Press, 1970.

Malone, Ann Patton. *Sweet Chariot: Slave Family and Household Structure in Nineteenth-Century Louisiana.* Chapel Hill: University of North Carolina Press, 1992.

Manfra, Jo Ann, and Robert R. Dykstra. "Serial Marriage and the Origins of the Black Stepfamily: The Rowanty Evidence." *Journal of American History* 72 (1985): 18–44.

Marshall, Anne E. *Creating a Confederate Kentucky: The Lost Cause and Civil War Memory in a Border State.* Chapel Hill: University of North Carolina Press, 2010.

McColley, Robert. *Slavery and Jeffersonian Virginia.* 2nd ed. Urbana: University of Illinois Press, 1973.

McKinney, Gordon B. *Southern Mountain Republicans, 1865–1900: Politics and Appalachian Community.* Chapel Hill: University of North Carolina Press, 1978.

Melton, J. Gordon. *A Will to Choose: The Origins of African American Methodism.* Lanham, Md.: Rowman and Littlefield, 2007.

Minutes of the Annual Conferences of the Methodist Episcopal Church for the Year 1867. New York: Carlton and Porter, n.d.

Minutes of the Annual Conferences of the Methodist Episcopal Church for the Year 1868. New York: Carlton and Lanahan, n.d.

Minutes of the Annual Conferences of the Methodist Episcopal Church for the Year 1869. New York: Carlton and Lanahan, n.d.

Minutes of the (Colored) Valley Baptist Association of Virginia Held at Abingdon, Washington County, Va., August 6–9, 1875. N.p., n.d.

Minutes of the (Colored) Valley Baptist Association of Virginia Held at Buchanan, Botetourt County, Va., August 7–10, 1874. N.p., n.d.

Minutes of the Colored Valley Baptist Association of Virginia Held at Christiansburg, Montgomery County, Va., August 10–14, 1871. Lynchburg, Va.: Chas. H. Bryant, 1871.

Minutes of the (Colored) Valley Baptist Association of Virginia Held at Marion, Smyth County, Va., August 8–11, 1873. Marion, Va.: Patriot and Herald Office, 1873.

Minutes of the Colored Valley Baptist Association Held at Salem, Roanoke County, Va., August 12–15, 1870. Fincastle, Va.: Camper and Mason, 1870.

Minutes of the Valley Baptist Association, Held at Alleghany Meeting House, Montgomery County, Va., August 16th, 1867. Lynchburg, Va.: Virginian Power-Press Print., 1867.

Minutes of the Valley Baptist Association, Held at Fort Lewis, Roanoke Co., Va., August 13–16, 1869. Lynchburg, Va.: Virginian Power-Press Printing House, 1869.

Minutes of the Valley Baptist Association, Held with the Enon Church, Roanoke County, Virginia, August 15th, 16th, 17th and 18th, 1871. Lynchburg, Va.: Chas. H. Bryant, 1871.

Minutes of the Valley Baptist Association Session of 1865 at Bell Spring, Pulaski Co., Va., August 18–21, 1865. Lynchburg, Va.: Johnson and Schaffter, 1865.

Minutes of the Valley Baptist Association Session of 1866, Held at Laurel Ridge Church, Roanoke County, Va., August 17, 18, 19, 20th, 1866. Lynchburg, Va.: Virginian Book and Job Office, 1866.

Mitchell, Mary Niall. *Raising Freedom's Child: Black Children and Visions of the Future after Slavery.* New York: New York University Press, 2008.

Mjagkij, Nina, ed. *Organizing Black America: An Encyclopedia of African American Associations.* New York: Garland, 2001.

Montgomery, William E. *Under Their Own Vine and Fig Tree: The African-American Church in the South, 1865–1900.* Baton Rouge: Louisiana State University Press, 1993.

Morgan, Lynda J. *Emancipation in Virginia's Tobacco Belt.* Athens: University of Georgia Press, 1992.

Morris, Robert C. *Reading, 'Riting, and Reconstruction: The Education of Freedmen in the South, 1861–1870.* Chicago: University of Chicago Press, 1976.

Mullins, Foney G. "A History of the Literary Fund as a Funding Source for Free Public Education in the Commonwealth of Virginia." EdD diss., Virginia Tech, 2001.

Nash, Steven E. *Reconstruction's Ragged Edge: The Politics of Postwar Life in the Southern Mountains.* Chapel Hill: University of North Carolina Press, 2016.

Nieman, Donald G., ed. *The African American Family in the South, 1861–1900.* New York: Garland, 1994.

Noe, Kenneth W. *Southwest Virginia's Railroad: Modernization and the Sectional Crisis.* Urbana: University of Illinois Press, 1994.

O'Donovan, Susan E. *Becoming Free in the Cotton South.* Cambridge, Mass.: Harvard University Press, 2007.

Pargas, Damian Alan. *The Quarters and the Fields: Slave Families in the Non-Cotton South.* Gainesville: University Press of Florida, 2010.

Peirce, Paul S. *The Freedmen's Bureau: A Chapter in the History of Reconstruction.* New York: Haskell House, 1971. Originally published in State University of Iowa Studies in Sociology Economics Politics and History 3, no. 1 (1904).

Penningroth, Dylan C. *The Claims of Kinfolk: African American Property and Community in the Nineteenth-Century South.* Chapel Hill: University of North Carolina Press, 2003.

Perkins, Linda M. *Fanny Jackson Coppin and the Institute for Colored Youth, 1865–1902.* New York: Garland, 1987.

———. "Heed Life's Demands: The Educational Philosophy of Fanny Jackson Coppin." *Journal of Negro Education* 51 (1982): 181–90.

Perman, Michael. *Struggle for Mastery: Disenfranchisement in the South, 1888–1908.* Chapel Hill: University of North Carolina Press, 2001.

Pincus, Samuel N. *The Virginia Supreme Court, Blacks and the Law, 1870–1902.* New York: Garland, 1990.

Poole, Donald, and Frances Poole, eds. *Voices from Eastern Montgomery County by Those Who Lived There.* Blacksburg, Va.: Pocahontas, 2012.

Potet, G. F. "Secondary Education in Montgomery County, 1776–1936." MA thesis, University of Virginia, 1937.

Proceedings of the Connecticut Medical Society. Bridgeport, Conn.: Farmer, 1905.

Pudup, Mary Beth, Dwight B. Billings, and Altina Waller, eds. *Appalachia in the Making: The Mountain South in the Nineteenth Century.* Chapel Hill: University of North Carolina Press, 1995.

Raboteau, Albert J. *Canaan Land: A Religious History of African Americans.* New York: Oxford University Press, 1999.

Rainville, Lynn. *Hidden History: African American Cemeteries in Central Virginia.* Charlottesville: University of Virginia Press, 2014.

Records of the Field Offices for the State of Virginia, Bureau of Refugees, Freedmen, and Abandoned Lands, 1865–1872. Washington, D.C.: United States Congress and National Archives and Records Administration, 2006.

Regosin, Elizabeth. *Freedom's Promise: Ex-Slave Families and Citizenship in the Age of Emancipation.* Charlottesville: University Press of Virginia, 2002.

Reid, Debra A., and Evan P. Bennett, eds. *Beyond Forty Acres and a Mule: African American Landowning Families since Reconstruction.* Gainesville: University Press of Florida, 2012.

Reiff, Janice L., Michel R. Dahlin, and Daniel Scott Smith. "Rural Push and Urban
Pull: Work and Family Experiences of Older Black Women in Southern Cities,
1880–1900." *Journal of Social History* 16, no. 4 (1983): 39–48.

Richey, Russell E., Kenneth E. Rowe, and Jeanne Miller Schmidt. *The Methodist
Experience in America: A History. Vol. 1.* Nashville: Abingdon, 2010.

Rushdy, Ashraf H. A. *American Lynching.* New Haven, Conn.: Yale University Press,
2012.

Russell, John Henderson. *The Free Negro in Virginia, 1619–1865.* Baltimore: Johns
Hopkins Press, 1913.

Sarris, Jonathan Dean. *A Separate Civil War: Communities in Conflict in the Mountain South.* Charlottesville: University of Virginia Press, 2006.

Scattergood, J. H. "Work of the Friends' Freedmen's Association and Christiansburg
Industrial Institute," *Westonian* 13, no. 3 (1907): 45–50.

Scharf, John Thomas. *The Chronicles of Baltimore; Being a Complete History of
"Baltimore Town" and Baltimore City from the Earliest Period to the Present Time.*
Baltimore: Turnbull Brothers, 1874.

Schwalm, Leslie A. *A Hard Fight for We: Women's Transition from Slavery to Freedom
in South Carolina.* Urbana: University of Illinois Press, 1997.

Schweninger, Loren. *Black Property Owners in the South, 1790–1915.* Urbana:
University of Illinois Press, 1990.

Schwieder, Dorothy, Joseph Hraba, and Elmer Schwieder. *Buxton: A Black Utopia in
the Heartland.* Iowa City: University of Iowa Press, 2003.

*Second Annual Report of the Freedmen's Department of the Presbyterian Committee of
Home Missions.* New York: Presbyterian Publication Committee, 1870.

Sharpless, Rebecca. *Cooking in Other Women's Kitchens: Domestic Workers in the
South, 1865–1960.* Chapel Hill: University of North Carolina Press, 2010.

Simmons, William J. *Men of Mark: Eminent, Progressive, and Rising.* Cleveland:
Geo. M. Rewell, 1887.

Slap, Andrew, ed. *Reconstructing Appalachia: The Civil War's Aftermath.* Lexington:
University Press of Kentucky, 2010.

Smith, Charles Spencer. *A History of the African Methodist Episcopal Church.* Philadelphia: Book Concern of the AME Church, 1922.

Smith, James Douglas. "Virginia during Reconstruction, 1865–1870: A Political,
Economic and Social Study." PhD diss., University of Virginia, 1960.

Smith, James W., and Amanda E. DeHart. *Christiansburg Institute: A Proud Heritage.* Petersburg, Va.: Westar, 1991.

Smyth, Ellison A. *A History of Blacksburg Presbyterian Church: Its First 150 Years.*
Blacksburg, Va., 1982.

Smythe, Victor. *Asbury United Methodist Church (Washington, D.C) Records,
1836–1986.* New York: Schomburg Center for Research in Black Culture, New
York Public Library, n.d.

Snavely, Tipton Ray. *The Taxation of Negroes in Virginia.* Publications of the University of Virginia, Phelps-Stokes Fellowship Papers, 1916.

Sternhell, Yael A. *Routes of War: The World of Movement in the Confederate South.* Cambridge, Mass.: Harvard University Press, 2012.

Stevenson, Brenda E. *Life in Black and White: Family and Community in the Slave South.* New York: Oxford University Press, 1996.

Stewart, Bruce E., ed. *Blood in the Hills: A History of Violence in Appalachia.* Lexington: University Press of Kentucky, 2012.

Stowell, Daniel W. *Rebuilding Zion: The Religious Reconstruction of the South, 1863–1877.* New York: Oxford University Press, 1998.

Swain, Ann. "Christiansburg Institute: From Freedmen's Bureau Enterprise to Public High School." MA thesis, Radford College, 1975.

Swann-Wright, Dianne. *A Way Out of No Way: Claiming Family and Freedom in the New South.* Charlottesville: University of Virginia Press, 2002.

Tarter, Brent. "When Kind and Thrifty Husbands Are Not Enough: Some Thoughts on the Legal Status of Women in Virginia." *Magazine of Virginia Genealogy* 33 (1995): 79–101.

Thompson, S. Millett. *Thirteenth Regiment of New Hampshire Volunteer Infantry in the War of the Rebellion.* Boston: Houghton, Mifflin, 1888.

Thorp, Daniel B. "The Beginnings of African American Education in Montgomery County." *Virginia Magazine of History and Biography* 121 (2013): 315–45.

———. "Cohabitation Registers and the Study of Slave Families in Virginia." *Slavery and Abolition* 37 (2016): 744–60.

———. "Soldiers, Servants, and Very Interested Bystanders: Montgomery County's African American Population during the Civil War." *Virginia Magazine of History and Biography* (forthcoming).

Tripp, Steven Elliott. *Yankee Town, Southern City: Race and Class Relations in Civil War Lynchburg.* New York: New York University Press, 1997.

Trotter, Joe William, Jr. *Coal, Class, and Color: Blacks in Southern West Virginia, 1915–32.* Urbana: University of Illinois Press, 1990.

Turner, William H., and Edward J. Cabbell, eds. *Blacks in Appalachia.* Lexington: University Press of Kentucky, 1985.

Twenty-Sixth Annual Catalogue, The: 1924–1925. Cambria, Va.: Christiansburg Industrial Institute, n.d.

Von Daacke, Kirt. *Freedom Has a Face: Race, Identity, and Community in Jefferson's Virginia.* Charlottesville: University of Virginia Press, 2012.

Wallenstein, Peter. *Virginia Tech, Land-Grant University, 1872–1997: History of a School, a State, a Nation.* Blacksburg, Va.: Pocahontas, 1997.

Walker, Clarence E. *A Rock in a Weary Land: The African Methodist Episcopal Church during the Civil War and Reconstruction.* Baton Rouge: Louisiana State University Press, 1982.

Washington, Booker T. *The Booker T. Washington Papers.* 14 vols. Edited by Louis R. Harlan and Raymond W. Smock. Urbana: University of Illinois Press, 1972–1989.

———, ed. *Tuskegee & Its People: Their Ideals and Achievements.* New York: D. Appleton, 1906.

Washington, Reginald. "Sealing the Sacred Bonds of Holy Matrimony: Freedmen's Bureau Marriage Records." *Prologue* 37 (2005): 58–65.

Wedin, Laura Jones. "A Summary of 19th Century Smithfield, Part I: The Years before the Civil War." *Smithfield Review* 18 (2014): 79–95.

Whitt, R. Michael. "'Free Indeed!': Trials and Triumphs of Enslaved and Freedmen in Antebellum Virginia." *Virginia Baptist Register* 50 (2011).

Williams, David. *I Freed Myself: African American Self-Emancipation in the Civil War Era*. Cambridge: Cambridge University Press, 2014.

Williams, Heather Andrea. *Help Me to Find My People: The African American Search for Family Lost in Slavery*. Chapel Hill: University of North Carolina Press, 2012.

——. *Self-Taught: African American Education in Slavery and Freedom*. Chapel Hill: University of North Carolina Press, 2005.

Woodward, C. Vann. *The Strange Career of Jim Crow*. 2nd rev. ed. New York: Oxford University Press, 1966.

Wynes, Charles E. *Race Relations in Virginia, 1870–1902*. Totowa, N.J.: Rowman and Littlefield, 1971.

Zipf, Karin L. *Labor of Innocents: Forced Apprenticeship in North Carolina, 1715–1919*. Baton Rouge: Louisiana State University Press, 2005.

INDEX

Richmond Theological Seminary, 160
Roanoke, 28, 31, 34, 135, 218, 227
Robinson, Silas, 217
Roer, Ferdinand, 90
Rollins, Steward, 78
Russell, George, 188
Russell, George Washington, 90
Russell, Sarah, 188

Sanders, Frank, 83
Saunders, Alexander, 51, 52
Saunders, Granville, 221
Saunders, Robert, 90
Saunders, Sarah, 51
Scattergood, J. Henry, 157
Schaeffer, Charles S.: attitude toward African Americans, 15, 17, 92, 123, 176; early life, 15; educational activity, 34, 121–24, 126–32, 136–38, 140, 141, 145, 148, 149–51, 153–55, 158, 159; Freedmen's Bureau agent, 15, 24, 41, 48, 49, 51, 58, 73, 78, 82, 84, 85, 121–24, 126–32, 136, 137, 165, 168, 173, 188, 190–94, 196–201, 204, 205; religious activity, 34, 92, 161, 168, 173–78, 180
Schaffer, Fanny, 221
Schofield, John M., 202
schools: administration of, 139–41, 145, 148, 150; African American, 118–60; creation of, 118–32, 227; curriculum, 118, 137, 144, 145, 148, 150–52, 154, 155, 157–59; demand for, 119, 120, 123, 126, 128, 134, 135, 142; distribution of, 38, 129, 135, 136, 142, 143; enrollment in, 126, 135, 143, 144, 158, 159; facilities, 124–28, 132, 133, 140, 149, 150, 155, 158; funding, 123, 124, 126, 127–33, 137–42, 149; principals in, 148; public, 138–41, 206; reaction to, 118, 120, 122, 124–29, 157–59; schedule in, 126, 136, 144; segregation of, 139, 228; teachers in, 106, 109, 118,

122, 123, 128–34, 140, 141, 145, 146, 153, 154; white, 120, 143, 144
Scott, Mary, 65
Scott, Robert, 65
sharecropping, 70, 75, 76, 79, 81–84, 88, 94, 99
Shaver, Martha, 112
Shawsville, 13, 38, 74, 95, 129, 182
Shaw University, 160
Shelton, Sallie, 64
Sherman, Amos, 90
Sherman, Granville, 90
Sherman, Howard, 65
Sherwood, George W., 120, 121
Simpkins, Thomas, 216
slavery, 9–13, 21, 23, 24, 33, 35, 36, 40, 44–46, 162, 226, 229; and families, 23, 24, 45; and marriage, 23, 24, 44, 64
Smiley, Sarah, 130
Smith, Floyd, 73
Smith, Madison, 112
Smith, Olivia, 68, 107, 117
Spindle, Thomas, 112
Spindle, William, 112
Spotts, Ann, 203, 204
Staples, Waller R., 87, 90, 194
Strother, Amos, 146
Stuart, Samuel, 107
Sullivan, Arthur, 203
Sullivan, Mary, 202
Sweeney, Sarah Jane, 146

Tallant, William F., 94
Taylor, Anne, 86
Taylor, Henry, 212
Taylor, James, 84
Taylor, James C., 124
Taylor, Margaret, 87, 88
Taylor, Richard, 40, 161, 162, 165, 174, 175, 177, 229
Taylor, Samuel, 64
teachers: African American, 105, 106,

The American South Series

Anne Goodwyn Jones and Susan V. Donaldson, editors
Haunted Bodies: Gender and Southern Texts

M. M. Manring
Slave in a Box: The Strange Career of Aunt Jemima

Stephen Cushman
Bloody Promenade: Reflections on a Civil War Battle

John C. Willis
Forgotten Time: The Yazoo-Mississippi Delta after the Civil War

Charlene M. Boyer Lewis
Ladies and Gentlemen on Display: Planter Society at the Virginia Springs, 1790–1860

Christopher Metress, editor
The Lynching of Emmett Till: A Documentary Narrative

Dianne Swann-Wright
A Way out of No Way: Claiming Family and Freedom in the New South

James David Miller
South by Southwest: Planter Emigration and Identity in the Slave South

Richard F. Hamm
Murder, Honor, and Law: Four Virginia Homicides from Reconstruction to the Great Depression

Andrew H. Myers
Black, White, and Olive Drab: Racial Integration at Fort Jackson, South Carolina, and the Civil Rights Movement

Bruce E. Baker
What Reconstruction Meant: Historical Memory in the American South

Stephen A. West
From Yeoman to Redneck in the South Carolina Upcountry, 1850–1915

Randolph Ferguson Scully
Religion and the Making of Nat Turner's Virginia: Baptist Community and Conflict, 1740–1840

Deborah Beckel
Radical Reform: Interracial Politics in Post-Emancipation North Carolina

Terence Finnegan
A Deed So Accursed: Lynching in Mississippi and South Carolina, 1881–1940

Reiko Hillyer
  Designing Dixie: Tourism, Memory, and Urban Space in the New South

Luis-Alejandro Dinnella-Borrego
  The Risen Phoenix: Black Politics in the Post–Civil War South

Clayton McClure Brooks
  The Uplift Generation: Cooperation across the Color Line in Early Twentieth-Century Virginia

Henry Kamerling
  Capital and Convict: Race, Region, and Punishment in Post–Civil War America

Daniel B. Thorp
  Facing Freedom: An African American Community in Virginia from Reconstruction to Jim Crow